NAKED
PLAYWRITING

NAKED PLAYWRITING

The Art, the Craft, and the Life Laid Bare

by William Missouri Downs
and Robin U. Russin

SILMAN-JAMES PRESS   LOS ANGELES

First Edition
10 9 8 7 6 5 4 3 2 1

Library of Congress Cataloging-in-Publication Data

Cover design by Wade Lageose

Printed and bound in the United States of America

Silman-James Press
1181 Angelo Drive
Beverly Hills, CA 90210

This book is dedicated to the memory of Adele M. Russin,
who relished every moment, and always looked forward to the next act.

Contents

FOREWORD   *vii*

ACKNOWLEDGMENTS   *xii*

INTRODUCTION   *xiii*

BEGINNING A PLAY

Chapter 1 - What on Earth Gave You That Idea?   *1*
Chapter 2 - Schools of Thought   *22*

BUILDING A PLAY

Chapter 3 - Structure, Part One: Story & Plot   *55*
Chapter 4 - Structure, Part Two: Creativity, Scenario & Writing   *88*
Chapter 5 - Getting Into Character   *111*
Chapter 6 - Dialogue in Action   *140*
Chapter 7 - Looking Good   *170*

FINISHING A PLAY

Chapter 8 - Copyrights, Rewriting and Development   *199*
Chapter 9 - Two Ten-Minute Student Plays Dissected and Discussed   *218*

MARKETING A PLAY

Chapter 10 - I'm Finished, Now What Do I Do?   *255*
Chapter 11 - Getting Real: Production and Contracts   *279*

CONCLUSION   *303*

APPENDICES   *307*

A: Overcoming the Naked Chiropractor: How Not to Navigate
   the Professional Script Analysis Process   *309*
B: Sample Character Sketches   *317*
C: Formatting Template   *321*
D: Playwriting Programs   *324*

Bibliography   *327*
Index   *329*

Foreword

BY MILAN STITT

Only in the last one hundred years has the notion of "learning" playwriting as a professional skill become widely accepted and practiced. Both publishers and universities have vigorously aided and abetted this. And, as history has shown, this new occupational training has proven valuable for the American theater.

In various golden ages of theater, actors were playwrights. Aeschylus (he played Clytaemnestra in *Agamemnon*), Shakespeare, and Molière were actors. The necessary "training" happened naturally. Rhythms, techniques, and style were incorporated into the artist's knowledge base without him realizing it was happening. The language of theater creation was learned as easily as children learn language.

Eugene O'Neill, a university-trained playwright, learned a great deal from touring with his father's production of *The Count of Monte Cristo*. He certainly learned what he did *not* want theater to be, but he also learned a great deal that did inform his plays. If one reads all his plays and then *The Count of Monte Cristo*, it is astonishing to discover how many relationships and plot devices O'Neill borrowed from the hated melodrama. In fact, without his intimate knowledge of this play, it is hard to imagine what O'Neill might have written.

Literary impulses (particularly in the Irish theater) increasingly brought non-actors, even non-theater people, to the field of playwriting. In America, however, Henry James, Ernest Hemingway, and Norman Mailer demonstrated that a lack of theater knowledge does not help to write an effective play, no matter how gifted the writer is in other literary forms. More importantly, during the twentieth century, technical innovations such as radio, movies, and television marked the end of theater as a primary entertainment medium. Touring and resident companies closed, thereby eliminating the possibilities for future playwrights to "learn on the job."

That specific things can be learned about writing for the stage is implicit in the word "playwright." Cartwrights, shipwrights, and playwrights are all skilled builders of vehicles meant to move people from one place to another. Clearly, one would not want to set off in a ship built by someone who didn't know what he or she was doing. And it probably wouldn't happen, because the vessel would sink before you got to the gangplank. Similarly, plays from untrained playwrights sink long before anyone can see them. It's curious that the only playwrights who think that training is not helpful are those who did not have the advantage. One has never heard from Eugene O'Neill, Arthur Miller, Tennessee Williams, Lynn Nottage, or Tony Kushner that their training was a waste of time.

The first school to offer a playwriting course was Harvard, where George Pierce Baker's English 47 (playwriting) had such students as George Abbott and Eugene O'Neill. There came a time when Professor Baker decided that his writers needed to see their works realized on stage, but Harvard was not interested in building a theater. Fortunately, Yale University was willing, so Professor Baker moved his training there, where it became the foundation of the Yale School of Drama. Realizing he would need actors, directors, and designers, instruction in these departments was added. Most likely, he used the model of Carnegie Mellon University (then, Carnegie Tech), which became America's first theater school in 1902. Another major playwriting school for many years was the University of Michigan, thanks to the classes of Kenneth Thorpe Rowe. His students included Arthur Miller, Lawrence Kasdan, and Dennis McIntyre.

Until the twentieth century, there were surprisingly few how-to texts for dramatists. Aristotle's *Poetics* has served as a guide for many writers, but its purpose was descriptive, rather than prescriptive. Aristotle noted this popular new form of poetry (i.e., tragedy) and described it, principally to differentiate it from long narrative poetry. His description has proven to be the bedrock on which subsequent how-to books have been built.

Both professors Baker and Rowe wrote significant playwriting textbooks. George Pierce Baker wrote *Dramatic Technique* (1919), America's first, and quite possibly the world's first, actual playwriting textbook. It has not stood the test of time well. Most of the plays it used as examples, which were drawn from the popular theater of its time, are now forgotten and no longer in print. The only writer I know who has read Baker's whole book is Lanford Wilson, who did not have a university theater education but studied the central texts with vigor in the seventies. Professor Rowe's *Write That Play* (1936) has held up better. His choice of plays such as *A Doll's House* and *Riders to the Sea* and others similarly significant has made his book easily accessible to today's reader, if one can find a copy. (Long out of print, copies sell for $100 to $300.) He invented the Major Dramatic Question method of developing an effective theatrical rhythm and story.

Rhythm has become a problem for many current playwriting students, since they are most familiar with the disjointed rhythm of television, which is directed to induce sales, rather than the ceremonial. Interestingly, the rhythm that Professor Rowe suggested is as applicable to avant-garde and the misnamed non-linear styles of contemporary theater as it is to more standard forms.

Following in the tradition of past significant texts, *Naked Playwriting* adheres to time-tested principles and guidance, including Kenneth Thorpe Rowe's Major Dramatic Question. It also acknowledges an important sign of the times with regard to "what a playwright needs to know," which now includes marketing, protecting the text, and utilizing the American theater's extensive play-development opportunities—a most welcome bonus for all writers who not only wish to write effectively but also want to see their plays produced.

Milan Stitt
July 21, 2004
Chelsea, New York

Acknowledgments

This book would not be possible if it wasn't for the loving support and careful editing of Lou Anne Wright—the best pal a writer could have. I'd also like to thank Rebecca Hilliker, Ollie Walters, Philip Dubois and all those at the University of Wyoming who make my job easy because they support the arts and freedom of speech. Thanks also to the Utah Playfest and the Mill Mountain Theatre for letting us reprint their play critique forms as well as Thomas Campbell and Todd McCullough for allowing us to analyze and examine their ten-minute plays—they have guts. Special thanks goes to Karen L. Erickson, Joel Murray, Clifton Campbell, Gordon Reinhart and Erik Ramsey for sharing their years of experience, as well as Barbara Rosenberg and Holly Allen for their encouragement and support. A special thanks to all the playwrights of the Denver Center for the Performing Arts Playwright's Unit. And finally thank you to my writing teachers—Lew Hunter, Stirling Silliphant, Lanford Wilson, Richard Walter, Rod Marriott, Hal Ackerman, Milan Stitt and James Livingston—who taught me that writing is more fun than therapy.

—William Missouri Downs

First and foremost among those I need to thank are our editors at Silman-James Press, Gwen Feldman and Jim Fox, who trusted us with this project and then did what all superb editors do: let the book be ours, while helping us to ensure that it measured up to their high standards. I'd also like to thank my colleagues at the University of California, Riverside, Professors Eric Barr, Richard Hornby and Rickerby Hinds, who were undeterred by the five pound manuscript I left on their desks, read it through and offered experienced and thoughtful feedback. This book could never have been written without the wisdom passed along by my teachers and role models at UCLA, Professors Richard Walter, Lew Hunter and Hal Ackerman. Thanks must go to my father, Robert Russin, an artist and scholar for all of his 90 years; my loving and endlessly supportive wife Sarah; and our two kids, Olivia and Ben, both master thespians, especially at bed time. Lastly, I'd like to offer my gratitude to my students, who over the years have taught me far more than I ever taught them about the pain, sweat, tears and joy of writing.

—Robin U. Russin

Introduction

****

Writing is like prostitution.
First, you do it for the love, then you do it for a few friends,
and finally you do it for money.

Molière

****

There are a lot of books out there covering various aspects of the craft of play-writing. Some are even pretty good. Most, however, are either no longer current or comprehensive. This book attempts to be both. It looks at all it takes to become a playwright in today's world, from your first scribbled notes to closing night. We've called it *Naked Playwriting* because this is where we attempt to lay bare the essentials of the craft and the career. (Also because we thought it would attract your attention—and as you'll see, a good title is half the battle toward getting your play read.) But before we get to all that, there's one question you have to answer. Why do you want to write a play? We can only hope that you're not in it for the money. If riches are your main concern, just go to business school. The naked truth is that the chances of making a living as a playwright are remote. True, some playwrights do make a living, even a pretty good one, but when it comes right down to it, you don't see a lot of playwrights cruising around in Porsches. You could probably fit those who do in a minivan. People who write plays don't do it for the money (although it's nice to be paid), they do it because they have something to say—something they want to see enacted.

IGNORING THE ELEPHANT IN THE ROOM

So why write a play for peanuts and relatively small audiences when you could write for TV or the movies? In today's world, playwriting may seem a poor cousin, a quaint relic, a dying star fading at the fringes of the brilliant new entertainment universe. But, in fact, playwriting remains as important as it ever was—perhaps even more so—for the simple reason that it is one of the last bastions of true individual expression. The playwright's voice isn't compromised. This is what makes writing for the stage unique. Even if you do write a Hollywood screenplay and sell it for lots of money, you will, like Ariel in *The Little Mermaid*, also have sold your voice. Screenwriters sell not only their words, but their copyright. This means that once the writer cashes her check, producers, directors, and even actors can change her script's theme, story, dialogue, characters—anything they want—without the writer's permission, or even her knowledge. It also means that other writers can be hired to cut, alter, even totally rewrite the story you created, and there isn't a damn thing you can do about it. (Except, of course, go for long, soothing rides in your Porsche.) This isn't a new situation. Years ago playwright and screenwriter Maxwell Anderson (*Anne of the Thousand Days*) said that playwrights in L.A. quickly discover Hollywood movies have no authors "because the picture companies own all the copyrights and are registered in Washington as the writers of the scripts turned out by the hired hands... After you've written your damnedest, they'll set seven galley slaves to work on it, singly and in groups, and by the time the product is ready for consumption, it will taste like all the rest of the soup in all the other cans labeled with the trademark of your studio."

In fact, it's not uncommon for screenwriters to attend the opening night of their movies and not recognize a single line of dialogue. It's almost as common for them not to attend at all. The experience is just too painful. Sometimes screenwriters even argue over who wrote which line. For example, the late Dean Riesner—one of Hollywood's best-known script doctors—was famous for writing Clint Eastwood's legendary line, "Go ahead, make my day." He also wrote Eastwood's most famous *Dirty Harry* speech: "I know what you're thinking. Did he fire six shots or only five? Well, to tell you the truth, in all this excitement I've kind of lost track myself. But being as this is a .44 magnum, the most powerful handgun in the world, and would blow your head clean off, you've got to ask yourself a question: 'Do I feel lucky?' Well, do ya, punk?" It was a pretty good little monologue. Riesner had a pretty good voice. The problem is that screenwriter John Milius, who had also worked on the script, publicly claimed that he was the one who wrote that speech. No one knows for sure which writer wrote it.

This can't happen to a playwright because, unlike screenwriters, playwrights don't sell their copyright, so they retain ownership of their voice. As a result, no doubt exists as to who wrote what. (For more on copyrights see Chapter 8.) Your story, your play, remains yours, and if you can get it staged—a far easier proposition than getting a movie made—you will find an audience. After his experience with screenwriting, Maxwell Anderson concluded: "A playwright [is] nobody's hired man. What he has written is his own and may be changed only with his consent."

Voice Lessons

Having a voice isn't enough. Being a playwright isn't a birthright. It takes work. Seldom do playwrights find a strong, mature voice before their middle to late twenties. Having something to say is great, but having the ability to say it is another matter. Whether you have talent is out of your control. But you can master the technique, structure, and practical side of the art. "Most playwrights go wrong on the fifth word," said Meredith Willson (*The Music Man*). "When you start a play and type 'Act One, Scene One,' your writing is every bit as good as Arthur Miller or Eugene O'Neill. It's that fifth word where beginners start to go wrong." This book is devoted to those lessons of craft that playwrights must learn in order to reveal their talent, find their voice, and write that fifth word.

That said, there's really no such thing as a how-to book when it comes to playwriting. A how-to book could perhaps show you someone else's techniques and formulas, and that's not all bad. Good playwrights learn from the past and go through a period of apprenticeship and acquired knowledge of technique, without which their creativity would be limited. But creativity is the one element that can't be taught, so the goal of this book is to demystify and explain the elements that can. This is a down-to-earth, practical guide and as close to a how-to book as possible. It will solve many of your writing problems, but it can't make you a playwright.

Messing with the Muse

Some writers, both beginners and the more experienced, rebel against structure and technique, rejecting what they consider soulless formulae. They may feel that once the Muse whispers in their ear and the words flow onto the page, it's wrong to change anything. They may worry that the Muse might abandon them if they distrust her and actually lower themselves to studying the craft of writing. They believe structure and technique are mere constraints that limit creativity and result in manufactured, fill-in-the-blank, mechanical plots. Or they may just be lazy. Sometimes these writers strike out to invent "new traditions," only to discover that their pages of deep emotions and private thoughts don't connect with an audience. Confounded by this lack of appreciation, they might defend their failure by thinking of themselves as ahead of their time. More often than not, the problem isn't their advanced ideas, but their lack of simple storytelling skills. The Muse, like all the gods, needs to assume recognizable form for us to make sense of her messages. She needs structure.

Consciously or unconsciously aware of their lack of technique, and therefore of their inability to give full expression to their own voices, many beginners imitate favorite playwrights. University playwriting classes are filled with young Churchills, Mamets, Becketts, even Shakespeares who have substituted someone else's approach for their own. They imitate because the empty page is hard to face without a crutch. They imitate for security, as a safeguard against false starts and half-finished plays. And it's true that many famous dramatists began by imitating other writers' voices, but they only became famous after finding their own. This book is about helping you find and develop your own voice.

A PLAY FALLS IN A FOREST...

Writing a play that doesn't get produced and seen is pointless. You have to find your audience. So this book also covers the basics of self-promotion and how to appear professional. Many good playwrights finish a script, but don't know how to market it. Even with an agent, you can't just sit back and hope the world beats a path to your door. You must enter contests, contact producers, and get yourself out there in any way you can. Knowing how to properly format a play, write a good synopsis, an effective cover letter, and résumé are skills almost as crucial as those for writing the play itself. Theaters generally reject scripts or letters that don't look professional. This is of course literally judging a book by its cover, but they're usually right to do so. If the writer is too lazy to figure out the right format and presentation, it's a safe bet that she was probably lazy in writing her play, too.

Lastly, this book is about helping you make the transition from the page to the stage. Once they finally succeed in getting a production, some playwrights find it difficult to go from solo artist to member of an artistic ensemble. A playwright must work with actors, designers, and directors. He must learn how to rethink his words based on how those words sound coming out of an actor's mouth, and be ready and able to rewrite when necessary. Those who can't make this transition often go no farther than their first play; it never gets produced or is panned, and they give up. They may question their talent or lapse into bitterness over being misunderstood or attempt to justify failure by saying, "Playwrights are born, not made." They're wrong. Talent needs guidance and structure in order to succeed. So this book is dedicated to the belief that playwrights are made, not born.

Beginning a Play

1

What on Earth Gave You That Idea?

****

If you don't have the initial inspiration,
put down the pen, put the pencil back in the jar,
switch off the computer and go and dig in the garden instead.

Alan Ayckbourn

****

Maybe the most common question fans ask their favorite writers is, "Where do you get your ideas?" The answers to this question are as varied as there are writers—which leads surprisingly to the conclusion that there is in fact just one answer. Ideas come from each writer's personal obsessions. That isn't to say that an idea springs Athena-like, fully formed, from the mind of its creator. The original seed of excitement, the "germinal idea," may come from a newspaper article, a local event, a poem, a photo, a conversation overheard on a plane—from almost anywhere. But it's sure to be something that stirs a particular and deeply felt emotion in the writer, something connected to that writer's intimate experiences, fantasies, dreams, nightmares, resentments, unfinished business, or the writer's reaction to some form of social injustice.

Something to consider when evaluating an idea is whether it can stand up to what Aristotle called "a certain magnitude"—the idea must be potent enough to carry your thematic message and maintain both your own and your audience's interest. What creates this potency? Kurt Vonnegut taught his students "to make their characters want something right away—even if it's only a glass of water." That may be enough for a short story, but Lajos Egri, in *The Art of Dramatic Writing*, takes that idea one step further for a drama: "Whenever you have a fully rounded character who wants something very badly, you have a play." The key here is "wants something very badly," which suggests a crisis in that individual's life that must be resolved in the face of strong opposition. It suggests a character who will force a conflict. "Write about people only when they have arrived at a turning point in their lives. Their example will become a warning or an inspiration for us." And it will provide the "magnitude" for the original idea to succeed as a finished play.

Just as anything that stimulates the playwright's imagination can be the source of an idea, the same source may stimulate many different writers—but always with different results. What makes such an idea "original" to each playwright depends on how this raw burst of illumination refracts through the prism of each one's unique point of view. David Mamet, in *Three Uses of the Knife*, defines the difference between an incident and the beginning of a drama: "We dramatize an incident by taking events and reordering them, elongating them, compressing them, so that we understand their personal meaning to us... If you said, 'I waited for a bus today,' that probably wouldn't be dramatic." But "'I waited *half an hour* for the bus today" is a dramatic statement. It means: 'I waited that amount of time sufficient for me to be sure you will understand it was 'too long.'"

Drawing a distinction between the idea for a drama and its plot or the characters that enact it (both of which we'll examine in great detail later on) is important. It is the distinction philosophers draw between form and content. Millions of plays have been written in the last 2,500 years, so there's very little chance that your play's plot or basic character types will be completely new. In his book *The Thirty-Six Dramatic Situations* (1921), Georges Polti proclaimed that, because there are a limited number of human emotions, there are also a limited number of story ideas—thirty-six, as his title implies. All plays, novels, and short stories are variations of these thirty-six plots. His categories include "Fatal Imprudence," "Daring Enterprise," and "Murderous Adultery." Following a similar vein of thought, William Wallace Cook's book *Plotto* (1928) proposed to help writers construct plots by stringing together hundreds of standardized, interchangeable events, complications, conflicts, and motivations. According to Polti and Cook, if you categorize all the stories ever written, you'll find that there are no new plots. Even those that seem new are really just rearrangements of existing plot elements. But even if you disagree with Polti and Cook, all this is beside the point because plot, like your skeleton, is about structure, and just because every human on the planet has a bony structure similar to yours doesn't take away the uniqueness of the individual (you) who is supported by it. Shakespeare borrowed most of his plots. So does Quentin Tarantino. But their dramas remain unique because of their original points of view, their particular obsessions, and their experiences.

Similarly, characters tend to fall into types, which fulfill certain functions within the story structure. In *The Writer's Journey*, Chris Vogler examines how the universal mythic prototypes identified by Joseph Campbell (such types as the Hero, the Shape-Shifter, the Wise Old Man, the Shadow, the Trickster, the Elixir, and so forth) can be turned into useful tools for the writer. Characters in drama, as in myth, fulfill certain functions—often the same functions: the Leading Man

(Hero), the Love Interest (Elixir), the Comic Sidekick (Shape-Shifter or Trickster), etc. While these may be both limited in number and prototypical, they don't have to be stereotypical. The myriad ways you can reinvent them and the attributes you give them can make them unique. It's all a matter of finding them within the inner cast of characters that make up your personality and experience of humanity.

PREMISES, PREMISES

An idea is never enough on its own. It must serve a theme, a deeply held belief on the part of the writer. Lajos Egri calls this the "premise," and he regards it as both the starting point and the core of the drama, the organizing principle that defines everything else in the play. The premise, like the plot, need not be original for the play to be. As Egri puts it, "Ten thousand playwrights can take the same premise...and not one play will resemble the other except in the premise. Your knowledge, your understanding of human nature, and your imagination will take care of that." What a premise is, in essence, is what the central idea of your story is about, its moral, the punchline to its joke. Any play without a premise is like a joke without a punchline; it just sort of hangs there. What's the point of all this conflict? What are you trying to say to us, to prove to us, to make us feel? This doesn't require you to come up with a long thesis; in fact, the shorter and simpler the better. A premise is a clear statement reflecting your belief about some aspect of life or some point of view you want to explore. The premise of *Hamlet* could be stated this way: The ghosts of past injustice will torment us until those responsible are punished. *The Importance of Being Earnest* practically declares its own premise, but it might be rephrased: Only by being earnest in spirit as well as name can you find happiness. Your task as a writer is to find the "why" and "what" of your play. Why this story? What are you trying to say with it?

EXPERIENCE OF A LIFETIME

This leads us to each writer's individual experience. There are two ways to experience life: directly and indirectly. Both are important. Direct experience is tasting life firsthand. It's a heightened experience because it comes from actually probing, participating, watching, and even daydreaming (as long as those daydreams are not just a means of escape, but are analyzed and remembered, as in Proust's *Remembrance of Things Past*). It's been said that most people are truly aware of their lives for only a few short moments each day. Humans are creatures of routine and will find any reason to go on automatic pilot. To be a playwright, however (or any other type of creative writer), you can't go on autopilot. Instead, you must strive for a deeper awareness that can make even the most mundane, ordinary moments interesting. Wake yourself up and go out of your way to meet people, see new places, feel, think, and above all, listen, remember, and interpret the noise of life. That noise, refined by choice and talent, becomes the music of drama.

Indirect experience is viewing life through someone else's eyes. The most common ways to do this are through reading and listening to others. History books, novels, biographies, plays, true confessions, and newspapers are all sources of indirect experience. All are good, so read anything that can expand your view of the world, from *The National Enquirer* to Plato's *Republic*. As Nobel Prize-winning poet Joseph Brodsky said (at the Washington, D.C. press conference where he accepted the U.S. poet laureateship), "There are worse crimes than burning books. One of them is not reading them." A playwright also gains indirect experience by listening: by interviewing interesting people, by eavesdropping on conversations at the next table, by hanging onto the chitchat of everyday life. In short, a playwright isn't an isolated genius who relies solely on the resources of her imagination. No one is creative enough to write about that which they have never experienced, either directly or indirectly.

So, once again, where do ideas come from? They come from watching junk TV, climbing Mount St. Helens, talking to the guy at the convenience store who is proud of the fact that he's been robbed twenty-seven times, chasing down blue-light specials, contemplating a spider hanging in mid-air, falling in love, falling out of love, hiking, reading old comic books, lending an ear to door-to-door evangelists, scanning the news, fearing takeoff and landing, fighting with your boyfriend, dating a urologist, arguing with your stepfather, having your prostate checked, getting scammed, and absorbing, one page at a time, the pocket edition of Voltaire's writings. Oh, and don't forget the obituaries, jazz, pissed-off overweight middle-aged men, unprovoked anger, unexpected love, premature ejaculation, missed periods, the Hindu temple in Queens, the sound of twins crying, *War and Peace*, war and peace—or even the experience of being creatively blocked.

The point, ultimately, is who cares? No idea necessarily promises to become a good play, unless you can transform it through the alchemy of your talent, passion, and hard work. As Egri writes, "The great plays came down to us from men who had unlimited patience for work." Wherever your ideas come from, they will become yours and yours alone only if you are true to your own take on life—your philosophy. Don't have one? Then find it. By philosophy, we don't mean some bloodless analysis of the meaning of meaning. (Although some playwrights have found apt material even here, as Tom Stoppard did in *Rosencrantz and Guildenstern Are Dead.*) For the ancient Greeks, originators of what we regard as theater, playwrights were philosopher-poets. Philosophy and poetry were matters of life and death, both essential to drama. A poet was literally a "maker," a creator, and at the heart of his creation was a passion for understanding—a "philosophy."

More than just an opinion, a philosophy is a definable, deeply felt perspective about what and how life is, isn't, and/or should be. It's about what matters to you, which is often—in fact, mostly—an emotional issue. What moves you to joy, pain, satisfaction, despair, enlightenment, fury? Your philosophy is your slant on the basic values and importance of life, as well as the relationships between human beings, nature, and the individual and society at large. In order to find and define it, you as a writer must be curious and actively engaged in the world. Like an actor (and every playwright is both an actor and director on the page as she creates her characters and actions), you must be in touch with your goals and emotions as you experience, interpret, and evaluate life. All these will inform your philosophy and, ultimately, the themes your writing will explore as you become a creator with a passion for understanding—a playwright.

GETTING EMOTIONAL

As noted, powerful emotional content is at the core of a good dramatic idea and flows directly from a character's wanting something badly. Yet real people habitually avoid overwhelming emotion. Real people don't often act on their wants, because they're afraid of disappointment. Great joy carries the risk of loss and greater pain; if we summit the highest mountain, we may also fall into the lowest valley. So we often do everything in our power to live in the gray, safe area between peak and valley, sacrificing the highs so we can avoid the lows. Playwrights never shrink from emotional experience, and once they've experienced it, they never forget it. The great Russian acting teacher Konstantin Stanislavski (1863-1938) taught actors to "save" their sensory impressions and emotional experiences so they could be recalled and experienced again. The same applies to a playwright: Her emotions are always on standby, ready when she needs to invest them in her characters. These "sense memories"—strong, stored emotions—lead to a heightened awareness, a deeper sense of character, and a stronger ability to transform an idea into a drama. A playwright is no better than his ability to draw upon the sum of his emotions and experiences. In short, he must explore life, welcome its passions, and remember what he's learned. Then, no matter how few the number of possible plots, the number of possible original stories is unlimited.

This doesn't necessarily mean that a playwright should get sloshed, start a brawl, and end up in jail every night, then relive his misery each following day. Raw emotion by itself does not guarantee a gripping drama—that requires *directed* conflict. Emotion without purpose or premise is like a drunk at a bar crying in his beer. It just sits there and doesn't really involve us. Emotion must serve the story's premise and rising conflicts. A wedding or funeral or sexual experience can be wildly emotional and still not be in the least dramatic or even interesting. Drama requires characters who want things they don't yet have, who need things they don't yet recognize, who are in conflict with people and forces arrayed against them. Then, when they get emotional, so will we.

IS THE IDEA HALF FULL, OR HALF EMPTY?

A good idea has several necessary characteristics: It must be exciting enough to spark months of brainstorming and long hours of reflection, and sustain days and nights of creative writing. It must contain a central conflict resulting from characters with deeply held desires and differences, who are shown at a critical moment in their lives. And, it must be stageable.

Half-ideas may lack clarity, proper scope, or insufficient knowledge of the subject. Without any one of these, it is impossible to build character, plot, action, unity, crisis truth—in short, drama. A half-idea at first may seem promising, but when you begin developing it, it will probably come up short because it lacks an essential ingredient or two.

In a recent beginning playwriting class, twelve students were asked to write a short paragraph stating (or "pitching") an idea for a play. Most of the students came up with half-ideas. Let's examine their pitches and see where they went wrong.

Playwright #1 (Working Title: *The Forgotten*)

> The play I want to write is inspired by the fall of Saigon in 1976. The last helicopter left the roof of the U.S. embassy only hours before the North Vietnamese entered the compound. What the departing Americans didn't know is that they have accidentally left four Marines on the roof of the building. Back on the ship, their absence was not detected for more than two hours. I think I can make a strong statement about America's involvement in war. In the end, of course, they're rescued, but for two hours they wouldn't know, so there'd be much arguing and inherent conflict.

This is certainly an interesting starting point for a play, but at this point it's a half-idea because it has no characters. Who are these four Marines? Beyond the obvious and generic desire to escape Saigon, what does each of them want? How does this create drama and conflict? Whatever happens on the roof of the embassy will depend on their four distinct personalities, their wants, desires, and resulting conflicts.

Until this student writer has at least a vague notion of who the characters are, he doesn't have a full idea—all he has is a location and situation, which is a fine place to start brainstorming, but it's not enough to start writing. As it turned out, this student had never spoken with a Marine, never been in the armed forces, and had quite of bit of research and indirect experience to gain before he could flesh out his idea.

What separates theater from the other performing arts is that it is the only art form in which the medium and subject are the same. In opera or dance, as in theater, the subject may be human drama, but the medium is music and/or choreography. In theater, however, the medium is live human action and interaction. Some of you out there may be exclaiming: "Oh, yeah? Well what about the musical *Cats*? That's not about humans, it's about, well, it's about cats." Not true. There are human beings in those cat outfits, and the emotions, ideas, and the actions they play are human. The musical would make little sense if it were truly about feline thoughts and emotions—not to mention feline vocal styling. In short, if you don't have even a vague inkling of who your characters are, you have a half-idea and are not ready to write.

Playwright #2 (Working Title: *A Hard Act to Follow*)

I want to write about my grandfather, a man who lived to be over a hundred. He didn't talk much, but everyone knew he had had a hard life. He lost three children at birth, was widowed twice, but he never seemed to let the world get him down, and so he was a source of hope and inspiration for my whole family. He had a gold tooth and was missing a finger, which he claimed he lost to a bear. We never believed it. By writing about the last years of his life, I think I can make a statement about not taking life too seriously and enjoying the time we've got.

Again, this is a half-idea. The playwright has the beginnings of a character, but what's the *story*? What happens in the play? What does the grandfather do? What does he want? How, if at all, do his desires provide crisis and conflict? Plays must be acted, and actors tell a story by doing something—performing actions. Before you start writing you don't need to have your whole story worked out, but a good idea contains at least a hint of what will transpires in the play, of what the characters ultimately want and what or who will try to stop them from getting it. This grandfather idea could work as a short story, an essay, or a poem, but dramatically it's a half-idea until the playwright comes up with the play's action.

Action is how characters create a story, and how a story reveals its characters. Action is what characters do in order to change the circumstances of their lives.

It is more than just physical movement; action includes the strategies, reactions, conflicts, and thoughts that drive a story forward. Action is the continuous, progressive growth and change in the characters and the story.

Even if a play has no physical action, its characters must express mental action through dialogue. (This is certainly going to be a problem with this non-talkative grandpa.) In his book *Backwards & Forwards*, David Ball states, "Action occurs when something happens that makes or permits something else to happen." Hamlet's "To be or not to be" soliloquy is full of action—including its opposite, the paralysis of action denied—even though little is physically happening on the stage. In short, a play without action is simply not a play, because action and character are inseparable, and a character cannot be realized without it. Who characters are determines what actions they will take; simultaneously, the actions that characters take define who they are. A scene or sentence lacking action—lacking a character's attempt to act upon his or her goals—will freeze a play in its tracks.

But characters taking action, in and of itself, isn't enough to create a gripping story. It's worth reiterating: The action taken must be based on strong desires, it must encounter opposition, and it must be in the service of sufficient stakes hanging on the outcome of the ensuing conflict to make us care. Play action must be "dramatic action." Dramatic action occurs when a character decides to do something either because of or in spite of the consequences. This grandpa play will fail, unless the playwright comes up with something the family or grandpa is willing to do in order to change their given situation, and there must be consequences hanging in the balance should they fail.

The need for dramatic action can cause a problem when trying to write characters who are based on "real people." While everyone takes dramatic action now and then, most of us go about our lives trying to avoid conflict. We receive an unjust parking ticket and we pay it rather than go to court. Our boss insults us and we bear it rather than confront her. Most real people try to maintain the status quo; they occasionally may want or feel deeply about something, but only rarely do they do anything about their situation. Most real people would make lousy characters in a play because until characters do or say something that changes their circumstances, the playwright has no way to get a handle on them or write a play about them. Unlike real people, play characters are willing to force the issue, to take a chance, to engage their opposition, to take a stab at changing their world—in short, to take dramatic action. Most importantly, it is the *choice of action they take*, from among many possible alternatives, which defines who they truly are.

THE PATHS NOT TAKEN

Now, let's reverse ourselves. Even the experience of having not acted because of fear of the consequences can provide the playwright with an idea, if the result provides an experience of emotional truth. Several successful plays have characters who take no apparent action, or the action they do take has little to do with what needs to be done (just as in real life). Anton Chekhov (1860-1904) thought that if one were going to write realistically about people, then taking action (which according to most playwriting teachers is at the top of the list of things needed to write a good play) would be at the bottom of the list of likely human behaviors. For example, Chekhov's *The Cherry Orchard* has several major characters who do little or nothing to correct their situations. At the beginning of the play, the family is told that their estate and its cherry orchard are to be sold to pay back taxes. A friend suggests that they cut down the cherry orchard and rent the land for summer cottages. This will at least give them the funds they desperately need, but the family does nothing. Four acts later, the estate is sold at auction and they move out. Stories like this often result in a funny, absurd, or frustrating play that makes a statement about how people really are. Such stories hold up a mirror that reflects our own passive existence, paradoxically showing us how absurd the commonplace can be. In a letter from 1887, Chekhov wrote to a friend:

> The demand is made that the hero and heroine should be dramatically effective. But after all, in real life people don't spend every minute shooting each other, hanging themselves, and making confessions of love. They don't spend all their time saying clever things. They're more occupied with eating, drinking, flirting, and talking stupidities—and these are the things that ought to be shown on the stage. A play should be written in which people arrive, go away, have dinner, talk about the weather, and play cards. Life must be exactly as it is. And people as they are—not on stilts... Let everything on the stage be just as complicated, and at the same time just as simple as it is in life. People eat their dinner, just eat their dinner, and all the time their happiness is being established or their lives are being broken up.

If you intend to write a Chekhovian and/or absurdist play (which we don't think Playwright #2 was intending to do), then be warned that it too must still have action. The main story in *The Cherry Orchard* may seem to have little or no action, but in fact it is governed by conflict: In the face of necessity, its characters are incapable of action—and the refusal to act is a dramatic choice, an action, with consequences that resolve the play's premise. Meanwhile, its subplots are full of dramatic actions that keep the play from grinding to a halt. One of the paradoxes of playwriting is that in order to show people who are static or paralyzed, you must demonstrate it through a story that contains active choices—even if those choices are to avoid dealing with the problems at hand.

Playwright #3 (Working Title: *My Kinda Heaven*)

> I want to write about real people and real lives. In particular, my childhood. I came from a loving family. I think people have forgotten that there are loving, dare I say, perfect families out there. I want to tell the story of a vacation my family took when I was twelve. We did everything, camped in Yellowstone, met new and interesting people, saw wonderful sights, and drew together as a family. In the end, we reaffirmed our love for one another.

This idea has characters (though the playwright didn't go into much detail) and some action, but it's still a half-idea because it lacks conflict and/or crisis.

A play is essentially the history of a particular conflict. It begins with a character's need or desire, which leads to the first inkling of the conflict and develops this conflict through a series of dramatic peaks as the action grows to a climax. Conflict (explicit and/or implicit) should be at the core of every scene and character. As noted, even in Chekhov's work there is the conflict between what the characters know they must do and how they avoid acting on that knowledge.

Those elements of life that don't contain conflict, that aren't about characters wrestling with an intractable dilemma or entanglement, don't work in a play. David Mamet writes in *Three Uses of the Knife*, "A play is not about nice things happening to nice people. A play is about rather terrible things happening to people who are as nice or not nice as we ourselves are." And UCLA screenwriting professor Richard Walter puts it this way: "No one wants to see a play about the village of the happy people. Unless something really unhappy is about to happen to them." Those elements of life that don't contain at least the promise of conflict and crisis don't belong in a play. Drama is conflict. It's that simple.

Playwright #4 (Working Title: *Cry for the Moon*)

> I want to write about a woman who has traveled across country in a minivan. She's running away from a horrible relationship. Married three times, her last husband was a truck driver who loved to get drunk and beat up women. The policewoman who arrested the wife-beater was a good person. She didn't want to make the arrest but instead wanted to teach him how to control his temper. The policewoman was kicked off the force because she cared too much. The policewoman's son Max never recovered from his mother being unemployed and so he grew up

to be a bum. One day the son became so depressed about his grades, he jumped off a bridge. It's a sad ending, but sometimes life is sad.

This idea has characters, there's action, plenty of opportunities for conflict and crisis, but it's still a half-idea because it lacks *unity of action*—the cohesiveness that brings all the elements—conflict, crisis, characters, and action—to bear on a single subject or spine (sometimes called the "through-line"). *Cry for the Moon*'s half-idea begins with a woman who runs away from an abusive husband, but then we never hear what happens to her. The story wanders without sufficient cause and effect and therefore lacks unity. This idea might work for a novel, but not a play. For this idea to succeed as a play, the writer needs to choose a *central conflict* and develop it. This is because plays (and movies) develop through real, linear time. But it is a heightened reality, charged with the urgency of conflicts unfolding before the audience's eyes. You can't stop the play to ponder some tangential, if fascinating, philosophical problem. You can't rewind it to re-examine where a secondary storyline might have some kind of thematic connection to the primary action. Watching a play, we're in a state of constant present-tense, following a chain of immediate needs and desires, of action and reaction in response to a central problem, that keeps us involved and informed. If this urgency and forward momentum is lost, so is the play's audience.

Although "unity of action" is a general dramatic rule, some forms of experimental or religious theater do employ large, sweeping and occasionally non-linear stories. In certain Eastern traditions, long epic narratives such as the *Ramayana* and *Mahabharata* are communal, episodic retellings of religious stories. The medieval "*Miracle*" and "*Mystery*" *cycles* similarly took their audiences on a tour of the Bible. But these drew and kept their audiences primarily because they reiterated and reinforced shared communal narratives and religious beliefs.

More recently, we have the Epic Theater created by Bertolt Brecht (1898-1956), which challenged traditional cause-and-effect plots and substituted stories made up of episodic sequences that may or may not be related to each other. Epic Theater, promoting mainly Marxist ideologies and Hegelian dialectics, encouraged plays with a grand scope, longer timespan, wider range of incidents, and, therefore, a broader social reach. For example, one Epic Theater production in postwar Germany staged Tolstoy's *War and Peace*. Where traditional plays attempt to structure their events according to unity and rising action in a linear progression (a series of progressively more extreme actions taken to solve a single, overarching dilemma), Epic Theater presents an irregular path of sometimes unrelated (and usually political) events; each scene stands as an independent unit rather than a part of a causal sequence.

More recently we have experimentalists such as Robert Wilson, whose plays like *The Civil Wars* challenge both dramatic structure and their audience's patience with long spectacles united primarily by imagery and music rather than by story. But even viewed in relation to these looser formats, Playwright #4's story wanders too much without a unifying social, political, or artistic message. Besides, while a few playwrights continue to write epics—such as David Edgar's marathon adaptation of Dickens' *Nicholas Nickleby*—such plays are an enormous challenge for theaters to mount and far less likely to be produced. (For more on Epic Theater see Chapter 2.) Also, these unorthodox efforts, however brilliant, are difficult for general audiences to understand or connect with. However proletarian in intention, as with "art films" and twelve-tone music, they tend to find an audience only among a limited, sophisticated elite.

If you are just starting out, stick to the basics. Write a play with a clear thought-line.

Playwright #5 (Working Title: *Innocent Revenge*)

This play is about a man who was furious with his wife and wanted her dead. One day he got a baseball bat and waited in Central Park for her. When she passed by, he jumped out and whacked her. She fell and impaled herself on a park bench. My story is about the trial and how the man is really innocent. In the end, the jury agrees, because the park bench is what killed the woman, not the husband. He leaves the courtroom, starts his life over, and this time he gets it right.

Hmm, what's wrong with this idea? It has action, characters, crisis, and unity—but it's lacking something: *plausibility*. It just doesn't feel true. The action of the play is illogical, and no audience will buy it. What jury would find the park bench and not the husband responsible for the death? The only possible justifications might be that this is an absurdist satire and/or that the playwright wants to make some sort of statement about our screwed-up judicial system, in which case the central character might be a shady lawyer bending the law to defeat common sense. But the playwright doesn't say that, doesn't even suggest this notion. So the story is a contrivance. A good playwright seeks out the truth inherent in her premise and reveals it for the audience through a plausible sequence of related actions. This idea as stated is implausible, and until a premise is provided to justify the plot, it remains a half-idea.

Playwright #6 (Working Title: *Dancing in Dark Cells*)

My concept involves the manifestations of the bleaker goals and aspirations of mankind. An exploration of how we extrapolate the truth upon the steel traps of false souls; the materialistic actualizations of two main conventionalists, both of whom remain close despite the demagnetized roles of society and anticlimactic roles of the media. I explore the duality of the human condition as opposed to the singularity of our hostility; a single set of which may gain ascendancy over the commonplace "mortal coil."

Uh, yeah. What can we say? Between the two of us, the authors of this book have about a dozen years of post-graduate education, we've attended every type of performance (including cricket matches), read everything from Heraclitus to Derrida, and written every thing from Kabuki plays to sitcoms to action/adventure movies—and we still haven't the vaguest idea of what this student is trying to say. A good playwright is a communicator. If you can't communicate your ideas, you're not ready to write. This is a half-idea because it is nothing more than pseudo-philosophical gobbledygook. Not only does this emperor wear no clothes, there does not even seem to be an emperor. *Dancing in Dark Cells* doesn't even come close to answering the basic questions: Who are the characters? What do they want? What is the conflict? This playwright should go back to the proverbial drawing board to redefine his conceptualizations with greater underlying dramaturgical perspicacity.

Playwright #7 (Working Title: *The First Annual Chicago Historic Bar Tour*)
My play is going to be about a group of professionals who take a tour of the historic bars of Chicago. The characters are all like historians, lawyers, professors, and doctors. At the first bar they play superior games with each other by discussing obscure Cambodian writers and outdoing each other with witty puns. Then, about the third bar, they begin getting drunk. By the fifth bar they are telling each other what they really think. Soon, total social order breaks down as they fall in love with each other's spouses and slap-fights break out between the most sophisticated. I see them telling the bus driver how to drive, mooning people they see out the bus windows, and swimming in the Chicago River. The next morning they wake up in jail and act like nothing happened. I think it would make a good comedy that'd show the fundamental hypocrisy of people.

This might be a very good story, but it is a half-idea because it relies on *cinematic thinking*. In other words, it's almost unstageable. The playwright sees the story as a movie, not a play. Cinematic thinking is a common problem with young playwrights who grow up on a steady diet of television and movies, in which sustained scenes are the exception. In the theater an abundance of scenes can give a story an intermittent feeling, actually slowing it down as sets have to be changed, and be difficult and expensive to stage. The frequent jumps in time and location as the tour moves from bar to bus to the Chicago River could only be staged by only the largest of theaters and would seldom be produced for reasons of cost alone. Movies and television can use an unlimited number of sets and characters, but the theater is limited. Broadway may produce massive pageant dramas and huge spectacles, but they're rare and tend to be devoted to musicals and entertainments of mass appeal, not serious drama. For every *Miss Saigon*, where a helicopter lands on stage, there are a thousand small plays that stay within the physical and economic limitation of most theaters.

Cinematic thinking can infect a script on many levels. It doesn't have to be as big as this bus tour idea, it can be quite small. A screenwriter-turned-playwright might come up with a final stage direction like this: "Sam, holding the molotov cocktail, hurls Bill over a table and dashes out the door. He jumps on a motorcycle parked there by the curb, hot wires it, and guns it. Before he can throw the bomb, Bill runs out to stop him. Sam hops the curb, driving over Bill while launching the cocktail back into the room, then peeling down the street (offstage). Bill, bleeding and broken, reaches after him before collapsing dead, as the house erupts in flame." This is the end of a movie, not a play. How could a director block all this safely and predictably, night after night? Perhaps if both actors are seasoned stunt professionals and there's a large pyrotechnics budget it can be done, but the cost and headaches for the designer and technical director wouldn't be worth it. As you imagine your play, are you seeing close-ups and camera angles? Do you see the action taking place in real locations rather than on a stage? Are you seeing effects that in a film would require separate setups and skilled technicians and stuntmen to pull off? If so, then you're guilty of cinematic thinking. For a screenwriter, cinematic thinking is a requirement, but for a playwright, it's a liability. In a way, the restrictions of the stage are liberating: You know your restrictions, now you can write for them, just as the rhyme scheme of a sonnet frees you from the intimidating formlessness of blank verse.

One way to break yourself of cinematic thinking is to sit in an empty theater and try to imagine your play being staged there. Try this before, during, and after you write the first draft. Make sure it's a small theater, not some massive house. Most theaters have tiny budgets and little storage, fly, or wing space. Get up on the stage and try to imagine how you (with little time and less money) would stage your play. After all, Sophocles could summon the gods, and Shakespeare could describe history-changing battles, within the confines of a nearly bare stage. Jerzy Grotowski, director of the Polish Laboratory Theatre, called for a "poor theatre," a theater that eliminated technological aids and effects and concentrated on the actor–audience relationship. You can take away the costumes, scenery, makeup, lighting, and sound, but you can't eliminate the actor. Limit yourself to the confines of the poor theater and you will find true freedom (and more productions).

Playwright #8 (Working Title: *The West*)

I have always wanted to tell the story of the cowboys: from the first explorers to Custer's Last Stand to the last real cowboys of Alaska. This play would deal with the Indian question, the devastation of the buffalo herds, the coming of the Iron Horse, and the depletion of our national resources. There would be scenes depicting the Donner party, the outlaws, Butch Cassidy and the Sundance Kid, the O.K. Corral, and the simple sheep rancher. There is a statement here about part of the American character that I think we've lost.

This idea has tons of conflict/crisis, plenty of characters, an abundance of action. But, on top of suffering from cinematic thinking, it suffers from an over-abundance of scope. How on earth would you show the coming of the Iron Horse or the devastation of the buffalo herds on stage? It's not a half-idea; it's dozens of ideas, and so its scope is too wide for a play. It might make a great novel or miniseries; James Michener would've loved it. But it's not a play. For one thing, it's episodic, and while it may seem to have unity—the story of the rape of the West—that in itself is too all-inclusive. When it comes to a single man's life, Aristotle wrote in *Poetics* that "the infinitely miscellaneous incidents cannot be reduced to a unity." How much more difficult, then, to reduce to unity an entire chapter in a nation's history. A good play has a more focused scope. It generally concerns itself with a limited number of characters and only a few hours in those characters' lives (although the hours may be spread over many years, as in *Same Time, Next Year*). Even Epic Theater is necessarily limited when compared to a movie or novel. A play falls closer to a poem than a novel. Scope means more than just a story that's small enough to fit within the confines of a play. It involves a creative selection and compression of the important parts of the story into a unified, premise-driven work of art. This western history could be written, but it would need to be much more specific. The playwright can still make his point about the American West by concentrating on and telling a tenth of the story he originally intended. Let single locations, fewer characters, and stageable situations represent and stand in for the larger events surrounding them. Shakespeare opened *Macbeth* with a brilliant dialogue description of the battle just won; he didn't attempt to reenact the whole battle on the stage.

IT'LL COST YOU

Closely related to scope is budget. Today, most professional theaters are fiscally strapped. In order to keep the payroll down and set-construction costs to a minimum, they're forced to look for plays with small casts and simple sets. If you have more than six characters and more than one set, you're reducing your chances of getting produced. This isn't a hard-and-fast rule, but it's generally true, and so, for practical reasons alone, a playwright should make sure all the characters are necessary. If you have small parts that serve only one function or appear for only a few minutes, try to combine them into a major character or, as is often done, design those roles so they can be double- or triple-cast—so one actor can play two or three small roles.

Playwright #9 (Working Title: *Dinner with the Smiths*)

> **I want to write a short one-act about a family dinner that turns into a nightmare. The Smith family gathers to welcome home their son. They think he's been in Spain for over a decade; in fact, he just escaped from a mental institution. The son desperately wants to tell everyone that he's spent the last ten years in a straightjacket, not Madrid, but before he can, his father announces that he doesn't love his mother, that he is gay, and that he has AIDS. The father then attempts suicide but fails. The daughter explains that she just flunked out of medical school. She's so ashamed that she attempts suicide and succeeds. Meanwhile, the mother reveals that the son is adopted, but the truth is too much for her—she has a heart attack.**

There are several problems here. First, this idea lacks focus. Whose story is it—or, more precisely, which character is central and carries the premise and action to a conclusion? Is it about the crazy son, the suicidal father, the embarrassed daughter, or the mother with the heart problem? Even if it's about all of them, what is the point of it all? This might make a good play, but some choices have to be made. And if you're just starting out, you're less likely to defeat yourself and grow discouraged if you create a play with a single protagonist, a clear premise, and concentrate on how that protagonist's story works out that theme.

The protagonist is a story's central character, around whom the play is written and the one in whose story the audience invests itself. The protagonist is also the one who takes action and drives the main conflict. In this student's idea, none of the members of the family seems to be the main focus of the story. As result, it is a half-idea. There is simply too much going on, all at a high pitch. If you press too many high-wire events into a short period of time, the result will be not only unbelievable but also unintentionally comic. Unless this play is a farce (which it isn't), Playwright #9 would be better off fully exploring one of the four stories she presents here. Give yourself time to develop your characters' conflicts before you move on to new complications.

Playwright #10 (Working Title: *Above Suspicion*)
> This is the story of a famous athlete who is on trial for murder. It's a lot like the O.J. Simpson story only I'm going to make it a hockey player. I think the idea is very topical and will attract a lot of interest. The conflicts would come from his relationship with his lawyer, missing his children, and the final verdict.

When asked why he wanted to write this play, the student answered, "It's a hot topic, and I think if you want to get on Broadway it's a good idea to be on top of popular current interests." The problem is, by the time you finish your "Broadway play," current interests, like all ephemera, will have changed and Broadway will be producing something different. Write what you need to write, what you want to write, and with a lot of luck and a damn good play, maybe Broadway (or to be totally truthful, Off Broadway or Off Off Broadway) will look your way. While certain theatrical hits—*The Vagina Monologues*, *The Laramie Project*, *The Bloodknot*—were topical and certainly written with that in mind, we can guarantee you that popular current interest had nothing to do with the writing—or the success—of such enormously successful plays as *Amadeus* or *Equus*. The point is that your play must first and foremost be something you yourself would want to see, something you care about and will be glad to have written, even if it never gets to Broadway. Like those quickly produced paperbacks that emerge after every news or celebrity sensation, trendy plays (sometimes called flavor-of-the-month plays) seldom stand the test of time; they're a hit while the trend lasts, then they're forgotten. The truth a playwright seeks must be true tomorrow as well as today. Don't write what you think will be popular or successful or what people want to see. Write what you need to write or want to write. Make it good, communicate truthfully, and perhaps popular current interest will turn in your direction of its own accord. Commercially successful or not, you'll be a happier writer.

Playwright #11 (Working Title: *Meet the Press*)
> I want to write a fake state-of-the-union address in which the President of the United States must admit that he has an IQ of only 50. He'll show how he gets all his good lines through an ear piece from the Vice President (who is standing offstage) and that he really doesn't

even know how to read. He'll also show off his certificate for winning the Special Olympics and much much more.

The problem with this is that it's not a play. It's a *skit*—a short, humorous, or satirical sketch that plays a single joke to its extreme. True, skits are a form of theater (they need actors, a stage, and such), but skit concepts will not sustain a full play—as you know if you've seen any of the movies made from *Saturday Night Live* skits. If your idea feels like it belongs on *Saturday Night Live*, then write it for that sort of skit-based venue. We're not saying you shouldn't make a political point—a lot of theater is about making political points. But if your idea revolves around a single joke, there's probably not enough substance to justify interest or a professional production.

Playwright #12 (Working Title: *Black as Snow*)
I have this idea about a black family who moves into an all-white town. It's based on a story I heard about a black doctor who moved to the Upper Peninsula of Michigan, a predominantly white part of the United States. Even though this small town desperately needed a doctor, they drove him and his family out. We always hear about how well America is coping with racism and how progressive legislation has become, but it still exists and is still pervasive. This play would show how the black family deals with the hatred as the father's medical practice goes bankrupt and the family falls apart.

The twelfth time is a charm. This is a good idea for a play. It has conflict, crisis, unity, action, and the beginnings of character. Its scope is well within the confines of a play, and it deals with a basic truth. So far, each element is only partially worked out, but it's a beginning, and a good one. The one potential problem this writer faces is that she risks preaching to the audience. David Mamet in *Three Uses of the Knife* calls this kind of drama a "Problem Play" and declares it "cleansed of invention" because it focuses on a societal problem with obvious right and wrong sides of an obvious, politically correct argument. Both writer and audience may feel a smug power in siding correctly, because their moral sensibility has not been challenged, only reaffirmed. Presuming an enlightened audience, it is literally an exercise in preaching to the choir, and therefore both sanctimonious and pointless. Louis Catron, in his excellent text *Playwriting*, repeatedly hammers the point home: Show, don't tell—prove your premise through characters we believe and care about, not through speechifying. Lajos Egri states outright: "Never use your play as a soapbox. Have a message, by all means, but have it naturally and subtly" grow out of a genuine human situation.

Assuming our writer avoids the soapbox problem, one question remains: Can she deliver? The oldest adage in writing is, "Write what you know." This doesn't mean just write about your own life—which is unlikely to contain the stuff of gripping drama—but about the emotions and characters you personally understand, situations you can grasp, and the kinds of stories that you yourself like. In the case of *Black as Snow*, does this student understand the problems and feelings associated with discrimination? This budding playwright was a Korean exchange student in the United States for a year's study. Could she understand and write about the feelings of a black family in the midst of a white majority? As it turned out, she was born and raised in Japan, where she was considered an "alien" by the Japanese government. Even though her family had lived in Japan for three generations, she was denied Japanese citizenship and treated as a second-class member of society because of her Korean ancestry—so she did know a great deal about discrimination. She still had research to do about the black experience in America, but she had what it took to write what she knew. Perhaps writing her own story about growing up Korean in Japan would be easier, but sometimes a writer needs to make a story less personal by putting some distance between herself and the subject.

Writing what you know is really just a place to begin. The excellent screenwriter Katherine Fugate suggests that you should write what you don't know—in other words, write to explore the world and enrich your experience. But, as you will always be you, whatever you learn will become, necessarily, what you know. It will just take longer to get there.

At their most basic, all plays are about characters, what they want, what they do ("action"), what stymies them, and the conflicts and crises that result. A central, organizing theme with clear focus and unity of action drives all of these elements. Experienced playwrights have a natural (meaning well-learned) sense for these requirements, but a beginner must carefully analyze his or her idea before starting down the long path of writing and development. You don't want to work for months only to find that your basic idea is flawed. If all you have is a half-idea, that's not half-bad as long as you can find the other half. Most good ideas start off as half-ideas. Rarely does a brilliant play emerge fully formed from the writer's mind. Ideas come in fits and starts, and each one has an incubation period. If you can recognize a half-idea's missing elements, stay with what excites you about it, and take it down a clear, logical path, chances are good you'll write a good play.

I Can't Define It, But I Know It When I See It

No, we're not talking about obscenity, though Supreme Court Justice Potter Stewart's words on that topic apply here too. We're talking about premise, or theme. While we firmly believe that it will help you immensely to find and define your premise as early as possible, sometimes your theme simply doesn't become clear until you begin to write. Arthur Miller (*All My Sons, Death of a Salesman*) said that often the theme of his plays was not clear to him until his second or third draft. Theme is critical to any play, but isn't strictly necessary in order to begin writing, and it can happen that a writer who's locked into a particular theme may sacrifice character and story and resort to speechifying to prove the theme correct. As we said, you don't want a propaganda or "problem" play in which the characters are only mouthpieces for the author's message. Whether you have a complex or a simple idea, its theme must be embedded in and revealed by character and action. If you start with strong characters and the other playwriting essentials we've just discussed, you most likely will find your theme before too long.

Now that you have a basic idea for a play, you should ask yourself a few basic questions before you start down the long path of development and writing:

Is That Diverse Play I Ever Saw?

A play should appeal to different races, genders, and regions. If you say you're writing to a select group of people, then you're defeating the purpose of writing a play. A play should never be so personal that only a select group can understand it. For example, one student from Beverly Hills finished a scenario in which the antagonist was a leaf-blower. Needless to say, it was an avant-garde piece. The leaf-blower was never explained, for it made perfect sense to the playwright, because at that time there was a great deal of controversy in the city of Beverly Hills because the city council was thinking of banning the use of leaf-blowers due to the noise. But, to anyone who didn't live in or near Beverly Hills, the leaf-blower analogy was totally meaningless. The art of playwriting is the art of communication. So, before you go any farther, you must ask yourself if your play will communicate to a diverse audience.

Why Do I Want to Write It?

Writing is like a painful rash; you have to scratch it or be miserable. But to write well requires hard work and long hours, so be sure to ask yourself why you want to write. If your sole reason is that you need a play idea for class tomorrow, and any idea will do, you're in trouble. Your interest will surely wane. If you want to write to make money, you're in even deeper trouble. Few playwrights make a living at their craft. If your sole reason is to tickle your own fancy, regardless of whether anyone else cares or understands what you write, you're also in trouble. Expressing yourself is essential, but playwrights must communicate as they do so. The playwright whose sole desire is to express himself selfishly, who writes only as therapy, ends up with a diary entry, pages of deeply personal emotions that mean nothing to anyone but himself. Writing is a painful, lonely enough process as it is, that more often than not leads to failure. Why put yourself through it, if not for some larger purpose? The only reason to write a play is because you are compelled to understand the world and to communicate your thoughts and discoveries to others.

IS MY PLAY UNIQUE?

Thousands of plays are published and produced every year; tens of thousands are written. How will mine stand out from the crowd? You must ask yourself, What makes my play unique? True, as we noted at the beginning of this chapter, your own special take on things will certainly help, but you should also look at your subject, characters, and plot. Do they imitate those found in other plays or do they each have some point of view or device (some fresh situation, structural approach or narrative hook) that will make your play one of a kind? For example, countless plays have been written about love affairs, love triangles, unrequited love, you name it. When it comes to love, the subject has been pretty much explored. Yet, the play *Betrayal* by Harold Pinter (*The Dumbwaiter*, *The Birthday Party*) is unique. It's the story of a woman who falls in love with her husband's best friend. Certainly, this love triangle story isn't new. One can argue that Pinter's distinct point of view, his original take on things, makes his story different, but what made the play unique was a structural device that makes his play different from all other love triangle plays. He tells the story backwards. He starts with the breakup and moves back through time from the characters' last to their first meeting. The scenes flowing backward through time allows him to look at an old story in a new way.

PSYCHO DRAMA?

Playwriting has been compared to therapy, because playwrights are constantly trying to heal the psychological and social problems that plague them and our society. It's been said that playwrights "write to get well," as if once they're well, they no longer have the need or desire to write. Perhaps there is some truth in this. Playwright Christopher Hampton gave his character Celia in *The Philanthropist* this arch line: "It is our belief that no human being who devotes his life and energy to the manufacture of fantasies can be anything but fundamentally inadequate." Therapy can be wonderful, but the play will remain nothing more than therapy, a comforting diary entry, if the playwright doesn't have a deep desire to communicate her particular view about how the world is or should be.

2

Schools of Thought

I'm back in fashion again for a while now. But I imagine that three or four years from now I'll be out again. And in another fifteen years I'll be back. If you try to write to stay in fashion, if you try to write to be the critics' darling, you become an employee.

Edward Albee

Good playwrights don't deliberately set out to become the critics' darlings, but instead try to find their own voices. Your voice comes from your experiences, the rules of your society, your culture, your lifestyle, upbringing, the age you live in, the part of the world you occupy, and so forth. The various schools of thought that exist at the time you're writing can also affect it. By "schools of thought" we mean the distinctive systems and/or theories (structural, aesthetic, moral, political) on how a play should be written. In the long history of playwriting, tens of thousands of playwrights have developed, contributed to, blindly followed, and attacked various schools of thought.

In this chapter we'll look at the definitions, methods, and histories of several of these schools of thought that are popular today in the West: Realism, Romanticism, Expressionism, Absurdism, Epic Theater, and Brechtian Alienation. Our hope is that by defining them, you'll be able to choose the one that works best for your play, combine them to fit your needs, or perhaps even cast them aside and create a new one. Before we get to the "isms," however, we first must examine the two great over-arching theatrical categories, of which all the rest are subsets.

TO LAUGH OR NOT TO LAUGH, THAT IS THE QUESTION (COMEDY AND TRAGEDY)

Comedy and tragedy have been recognized genres for thousands of years. The ancient Greeks had play festivals dedicated to both (tragedy by 534 B.C. and comedy starting in 442 B.C.), and any of the schools of theater mentioned below (Realism, Romanticism, Expressionism, Absurdism, or Epic) can be made into either serious or comic plays. Comedy and tragedy have stuck around so long because they signify the basic yin and yang of life. They describe the vast differences in human experience (and interpretation of that experience), and yet they're separated by the thinnest of margins. The lightest comedy ever written has within it the makings of a good tragedy, while the darkest tragedy ever to grace the stage has at its core the makings of a good comedy. "Comedy," Peter Ustinov once said, "is simply a funny way of being serious." To which we'll add, tragedy is a serious way of being funny. Or as Mel Brooks said, "Tragedy is when I cut my finger. Comedy is when you fall into an open sewer and die." But comedy also offers a release from life's troubles. In his televised interview in *Inside the Actor's Studio*, Mike Myers called silliness "a state of grace."

MAKE 'EM LAUGH (COMEDY)

Ideas of what's funny have changed through the centuries. In the Middle Ages, the handicapped were often the butt of jokes, while during the Restoration the bedroom escapades of the upper class provided most of the laughs (at least for the upper class). And don't get us started on Shakespeare's fart jokes. Come to think of it, maybe not that much has changed. It was only until well past the mid-twentieth century that jokes based on race and ethnicity became socially unacceptable, but these still thrive in private conversation. Barely hidden under a thin social veneer of good taste or political correctness that restrains our more coarse or even cruel instincts, much of comedy remains by its nature as dependent on humanity's baser side as it is on sparkling wit, light entertainment, and good humor. The success of the Farrelly Brothers' movie *Dumb and Dumber* proves the point that we haven't evolved all that much from the days of Chaucer's *The Miller's Tale*, or of the Athenian satyr plays (the latter being the lineal ancestors of the more sophisticated comedy of satire). They don't call it a belly laugh for nothing; much of comedy has always been gut-level. That being said, there has also always been a brighter side to comedy, where rapier wit, character incompatibilities, and social lampooning are at the heart of the humor, as exemplified by the comedies of Shakespeare, Oscar Wilde, and Alan Ayckbourn. This ebb and flow between the base and brainy has gone on since the beginning.

Today, there are several prevalent types of comedy. First, there is the standard "sentimental comedy," which takes an entertaining look at the problems, fears and troubles of common people, and of course has a happy conclusion in which those troubles end, at least temporarily. Sentimental comedies allow us to laugh with and/or at people who are like us, while reinforcing our hope that everything will work out for the best. Plays like *The Dinning Room* by A. R. Gurney and *The Man who Came to Dinner* by Moss Hart and George Kaufman are examples of sentimental comedies. Next there's the "farce," in which characters are caught in fast-paced, improbable, and often broadly satirical circumstances. The fastest farces are sometimes called "door-slamming farces" because so many characters are entering and exiting that the hinges are constantly in use. One of the most successful farces of late was *Noises Off* by Michael Frayne. Lastly there are "dark comedies" (sometimes called black comedies), which allow the audience to laugh at the bleaker and/or absurd side of life, those things that would normally not be considered amusing (such as death). Dark comedies are a nervous chuckle as we waltz past the graveyard, and they don't always have a happy ending. An example of a dark comedy would be *Little Murders* by Jules Feiffer. The raw, raunchy humor found in teen-oriented movie comedies (such as those of the Farrelly Brothers) tends not to have a home in the theater, but there's always hope.

When writing funny for the stage, one thing you might want to steer clear of is a subset of the sentimental comedy known as the "situation comedy" (called "sitcoms" on television). Many theaters will state in their call for scripts (see Chapter 10), "No situation comedies." At its most basic, a sitcom is a humorous story that depends on the situation more than the characters. Sitcom writers place stock characters (in other words, basic character types such as evil mother-in-laws, dumb blondes, and bickering parents) into funny situations and explore the predicaments that result. Simple (and simple-minded) jokes and characters who seldom grow or change dominate sitcoms. They also usually have "safe" themes and commonplace subject matter that never insults the audience or troubles them to think too much.

And yet, sitcoms have been a part of the theater for thousands of years. One of the most famous of the ancient sitcom writers was Menander (342-292 B.C.) who wrote more than one hundred such comedies. In the thousands of years since, sitcoms haven't changed much, except for the fact that fewer and fewer theaters are willing to produce them. This is because they dominate television and, as a result, the feeling is that theater audiences won't be willing to fork out fifty bucks a ticket (more or less) to see something they get for free at home. Most theaters want to present plays that have a deeper meaning than that provided by the typical sitcom, though some exceptions come to mind: Neil Simon's early plays, for example, strongly resembled sitcoms in form and dialogue, and made him extremely famous and extremely rich. However, when he wrote those plays (i.e., *Star Spangled Girl, Barefoot in the Park, The Odd Couple*) television was in its infancy. Today, sitcoms are pretty much dead as far as most professional theaters are concerned (though community and high school theaters may still appreciate them, and in the wake of monetary successes like the recent theatrical staging of episodes from *The Brady Bunch*, one never knows).

You can steer clear of sitcom writing by focusing on well-developed characters who *change* over the course of your play and stories that make audiences think, rather than just entertain them. As a general rule, if your comedy is more dependent on character than situation, it is considered more sophisticated. If your comedy is more dependent on situation and events, it's considered less sophisticated. Whichever is the case, reputable theater companies never consider either type of comedy easier to pull off than drama. And most playwrights feel that, of the two, comedy is the more difficult to pull off successfully.

Make 'Em Cry (Tragedy)

Serious dramas, just like comedies, can follow the tenets of Realism, Romanticism, Expressionism, Absurdism, or Epic style. The oldest form of serious drama is tragedy. The word "tragedy" today means an unfortunate, sad, or disastrous turn of events, yet to the ancient Greeks, who (as far as we know) were the first to produce these plays, the subject of a tragedy was serious but not necessarily depressing. In fact, the origin of the word tragedy has nothing to do with grief and sadness, but comes from the ancient Greek words "tragos" (goat) and "oide" (song) and meant "goat song." This connected the drama to the fertility rites that the ancient plays grew out of. (The Greeks considered the goat a sexually potent animal, as well as the vehicle for ritually cleansing the society through its slaughter as a "scapegoat.") Greek Tragedies were concerned with the search for the meaning of life and were designed to help the audience understand the factors that cause suffering and dilemma. Because tragedy dealt with such high-minded topics, the Greeks also felt that tragedies could not be about lower-class citizens or the poor, but could only revolve around an extraordinary hero of noble birth. The idea was akin to the adage "the bigger they are, the harder they fall," and falling far and hard was an important part of ancient Greek drama (as, indeed, it was for Shakespeare two thousand years later).

Today, theater purists insist that real tragedies are no longer possible because there just aren't that many extraordinary people of noble birth lounging around our communities. As a result, modern versions of tragedy have been called "tragedies of the common man." These take a serious look at our search for the meaning of everyday life and ask powerful questions such as: What's our purpose? Can we rise above our apparent destiny? Are we doomed by the simple emotions of love, jealousy, and revenge? Can we perceive our character flaws before they destroy us? Tragedies of the common man generally end tragically (no big surprise), and, as the ancient tragedies did, they should leave the audience with a feeling of catharsis. They're also intended to inspire the members of the audience to examine their own lives and purge themselves of flaws they share with the main characters. Some good examples of tragedies of the common man are Arthur Miller's *Death of a Salesman* and Tennessee Williams' *A Streetcar Named Desire*.

THE TEARS OF A CLOWN (MIXING COMEDY AND TRAGEDY)

Aristotle wrote in *Poetics* that tragedy and comedy should never co-mingle in the same play. During the Renaissance, most playwrights (particularly in France and Italy) would've agreed, but that's not the case today. Mixing comedy and tragedy in the same play is perfectly acceptable as long as its basic style remains the same—you might think twice about having broad slapstick comedy in the middle of a serious play about AIDS—but then again, you might not, depending on how much pathos you can subsequently squeeze out of the situation. Juxta-posing emotions can create powerful contrasts and emotional highs and lows that pure comedy or pure tragedy alone may not be able to create. One old dictum in the theater is, "If you want to make someone cry, first make 'em laugh." Modern "serious" plays no longer need to be unrelievedly serious, or to have sad endings for that matter, but they do need to seriously explore the emotional, intellectual, and psychological elements that make up the human condition. Above all, when writing a serious drama or a comedy with heart, do not write just a diary entry. The story might be highly personal, but the theme—the unifying idea of the play—must be universal and the stakes high enough to justify the use of drama.

The basic elements life (love and war, birth and death, pain and happiness) can be both serious and incredibly funny (often at the same time). About comedy and drama, Alan Ayckbourn says in his book *The Crafty Art of Playmaking*: "I certainly don't decide when I sit down to write: Today I'm going to write a comedy. Simply, I'm going to write a play. The degree of lightness or darkness is often initially dic-tated by the theme, but never to the extent that I would ever want the one totally to exclude the other." The same is true when it comes to basic theatrical schools of thought. Sometimes a playwright will sit down intending to write a Realist or Romantic or Absurdist play. But more often than not, these decisions are made by the play. As it flows from you, it will tell you what type of play it's going to be. And once the play speaks to you, it's important to have at least an idea of theater's basic schools of thought and which will best suit your purposes. Here, then are some guidelines.

JUST THE FACTS, MA'AM (REALISM)

Without thinking about it, most novice playwrights automatically write in a realistic form. To most, this means writing authentic situations, psychologically motivated characters, and dialogue designed to reflect how modern people talk when they're in the kitchen, bedroom, or corner café. Yet, Realism as a school of thought is about far more than just being authentic. Realism is a style of theater that examines problems and assumes that solutions are possible because, since the Enlightenment (or even since the Renaissance and the Humanist movement), we in the West have developed a sense that there's a cause-and-effect logic at work in the world, a definable perspective, a progressive narrative as to how society and human beings operate. Realism's underlying principle is that we can talk things out, take action, analyze our problems, and in so doing change our lives, set a new course, and come up with solutions to the problems that plague everyday existence.

This doesn't mean that Realism always presents solutions. In a tragic Realist play, the characters may end up trapped by their inability to see their way through to one. (Although we, the audience, often are meant to—we can see what the characters can't, and therein lies both the lesson and the pathos of the drama.) Rather, Realism is more concerned with the problems themselves, the idea being that before we can ever hope to come up with a solution, we must clearly identify the problem and confront it if we want to change the status quo. In this, Realism reveals itself to be rather unrealistic (except perhaps in the case of tragic Realism), for seldom do ordinary people in everyday life really understand and confront the problems afflicting them. Most people go through life avoiding problems, sweeping them under the rug and out of sight. When images of starving babies flicker on the TV screen, we change channels; we immediately flip to the sports section, rather than face scary headlines; we hope for the best, but avoid taking a stand, rather than confront injustice. Humans are so proficient at avoiding problems that we can become blind to the fact that problems even exist, or if we do see them, we beg off with the excuse that there's nothing we can do about them. We sail through a sea of troubles, convincing ourselves that our relationships, society, and government are doing the best they can, or at any rate could be worse if we rocked the boat. Since we fail to perceive problems, we also fail to solve them. Theatrical Realism, then, is a heightened or directed manipulation of "reality" that sets out to help the audience recognize problems, dissect them, sometimes solve them, and perhaps even admit that they themselves may be part of the problem.

Realist playwrights may see no need to present solutions to the problems they present, because once the audience is fully cognizant of the problems, the solutions should be apparent. Realist plays are sometimes called "problem plays" because they concentrate more effort on defining problems than on proposing answers. For example, one of the first Realist plays was Henrik Ibsen's (1828-1906) *A Doll's*

House, the story of a young woman, Nora, who is dominated by her husband and a patriarchal society. At first, Nora is blind to her situation and inadequacies. But the events of the play force her to see that she's hardly more evolved than a child, and that the only way she can become a fully functioning human being is by leaving her husband and children. So she strikes out on her own, slamming the door behind her. This can hardly be called a solution to Nora's problems, for the play was written and takes place in 1879, when a woman walking out on her husband and children was an outrageous act that would certainly have led her to be shunned by society. But Nora's action wasn't designed by the playwright to solve her problem. He wanted theatergoers to look at themselves and realize that their patriarchal societies gave people—especially women—little chance at self-actualization. With this epiphany, some solutions might be found in real life.

The audience certainly did do something when *A Doll's House* was first performed. The theater patrons were so outraged and insulted they ripped off the theater's billboard. To avoid trouble, other theaters that produced the play simply rewrote the ending so that Nora reconsidered and begged her husband for forgiveness. (International copyright laws weren't yet in effect; for more on copyrights see Chapter 8.)

Ibsen's other Realist plays were considered an affront to public decency and banned in many countries. Reviewers dubbed Ibsen a "lunatic" and a "pervert," while his plays were labeled "revolting" and "blasphemous." The same thing has happened on many occasions with Realist plays. For example, when Sean O'Casey's *The Plough and the Stars* (1926) was first performed at the Abbey Theater, the audiences rioted in the streets, because they didn't like how O'Casey portrayed the leaders of the Irish nationalist movement as half-wits and their conflict as one in which men indiscriminately slaughtered each other.

Realist playwrights usually discard such devices as soliloquies and asides to the audience as being, well, unrealistic. The exception—in fact, the opposite—arises in a different, more recent form of Realism growing in popularity today: the one-person autobiographical or confessional performance, such as Eve Ensler's *The Vagina Monologues*. This work, too, initially generated a powerful and often vehemently negative critical reaction, although by and large it has come to be accepted. This monologistic type of theater has ties to (one might even say roots in) the stand-up comedy tradition, going back to Lenny Bruce and continuing through Lily Tomlin, George Carlin, Richard Pryor, Jackie Mason, Chris Rock, Julia Sweeney, John Leguizamo, Eddie Izzard, and others. While the one-person monologue is somewhat outside of the focus of this book (where we're focusing on multi-character conflict-driven drama), it nonetheless is a form of realistic, truth-telling theater designed to figuratively smack the audience awake, either through humor or shock tactics, to confront contemporary personal or political problems.

"But wait," you complain, "I just want to write something that moves me, and hopefully other people. Are you saying it isn't realistic if I don't tick people off?" No, we're not. We're saying that part of your goal, if you are writing a Realist play, ought to be at the very least to challenge your audience to examine personal and societal problems (an act which sometimes ticks them off).

All this may make Realism sound rather dark or negative, if not outright dangerous to the playwright, but in fact Realism is a rather positive genre—in presenting a problem, it necessarily suggests the corollary idea that there may be a solution. The playwright who writes in the Realist style is saying that, if we are willing to face the rocky road ahead, we can with optimism live better lives. Through Realism, playwrights hope they can change the world, or at least nudge it a bit in the right direction.

BACKGROUNDS OF REALISM

Realism as a movement in theater started around 1850. Its godfather was the great Norwegian playwright Henrik Ibsen (1828-1906), author of *A Doll's House*, *Hedda Gabler*, and *Enemy of the People*. It was inspired by such innovative thinkers of the time as Charles Darwin, Sigmund Freud, and Karl Marx, as well as inventors like Thomas Edison and Fox Talbot, who came up with many of the processes behind modern photography. Photography changed how people saw the world. Suddenly, if a farmer in Nebraska wanted to experience Paris, he could see an accurate photo of it, not some painter's varnished impression.

In the 1850s, "authenticity" was all the rage, and the theater followed suit by giving audiences "honest" acting and "natural" looking sets. This was helped by Edison's electric lights, which quickly replaced the dangerous gas- and candle-powered fixtures used up until then. By 1881 the world's first electric powerplant was up and running in New York City and, only four years later, the New Lyceum became the first electricity-powered theater in the world. Electric lights allowed designers to create "realistic" illumination: If the director wanted the morning sun shining in through a set's windows, it was now possible. If the director wanted a raging storm on stage, it could be done with controlled flashes of light; electricity-powered fans that could not only give the audience the feeling that they were in the core of the action, but could blow King Lear right off the stage.

Realism was part of larger, worldwide scientific and philosophical movements intent on revealing the complex psychological reasons behind human actions. Forms of psychology and even pyschotherapy had been around since Aristotle, but they weren't codified into a science until the 1800s, when detailed methodologies were developed. In 1875, the American philosopher William James founded what was probably the world's first psychology laboratory. Other budding psychologists were soon analyzing human instincts, sexual drives, dreams, and what they called our "death wish."

Two of the greatest influences on the perception of human psychology were Charles Darwin and Sigmund Freud. Darwin, author of *The Origin of Species by Means of Natural Selection* (1859), suggested that heredity and environmental factors could be used to explain human behavior. This meant that humans were a scientifically quantifiable product of their surroundings, inherited characteristics, and method of upbringing, and that human actions could be understood, explained, and even predicted and altered through scientific methods. In other words, the human character could be analyzed—a notion that a doctor from Vienna, Sigmund Freud, took up and developed. Freud said that our subconscious plays an important role in shaping our behavior. Subconscious motivations might be suppressed memories from early childhood or traumatic events that we've blocked out of our conscious awareness. Freud theorized that we spend vast amounts of energy forming defense mechanisms to cope with such memories, which result in neuroses or aberrant behaviors. He argued that our basic instincts can only be controlled through socialization, yet socialization often causes us to suppress many natural biological desires and urges, which then submerge into the subconscious. By the turn of the twentieth century, most plays were dominated by Freud-influenced explorations of motivations, heredity, and subconscious.

Although most of Freud's theories have recently been discredited in the practice of psychology, characters in Realist plays are still usually constructed psychologically, and Freud's work remains a vital source of inspiration in the artistic world. This means that a deep, Freudian-like analysis of your characters is possible, and that your characters have reasons and motivations for their actions: Even the smallest walk-on should have an inner life and not be a stereotype. Just like the plot they're enacting, Realist characters are built on cause-and-effect logic, in which every word they speak and every action they take can be traced back to their heritage, and their physical, sociological, and psychological traits. This means that it's a good idea to write character histories dealing with relevant formative elements in their lives up to the moment they walk into the play. (For more on building a character, see Chapter 5.)

Theatrical Realism was also shaped by the German philosopher and social scientist Karl Marx, the chief founder of two of the most powerful political movements in modern history: democratic socialism and revolutionary communism.

Reacting to the economic and social inequities of the burgeoning industrial revolution, Marx expressed his disgust for capitalism, saying that it causes human misery because it takes advantage of the poor and creates a hierarchical social structure in which workers are exploited by the ruling class. Playwrights followed Marx's lead by throwing a limelight on the evils of unregulated profit, the dark side of the industrial revolution, and the exploitation of common people. More and more playwrights began to see themselves as literary scientists, whose job it was to study, critique, and improve humankind and society. Just as the so-called "Impressionists" were attempting to challenge the ossified, mythology-driven art of the Academy with "realistic" and "scientific" portrayals of reality, the Realist playwrights' desire was to overthrow the simplified, sugar-coated views that dominated the stage in favor of drama that would awaken the social conscience, attack provincialism, point out hypocrisy, destroy popular illusions, diagnose the ills of humankind, and cause change by showing us as we really are (at least from their point of view). They argued that only when we look in a mirror and don't like what we see can we begin to change, grow, and improve.

Realism evolved into several stylistic variations. For example, in the 1880s there arose a stringent version of Realism known as "Naturalism." (Although Naturalist playwrights would argue that Naturalism isn't a variation of Realism, but an "ism" all to itself.) The Naturalists wanted to capture onstage life as it is, not as it should be, without formulas, schools of thought, or didactic themes. This meant that most Naturalist playwrights wrote on subjects like poverty, disease, and prostitution. The Russian playwright Maxim Gorky (1868-1936), in *The Lower Depths*, took a stark look at poor people huddled in a cellar of a Moscow flophouse. Anton Chekhov (1860-1904), author of *The Seagull*, *Uncle Vanya*, *The Three Sisters*, and *The Cherry Orchard*, sought only to be an "objective observer" who eavesdrops on life and reports the facts without distortion or revision: "All I wanted was to say honestly to people: 'Have a look at yourselves and see how bad and dreary your lives are!'"

Some playwrights combined Realism with other isms in what has been called "Selective Realism." Arthur Miller did this with *Death of a Salesman*, in which he combined Realist elements with Expressionism (see below). Tennessee Williams combined Realism with heightened language in what came to be called "Poetic Realism."

LET'S BE REALISTIC

If you're going to write a realistic (or Realist) play, you should keep a few things in mind: First, make sure that you have a "take" on a particular problem in life, a theme you want to explore. Fine. But get to know your topic so well that you don't indulge in generalities; details are critical. Let's say you're writing about same-sex marriages in Utah. You'll want to do a lot of research, so that you can show the audience realistic characters (not stereotypes) and a nuanced analysis of the problem. The problem must be so clear that the audience will be able to recognize it, as well as perhaps arrive at possible solutions. Make sure that your characters are not mouthpieces for your political point of view—they shouldn't be aware of the theme of the play, because they're caught up in the events. Let the theme be revealed through subtext, not actual text. Just as with real people, characters in a Realist play don't know how they fit in to the overall scheme of things and don't have such keen insights that they overtly spout the playwright's point of view.

Some contemporary playwrights, like David Mamet, have little patience for the Realist "Problem Play." In *Three Uses of the Knife*, Mamet calls it "a melodrama cleansed of invention" which "allows the viewer to indulge in a fantasy of power…we indulge a desire to feel superior to events, to history, in short, to the natural order." (More on melodrama below.) In other words, we are on our soapbox, preaching—"to the choir" if our message is too obvious and politically correct. What's more, solutions are dishonest and illusory, because events in real life are out of our control. To playwrights like Mamet, tragedy is the only honest form of Realism because it "is a celebration not of our eventual triumph but of the truth—it is not a victory but a resignation."

To avoid the Problem Play's self-indulgence, you must make its actions and conclusions seem not only plausible but also inevitable. Make sure that your plot follows a cause-and-effect, scientific logic. Remember, if you want to suggest that change is possible, your characters' actions and dialogue must be well-motivated and have direct, observable results within the play. You should have no nonessential elements in your story—and especially no reliance on coincidence. Little or nothing in a Realist play can happen by chance or at random, even though real events might. The old argument that "truth is stranger than fiction" doesn't work when writing a compelling Realist play.

By coincidence, we mean an event or sequence of events or story twists that, although accidental, somehow conveniently complicate or solve a play's problem in a way that reveals the writer's hand at work. In a Realist play, you are allowed only one coincidence before the audience will begin to question your plot's plausibility. For example, if two old friends bump into each other on a street corner in Times Square, the audience will accept it as possible (even if one is now living in Wyoming and the other in Los Angeles). But if you start adding more coincidences, such as the two old friends have both traveled to New York to find the same mail-order bride, and then coincidentally find that she's actually a long lost sister, you're stepping away from realism, because the chances of that happening are highly unlikely. (Cornell Woolrich's stories provide many examples of how coincidence can destroy plausibility.) Eliminate coincidences and your play will feel more realistic.

Realist plays don't have leaps of faith, supernatural moments, dream sequences, or unbelievable endings. They also usually take place in the present. This is because Realist playwrights usually want to deal with the problems that plague society in the here and now. Even Arthur Miller's *The Crucible*, which is set in the seventeenth century, uses the lens of hindsight to illuminate contemporary problems. Ostensibly about the Salem witch trials, this play is the definitive theatrical commentary on the Red Scare of the fifties.

A Realist play's sets should feel real, but they don't have to be exact down to the last detail. Once, Realist doctrine demanded a realistic set, but this rule has been pretty much suspended—because most theaters are too poor to build detailed sets. So your Realist play should allow for selective realism in its production design. This means that you don't want to write a play that can't be staged without authentic walls, windows, and doors. Make your story and characters real, but allow the set to be so simple and adaptable that even small, poor theater companies can afford to build it.

Realism isn't a barrier to getting produced. Most readers, artistic directors, and literary managers expect your play to be some form of Realism. But be warned, there are some theater companies that are so tired of realism they even advertise in trade magazines (The Dramatists Guild's *Resource Directory*, *Dramatists Sourcebook*, and *Insight for Playwrights*—see Chapter 10) that they no longer accept "Kitchen-Sink Realism." By "kitchen sink" they mean generic Realist plays (ones usually set in a kitchen, a living room, or on a front porch) in which the characters spout their problems in what Freud called "talking therapy." These theaters aren't interested in plays that contain yet another "mirror held up to reality" or "slice of life." But don't worry; most theaters accept Realist mirrors and slices without question.

HEARTS ON FIRE (ROMANTICISM)

Romanticism, in its pure form, dominated theater for a little more than fifty years in the early 1800s. In the long history of the theater, this was but a blink of the eye, but the effects of that brief period are still with us today. Romantic playwrights emulated their hero William Shakespeare by writing plays with heightened (poetic and sometimes effusive) language and emotional plots that stressed instinct and feeling rather than logic—for instance, who has ever watched *Romeo and Juliet* and not wanted to scream at them, "Just tell your parents or the

Prince that you're married!" And for heaven's sake, why have the Friar subject Juliet to a near-death experience so Romeo can come find her? He could just have sent her off to Mantua! But then there would've been no wrenching tragic-death scene.

The Romantics felt that the heart could understand things that reason and intellect weren't equipped to comprehend. The heart—as Pascal, the French physicist, mathematician, and philosopher wrote in his *Pensées*—"has its reasons of which reason knows nothing." Romantic plays include everything from Goethe's *Faust* and Edmond Rostand's *Cyrano de Bergerac* to modern musicals like *Les Misérables*. Romantics claim as their own any character that feels that the intellect can't be totally trusted, that only the heart knows truth, that we must, as Luke Skywalker does in *Star Wars*, "feel the force," turn off the ship's computer, and aim our torpedoes at the Death Star by intuition alone.

If you have your heart set on writing a Romantic play (and to remain consistent, only your heart can tell you to write one), you'll want to avoid falling into the trap of making your story a "melodrama." Melodrama is an offspring (some would say the bastard child) of the Romanticism that came to dominate theater and consumed the Hollywood film industry from its inception. The term "melodrama" dates to the nineteenth century, when the dialogue in many plays was often accompanied by background music, much as today's movies employ a musical score to underline what we're supposed to be feeling. Melodrama is associated with flimsy "good versus evil" plots, all of which seem to have a falsely accused hero who fights the good fight, struggles against evil, and puts the audience through enough twists and turns to keep even the most entertainment-weary members on the edge of their seats. Melodrama is plot-oriented. It concentrates on the story's action rather than its characters; it stresses what the characters *do* rather than *who they are*, and what they do falls within a very limited range of possibilities, dictated by a reliance on formula.

The consummate formula playwright was the suitably named Eugene Scribe (1791-1861), who wrote more than 400 dramas (with the help of hack assistants), and whose plays are today all but forgotten. He's remembered almost solely for his machinelike technique for structuring plays. His formula included: a secret known to the audience but unknown to the characters, intense action and suspense, a series of ups-and-downs for the protagonist, an obligatory scene in which secrets are exposed, and an ending that was pure deus ex machina (see Chapter 3).

Today, melodramatic plots like Scribe's are often called, somewhat ironically, "Well-Made Plays," because they have perfectly structured plots that sacrifice characterization, logic, and truth to give undiscriminating audiences an evening of mindless entertainment. A hundred and fifty years ago, Scribe's formula plays were popular with homespun theater audiences, but these people long ago abandoned the theater for television and movies (with the possible exception of the popular, light entertainments offered by dinner theater). Today's more discriminating theatergoers find Scribe's melodramas unacceptable—and even in is own day, sophisticated audiences condemned him. The German poet Heinrich Heine was on his deathbed, his breath failing, when a doctor asked him if he could make a hissing sound. Heine answered, "No, not even for a play by Scribe."

ROMANTIC BEGINNINGS

Jean-Jacques Rousseau (1712-1778), the French philosopher, is often called the father of Romanticism. Rousseau believed that society corrupted the individual, in whom it brought out selfishness and aggression. Rousseau believed that people should learn from nature rather than from society, which he felt was full of artificiality, inequality, and oppression. Rousseau stressed individualism. In one of his most famous quotes (from his *Confessions*), he said, "I venture to believe that I am not made like any of those who are in existence. If I am not better, at least I am different." Rousseau's thoughts inspired Romantic writers to create headstrong protagonists who were often full of despair because they were isolated from society, but who basked in their individuality, felt awe-inspiring emotions (particularly love), and knew in their unique hearts that they were right, even though the "logical" society around them could come up with a hundred reasons why they were wrong.

Among those inspired by Rousseau were the English poets John Keats (1795-1821), who wrote in *Endymion*, "O for a life of sensations rather than of thoughts"; and William Wordsworth (1770-1850), whose introduction to his *Lyrical Ballads* states, "All good poetry is the spontaneous overflow of powerful feelings." To this list we should add William Blake, Percy Bysshe Shelley, and Americans Nathaniel Hawthorne and Henry David Thoreau. In Germany, the Romantic Movement was called "Sturm und Drang" (Storm and Stress) and inspired playwrights like Johann Wolfgang von Goethe (1749-1832), whose Faust exemplified all the traits of the Romantic hero. In France, Victor Hugo (1802-1885), famous for such novels as *Les Misérables* (which was adapted into the play of the same name), wrote his most famous Romantic play, *Hernani*. In England, Friedrich von Schiller (1759-1805) wrote *The Robbers*, which has been called Romanticism in its purest form.

Rousseau also inspired non-writers. A man named Freidrich Froebel created a new method of teaching children called "Kleinkinderbeschäftigungsanstalt." He later gave it the more economical name of Kindergarten—a place where children wouldn't be pushed to memorize society's artificial rules, scientific constructs, or religious dogma, but would be free to explore and learn about nature through their senses (just like Romantic heroes).

Romanticism became a movement of enormous scope. It embraced literature, politics, architecture, criticism, philosophy, and all the arts, yet literary critics and historians have quarreled over the actual meaning of the term for decades.

Romantic writers included liberals as well as conservatives, the deeply religious as well as atheists, revolutionaries as well as moderate reformers. The only thing they all had in common was dissatisfaction with a purely rational, empirical, "realistic" view of the universe.

In fact, the Romantic Age was so diverse and contradictory in the notions it engendered that some scholars suggest that the best thing to do is to abandon the expression all together. There is no one book, play, painting, or poem that all critics can agree is definitively "Romantic." The great historian Will Durant wrote in *Rousseau and Revolution* that Romanticism is:

> ...rebellion of feeling against reason, of instinct against intellect, of sentiment against judgment, of the subject against the object, of subjectivism against objectivity, of solitude against society, of imagination against reality, of myth and legend against history, of religion against science, of mysticism against ritual, of poetry and poetic prose against prose and prosaic poetry, of neo-Gothic against neoclassical art, of the feminine against the masculine, of romantic love against the marriage of convenience, of "Nature" and the "natural" against civilization and artifice, of emotional expression against conventional restraints, of individual freedom against social order, of youth against authority, of democracy against aristocracy, of man versus the state—in short the revolt of the nineteenth century against the eighteenth, or, more precisely, of 1760- 1859 against 1648-1760: All these are waves of the great Romantic tide that swept Europe between Rousseau and Darwin.

LET'S BE ROMANTIC

Today, Romanticism works best if you're writing a love story, musical, myth, gothic tale, religious drama, children's play, or any story that requires unquestioned universal truths (within the world of the story) and a protagonist who sets out against impossible odds simply because he knows in his heart that he's right. Romantic plays are all about the protagonist. The Romantic protagonist is an idealized hero and an idealist himself who is attractively out of step with society. He often knows that he doesn't fit in, but isn't sure why. To get away from people, the Romantic protagonist often spends time planting flowers or contemplating his navel in the forest—whatever it takes for him to get away from civilization and back to nature. (As in Shakespeare, the woods of Arden and not the halls of the castle are where the truth comes out.) The Romantic protagonist is also brave, although he may not know it until he's tested. Often he can't articulate it, but he knows in his heart (or if he's a rough-and-tough character, his gut) that absolute truth exists and is somehow connected to purity of heart and to love.

This, of course, implies that universal, absolute truth exists, and that humans can comprehend it. This also implies that the liberal idea that there is more than one way to look at things is wrong, and denies that each person's morals, values, point of view, and/or take on things should be respected. Instead, there must be one truth, felt rather than reasoned—so cold, calculating logic can only lead one astray. As the bearer of absolute truth, the Romantic protagonist must be willing to fight for what she believes. She will risk everything for truth, personal freedom, and love. When the going gets tough, the Romantic hero doesn't back down and seldom questions her own actions. So, unless you're careful, all of this baggage can make Romanticism seem strangely reactionary and even somewhat totalitarian in its worldview, for all its emotional insistence on personal freedom.

If you're writing a Romantic play, you can avoid these pitfalls by making sure that your protagonist isn't one hundred percent good and your antagonist isn't one hundred percent pure evil. This type of black-and-white thinking might work well in a Hollywood action-adventure flick, but it falls flat in a play, because Hollywood can amplify melodrama with spectacle; theater depends more on thoughtfulness. Give your protagonist a few flaws (for instance, Cyrano had his nose and his nasty temperament) and give your villain some redeeming or sympathetic qualities (as when Shylock cries out, "Hath not a Jew eyes? Hath not a Jew hands, organs, dimensions, senses, affections, passions…").

BRIGHTER COLORS (EXPRESSIONISM)

In the early part of the last century, movies began taking a heavy toll on the theater. By 1910, there were over 10,000 nickelodeons in the United States. By 1915, the number of touring theater companies had been cut from 300 to 100, and soon the number fell to less than ten. By 1911, 1,400 "legitimate" or live-theater stages in the United States had been converted to movie houses. Theater certainly looked as if it were dying. One of the problems, as many playwrights saw it, was Realism. For example, if you want to depict a realistic-looking sunset on stage, you need a battery of lights plus a crew of stagehands, and even then it doesn't look that real. If you want a realistic-looking sunset in a movie, all you've got to do is find the right location, set up a camera, and show up at sundown. Today, if you can't find the exact sunset you're looking for, a computer can manufacture it for you. As attendance diminished, a call arose for theater to redefine itself, to do what the camera could not do, to "re-theatricalize" the theater. As the great theater designer Robert Edmund Jones wrote in *The Dramatic Imagination*, "When we succeed in making a production that is the exact antithesis of a motion picture, a production that is everything a motion picture isn't and nothing a motion picture is, the old lost magic will return once more. Realist theater, we may remember, is less than a hundred years old. But the theater—great theater, world theater—is far older than that. So many centuries older that by comparison it makes our little candid-camera theater seem like something that we thought up only the day before yesterday." Expressionism was a form this revolt took.

Where Realism focuses on creating the illusion of an objective authenticity, Expressionism attempts to capture the inner mysteries of the human psyche in ways that direct observation, like viewing a photograph, could never reveal. It does this by recreating the world as the characters see it, subjectively, with their emotions and subconscious thoughts made visible in the set design and/or other, non-realistic characters. Expressionism is a different kind of realism, in a way— because we don't see things as *they* are, but as *we* are, and that is the only reality we can know. For example, if an intoxicated person were to say that he sees pink elephants on the wall, he wouldn't be expressing a truth about the wall (if in fact no pink elephants were on it), but would be revealing a truth about his own internal reality, which exists in defiance of what others might perceive to be real. If we go one step farther and allow the audience to see what the drunk sees, the result is a kind of virtual reality of the character's point of view, in which everything (even pink elephants) is filtered through the character's psyche.

Expressionist plays, therefore, try to dredge up the subconscious, the dream-state, the fevered imagination, and make it visible. They often start with an intolerable situation that becomes even more intolerable and often leads to the failure or death of the protagonist. At the end of such a play there is often the feeling that nothing has changed—but also that life in all its illogical complexity will go on. Subtext becomes text. The staging of Expressionist plays is often highly stylized, and can take on dreamlike qualities or nightmarish distortions that reveal the tortured minds of the characters or, for that matter, the playwright. Sets contain distorted views, including such things as slanted walls that make the set feel claustrophobic (not because the location is, in fact, claustrophobic, but because a character feels claustrophobic there), and wallpaper that imitates prison bars and trees that look like huge strangling hands (again, not because they are, in fact, bars or hands, but because the characters feel trapped, as if behind bars or in a stranglehold). To Expressionists, truth (or beauty for that matter) isn't what the eye sees, but what the mind projects.

BACKGROUNDS OF EXPRESSIONISM

Artistic Expressionism started in Germany around 1910 as a reaction to Impressionist and Post-Impressionist painters such as Monet, Renoir, and Cezanne. These painters were mainly concerned with how the surface of any given subject appeared to the eye at a particular moment in time—an objective rendition of an objective perception. Expressionist painters instead looked inward, abandoning the quest for perceptual accuracy in favor of visualizing their own strong inner emotions—a subjective account of a subjective perception. Sometimes lines separating artistic schools blurred. Although he insisted he was being objective and observational, the Post-Impressionist painter Van Gogh created in his *Starry Night* an Expressionist work. Edvard Munch's *The Scream*, on the other hand, is clearly and intentionally Expressionist.

Expressionist plays were made popular by such writers as August Strindberg (1849-1912), Elmer Rice (1892-1967), and Eugene O'Neill (1888-1953), and Expressionism certainly influenced Austrian novelist Franz Kafka (1883-1924). O'Neill summed up the idea of Expressionism in a program note prepared for a production of a Strindberg play at the Provincetown Players. He said that Naturalism and Realism no longer applied to society. They "represent our fathers' daring aspirations toward self-recognition by holding the family Kodak up to ill-nature... we have taken too many snapshots of each other in every graceless position; we have endured too much from the banality of surfaces." The irony of this remark is that photography and movies almost immediately co-opted Expressionism for themselves, as is evidenced by the works of still photographers like Man Ray and filmmakers like Robert Wiene (*The Cabinet of Dr. Caligari*) and Fritz Lang (*Metropolis*).

Expressionism hit its peak in the 1920s, when such plays as Elmer Rice's *The Adding Machine* and Eugene O'Neill's *The Hairy Ape* dominated Broadway. *The Adding Machine* is about an accountant named Mr. Zero, who is fired from his job and replaced by an adding machine. Rice used distorted settings and nonrealistic acting to show the tortured mind of Mr. Zero, who kills his boss and is subsequently executed. At the play's end, he finds himself in the afterlife, where he's assigned to a meaningless accounting job. *The Hairy Ape* is the story of a character named Yank, a stoker in the engine room of an ocean liner. At the beginning of the play, Yank feels that his life is important and useful because he's one of the men who makes the great ship move. But when the ship owner's daughter visits the engine room, she's shocked by what she sees. From her point of view, the engine room is nothing but a steel cage, and Yank and his fellow stokers nothing but Neanderthals. Later, while on leave in New York City, he walks down Fifth

Avenue. The audience now sees Yank's perception of a city inhabited by identical, robot-like people. When these robots ignore Yank, he strikes one and ends up in jail. In the end, Yank goes to the zoo, where he finds a gorilla that seems to understand him, but when he frees the beast, it crushes him. Yank dies bewildered and humiliated, but realizing that he had no power over the massive machine that dominated his life.

Though Expressionism in its pure form is seldom seen on stage today, many Expressionist set and lighting techniques are still used, and its influence is obvious in many plays. For example, Arthur Miller's *Death of a Salesman* is largely Realist, but it has several Expressionistic sequences, where the audience sees Willy's limited view of what life should be like. Others who've incorporated elements of Expressionism into their work are Sam Shepard (*The Tooth of Crime*) and Nobel Laureate Dario Fo (*Accidental Death of an Anarchist, Orgasmo Adulto Escapes from the Zoo*).

Expression Yourself

When writing an Expressionist play, remember that the main character's psyche, rather than objective behavior, is what you're trying to physicalize. This character is often a common person with few heroic traits, a being full of fear and/or anxiety about an oppressive, incomprehensible world. Protagonists in many Expressionist plays see themselves and/or the other characters as puppet-like cogs in a grotesque industrial machine, over which they have no control. (Fritz Lang and Charlie Chaplin also incorporated this dehumanizing element in their films *Metropolis* and *Modern Times*, but had their protagonists rebel against it.) Because of this attitude, Expressionistic plays are often very political and supportive of socialist or pacifist themes as they criticize the evils of society. An Expressionist plot is driven by the author's agenda more than by realistic-cause-and-effect structures. This can make Expressionist plays feel disjointed, which is often a desired effect, because the story is told from the main character's often-fragmented point of view: Who in this life sees their existence following a structured or logical order? That only happens in the movies (or Realist theater).

LIFE SUCKS, AND THEN YOU DIE (ABSURDISM)

Absurdist playwrights would argue that Realism is false, because it imposes dishonest, tidy structures on chaotic reality and leads the audience to conclude that they can take meaningful actions to change the world. Romantics, according to the Absurdists, do the audience an even greater disservice by assuming that life has meaning and that universal truths exist. Melodrama is almost criminal, foolishly assuming that good shall win over evil. Absurdists cheerfully proclaim that life has no rationale or morality, and that German philosopher Friedrich Nietzsche (1844-1900) was right: God is dead. But this negativity isn't necessarily a bad thing, because it can make for some pretty good theater.

To understand the Absurdist mind we must go all the way back to Aristotle (384-322 B.C.) and Saint Thomas Aquinas (1225-1274 A.D.), and consider Absurdism's opposite. Aristotle in *Physics* identified four "causes," which he believed explained how the world works. The first was "material," simply the physical stuff of the world. For example, the material cause of a statue would be raw marble. The next was the "formal," physical stuff whose potential has been actualized (for example, a finished, carved statue). The third was the "efficient," the being or thing that caused the material to become formalized (in this case, the artist). The "final cause" was that which brought it all together, the purpose, meaning, or "end in mind" (the statue's point, theme, or intent)—what later philosophers would call teleology. To Aristotle, everything had a purpose, so to understand God one must understand His purpose. When His purpose is too difficult for human minds to comprehend, we depend on faith. But faith doesn't mean a lack of purpose, only a limit to human knowledge and perception. This way of looking at the world, of course, implies that everything has a purpose, an idea that was picked up again by theologians such as Thomas Aquinas during the late Middle Ages and early Renaissance.

Today, most people are Aristotelians (whether they know it or not). They live their lives believing—or at least hoping—that everything has a purpose (a final cause). For example, when horrible things happen to us, what do we do? We justify them by saying that "God is testing me" or "It's all part of God's plan." Religious and political leaders love to contend they've got God's permission to go to war, to stamp out "evil" (i.e., fulfill God's purpose). An airliner goes down killing hundreds. That evening the TV news interviews the one person who missed the flight and their appointment with death. Dumbfounded, the tardy passenger turns to the camera and says, "God must have a purpose for me or there wouldn't have been so much traffic on the 405 freeway." Now all this survivor has to do is figure out God's purpose for him. (And we're left with the question of how and why the other two hundred dead folks managed to tick God off all at once.) His belief in a final cause may move him to improve his life, use his time more productively, and maybe help the poor. He may believe he's found out, like Moses on the Mount, what God wants from him.

The key to understanding Aristotelian thinking might be the word "because." (This happens *because*... That happens *because*...) If you can figure out the *because*, you can find your direction, design, and purpose. But what if you find no answer to "because?" What if the horrible things that happen to us are not God's test, but pointless, random acts of chance? What if there is no divine plan—no good or evil? How can we fulfill God's purpose by killing the enemy or helping the poor? Absurdist playwrights eliminate Aristotle's final cause and explore a world without purpose or faith. Absurdism strips away the stories, the narratives, the mythologies that people use to define their beliefs and behaviors, refuting the many ideologies that we think we can't live without. From the Absurdist point of view, it's ridiculous to say that we are being tested or to disguise our naked animal aggression as a divinely directed force of salvation or to kill in the name of God or read into life any purpose whatsoever. The Absurdist's only truth is that there is no truth, so playwrights should do the audience a favor and strip away the delusions that Realism, melodrama, and Romanticism—as well as religious and secular ethics—have created.

In his book *Mysticism and Logic*, Bertrand Russell begins his essay "A Free Man's Worship" with Mephistopheles telling Dr. Faustus about the creation of the world. Mephistopheles says that the earth was created because God had become weary of angels constantly singing his praise, and so he resolved that a great drama should be performed for his entertainment. So the cosmic stage was set with a hot nebula whirling aimlessly through space, from which grew planets, life, and mankind. Soon, tiny humans were struggling to find their purpose and fighting against each other and against sin. At the end of the tale, God sends another sun crashing through the sky, which collides with Man's sun and returns everything to a hot, whirling, nebula. After which He murmurs, "It was a good play; I will have it performed again." In Russell's comments to this story we find the heart of Absurdism:

> Man is the product of causes which had no prevision of the end they were achieving; that his origin, his growth, his hopes and fears, his loves and his beliefs, are but the outcome of accidental collocations of atoms; that no fire, no heroism, no intensity of thought and feeling, can preserve an individual life beyond the grave; that all the labours of the ages, all the devotion, all the inspiration, all the noonday brightness of human genius, are destined to extinction in the vast death of the solar system, and that the whole temple of Man's achievement must inevitably be buried beneath the débris of a universe in ruins—all these things, if not quite beyond dispute, are yet so nearly certain, that no philosophy which rejects them can hope to stand. Only within the scaffolding of these truths, only on the firm foundation of unyielding despair, can the soul's habitation henceforth be safely built. (Bertrand Russell, *Mysticism and Logic*)

Absurdist playwrights fall into three broad categories: fatalist, existentialist, and hilarious. The fatalists believe that we are trapped in an irrational universe where even basic communication is impossible. Words, symbols, gestures, even facial expressions only *seem* to have meaning; in fact, they don't because we understand others only from our own limited point of view. This solipsism means that even basic empathy is impossible. Fatalists also believe that we have no ability to influence or control events and that our foolish attempts to do so only lead to frustration and violence. The existentialists hold that God being dead is a good thing, for it's now up to us to do everything for ourselves—no excuses. Existentialism teaches that humans have free will, but we have no gods to thank, no devils to blame, no original sin to account for our situation, no ultimate moral truth to be revealed, and no alibis to justify our actions. Existentialism brings a ray of hope to Absurdism, for it says that we must rationally create ourselves and not derive our essences from false assumptions, like trying to understand divine purposes. Finally, the hilarious Absurdists highlight the insanity of life in a comical way. Their hope is that laughing at the absurdities of the world will allow us to face our problems, deal with life, and perhaps even maintain rationality; after all, it's an old truism that pain is a prerequisite for comedy. According to Nietzsche, man had to invent laughter to preserve his sanity.

THE ROOTS OF ABSURDISM

The Absurdist movement grew out of the insanity of the period encompassing the two World Wars. Before that, the prevailing belief was in the perfectibility of society, and even of man. But in World War I millions died, if not on the battlefield then from outbreaks of disease. This carnage turned patriotism into cynicism and apathy. The Roaring Twenties were an epicurean bath in the river Lethe, and then came the Great Depression. World War II brought even greater devastation, but added to the mix genocide and slave labor camps, which were replicated in Stalinist Russia. Combined, these events brought death on an unparalleled scale. For many it became impossible to remain optimistic: To them, the only sane response was to admit that the world was cruel, unjust, and absolutely meaningless. If there was a God, he was either a sadist or completely absent from the scene. The Scottish psychiatrist Ronald D. Laing said, "Madness is a sane response to an insane world." Taking this further, the French novelist Albert Camus wrote in *The Myth of Sisyphus*, "A world that can be explained even with bad reasons is a familiar world. But, on the other hand, in a universe suddenly divested of illusion and light, man feels an alien, a stranger. His exile is without remedy since he's deprived of the memory of a lost home or the hope of a promised land. This divorce between man and his life, the actor and his setting, is properly the feeling of absurdity."

The most famous fatalistic Absurdist playwright would have to be Samuel Beckett (1906-1989), author of *Endgame*, *Krapp's Last Tape*, and *Happy Days*. In his play *Waiting for Godot*, two clown-like tramps wait on a barren plain, a dreamlike vacuum (which some critics say is an aftermath of nuclear holocaust), waiting for Godot, a character or thing that never comes. When the play was produced at San Quentin penitentiary, the prison newspaper said, "It forced no dramatized moral on the viewer, it held out no specific hope... We're still waiting for Godot, and shall continue to wait. When the scenery gets too drab and the actions too slow, we'll call each other names and swear to part forever—but then, there's no place to go."

Jean-Paul Sartre (1905-1980), author of *The Respectful Prostitute* and *The Condemned of Altona*, is the most notable of the existentialist Absurdists. Sartre believed that humans are incomplete because there is no God. Without God, we are left without a predefined nature, so we must take control and define our own essence—in other words, our existence precedes our essence, which is the opposite of what most religions teach. In Sartre's play *No Exit*, three people are confined to hell. Hell turns out to be other people. Sartre commented in *Portrait of the Antisemite*, "Man is nothing else but what he proposes, he exists only in so far as he realizes himself, he is therefore nothing else but the sum of his actions, nothing else but what his life is."

Eugene Ionesco (1912-1994), author of *The Bald Soprano*, is one of the best examples of a playwright who emphasizes the hilarious side of Absurdism. For example, in his play *Rhinoceros*, the lead character slowly transforms into a rhino (echoing the bitter humor of Kafka's *Metamorphosis*). Ionesco's comedies convey the meaninglessness of modern man's existence in a universe ruled by chance, but he also allows us to laugh at the situation. Ionesco said, "I have always been in front of a locked door. There is no key. I am waiting for the answer, whereas I ought to provide it myself, to invent it. I keep waiting for a miracle, which does not come. Presumably there is nothing to understand. But one's got to have a reason, to find a reason. Or else to lose one's reason."

ARE YOU BEING ABSURD?

Let's say that life seems to you a cosmic crap game. If your play falls into the fatalist category, your theme is likely that every toss of the dice comes up snake eyes. Everything is bleak, the universe is irrational, and we can't communicate or have meaningful relationships. All of this leads to pathetic attempts to influence events that always fail (or end up where they started), as well as overwhelming feelings of despair, terror, and anger and acts of brutality. Of course this begs the question, Who would want to watch such a play? Playwrights, focused on revealing the yawning void to their audiences, often don't realize that a basic paradox of writing is that in order to write a scene about the futility of life, one must construct a stable, consistent, meaningful plot, just as the only way to show that a character is bored is to write an *interesting* scene about boredom. In order to maintain a structural framework for their take on chaos, fatalists may fill their plays with pointless yet engaging philosophical arguments, notable small talk, detailed analyses of unimportant things, action-filled moments that go nowhere, characters who make detailed plans for situations in which they can do absolutely nothing, all forcing the characters—like the audience—to kill time. However, even the most intriguing spectacles can sometimes fail, as Eric Ristad lamented in his review for *The Tech* of Robert Wilson's *The Civil Wars*: "*The Civil Wars* is private theater with a vengeance; it is without content, and immune from criticism. It consists of a sequence of structured images, not related in any generally meaningful way. Robert Wilson may have been thinking about civil wars, but I was thinking of everything from doing sit-ups to feeding actors to food processors."

Writing existential Absurdism means allowing a tiny ray of sunshine into your bleak world. There's still no God, and existence is still inherently meaningless, but your characters can create meaning for themselves if they accept responsibility for their actions, which may lead to improving their basic situations. Existential Absurdism leads to a logical, hopeful atheism that frees characters from the absurd ethics of the church, government, or society. The existential Absurdist often sets out to show the audience the absurdity of existence by creating characters who blindly follow rules, seldom question premises, or blame all their problems on outside influences. Some characters may have irrational hope that something better is coming, yet do nothing to help themselves. Into this stew, this insane world, is placed the sane character, who attempts to free himself from the madness around him. That character may succeed or fail. Success doesn't matter, as long as the audience gets the message that they too must take control and define their existence, and not let predefined notions of God, the devil, government, church, or society do it for them.

To write a comic Absurdist play, you should first define for yourself what makes our lives pathetic and then why you find that pretty darn funny. For example, a few years ago, an Ohio man was given an award for being the father-of-the-year. A few days later, he decided to do something very special. It was his son's last home football game and father-of-the-year wanted to make it memorable, so he took skydiving lessons and hired a plane to drop him off 10,000 feet above the stadium. He was going to parachute down to the fifty-yard line and surprise his son, the quarterback, with the game ball. Everything was set, the announcer asked everyone to look up, and…you guessed it, father-of-the-year's parachute failed to open. In front of the homecoming crowd, he fell to his death, landing on a car in the parking lot. Now, if this story makes you laugh, you may be a good candidate for writing a comic Absurdist play. To this end, your goal is to take life's inexplicable downers and make the audience laugh, because if we can laugh at death, mass murderers, the dying solar system, and this Ohio father-of-the-year falling to his death, then we will be drawn together, kept from going insane, and find at least a false sense of courage—which is better than none at all—in our mutual recognition of our hopeless place in an inane world. This, in turn, liberates us from responsibilities that we can never live up to, and problems we can never surmount.

THE GRAND SCALE (EPIC)

The vast majority of plays have limited scope. They tell a story using a small number of characters during a few critical hours or minutes within their lives. But not all stories fit within such limitations. Epic plays open the narrow confines of the stage and allow for wide, sweeping plots, with frequent shifts in location and large casts. The great scope of Epic drama allows it to be less structured, less focused—more like real life. For example, imagine a play as a photograph. Realism would be a detailed close-up. Close-ups are easy to frame because they deal with few elements and circumstances. Epic Theatre is more like a wide, panoramic shot. As you pull the camera back, you find more factors to deal with, making the shot much more difficult to frame. Epic playwrights deal with this framing issue by allowing their plays to be a little less organized. As a result, Epic Theatre often has more coincidences, outside influences, and random events (just like real life). Epic Theatre's expansive time period tends to negate the use of traditional cause-and-effect plots and substitute stories made up of episodic sequences that cover a wide range of incidents, which may or may not be related (once again, just like real life). As a result, where Realist plays attempt to build stories in a linear progression, Epic Theatre's broad boundaries allow it to simply relate events that follow the irregular curves of life. This means that Epic plays often have complicated stories with multiple storylines that can even involve several different protagonists.

Epic Theatre's grand scale allows it to examine and confront sweeping political, historical, and social issues. This can be particularly attractive for a playwright frustrated by the ever-diminishing attention brought to serious issues. For instance, the average-length sound bite on the evening news declined from 42.3 seconds in 1968 to 9.8 seconds in 1988, and it's even shorter today—so brief that hardly any real information can be conveyed. Politicians design their speeches so that catchy, ad-like sound bites can be extracted from them. But how do you explain or understand the complicated issues of international strife, politics, economic events, or just plain ordinary life in only 9.8 seconds? It's impossible. Epic playwrights believe that the same is true in the theater, that subjects like hatred, war, religious intolerance, and love can't be reduced to a modest play with a tiny cast and limited set. To truly see the issues that confront mankind, they go for the panoramic shot, the long and unabbreviated examination, where even the slightest problem is a reflection of much broader issues.

EPIC BEGINNINGS

Epic plays have been around for centuries. During the Middle Ages, huge "cycle" plays told the story of the Bible and could last for days, usually put on during religious festivals surrounding Easter or Christmas. Some of Shakespeare's plays might also be called epics, for they had huge casts and stories that covered decades, and some, like the Henry plays, build upon each other. During the Romantic age, playwrights often refused to be limited by rules, so they wrote plays as big and long as they felt necessary. Goethe's *Faust* has two parts and is so extended that it can seldom be produced, even on multiple nights. One Epic Theatre production in postwar Germany even staged Tolstoy's *War and Peace*.

The playwright who most popularized the form in modern times was Bertolt Brecht (1898-1956). Brecht felt that Epic Theatre's grand scope and broad political reach allowed the theater to confront the social problems emerging from the economic unrest after World War I. For example, his masterpiece *Mother Courage and Her Children* tells the story of a woman who travels with a canteen wagon, profiting from war by selling goods to the soldiers. The play has twelve scenes, a cast of over twenty, and takes place during the Thirty Years' War. The broad scope of the war allowed Brecht to make sweeping statements against war and capitalism. Today, Epic Theatre is rare, but it can still found with plays like Wendy Wasserstein's *The Heidi Chronicles*, which spans more than twenty years and has nineteen characters; David Edgar's *Nicholas Nickleby*, which attempts to bring Dickens' novelistic range to the stage; and Tony Kushner's *Angels in America*, which has a large cast and multiple storylines. It is also reflected in today's various interpretations of Wagner's *Ring Cycle*, as well as the marathon stagings of Shakespeare's plays that occasionally pop up at theater festivals.

GOT AN EPIC TALE TO TELL?

The Epic play presents one major problem: Almost no one will produce it! Few theaters have the money to build the many sets and hire the dozens of stagehands and actors that Epic Theatre requires. Exceptions to this are made for already extremely famous playwrights, or if you're writing plays for your local church groups, or high schools, where the actors aren't paid and large casts are desirable. But, in the professional theater, you are most likely shooting yourself in the foot if you write an Epic. Once most theaters take a look at your cast-of-characters page, they'll drop your script in the rejection pile before reading farther.

"Hey, wait a sec," you say, "I saw *Angels in America* at a local theater. Why wouldn't they consider my new Epic play *Frenched in 'Nam* about the history of homosexual love during the thirty-year Franco/American/Vietnamese war?" Well, they did *Angels in America* because it is a proven success. They knew going in that they would most likely make their investment back. And *Angels*, like the U.S. hockey team beating the Soviets in the 1980 Olympics, was a wild exception to the rule. Your unknown epic, no matter how good, has little name recognition and a much greater chance of failure and bankruptcy.

If you are still set on writing an Epic play, you can address some of its staging problems by double-casting the roles and simplifying the set. Double-casting means that actors will play more than one part. Generally, you don't want main characters to double up, as it may confuse the audience, but many smaller roles can be double-cast. The Epic set problem can be solved by imitating Shakespeare, whose plays (at least in his own day) were staged on simple, almost bare, platforms with only a few props and set pieces that represented a given location. To help the audience "see" the location, Shakespeare used "verbal scene painting," that is, his characters often describe and/or comment on their locations. For example, in *Macbeth* the King says, "This castle hath a pleasant seat; the air nimbly and sweetly recommends itself unto our gentle senses." The audience can now employ their imagination to see the modest stage as a cheerful castle. As a result, there is no need for a set designer to create huge castle walls or a lighting designer to hang dozens of gelled lights aimed to imitate the gentle illumination of the morning sun, or for a sound designer to find recordings that contain realistic intonations of distant birds chirping—or for a poor theater company to come up with the cash to pay for any of it. Our final words of advice regarding Epic Theatre are that you follow two basic rules: Allow yourself a sprawling story that imitates life's many twists, and design a theme that justifies this sprawl by broadly attacking and/or analyzing the social, economic, and political problems of the world.

BRECHTIAN ALIENATION

As we noted above, consciously or not, plays tend to be either Aristotelian or non-Aristotelian. In *Poetics*, Aristotle famously listed his essential structural methods (see Chapter 4), which are designed to create plays that lure audiences into a kind of trance-like state—Samuel Taylor Coleridge's "willing suspension of disbelief"—where they have a vicarious experience and, in the end, what Aristotle called a "soul-cleansing," or catharsis. This requires creating a situation that the audience can identify with, as well as sets, costumes, characters, and polished dialogue that draw the audience into the illusion. Done right, the audience will laugh when the characters laugh, weep when they weep, and suspend their disbelief. Aristotelian drama can be a deep emotional experience that has theatergoers on the edge of their seats, or simply escapist entertainment that transports them away from themselves, lets them leave their humdrum lives and lose themselves in the story and the characters, and, above all, have a cathartic experience. Aristotelian stories rule Hollywood filmmaking and American television, and are the most common type of play.

Non-Aristotelian plays, obviously enough, don't follow Aristotle's structural methods. For example, Japanese Kabuki plays, Indian religious epics, and African ritual dramas have their own structural rules. In the West, non-Aristotelian plays represent a conscious rebellion: plays in which the audience is intentionally never allowed to forget itself or that it is watching action taking place in a theater. This type of theater was the brainchild of Bertolt Brecht (also famous for Epic Theatre —see above). Brecht felt that if a performance puts the audience into a trance-like state, topped off by catharsis, all they'll get from it is a shallow escapist experience in which they don't have to consider, think, judge, or take action once the play is over. Say you go to see a play in which the protagonist sets out against a sea of troubles: He/she falls in love or defeats the communist bad guy or blows the whistle on industrial polluters or walks away from a domineering husband or deals with AIDS. During the play, you lose yourself in the story, and in the end you have a cathartic experience, having identified with the character's plight and journey. You leave the theater feeling cleansed—the play has let you live through a painful experience unscathed, but emotionally awakened. The next day what do you do? Do you emulate the hero? Fall in love? Fight communism? Blow the whistle on your industrial-polluter employer? Help a friend walk away from her domineering husband? Deal with AIDS? Probably not. Brecht argued that this is because the play allowed you to leave the theater satisfied, with little need to go out into the real world and solve, or even confront, the political, social, or environmental injustices with which the story was concerned. You don't need to do anything, because the actors have done it for you—never mind the fact that all the actors did was to pretend.

Brecht is reputed to have said, "I'm not writing for the scum who want to have the cockles of their hearts warmed." He wanted to shatter traditional stage illusions by alienating the audience so that they were constantly reminded that they were sitting in a theater and that what they were watching was only a performance. Brecht called this the "alienation effect." Alienation in this context doesn't mean that the playwright wants to turn the audience off, but instead, wants to wake them up by not allowing them to suspend disbelief. He wants them to maintain an aesthetic distance from a play's action by forcing the fact of the production on the audience and alienating them from dream-like illusion. Brecht believed that the audience that is distanced or alienated from a story's going-ons will do more than be entertained. Instead, through the audience's objective grappling with it, what happens in the play will spill out into real life and lead to actual change. Playwrights and directors who employ this technique of alienation rebel against standard dramatic formulas and staging techniques by doing such things as having the actors address the audience out of character, exposing the lights so that the audience is always aware that it is only a play, removing the proscenium arch that separates the audience from the players, and doing away with theatrical conventions like curtains, realistic costumes, sets, and dialogue that add to the standard theatrical mirage.

BACKGROUNDS OF ALIENATION

Three hundred and fifty years before the birth of Christ, Plato attacked the theater because he said that it allowed people to luxuriate in passion and abandon reason. He warned in *The Republic* that people forget themselves and are manipulated, spellbound, and even irrational when under the influence of the arts. In the thousands of years since, most theater people would agree—indeed, it's what they most hope for, because that's what the theater does. It allows people to become spellbound, captivated, even charmed. Bertolt Brecht has been called the most important dramatic theorist in two thousand years because he challenged this aspiration. Instead of a theater that captivates the audience, he wanted a theater that confronted the audience and forced them to react rationally. Brecht felt that learning could only happen if the audience was thinking, and that this was just as exciting, if not more so, than being enthralled or charmed during a play.

Today, Brecht's influence on contemporary theater is considerable, but his alienation techniques, in their purest forms, are seldom seen in the mainstream commercial theater, which gives the general public hits like *Phantom of the Opera* and *Cats*. But in the more intellectual, elitist, and experimental theaters, alienation is understood and welcomed. Brechtian techniques can be seen in many plays, including Thornton Wilder's *Our Town*, Tom Jones' *Fantastiks*, and Caryl Churchill's *Cloud 9*. (One could even argue that Richard O'Brien's perennial cult classic, *The Rocky Horror Picture Show*, falls into this category.) Brecht has also inspired such theater groups as the San Francisco Mime Troupe, The Living Theatre and El Teatro Campesino.

One of theatrical alienation's modern proponents is Brazilian director Augusto Boal (*Theater of the Oppressed*). Boal attacks the idea that theater is a vicarious experience where the audience must sit quietly in the dark. This type of thinking, he says, grew out of performances that are controlled by the church, the government, or the ruling class. Boal believes that traditional theater's purpose is to promote the moral views of the dominant class, which makes it essential that the masses (the audience) play a passive role. It's critical that they sit there like sheep, tricked into accepting the illusion, for (just as Plato said) then they can be manipulated, told what to think and how to feel, and rewarded for upholding the values of the leaders (just like the characters in the play). Playwrights who are influenced by Brecht want the exact opposite—they want the audience to respond with their minds and not their emotions, they want a theater in which the audience will think for themselves, not blindly believe what they're told.

ALIENATION CREATION

A central need in the theater of alienation is a political point of view. Why wake the audience up and make them think if you don't have anything important for them to think about? You want your play to have a real-world impact and lead to grassroots activism, not just be an entertaining evening. Augusto Boal wrote in *Theater of the Oppressed* that theater is "a rehearsal for revolution," and so your alienationist play requires a clash of ideas, between the status quo and whatever you think it should be replaced with. In this case, it may seem desirable for your characters to know their subtext and even announce it; but again, remember that if they do so, your play runs the risk of feeling preachy and self-righteous instead of daring and provocative. Let the action of the story carry the message.

Next, you'll want to dissolve the illusion of stage "reality." This means you'll want minimal costumes and scenery that are not reflections of reality, but insist on being seen as costumes and set dressing. Exposed lights and a simple, bare-platform stage are often used, and not because of cost, but because it gives the audience visual cues that this is a work of art and not reality. The script should also include staging elements that break the illusion; Brecht sometimes borrowed heavily from Eastern theater, like the Peking Opera, which (in its original form) was produced with little or no scenery and lots of song, pantomime, and symbolic acts. For example, by circling the stage, an actor signified that he was on a long journey or, if an actor ran across the stage holding a piece of flowing cloth, it meant that it was windy. At other times Brecht punctuated his sets with political slogans and/or photos flashing on a huge screens.

Other Brechtian techniques include actors who fall out of character and, as themselves, speak directly to the audience. At other times, characters might interrupt the flow of the story by including unrelated anecdotes or singing irrelevant songs. You might specify in the stage directions that the actors, rather than using real glasses, pantomime the pouring and drinking of imaginary water, thereby breaking the illusion of reality, or you might stipulate that folding chairs must be used instead of real living room furniture—anything that defeats the illusion, wakes up the audience, and reminds them that they're in a theater. Again, none of this is done because it's cheaper to stage (which it is), but because it will, as one critic said, "irritate the audience into thought." So in order to alienate your audience, you need to make them admit that the stage is a stage, the actors are acting, the moonlight is but a lighting effect, and that the script was written by a playwright (with a political point)—not something that seems as if it were made up by the actors as they went along.

Building a Play

3

Structure, Part One: Story & Plot

****

My first rule of playwriting is that scenes must be rivers, not lakes.
They must go somewhere.

David Hare

****

The root word "wright" in playwright isn't a misspelling of "write"; it comes from the Middle Ages and means "one who builds." For example, a shipwright is someone who builds ships, a wheelwright is someone who builds wheels, while a playwright is someone who builds plays. (This is similar to the root for the word "poet," which in Greek means "creator.") Therefore, writers William Archer and Alan Ayckbourn have called playwriting "playmaking." Playwrights are builders because they structure and construct plays. Structure is the skeleton of the story, giving definition, coherence, and meaning to a story's plot or sequence of events. People and their actions, in real life, are usually in a raw, unorganized state; a play (realistic or unrealistic) structures life into a unified whole. This chapter is about developing your "wrighting" ability.

It's All a Plot

Plot structure, as it's sometimes called, is the means by which a playwright creates order, which allows a story's event sequence to develop and carry its theme. Without order, there is no meaning, and no art. (Even the apparent chaos of a Jackson Pollock painting reveals, upon careful viewing, an intricate display of order.) A play lacking structure is nothing more than random events that will fail to communicate specific thoughts to anyone but the writer (and even she may be confused). Václav Havel, the great playwright and former President of Czechoslovakia, said in a speech to the Academy of Performing Arts in Prague, "As soon as we begin to realize that one thing may follow another, that some things may be repeated, that different occurrences may be connected, that space-time, and thus the world, are structured, we begin to experience a sense of the dramatic. And as soon as we began to use ritual to communicate with the forces we believed responsible for the order of the world, we were doing theater. Because what else is theater but an attempt to grasp the world in a focused way by grasping its spatio-temporal [space-time] logic."

Some contemporary critics—looking to release playwrights from constraints they imagine keep them chained like Prometheus to his rock—view structure as superficial and perfunctory, if not arbitrary. These critics (often never having actually tried to write a play, all the while proclaiming their opinions in well-structured essays) fail to understand that all plays have some sort of artificial structure—the root of "artificial" being the Latin for "making art." Strindberg's expressionistic *A Dream Play* may appear to follow the flow of consciousness, but it has a logically unified plot structure. Japanese Kabuki plays, in which a performer's style is often more important than the story, have well-defined structures. Even the most incongruous of Absurdist plays have a plot structure. All good plays have structure, just as language (and even expressive movement, like dance or Kabuki) has syntax. A play without good plot structure will wander and be cluttered, erratic, and pointless. Some playwrights purposely write erratic, pointless plays with the intent of showing how erratic and pointless life is. All they do is confuse the audience, or bore them to tears. We've said it elsewhere in this book, but it's worth repeating: It's a paradox of playwriting that even if a dramatist wants to communicate that life is erratic and pointless, he can only do this successfully by constructing a stable, meaningful plot that gives structure to this theme.

THE BUILDING BLOCKS OF STRUCTURE

Books on writing are always filled with instructions; do this, don't do that (we plead the fifth), but it's important to understand that there are different kinds of instruction: There are dramatic rules, and then there are dramatic principles. Rules are the special techniques and conventions that are (or were) applied to playwriting during a particular period of history. A principle is a dramatic axiom that has survived largely unchanged throughout history, and therefore applies to all plays in all ages. Principles define the nature of drama and are the building blocks of structure. In the 2,500-year history of playwriting, there have been countless dramatic rules, but only a few basic dramatic principles. For example, during the Renaissance, mainly in France and Italy, dramatic rules known as the "three unities" dominated playwriting. The unities meant that in order for a play to be correct and proper, the action of the story had to (1) take place within a twenty-four-hour period—unity of *time*—the play had to (2) be set in locations that could be reached within a twenty-four hour period—unity of *place*—and (3) that it was a cardinal sin to co-mingle comedy with tragedy—unity of *action*. These three dramatic rules became sort of a classical correctness. Critics, audience members, and fellow playwrights complimented and condemned plays based solely on how well they measured up to the yardstick of the three unities. Many sixteenth-century French playwrights and critics would've insisted that the unities were more than just rules, but were eternal principles. They are, however, now outdated. They were just rules.

On the other hand, the same basic dramatic principles that bound French and Italian Neoclassic playwrights also applied to the ancient Greeks, to Shakespeare, to non-Western dramatists, and are still valid today. The most famous list of dramatic principles is found in Aristotle's *Poetics*. The overarching principle of this twenty-three-century-old text asserts that there are six essential components of drama:

Plot - the arrangement of incidents

Character - the personalities

Diction - modes of utterance

Thought - the ideas or themes behind the story

Spectacle - the performance, set, costumes, and special effects

Song – the musical component of the drama

Of these, the last is usually felt to be the least relevant today; certainly singing isn't necessary to a good play today, as it was in ancient Greece. However, if you think of "song" as the sound and rhythm of the dialogue, and how these flow through the orchestration of your play, you may find that the principles of song that Aristotle details apply, even here. Aristotle's approach is discussed and analyzed in many other books, and our intention here isn't to regurgitate all that. Rather, we hope to point out what have come to be regarded as the touchstone principles of dramatic writing, and how you can make them, among others, work for you.

The debate over what elements make up a play and their order of importance has raged ever since Aristotle laid the groundwork for discussion. Writers from Horace to John Dryden to George Bernard Shaw to David Mamet have attempted to define the essence of what makes a play a play. Some great thinkers attacked the whole notion of art and its artifices as misguided and fundamentally false to nature. Plato argued that, as the visible world was a mere shadow or imitation of the "real," eternal world, art was simply an imitation of an imitation, and therefore worthless. In his *Apology*, Plato has Socrates deride playwrights as being the least capable of "truth" because they themselves are unable to give a coherent account of their own work, implying that they're divinely inspired idiots. Unfortunately, that criticism still applies to many playwrights today, who may have little objective understanding of what they do or how they do it. This makes their work hit or miss. Assuming that Plato was wrong and that art has value, a playwright needs a practical understanding of dramatic principles, so that he can create with or without divine inspiration.

Therefore, we humbly submit to posterity our own list of dramatic principles, which focus on the following elements of drama: *conflict, truth, spectacle, structure/unity*, character, and *action*. We'll cover character and action in Chapters 5 and 6; here we'll concentrate on the remaining elements.

TO TAKE ARMS AGAINST A SEA OF TROUBLES (CONFLICT)

Our first principle is that *all plays are about human struggle*. Whether it's good against evil, good versus good, the individual versus society, man against nature, thesis and antithesis, or man against himself, a play is about a clash of human wills or needs or desires. John Howard Lawson points out in his *Theory and Technique of Playwriting*, "It is difficult to imagine a play in which forces of nature are pitted against other forces of nature." It's difficult because that wouldn't be a play. Plays are about human conflicts and the solutions and resolution that result (or at least anthropomorphized conflicts, as in *Cats* and *The Lion King*).

Conflict happens when a protagonist clashes with an antagonist over differing needs and desires, and when compromise is no longer an option. This last part is often neglected, yet it is at the heart of dramatic conflict, because if the protagonist has the opportunity to reach an agreeable compromise but fails to do so, he will seem like a jerk and lose audience sympathy. What's more, if either character is willing and able to compromise and does so, the problem is solved, the conflict is over—and so is the play. The only way for dramatic conflict to drive the story is to eliminate any possibility of compromise for any reason, moral, physical, or psychological. Drama occurs when no mutual agreement can be reached, because the antagonist won't allow it and/or the protagonist's desire is too great. The result is a power struggle of which the permutations and solution are the subject of your play. It's a simple equation:

Desire + Obstacle x Lack of Compromise = Conflict

THE WAY IT IS (TRUTH)

With due respect to Plato, our second principle is that playwrights are philosophers. This means that *a play is an attempt to understand some truth about human beings and their world*. A playwright's goal is to challenge and move the audience, not just to entertain them. If you have nothing challenging or moving to say, if your ambition is simply to entertain, then write a sitcom or a Hollywood movie. Playwrights want their words to change the world, if only in a small way. As Tom

Stoppard wrote in his play *The Real Thing*, words can build bridges across incomprehension and chaos. Words, he said, "deserve respect. If you get the right ones in the right order, you can nudge the world a little."

ENTERTAINING A THOUGHT

In order to nudge the world, the playwright must have a powerful truth to express; in order to change a heart, she must have the ability to capture an audience's attention. But this idea, that art can change society, has often been ridiculed because theater is usually viewed as an accessory to society—an entertainment. In his introduction to French philosopher Jean-Jacques Rousseau's *Letter to M. d'Alembert on the Theatre*, Allan Bloom paraphrases Rousseau: "Men can be forced to listen to sermons but can't be forced to enjoy a play. This constitutes the major difference between the thinker (philosopher) and the dramatist; the thinker states the truth as he sees it and is indifferent whether anybody reads or agrees with him, while the dramatist must appeal to the dominant concerns of the people at large, no matter what the status of those concerns might be... A writer can never be in advance of his times; he must be a sensitive instrument reflecting the desires, often still inarticulate, of his age." Obviously, we disagree. The answer lies in combining forces: Entertaining the audience while expressing a powerful truth can be the highest form of the art. Truth doesn't have to be castor oil. Rousseau said that human tastes and habits can only be changed in three ways: by laws, by public opinion, and by pleasure. In all of these areas, pure entertainment fails: Pure entertainment makes no laws, it is never a vanguard in public opinion, and the pleasure it causes will never change anything because it only reaffirms the audience's values. It is an opiate. However, a play that leavens its message with entertainment, that draws the audience in even as it forces them to re-evaluate, can bridge this gap and drive a theme home. A play that captures the audience's emotions will reach them more directly than any sermon.

Our third principle, then, is that *all drama is about emotional truth* (the truth we feel) as much, if not more, as it is about intellectual truth (the truth we see). This isn't to say a play has to be funny or toothless—but it should engage and not repel. *Medea* is entertaining. *King Lear* is entertaining. *Rosencrantz and Guildenstern are Dead* is entertaining. *Waiting for Godot* is entertaining. And each one of them nudged our world a little.

MAKING A SPECTACLE

Spectacle is the world of the play, the set, and the stage against which the actors perform. It's also the visual expressiveness of the actors' performance. Aristotle's term "spectacle" helps to define drama's requirements as a performing art (actions performed by human beings in front of an audience). This leads to our fourth principle: *The ultimate test of a play occurs when it goes in front of an audience, and what the audience sees matters almost as much as what they hear.*

Playwriting is the only form of writing that must not only work on the page, but live on stage. Many new playwrights, focused on what their characters are saying, neglect to think of what actions they will play while talking, and what if any visual impact the set should have. But all of this is part of the live presentation, of what engages the eye as the dialogue engages the ear. In a big Broadway production, spectacle might include the huge dance numbers of *A Chorus Line* or the landing helicopter in *Miss Saigon*. In a mid-sized production of *Hamlet*, it would include both the sword-fights and Hamlet's famous conversation with the skull of Yorick, one of the defining images of theater. In a French farce, spectacle might include the comic timing of arrivals, departures, and near-misses of cheating lovers. On a small equity-waver stage, it might include rear-projection imagery or a single spotlight cast on a lone, naked actor standing on an otherwise darkened, empty stage (a bit of spectacle that has also been used in large-scale productions of Peter Shaffer's *Equus* and Bernard Pomerance's *The Elephant Man*).

An important factor to consider when creating spectacle is that it must change with the flow of the scenes. Unlike a painting or a statue, a performed work of art exists only during its performance. Once the performer (actor, musician, dancer) is done, the work comes to an end—it no longer exists outside the memory, as far as the audience is concerned. And every playwright must understand that without attention to spectacle, those memories will be faint and soon forgotten.

KEEPING IT TOGETHER (STRUCTURAL UNITY)

Our fifth principle: *Without structural unity, there cannot be meaning.* Unity is the relation of all parts to the whole. Unity means that character, action, conflict, truth, and spectacle come together to bear on a single subject or "spine." As Aristotle pointed out, unity also emerges from the "likelihood" and "necessity" of each incident: The characters and their actions must be both probable and necessary to the story. This requires a cause-and-effect relationship between incidents. If each event has a cause, and each cause leads to an effect or change, then each incident in the play will be related to the ones preceding or following it. Cause and effect knit otherwise disparate events into a whole. Unity isn't always apparent in real life, which can be random, so writers must find or invent it. You can't just assume it will show up while you're writing from the heart. Tchaikovsky wrote in his diary, "What has been written with passion must now be looked upon critically, corrected, extended, and, most of all, condensed to fit the requirements of the form." A play's form requires passion to be molded into an inevitable-seeming sequence of events—into a unity. In *The Art of Dramatic Writing* (required reading in all theater programs), Lajos Egri went further, also demanding a "unity of opposites," by which he meant an appropriate set of opposing forces (characters and thematic points of view) in the story.

Moving a story along through a play's limited timespan affects structural concerns. It means that anything not directly bearing on the central conflict or subplots must be cut. There just isn't time to go off on tangents. For theater to give meaningful form to the visible and invisible stuff of life, playwrights must "select and arrange." They must emphasize certain parts and de-emphasize others as they build a structure that only develops into its final form as it moves through time. In a way, watching a play is almost like watching a building rise from its foundations, a work in progress until it resolves, revealing the final unified structure. And with this revelation comes meaning. But if the structure is out of whack, if its staircases lead nowhere and its porticos are unsupported by columns, so to speak, the edifice will appear misshapen, and may even crumble before our eyes. Because of the compressed nature of stage "reality," every detail carries great significance—so make sure you put in the right details, and only those that matter, that affect the outcome of the dramatic conflict. As Chekhov famously wrote in a letter to a friend, "If there is a gun hanging on the wall in the first act, it must fire in the last."

Another good way of looking at this heightened significance of detail comes from the book *What Art Is: The Esthetic Theory of Ayn Rand*, by Louis Torres and Michelle Marder Kamhi. Philosopher/novelist Ayn Rand said, "Imagine if you will that a beautiful woman in a lovely evening gown enters a ballroom. She's perfect in every way except for the fact that she has a rather large, ugly cold sore on her lip. What do we make of it? What does it mean? Not much—cold sores happen to a lot of people and are at most unfortunate, but they have little meaning. However, if a painter paints a picture of a beautiful woman in a lovely evening gown and includes the same massive, ugly cold sore, suddenly the blemish takes on great importance." This minor imperfection, says Rand, "acquires a monstrous metaphysical significance by virtue of being included in a painting. It declares that a woman's beauty and her efforts to achieve glamour (the beautiful evening gown) are a futile illusion undercut by a seed of corruption which can mar and destroy them at any moment—that this is reality's mockery of man—that all man's values and efforts are impotent against the power, not even of some great cataclysm, but of a miserable little physical infection." Artists and playwrights isolate and stress those aspects of existence that are needed to convey their themes. But for us to even see and recognize these details and their significance, we need a structure that provides guidance and context. In a letter to a friend, T. S. Eliot put it this way: "It is the function of all art to give us some perception of an order in life, by imposing order upon it."

But why do we need to impose structure on life? Because life is constantly shouting at us, drowning us in a deluge of unfiltered sensory overload. Finding or imposing order is the goal of almost all our spiritual and moral activities, that attempt to help us deal with life's fundamental agonies: Why are we born? Why must we die? What happens after death, and does it matter then how we've conducted our brief lives? Religion deals with these impenetrable mysteries through faith. We are told that there are just some things we cannot understand, so we must have faith that there is a God, and that this God has a purpose. This may be right, but we won't know for sure until we're dead, so if you can't make that leap of faith, it doesn't help much. The scientist's "faith" used to be that, given enough time and experimentation, eventually we would understand the nature of the universe rationally. Now that hope has evolved into a realization that we may never be capable of answering every question, because each answer seems to open ten new questions. We learn that the atom isn't the smallest particle, but, in fact, made of many others, some of which defy common sense, moving backward through time, having no weight or matter, and so on.

Artists deal with what doesn't make sense or what defies meaning by selecting and arranging the stuff of life until at least some part of it does have meaning. The marble statue doesn't include the pile of chips that were carved away, even though these were once part of the material from which the art was made. In a play, these "chips" are the words that have to be left out, all the events that simply aren't part of the structural unity of the play, no matter that real life might have contained them. In this way, the artist or playwright simplifies life until we can at last see some aspect of it clearly, through the fog. We need art (as well as science and/or religion) to make sense of it all, and find our place in the world.

THE CHICKEN OR THE EGG?

For thousands of years, playwrights and critics have been arguing about which comes first, character or plot. Aristotle kicked off the debate, claiming that character is subservient to story. Based on the subject matter and work of the dramatists of his day, he came to the conclusion that the story had to be mapped out first and then characters fabricated to enact it. His logic was that a drama is an imitation of a course of action, not of any particular person: "The drama interests us, not predominantly by its depiction of human nature, but primarily by the situations and only secondarily by the feelings of those therein involved." This, however, was largely a result of one assumption, that all plays were based on familiar myths. Furthermore, in Greek mythology each character's fate was pre-ordained (by the conveniently named "Fates"). Since the endings were already known, the dramatist's job, then, was to present the import of the themes inherent in these existing narratives, which obviously came first.

More recent playwrights and theorists, freed from this determinism, might pay lip service to Aristotle, but tend to choose character as their starting point. Without great characters, the feeling is, you don't have a story worth caring about. John Howard Lawson wrote that a story "may contain a duel in every scene, a pitched battle in every act, and the spectator be sound asleep, or be kept awake only by the noise." Or even worse, be heading for the exits. Lajos Egri tackles Aristotle head on, pointing out that even in the works of Aeschylus and Sophocles the characters are strongly developed, which is why we still watch them. Even here, he argues, character—along with premise, or theme—clearly comes first. Egri grumbles, "What would the reader think of us if we were to announce that we had come to the conclusion that honey is beneficial to mankind, but that the bee's importance is secondary, and that the bee is therefore subsidiary to its product?" According to Egri, the bee is the character, and its honey is the story.

And yet, without a strongly structured story, even the most interesting characters will buzz around as aimlessly as, well, bees without a hive. Either method—putting plot ahead of character, or character ahead of plot—can lead to failure. Go too far one way and you end up with a soulless clockwork formula that only works in rare whodunits, such as *The Mousetrap* or *Deathtrap* or some other thing with "trap" in its title. Go too far the other way, and you get a snooze-fest in which people meander around, talking endlessly without any apparent point (just like life). The Sicilian playwright Luigi Pirandello (1867-1936) has great fun with the confusions and complexities inherent in simply turning your characters (and actors) loose in *Six Characters in Search of an Author* in which, without a firm plot to go on, the character/actors' own lives and problems take over and ruin a production. In the end, the Manager throws up his hands in disgust: "To hell with it! I've lost a whole day over these people, a whole day!"

Somewhere in the middle, between plot and character, lurks the unique, involving story for which you're hoping. So, which approach is right? Well, after millennia of debate, we are happy to finally give the correct answer: *They both are.* Characters are aimless without a well-structured plot, and a plot is empty without well-motivated, multi-dimensional characters.

"Okay, great," you snarl. "That sounds good, but what the hell does it mean? How do I use that to write my play?" Calm down. We're getting to that. We'll start by analyzing plot structure and formula, move on to the character-centered approach, and then see if we can't find a way to bridge the gap.

PLOT AND FORMULA

The word formula has acquired a bad rap. It's deserved when it means a writer slavishly conforms to tired conventions. However, it is a tool, like any other, and has its place. Its danger is that, when you work out the plot first, whether consciously following a formula or not, the structure of your play comes into being before your characters do, which can lead to poor characterization. But this needn't be; after all, for thousands of years playwrights have used formulas to write powerful plays. Everyone from Aeschylus (ca. 525-456 B.C.) to Neil Simon (1927-A.D.) has used formula. And it's been around a lot longer than the days of ancient Greece. Joseph Campbell (*The Hero with a Thousand Faces*) examined myths and storytelling throughout the ages and found that the plot/structure of most ancient myths were similar no matter from what country, culture, or century they came. Storytellers from pre-literary (oral tradition) times to Hollywood writers have followed the same formulas.

Today, formula writing is so persuasive (and pervasive) that writers often forget it's a formula. Formula is constantly drilled into us, particularly by Hollywood movies and television. Even the first bedtime story you were told as a child most likely followed formula. We're so familiar with the conventions of the modern formula that we tend to treat it as a standard and measure other methods of storytelling as deviations. Modern formula has a few basic qualities. First, it relies on established, predetermined, common plot structures (as all formulas do). Its generic qualities can lead (but not always) to uninteresting plays with predictable outcomes. And formula is about story, not character. It adapts the characters to fit the story outline, rather than growing the story out of the characters' needs and personalities.

ONCE UPON A TIME (THE BEGINNING)

To many, a standard writing formula is simply something like "Boy gets girl, boy loses girl, boy wins her back," or "In the beginning you get your hero up a tree, in the middle you throw stones at him, and in the end you let him down." These are both formulaic, but formula itself is far more complex than these simple statements reflect. To learn the structure of formula we divide a story into its basic sections: Beginning, Middle, and End. By pinpointing the exact moment when one section of the story ends and the next begins, and what plot components are contained within each section, we can discover the mechanics of a formula story. The usual components contained in the beginning of a formula structure are an *event*; an *inciting incident* (sometimes this is the same as the event); a *major decision*, and a *major dramatic question*. (See below for a diagram of formula elements in comparison to those of a non-formula play.)

DO YOU BITE YOUR THUMB AT ME, SIR? (THE EVENT)

Most plays begin with an *event*. An event is a uniquely significant moment in the characters' lives. (All scenes are actually events, in which something of significance happens and something of significance changes, but in formula terminology, the event is what kicks the story off.) It can be an unusual incident, a special occasion, or a crisis. It could be a wedding, a funeral, a homecoming, preparing for a party, or anything that makes this opening moment a little more special than the normal humdrum of the characters' lives. For example, at the beginning of Sophocles' *Oedipus Rex* (430 B.C.), a plague has hit the city of Thebes. William Shakespeare's *Romeo and Juliet* (ca. 1595) begins with a brawl, as the Montague and Capulet clans fight in the streets of fair Verona. The Prince stops the battle and announces that anyone caught fighting again would suffer the penalty of death. Lorraine Hansberry's *A Raisin in the Sun* starts with the Young family excited about the impending arrival of a large life-insurance check. Scott McPherson's *Marvin's Room* begins with Bessie at the doctor's office because she's not been feeling well. In each case, the play begins with an event (plague, clan warfare, a sudden increase in fortune, a doctor's visit) that is designed to spark the audience's interest.

A play doesn't necessarily need to begin with an event, but the advantages to doing so become clear when you look at who is passing judgment on your play. Most playwrights think it's the general theatergoing public, but these are not the people who will decide if your play will be produced. Your first audience will be producers, directors, and other readers who are bombarded with thousands of plays to read, most of them horrible. And most of these readers will not finish a play that hasn't captured their attention by page ten (or sooner). Beginning your play with an event that grabs your reader's attention will start your story with a bang rather than a slow fade-in, and keep them reading. On the other hand, slapping an event on the beginning of a play simply to attract attention doesn't make for good writing. A good opening event must be germane to the story and not forced or tacked on. The event must be a natural place to begin, central to the plot, and must set up the chain of cause and effect that becomes your story. Aristotle defined this opening event as the moment before which nothing of immediate importance to the plot has happened, but after which everything is of importance. The best opening events contain the essence of the story that follows and usually involve the protagonist and antagonist. Their exact conflict need not be spelled out yet, but the audience wants a hint of what the coming conflict *might* be, even if no major conflict yet exists.

DID MY HEART LOVE TILL NOW? (THE INCITING INCIDENT)

Lajos Egri, describing the *inciting incident* as "the point of attack," said that "it must be the turning point in the life of one or more of your characters." The inciting incident (sometimes called the *disturbance*) is the moment in the play when the protagonist's life is upset and forces that oppose him are put into a situation rich with potential conflict. The inciting incident unglues the protagonist's comfortable life, forcing him into a situation where he must inevitably confront these opposing forces. For example, in *Oedipus Rex*, Oedipus learns that an oracle has proclaimed that the plague will not be lifted until the murderer of former King Laius is found and punished. In *Romeo and Juliet*, the inciting incident is the meeting of the young lovers at the masked ball. In *A Raisin in the Sun*, the family disagrees on how the insurance check should be spent. In *Marvin's Room*, Bessie discovers that she has leukemia. In each case, the protagonist is forced into a situation where taking action is not only critical but unavoidable.

Note that the protagonist always confronts the inciting incident from a position of disadvantage (less power). If your protagonist starts out stronger than your antagonist (or opposing forces), your story will be boring because it's essentially over before it begins. The resolution can only go one way: Your protagonist will win because he or she has the power to do so from the get-go. Therefore, the antagonist must have so much power that your protagonist's chances for success are always in doubt. The problem underlying a weak or boring story can almost always be traced to a weak antagonist or a too-powerful protagonist. Even a king like Oedipus was at a disadvantage before the power of Fate itself. What your protagonist must possess at the beginning isn't overwhelming power but the *potential* to rise to the antagonist's challenge.

HENCEFORTH I NEVER WILL BE ROMEO (THE MAJOR DECISION AND THE MAJOR DRAMATIC QUESTION)

The beginning portion of a formula play ends when the protagonist makes a *major decision* that sets him on a collision course with the forces that will oppose him. This decision and resulting action also defines what the play is about and clarifies the protagonist's goal. It's the core action of the play. For example, Oedipus decides to find Laius' killer at all costs, while Romeo and Juliet decide to act upon their love in spite of their warring families. In *A Raisin in the Sun*, Mama decides to go against her basic values and give her son, Walter Lee, a part of the insurance money so that he can open a liquor store. In *Marvin's Room*, Bessie decides to contact her estranged sister, who might be a possible bone-marrow donor. By ending the beginning with the protagonist's major decision, you make your protagonist active, someone who sets out to achieve a difficult goal or must satisfy some deep desire or is forced to move forward against great odds. Passive protagonists, tossed about by the winds of change, unable to make major decisions or at least try to change their world, are unacceptable in this formula, because they do not hold an audience's sympathy. The protagonist can be a victim only if she fails to act. If she takes action, she's no longer a victim.

As noted earlier, the inciting incident is sometimes called the *point of attack* because it's the moment in the story when the fuse is lit, the clouds of conflict appear, and the primary action of the story clearly declares itself. If the inciting incident and the protagonist's major decision seem to take a long time to get going, the play is said to have a late point of attack. If they appear within the first few pages, then the play has an early point of attack. Most plays have an early point of attack. This is certainly the case with *Oedipus Rex*, *Marvin's Room*, *Medea*, and *King Lear*. Some formula playwriting professors believe that the point of attack should fall about a tenth of the way into the play. This is called the "10 Percent Rule." So, according to this rule, if your play is 90 pages long, the point of attack should happen around page 9. If you're writing a ten-minute play, the point of attack should happen one minute (approximately one page) in. This sort of structure is a formula, because decisions as to when the point of attack should happen are made before the play is even written. We by no means feel that a playwright should strictly follow the 10 Percent Rule, but if your play seems to start slowly, if readers are bored early, or if audiences seem to rustle in their seats shortly after the beginning, check your point of attack. How many minutes into the play do the inciting incident and decision fall? In other words, where does the main action of the play begin? If you find that the protagonist makes his first major decision on page 50, chances are pretty good that you've found the problem.

Having a late point of attack isn't always a problem. On the one hand, if the protagonist makes a morally correct decision ("I will fall in love" or "I shall save my father from alcoholism" or "I must catch the killer of my friend"), then the stakes and action are pretty clear and a long beginning isn't advisable. But if the decision is more complex, muddled by moral ambiguity ("I need to steal the money so my kids can go to school" or "I shall cheat the boss in order to raise my wife's opinion of me" or "I must take another drink or I'll die"), then the beginning needs to be long enough to make the audience get under the protagonist's skin and believe that, in a similar situation, they too might make the same decision. For example, in *A Raisin in the Sun*, Mama decides to give her son a part of the insurance money to open a liquor story even though she's totally against the idea. The morality of this decision is questionable, so the play has a longer beginning (in other words, a late point of attack). On the other hand, if you spend too long with a protagonist who eventually makes a righteous decision, the audience will become bored long before the decision is made.

The inciting incident and the protagonist's decision not only lead to conflict but also introduce the "Major Dramatic Question" (sometimes called the MDQ). The MDQ is the hook that keeps the audience in the theater for two hours, because they want to know the answer. The MDQ is an electrifying question that provokes curiosity and suspense, and presents the first part of a play's thematic statement. For example, the MDQ in *Romeo and Juliet* might be stated, "Will love triumph over murderous hate?" which, when answered, gives us the theme of the play, which might be, "Murderous hate of others will lead to the destruction of those we love." The dramatic and definitional nature of the MDQ makes it critical that the playwright hold off answering it until the play's very end. The moment the major dramatic question is answered, the suspense ends, and so should the play. For example, in *Romeo and Juliet*, the major dramatic question is answered only in the very last scene of the play (after the lovers have taken their lives), when the warring families end their feud and the Prince tells us the lesson:

> See what a scourge is laid upon your hate,
> That heaven finds means to kill your joys with love;
> And I, for winking at your discords too,
> Have lost a brace of kinsmen: all are punish'd.

A SERIES OF OBSTACLES (THE MIDDLE)

George Bernard Shaw reportedly said, "Anyone can write a good beginning." And hundreds of would-be playwrights have done just that, only to discover that beginnings are easy compared to middles. When a playwright doesn't finish a play because it seemed to fizzle halfway through, it's most likely because the idea lacked the *three Cs: conflict, crisis,* and *complication*. The middle of a formula play is dominated by the three Cs and rising action (see below) that leads to apparent failure.

THE THREE Cs

Conflicts, crises, and complications are the obstacles that make sure the protagonist's course of action isn't clear-sailing, for calm waters are the death of drama. When the protagonist faces no further conflicts, crises, and/or complications, the play is over. (What are we going to watch him do, iron his shirts?) Recently, a student playwright wrote a play in which halfway through, the young lovers/ protagonists proclaim their devotion to each other. For five full pages, all of their problems were solved as they read poems to each other. When informed that this scene lacked conflict and was not dramatic, the student playwright defended his choice by citing the balcony scene from *Romeo and Juliet*. He said, "Nothing more happens in that scene, yet it works." But a lot more happens in the balcony scene. Yes, the lovers proclaim their love, but it's a forbidden love, so we know they're going to face difficulties. They're stealing a brief moment, fearful of being caught. If discovered by Juliet's family, Romeo could be killed. True, the source of the conflict isn't physically there on stage, but it's still present—*imminent conflict* maintains the suspense. As a result, the lovers are in a tight spot and the scene is full of tension and near-crises, such as the nosy nurse who keeps threatening to find them. There are also complications, such as the balcony itself, which prevents the lovers from easily talking face to face. (Where would the doomed clandestine lovers Pyramis and Thisbe be without their cracked wall through which to whisper?) If the scene was really about two young lovers proclaiming their adoration without any conflicts, crises, and/or complications, it would hardly be memorable. As Shakespeare wrote in *A Midsummer Night's Dream*, "The course of true love never did run smooth," to which we'll add, "or it wouldn't be interesting to watch."

UPPING THE STAKES (RISING ACTION)

The middle of a play isn't a spot for naps, although the audience may think so and doze off if nothing dramatic is happening on stage. Each solution to an obstacle at hand should generate a new and even more difficult problem, conflict, crisis, or complication that keeps your play's characters and story in a growing state of flux. The term *rising action* describes the dramatic escalation of conflicts, crises, and complications. Those that happen on page 40 shouldn't be as powerful as those that happen on page 50. The stakes get higher as the story moves forward: The protagonist has more and more to lose and faces a greater possibility of failure and a growing list of consequences should failure become a reality. As a result, the middle of a play must follow the path of *most* resistance. There may be moments of apparent success, but they must always lead to an even greater undoing. The middle of a play is a series of failures for the protagonist. The hard part for the writer is to construct these conflicts and obstacles so that it's clear to the audience that the protagonist can't take any but the hardest road.

In the middle of *Oedipus Rex*, the three Cs and rising action combine to create a rollercoaster ride. Oedipus sends for a blind prophet to help with his investigation, but the prophet points a finger at Oedipus himself. Next, Oedipus accuses his wife's brother Creon of murder and treason, but Creon refuses to confess. Then Oedipus' wife, Jocasta, tells him to ignore the oracle because this same oracle predicted her former husband, King Laius, would be killed by his son, yet everyone knows that he was killed at a crossroads by thieves. Of course, Oedipus knows that he killed a man at a crossroads and so he begins to doubt himself. The lovers in *Romeo and Juliet* succeed in getting secretly married, but their plan quickly unravels as Juliet's cousin, the fiery Tybalt, picks a fight with Romeo, kills Mercutio, and is then killed himself by Romeo. As a result, Romeo must avoid the Prince's wrath and go into exile, while Juliet is forced to take the drastic measure of feigning death. In *A Raisin in the Sun*, Walter Lee loses his (as well as his sister's) inheritance to a con man, while in *Marvin's Room*, Bessie must convince her sister's son Hank, to whom she's also not close, to have a bone-marrow test.

ALL IS LOST (THE DARK MOMENT)

The conflicts, crises, and complications in the middle of a formula play lead to a stunning reversal of fortune and a sense of failure known as the *dark moment*. This is the moment in the play when the protagonist seems to have totally failed, her quest collapses, her shortcomings have tripped her up, and her goal seems more unattainable than ever. It's the ultimate obstacle, because the antagonist has won the battle and the war appears to be over. At the dark moment, the protagonist, usually because of her own mistaken actions, falls to a new low, a place where recovery and/or success seem no longer an option.

In *Oedipus Rex*, the dark moment happens when Oedipus confirms his worst fears, that he has caused the plague by killing his father and unwittingly marrying his mother, Jocasta. When she hears the news, she makes the dark moment even darker by hanging herself. The dark moment in *Romeo and Juliet* happens when Juliet finds that her parents (who don't know that she's already married) have arranged for her to be wed to Paris. Alone and desperate, Juliet appears to have no options left. In *A Raisin in the Sun*, Walter Lee's dark moment occurs when he decides to make up for his mistakes by selling the family's dream house to the white homeowners' association for an inflated price. In *Marvin's Room*, the dark moment comes when Bessie learns that her sister's son won't give her a bone-marrow transplant and, to make things worse, the boy runs away from home.

In a tragedy, the dark moment signals the beginning of the end in a negative way: In fact, the protagonist has lost the struggle. In a comedy or play with a positive ending, the dark moment is a false moment of despair, because some new hope arises, some ally or news or realized ability, that allows the protagonist to drag himself to his feet and win the final conflict.

THE MEANS JUSTIFIED (THE ENDING)

A good ending to a story must be consistent with its beginning. The audience might be shocked or pleasantly surprised by the end, but they should never feel that they've been tricked and misled into a "shaggy-dog story" (a long-winded tale whose ending feels inane or anti-climactic because it has nothing to do with the tale itself). By the end of your play, the concluding events must appear to have been inevitable. In other words, the ending must not come from out of the blue, as it sometimes did when ancient playwrights wrote themselves into a corner and then depended on the character of a god, mechanically lowered onto the stage, to set everything straight (*deus ex machina*, "a god from a machine"). Today, the term deus ex machina may not involve a deity lowered onto the stage, but still refers to when a playwright fails to set up the ending of a play as a natural, logical consequence of the preceding chain of cause-and-effect. For example, in the old melodramatic Westerns, the wagon train circles, the Indians attack, the settlers run out of bullets, and then, out of nowhere, the cavalry arrives. The cavalry here is the deus ex machina. But so is any unprepared and totally coincidental solution to a drama. So if your play involves the plight of a family in abject poverty, it's not a good idea to solve that plight by having them discover in the last scene, by accident, that there's a million dollars hidden under a floorboard.

THE TRUTH REVEALED (ENLIGHTENMENT)

The beginning of the end is enlightenment. *Enlightenment* occurs when the protagonist understands how to defeat the antagonist or, in a tragedy, that the antagonist cannot be defeated. Enlightenment can come in many forms: The protagonist may join forces with another, a revelation may shed new light on the problem, or the protagonist, after falling into an emotional abyss, may now be able to see her error and know how to defeat the antagonist. Enlightenment must be something the protagonist could not have understood before enduring the conflicts and trials of the story's middle, which stripped away all pretense and illusion. It must be carefully set up earlier in the play, but if the setup is too obvious, you'll either have given away the ending or frustrated the audience, who will gain enlightenment before the protagonist and ask, "Why didn't the protagonist figure this out two hours ago, like I did?"

Enlightenment for Oedipus occurs when he realizes his own guilt, takes a pin from his deceased mother's dress, blinds himself, and begs Creon to forgive him. Juliet's (false) enlightenment comes when Friar Laurence convinces her to take a potion that will put her into a deep death-like sleep. Thinking her dead, her parents will take her to the tomb. Meanwhile, Friar Laurence will send a message to Romeo informing him that Juliet is really not dead, and that he can go to the tomb and claim his bride. The enlightenment in *A Raisin in the Sun* happens when Walter Lee realizes that his family's pride is more important than the money. In *Marvin's Room*, enlightenment occurs when Hank returns home and agrees to the bone-marrow transplant.

DRIVING IT HOME (CLIMAX)

As with the middle of a play, rising action dominates the final portion, leading to the play's dramatic *climax*. Now, armed with enlightenment, the protagonist is renewed and ready to defeat the antagonist. The outcome of the play becomes clear, so the pace should accelerate toward the climax. The climax, in a formula play, is the moment the antagonist is defeated. A climax doesn't have to be a violent or horrible moment. It can be quiet, even subtle. *Oedipus Rex* is rather unusual, for the enlightenment and climax happen at the same time: When Oedipus blinds himself, not only does he attain enlightenment but he also defeats the enemy (himself). In *Romeo and Juliet* the climax happens when they kill themselves and, in death, bring their warring families to peace. *A Raisin in the Sun* climaxes when Walter Lee becomes a man and throws Karl Lindner—the spokesman for the white community—out of his house. *Marvin's Room* climaxes when Bessie learns that Hank's bone marrow doesn't match hers. He can't save her life, but she has repaired the relationship with her estranged sister and has her family back.

Always keep in mind that in a satisfying climax, the protagonist is never a passive recipient, but the driving force. The protagonist always instigates the climax, which is a direct result of his actions.

THE WORLD RESTORED (CATHARSIS)

After climax comes catharsis, or emotional purging, as well as a hint at what the future might bring for the major players. In tragedy, according to Aristotle, the audience should feel great pity and fear, pity for the hero's plight and fear that they also might possess a similar tragic flaw. In other words, the catharsis should burn away the dross of life and lead to a deeper level of self-understanding. In a comedy, the catharsis can be a moment of equally clarifying ecstasy: The moment lovers freely proclaim their love or little Billy hugs his alcohol-free father or everyone finally understands the importance of being Ernest or the crotchety Grinch—minus the "garlic in his soul"—returns the Yuletide gifts to the singing Whovillians, and all's well that ends well.

At the end of *Oedipus Rex*, the plague is lifted. In the final scene of *Romeo and Juliet*, the Montague and Capulet families realize the folly of their feud. In *A Raisin in the Sun* the family moves from their inner-city flat into the better neighborhood. In *Marvin's Room*, Bessie learns to accept her fate, and also the importance of love. The key to writing this final step in a formula story is to make sure that it doesn't linger. Once the climax is over and the antagonist defeated, the audience wants out.

THE FORMULA TRAP

Although formula plays may have diverse characters and dissimilar stories, may be epic or personal, tragic or comedic, they follow the same basic structure. The fundamental elements (event, inciting incident, major decision, conflict, crisis, complication, dark moment, enlightenment, climax, and catharsis) all occur in the same order. They follow a method of storytelling as old as mankind. Again, let's make it clear that using a formula is a great way to structure a play. The problem is, the playwright who follows the rules of formula too slavishly can produce a predictable, uninteresting play, just as the poet who follows a perfect iambic meter will probably write a rather clockwork poem. (Even Shakespeare had some variance within his sonnets.) The trap of formula is that it can become comfortable, and being too comfortable can lead one to avoid the risk-taking that great art requires. Comfort can turn a landscape artist into someone who churns out sofa-paintings. It's easy, you know how to do it, and it sells. But it's not art. In Hollywood, when Joseph Campbell's *The Hero with a Thousand Faces* was published (or rediscovered, after his TV series with Bill Moyer), many producers and screenwriters were overjoyed. They had finally found their bible, the holy grail of storytelling. Now they could plug any idea into a simple (but eternal and mythic) blueprint and come up with a pretty good story. Experienced playwrights weren't so quick to proclaim the end of the quest. Perhaps, because they'd been around so much longer than screenwriters, formula was nothing new to them. And before long, even the screenwriters began to realize that it could be as much of a trap as a boon.

Most beginning playwrights are unaware that they're using a predetermined formula; they think they're simply following their instincts. Only by studying the formula do they become aware of what they're doing. Experienced playwrights use it because it has proven results. But formula's apparent safety can be deadly, and so the playwright must, strangely enough, find enough danger to keep his play alive. This danger lies in that messiest and least-predictable element of theater, the character.

SUCH STUFF AS DREAMS ARE MADE ON (CHARACTER)

William Archer wrote in *Play Making: A Manual of Craftsmanship*, "The difference between a live play and a dead one is that in the former the characters control the plot, while in the latter the plot controls the characters." Without formula, the playwright can let the story grow naturally from the characters rather than following preset guidelines.

Formula plays are full of plot points that follow a predetermined order. In a non-formulaic, character-driven play, each plot point is simply the next logical, motivated step in its characters' lives. In other words, when a formula writer asks, "What happens next?" she's really asking, "What is the next prescribed plot point—the step in the formula? Is it time for the inciting incident? The major decision the protagonist makes to cause conflict? The dark moment?" The non-formula playwright, on the other hand, asks: "What would these particular characters in this situation do next?" The answers to this question are then strung together to form a series of non-predetermined plot points that make a unique framework. If the characters are well-crafted and the playwright has an over-arching premise—a strong thematic statement—to build on, this approach can lead to brilliant new structures that work. If not, it can lead to a shapeless mess. Chapter 5 has specific techniques to help you build well-crafted, complex characters. Before we get into that much detail, let's first examine how such characters can generate a non-formula structure.

Let's look at Marsha Norman's Pulitzer Prize-winning play, *'Night Mother*. The following chart shows how different her unique character-driven play is from the standard formula. In column one are the standard steps of formula, in column two, their analogs in Norman's play.

STANDARD FORMULA	'NIGHT MOTHER
EVENT	Jessie tells her mother that she's going to kill herself.
Protagonist Antagonist	It's not clear which character is the protagonist and antagonist. This isn't a play about good against evil.
Inciting Incident	The disturbance happens long before the play begins.
Decision	Again, Jessie's decision to kill herself happens before the play begins.
MDQ	Will Jessie kill herself?
Conflict Crises Complications Rising Action	There is a great deal of crisis and conflict as Mother tries to talk Jessie out of killing herself, but few complications. Nothing happens that makes Jessie reconsider or blocks her attempted suicide.
Dark Moment	No one moment can be called the dark moment.
Enlightenment	Jessie kills herself. But the enlightenment that brings her to this point happens before the play begins. There doesn't appear to be any major enlightenment between Jessie and her mother.
Climax	Jessie kills herself.
Catharsis	Her mother calls for help, but is there catharsis? We don't know.

FREE VERSE (NON-FORMULA WRITING)

Using a character-first writing method is to enter into a deeply personal world of playwriting as varied as are playwrights. Back in Chapter 1 we examined several play ideas by students in a playwriting class. Here is another, with the working title *Fathers & Daughters*. The student playwright agreed to let us recount her process as she attempted to take an idea and build it into a character-driven, non-formula play. Here was the playwright's pitch:

> (Working Title: *Fathers & Daughters*)
> This is a play about the archetypal father-daughter relationship. I believe that mothers do not teach girls to be women, but through their rewards and punishments, fathers do. We all seem to look to the

```
other sex to reaffirm our own. I want to write about
a daughter who is incomplete. Her father is a macho
man who, in his heart, is afraid of women because
he doesn't understand them. As a result, she has
trouble valuing her own femininity. When the daughter
discovers that her father is dying, she comes home to
confront him and tries to get from him the one thing
all women need—the knowledge that being a woman is
not less than being a man.
```

The first question in writing a character-first play is, of course, who are the characters? Because playwrights (particularly beginning playwrights) often write about characters they generally know and/or have empathy with, this playwright began by looking at her own father, an amateur philosopher who had an opinion on everything.

The playwright spent the next few weeks mulling over her characters. She spent little time at the keyboard, but she was still "writing." (F. Scott Fitzgerald said that he could never convince his wife that the time he spent staring out his window was time spent writing.) In one of her staring-out-the-window sessions, our playwright remembered something that happened years before. One evening, her father came over for a visit and they somehow got into a heated argument about how screwed up the human race was and how it was destroying itself through overpopulation. Her father concluded that a responsible parent would only have, at most, a single child (like he did). The playwright broke down in tears, because she was holding her second child, his grandson. Her father muttered, "It's nothing personal," and left.

What does this tell us about their relationship? The father seems to need an audience for his ideas, but he doesn't consider their effects. The playwright went on to remember that her father only liked French vanilla ice cream. "All the time I was growing up, it was the only flavor of ice cream allowed in the house." She was in college before she discovered chocolate and strawberry. She made the following note about the characters:

```
The night of the "one-baby-per-woman fight," my father
couldn't deal with my "illogical tears" and left. Two
hours later, near midnight, he returned with a small
white paper bag. Inside was a half pint of peach ice
cream. He never said he was sorry. He just served up
two small plates of ice cream and we sat there eating
in the dark. I hate peach ice cream, but it didn't
seem to matter. That's the type of man he was—he
never took the time to ask what kind of ice cream his
daughter liked, but the fact that it wasn't French
```

```
vanilla was enough. Reaching out was so hard for
him—except for that night, just sitting in the dark
eating peach ice cream.
```

This is a good plot point. Could it be the end of the play? If so, what leads us to this final moment? The playwright began to toy with the idea, asking more questions about this father-and-daughter relationship. Who are they? What do they want from life? From each other? What makes them tick? What character elements will result in their taking actions that might be developed into a story?

The playwright's next note read:

```
I had this older friend who was a wonderful character
actor but never really made it big. One day I was
visiting when he told me he was dying of cancer. He
was very weak. He then asked if I'd do him a favor
and go into his attic and retrieve an old dusty box,
which I did. He then took the box, went outside, and
threw it in the trash. What could it have been? What
dark secret was he trying to hide? What about his
life did he want to hide after his life was over? I
had to find out. After we said our goodbyes, I snuck
around back and dug in the trash. The box was filled
with old, dusty 1960's porn magazines that hadn't
been touched in years. Here was a man who was facing
death and all he could think about was what would
people think if they found his old smut after he was
dead. He was just like my father, more interested in
appearances than reality.
```

A "mystery box" would create an interesting dramatic question. Maybe the daughter thinks that it's something very personal, something which, when revealed, may bring forgiveness and understanding, but when she discovers it's only ancient "stag-mags," it pisses her off and forces her to confront her father. Add this to the peach-ice-cream plot point and our playwright is getting a much clearer idea of this father, although what she has so far doesn't make a play. The playwright next remembered how her father seldom listened and never valued her opinion.

```
We were driving along one day. I was giving him
directions. I told him to turn here, but rather than
trust me, he flagged down another car and asked a
total stranger directions.
```

Another good character moment for the father, but what does it say about this daughter? The playwright wasn't sure. As is often the case, the character representing the playwright was the weakest, for this character requires not only self-analysis and understanding, but to be distanced from the playwright's own natural human passivity. In other words, the playwright/character had to be trans-formed a dramatic protagonist.

> What if the daughter has just gone through her second
> divorce? Often women seem to pick husbands that are
> just like their fathers. Darla is desperate to find
> a dominating man who'll value her. It's a paradox.
> Dominating men never value their wives. She's searching
> for a man who doesn't exist. After a failed second
> marriage, she comes home to confront her father.

Notice that a transition has been made. Rather than talking about real events that have happened to her, the playwright just made up something about the daughter, who suddenly has a name (Darla). The characters are starting to take on a life of their own. But why does she have to be divorced? Why is that important to the story?

> Two reasons. First, I've never been divorced and
> so I think it'll allow me to separate myself from
> a character who, let's face it, is part of me. And
> second, it'll give my two characters something to
> talk about. Perhaps the father really liked this
> ex-husband, because he was a lot like him, and
> the father and daughter can have conflict over the
> divorce, while in reality, they're talking about
> their own relationship. In the beginning, she doesn't
> realize the men she marries are just like her
> father. In fact, her problems with men revert back
> to childhood. During the course of the play, she'll
> discover the truth about her relationship with men.
> That discovery will make for another plot point.

Notice that her character now has direction and motivation. She has actions to play that will move the drama forward. (Sometimes these key actions are called *plot points*.) There isn't really an order to them yet, but the story is growing as the characters become more complete.

The playwright continued to analyze her memories and experiences as she searched for new possibilities. This process can take months, even years. (This is also why many writers rely on formula, because it takes much less time to come up with the story.) But in this case, the playwright had made new discoveries rather quickly. She questioned why so many fathers draw away from their daughters as they grow older.

> Something about reaching puberty causes the end
> of the "daddy's little girl" relationship. Perhaps
> fathers don't trust themselves, so they would rather
> break the emotional bond than take the chance of

```
being tempted. This doesn't mean that all fathers
want to go to bed with their daughters. It's just
that they hate themselves for even thinking about it.
```

This is good, but it's not yet specific to these characters and this play. Why does this *particular* father pull away? She didn't know yet. Several days later she created a scene between the daughter and father in which the daughter reveals that she's pregnant—a new plot point. The daughter wants to grow up, and having a child is the only way she knows how. The twist, however, is that the daughter's revenge is that she's having the child through artificial insemination. She's going to cut men out of her life altogether. At this point, the playwright was beginning to write bits of dialogue and brief scenes rather than notes:

```
                    DAUGHTER
Look, I paid fifteen hundred. Everything I had.


                    FATHER
And you don't even know who the father is!


                    DAUGHTER
Well, not entirely. I read his sperm report. Most of the
donors there are Texas A&M students. This one was, I think.
He was six foot two, curly hair, and brown eyes. From
the Midwest and a football player with 3.01 grade point
average.


                    FATHER
A sperm report?


                    DAUGHTER
They give you an information card about the donors and you
choose what you're looking for. You can find anything.


                    FATHER
How do you know it's true?


                    DAUGHTER
The donors only get twenty-five bucks per donation, the
difference is quality control.


                    FATHER
QUALITY CONTROL! This could be bull sperm they've implanted
in you and how would you know?!


                    DAUGHTER
I guess I don't know. But I have confidence in them. They
were awfully nice.
```

```
                    FATHER
Of course they were nice, they charged fifteen hundred
bucks per ounce! God, that's great! My daughter's been home
three weeks. Where was she? She spent the time downtown,
layin' there with her skirt up, legs all akimbo, bein' shot
full of bull sperm! I'm such a happy parent!

                    DAUGHTER
It's a very respected cryo bank! Highly recommended.

                    FATHER
Christ almighty, what do you want me to say?

                    DAUGHTER
I don't want your approval! I just want you to know. You're
going to be a grandfather.
```

Where does this chunk of dialogue come within the play? The playwright didn't know. She said, "It may not even fit. It may just be a character study." This is perfectly okay, because the playwright is still trying to understand the characters, and writing bits of their dialogue is a wonderful way to find their voices and their needs, fears, and motivations. After writing this, the playwright also said that the play might become a comedy. She didn't intentionally set out to write comedy; it's just that the characters seemed to be telling her that this play was going to be funny.

The playwright went on: "There has to be a climax, right? So, what if the climax was the moment of recognition, where the father learns a lesson about women and his daughter?" Of course, that's exactly what would happen in a formula play. She could use that as a safety factor, a crutch. But a character-first play doesn't have to have a formal climax. What were other possible plot points? What would be consistent with these characters? Could the daughter come to realize that the father is set in his ways and that it's essential she work out her problems on her own? Could the father die and leave the daughter alone, their differences never resolved? There are hundreds of other ways to end the play. Throw out the formula and explore. What does the daughter do next? What do her characters allow—indeed, what is the only honest path these characters would take, if they were true to themselves? Don't worry about the formula answers. Don't immediately do what so many Hollywood movies do, and force the asshole antagonist to suddenly have a heart of gold, like Darth Vader turning all mushy-touchy-feely when his mask comes off. These easy, formula solutions will always be there if all else fails. But risk those failures! Try for something new.

After several weeks of work, the playwright felt she knew enough about her characters to write down a list of possible plot points. She wasn't sure she would follow these points exactly; it was just an attempt to solidify her ideas and begin creating her plot structure:

Plot Point #1	The daughter comes home. Just divorced, she needs comfort, but doesn't want to admit it to her father.
Plot Point #2	She tells her father that she's getting another divorce. He really liked the guy and can't believe she's left him. They argue.
Plot Point #3	He wants her to go get a box from the attic. The daughter wonders what it could be.
Plot Point #4	She tells him she's pregnant and is going to raise the child alone. Set in his ways, he attacks her for trying to live without a man.
Plot Point #5	She sneaks a peek into the box and discovers that it's only old *Playboys*. She explodes.
Plot Point #6	She discovers that all of her husbands and lovers have been just like her father.
Plot Point #7	Peach ice cream scene.

There are still massive holes, but the writer is beginning to have an idea of what the plot structure will be. Notice that the process includes no mention of any formula signposts. In place of the formula, the writer is coming up with a string of character-motivated events that will soon logically link together to form a compelling story. But it has been a long process. Writing character-first plays can be frustrating because, in the beginning, the few strokes of story and character don't look like much. Unlike formula writers, who can work out the story in a matter of days (again, this doesn't have to be a bad thing!), character-first writers, in the beginning, often have trouble pinpointing their story. It's only after long analysis and much writing, throwing things out and rewriting, that the play becomes an organized plot built around real characters. It's hard work being original.

As the events she amassed took form, the playwright decided she was spending too much emotional time with the daughter and should spend more with the father. Who was he, really? Why was he so standoffish? What was his point of view? She had to find positive reasons for his coldness. Her meditation led to thoughts of her dog. The poor thing lived the last three years of his life with cancer and the time had come to put him to sleep. The playwright remembered that on that last trip to the vet's office she wanted to cry and hug her pet but couldn't. First, she was worried that it would upset her little friend, and, second, she wanted to ease the transition. She wanted to prove to herself that she could go through with this. She also felt as if once she started crying, she would never recover. Could the father be the same? Could he think that he must be strong for his daughter's sake, that if he wasn't strong he would never be able to let her go? Maybe, although he doesn't know how to express it, he actually loves her so much that it frightens him? The playwright had found a positive reason for the father's actions, which the daughter views as coldness.

The process continued until she discovered that she had made an almost seamless transition from making notes to writing a play. She stopped calling her instructor (Bill) for several weeks, so he called her. She didn't have time to talk. The play was alive. The number of plot points had grown from seven to twenty well-motivated, logical steps in a story that was still morphing as she wrote. She had to get back to it. She was living with the people in her play and had no time for any reality but theirs.

When the script *Fathers & Daughters* was finished, it followed the exact order of a formula play. That's fine, because that structure turned out to be what grew out a deep understanding of these particular characters—and so it didn't feel forced upon them. Character-first writing is about the process, a process by which both the writer and the play will grow.

THE YIN AND THE YANG OF IT

Plot and character are inseparable, and most successful playwrights build their plays using both. They'll develop a story starting with its characters until the story becomes bogged down, and then switch to plot formula to solve a few problems, and then switch back. Or they may sketch out the map of the story, but then step back and do some serious character construction to make sure they have exactly the right people inhabiting their story, people with the right backgrounds, needs, desires and motivations to drive the plot's conflicts. If either character or plot is neglected, the play will suffer.

Both character-based and plot-based writing use dramatic principles, techniques, and plot structure. The main difference is that with formula writing, the structure is always the same, while with character-first writing, the plot becomes more flexible. I (Robin) taught a class in which the students were to write two plays. In the first, they were asked to come up with some interesting characters, but no idea of what kind of story they'd be in, and go from there. In the second, they were to come up with a plot, without thinking about what kind of characters would inhabit it. As they tried each approach, it became apparent that there was no way to succeed by strictly following only character or only plot. The characters almost demanded the working out of a strong storyline, and the plots automatically began to generate specific characters appropriate to their stories. The lesson seemed to be that, even if you are still discovering your premise as you work, you must recognize that your plot and characters quickly grow dependent on each other; once you move past character descriptions and plot outlines, neither can exist without the other.

This leads to our sixth (and perhaps most important) principle: *Character is plot and plot is character.* Rather than wondering which comes first in the chicken-or-egg fashion, think of character and plot as the yin and yang of your play, each simultaneously necessary to the other.

TRICKS OF THE TRADE
(TECHNIQUES IN STORY BUILDING)

An old adage goes, "Before writers learn technique, they are fools; while learning it they are weak, and only after they master it can they become creative." A playwright—a builder of plays—is no different from any other artist/artisan. A cabinetmaker, before learning the techniques of working with wood and tools, struggles to make a simple box. While learning, he can build a pretty average cabinet, but he's not yet able to make the wood do exactly what he wants. Only when he's mastered the techniques, knows how to choose which wood to use, which tools to use, and how to use them, is the cabinetmaker free to be truly creative. All playwrights must be experts at technique. Dramatic techniques are those tools that have repeatedly been shown to work. Call them a bag of tricks if you wish, but techniques are part of the craft by which the complex task of writing a play is accomplished. This book is really a toolbox. Here are a few more tools that can help you build your play.

HIGH NOON (THE TIME LOCK)

Time limits everything. Whether we like it or not, we're all under deadlines. In a play, one deadline is the end of the amount of time you have on stage to tell your story, reveal your characters, and come to some sort of conclusion. But there are many other kinds of deadlines that can become story tools to generate excitement and tension in your play by forcing your characters to act under the pressure of limited time.

George Pierce Baker, Eugene O'Neill's playwriting professor, said in *Dramatic Technique* that "a play is the shortest distance from emotions to emotions." If your plot seems to lack energy, if there is a lot of distance between emotions, if the characters aren't driven to take action, you might try using a "time lock." This is an internal deadline put on the shoulders of the protagonist that heightens the sense of impending crisis. A time lock forces the protagonist to confront his problems *here and now*. It provides a reason why a character can't wait to deal with a difficult situation that they might rather put off until tomorrow. In a Hollywood movie, it might be a ticking bomb or a marriage date or the arrival of the bad guys on the train at high noon. In theater, a classic example comes from *Romeo and Juliet*, when Juliet is forced to take action because her parents have arranged for her to marry Count Paris (which is a problem because she's already married to Romeo). If this impending marriage weren't limiting her time, she might've considered her options and planned a less-risky strategy. Instead, the time lock forces her to act without delay. And so Juliet takes the potion—takes action—and the love story comes to its tragic conclusion. Notice that this plot device isn't forced on her unnaturally. It's perfectly in character for a love-struck, headstrong girl who's already married the son of her family's worst enemy the morning after first meeting him.

No Exit (The Trap)

Have you ever seen a play in which you can't understand why the characters don't just tell each other to shut up, screw off, and leave? Most of us don't like conflict and will walk away from a fight. But if the characters in a play walk away, there's no play. One solution is to create a trap, a reason why the characters must stay and must confront each other. It can be a physical trap; for example, in *Bus Stop*, William Inge locks his characters in a café/bus stop during a bad snowstorm. The same basic device is used in *Key Largo* (both the movie and the play by Maxwell Anderson on which it's based). Here, a hurricane traps the characters together. In Shakespeare's *The Tempest*, the characters are shipwrecked on an island. Bad sitcoms use cliché traps all the time: The writers will trap the characters in a stalled elevator or some other small space where they're forced to look back and remember past episodes, all while desperately needing to get somewhere else.

A dramatic trap doesn't have to be physical. It can be a psychological reason that traps characters in a given situation. The characters in *Long Day's Journey into Night* are trapped by guilt, haunting memories, and alcoholism. As long as the trap is justified and an integral part of the plot (not just a broken elevator), a trap can act as a pressure cooker and intensify the heat of any conflict. Of course, the ultimate trap is to make the characters want something badly enough (from the situation or each other) that they can't leave until they get it, as happens in *Oedipus Rex*, *Romeo and Juliet*, and *Glengarry Glen Ross*.

Sleight of Hand (Sarcey's Principle of Offstage Action)

Francisque Sarcey (1827–1899) was a French dramatic critic who theorized that an audience was less likely to scrutinize the plausibility of an event if it occurs offstage or before the play begins. In other words, if your story demands a questionable coincidence that tests the limit of believability, rather than staging that plot point, have it happen offstage or before the play begins. For example, in *Oedipus Rex* it seems rather strange (knowing the oracle's prophecy that Oedipus will kill his father and marry his mother) that Oedipus isn't careful about marrying a woman who is obviously old enough to be his mother and, while he's at it, inquiring into the circumstances of King Laius' death. But most audience members never question this because the killing of Laius and Oedipus' marriage occur outside the time frame of the play. So, if you have something that stretches the boundaries of believability, you might consider putting it out of sight, so to speak.

WHY DO YOU ASK? (ANSWERING A DRAMATIC QUESTION WITH A DRAMATIC QUESTION)

All plays have a Major Dramatic Question (see above), but they're also populated by smaller dramatic questions. For example, at the beginning of a play, a son comes home from the army and tells his mother he's been dishonorably discharged, but he doesn't want to talk about it. Of course, the dramatic question is why was he dishonorably discharged? A good playwright doesn't answer that question immediately but instead enjoys teasing the audience by holding off the answer. And when he finally answers the question, he does it by asking a new dramatic question—maybe the mother is told that her son was discharged for "psychological problems." Of course, this leads to a new dramatic question: What type of psychological problems? And what made them grounds for dishonorable, rather than medical, discharge? By answering dramatic questions with new dramatic questions, the playwright builds tension, creates rising action, and constantly whets the audience's curiosity.

BREAKING NEWS (INTERRUPTION)

Interruption is a technique that a playwright uses to temporarily suspend or interrupt a story's main action by injecting an event or crisis. For example, the arrival of the players and Hamlet's advice to them momentarily diverts the main action of the play. Many plays utilize the device of a character bursting onto the stage, interrupting a conversation in progress with some urgent news. This technique freezes a story's progress, and if applied at the right moment, will add suspense and tension to the primary action. The Victorian novelist Wilkie Collins said, "Make 'em laugh, make 'em cry, make 'em wait." Delays and interruptions in a story, however, must feel organic and be carefully planned and executed. They must come at the right moment, or they will kill the play. William Archer cautioned, "Once a play has begun to move, its movement ought to be continuous, and with gathering momentum; or, if it stands still for a space, the stoppage should be deliberate and purposeful. It is fatal when the author thinks it is moving, while in fact it is only revolving on its own axis."

Tell You What I Want, What I Really, Really Want

One of the most common errors beginning playwrights make is to write dialogue that doesn't advance the story. This happens when characters are simply chatting, without wanting anything from each other. In a play, when two characters converse, each must want something from the other. For example, let's take the *Fathers & Daughters* play idea that we used earlier in this chapter. Let's say that the playwright adds a scene in which the daughter talks about her problems with a friend. That scene will only work if the daughter *needs* something, anything, from that friend—even if it's only some reassurance that she's doing the right thing. If nothing is needed, the scene will just lie there, not advancing the story. Without an obvious need it can also feel like the character is talking to the wrong person—why is she telling all this to that guy? He can't do anything about it. To make sure that your characters are talking to the right person, make sure they want or need something from the person they're talking to now.

Deja View (Signposts)

It's been said that the present is pregnant with the future. This is certainly true with a play, for every current action (cause) contains the seed of a future event (effect). Sometimes called a setup or a foreshadowing, a *signpost* is dialogue or action that portends and justifies future events within the play. For example, in Act II scene iii of *Romeo and Juliet*, Friar Laurence gives a speech about his love and knowledge of plants and herbs. This speech is a signpost that sets up the fact that this simple man of God knows enough about herbology that he can concoct medicines and even poisons from the plants in his garden. Without this signpost, his later ability to produce a sleeping potion would seem unbelievable. But because the playwright has set it up—provided a signpost—earlier in the play (when the pressure was not on, we might add), the audience swallows the whole potion bit hook, line, and toxin. Chekhov's famous "gun on the wall" is also a visual signpost: We see there's a gun in the first act, so it doesn't come as a surprise out of nowhere if someone gets shot in the third act.

So let's say that you have a story in which one character forgets an all-important meeting and this action causes the play's dark moment. In order to justify that character's action, you would come up with a signpost earlier in the play, showing that same character forgetting something far less important. We see he's habitually forgetful—which will offer the possibility that this character would forget an all-important meeting. (This device is used to brilliant effect in movies like *Memento* and *Finding Nemo*.) The key to the signpost is to make it memorable, yet subtle enough that it only hints at future possible events without giving them away. If

Shakespeare had made Friar Lawrence's plants-and-herbs speech too obvious (perhaps writing a soliloquy about how to actually make a sleeping potion), the audience would've foreseen the potion solution long before the Friar comes up with it, thus losing the scene's sense of urgency when it arrives. Alexandre Dumas said, "The art of the theater is the art of preparations." William Archer added to this often-quoted remark: "On the other hand, it is also the art of avoiding laborious, artificial, and obvious preparations which lead to little or nothing."

OUR DOCTRINE: DON'T BE DOCTRINAIRE

Both character-first and formula playwrights can turn out quality work. To turn up your nose at formula, or to label yourself a character-first writer, might be good for the ego, but unless it turns out a quality play, the label is meaningless. You'll produce your best work if you're flexible enough to know how to use either or both approaches, as your play demands. Being doctrinaire might be fine for theorists, but it can produce a creative prison. For playwrights, what matters is getting the play built right, from a strong foundation to the last finely turned ornament.

4

Structure, Part Two:
Creativity, Scenario & Writing

Playwrights aren't always in the mood to write, and flashes of inspiration can be few and far between, so forget the notion that writing can be done only when you're inspired. Inspiration is wonderful, all writers long for it, but writing a play takes months, if not years, and, frankly, the Muse gets bored sitting there watching over our shoulder. So a playwright must learn to write without her. Art, written or anything else, isn't so much inspiration as discipline. Mozart wrote over 130 symphonies, concertos, and string quartets in 35 years, Einstein had 248 publications in 53 years, Darwin 119 publications in 51 years, Freud 330 publications in 45 years, Shakespeare wrote 37 plays (or 38, depending on whom you talk to) and more than 150 sonnets in 24 years. Thomas Edison, who said that creativity was "ninety-nine percent perspiration," conducted 2,004 experiments before he found the right light-bulb filament. And Pablo Picasso was so disciplined that he produced over 3,000 works of art before his thirtieth birthday—and he kept up that pace until his death at 92.

DON'T BE A BLOCK HEAD

Some writers blame a lack of creativity on "writer's block." This phrase seems to express some mystical reason for not writing, but the condition seems to be a form of hypochondria—many think they suffer from it, but most would simply rather complain than get down to work. So let's assume you're part of the vast majority and simply trim "writer's block" from your vocabulary. If you simply sit down and start working, it goes away. Will you immediately start writing Tony Award material? Probably not; the act of committing yourself to writing ANYTHING will unblock you like a mental high colonic, and what comes out at first may not be pretty. But don't judge it (yet) and don't hold back. Eventually the stream will clear.

We chose that rather earthy analogy because writing isn't a rarified, pristine thing. It's hard, gut-wrenching work, requiring you to get in touch with every aspect of your being, including its physicality. In this chapter we'll look at the hard work of creativity, building a scenario, and the methods that help a playwright maintain discipline. For no matter how talented you are, whether the Muse is present or on vacation, you must be able to generate your own creativity. To do this, you must provide yourself with a map, an idea of where you're going, and you must have the discipline to write every day. As Terrence McNally (author of *Corpus Christi* and *Love! Valour! Compassion!*) advised playwrights in a recent issue of *The Dramatist*, "Write. Just write. Even when you don't feel like it. Even when you're not inspired. Even when they want to smother you in your cradle. Especially when they want to smother you in your cradle. Write. Write when it's hard. Write when it's lonely. Write even when you think no one else in the entire world cares what you have to say." And don't pretend that tomorrow will be a better day; as the adage goes, "Procrastination preserves only the illusion of greatness, because the potential is never tested."

IN THE BEGINNING WAS THE WORD (CREATIVITY)

What is creativity, anyway? At the beginning, in perhaps the smallest percentage of time you will devote to your play, is a brief moment of insight. It's the adrenaline rush that occurs at the moment that you, like Archimedes in his bathtub, cry "Eureka!" because you have just invented something or solved something or transformed the familiar into the new. This is that moment when you feel you have something to add to the sum total of our culture. This flash of creativity can be a lightning strike that changes the world or a small insight that solves a minor but nonetheless intriguing problem. In playwriting, it can be the brainstorm that sees shattering revelations lurking in the story of an obscure Prince of Denmark, or a tiny moment in which a single line of dialogue comes together. (Just imagine the Bard at work: " 'To live or to die'…no, that's flat…' 'To hang around or to hang it up'…no, way too anachronistic…wait—I know…!!"). Whether overwhelming or modest, a flash of creativity is seldom as spontaneous as it looks: The ground has been tilled, the seeds are planted, and the rain falls. At that moment, whether consciously or unconsciously or subconsciously, something new and alive emerges. So we need to explore ways to prepare the soil and increase our chances for such moments to occur.

Creative people look for options to increase the range of their choices. They're the ones whose mental mobility allows them to draw analogies and metaphors and see order underlying apparent chaos. Creative people experiment and take risks. But, most importantly, creative people put themselves into situations where creativity is possible. The great French scientist Louis Pasteur said, "Chance favors the prepared mind." For a writer, being prepared means having studied people and life stories, having populated the mind with an ever-growing cast of characters and themes and possible plots. Then he sits down and starts writing.

Writers write, whether we feel like it or not. We write whether we're inspired or not. We write whether we're in the mood to or not. Creativity may hit at any time but, if we've been observant and thoughtful during the rest of our day, it's more likely to occur while we're actually putting thoughts down on paper. "But how," you moan, "how can I be creative when the baby is crying and the street is noisy and I'd really rather just have a beer and watch the game instead of sitting here staring at my blank page?" The answer, as with a tired tennis player who nonetheless wins the match, is to build stamina and master technique.

IT'S ALL IN THE WRIST (TECHNIQUE AND CREATIVITY)

If creativity is a brief moment of insight, technique is what allows us to capture that lightning in the bottle of our story. Like grammar in a sentence, it doesn't provide the thought, but it makes it comprehensible. In other words, technique is what gives structure to creativity. When you make a discovery about a story or a character, creativity is involved. In order to organize and express that discovery through your characters' actions and voices, you rely on technique. Techniques are those methods that have been repeatedly shown to work. Call them tools, or a bag of tricks if you wish, but techniques are devices and methods by which a complex task, like writing a play, can be broken into manageable bits and accomplished. Techniques can be learned from your own hard-won experience, or from someone else's. (That's why you're reading this book, which is really just a compendium of techniques.)

In our opinion, the arts and theater are more about technique than creativity. Say a talented actor is playing Hamlet. The audience is enthralled, the actor's performance is winning the critics, there is a feeling of magic in the air. But is the actor being creative? Not necessarily, not after he has done the initial work of deciding how to interpret Shakespeare's text. Night after night he may be acting with great talent, impeccable grace, deep emotions, and compelling passion, but what is creative about his performance on the fifth or fiftieth night? He's not inventing anything new. But his technique allows him to consistently tap into those emotions and expressive actions upon which he can depend to bring the play to life, whether he's in the mood to perform that night or not. Armed with sufficient technique, there is no excuse for an actor not to take the stage and give a good performance, even if he has the flu.

The same is true with playwrights. They can sit at the computer, not feel creative, not be in the mood, and still write something good; good enough, at least, that it can be the basis for a strong rewrite later on. For a playwright, if she's already working on a play, technique is applying the basics of good dialogue, plot structure, and character development. If she's still searching for ideas, technique is applying some of the methods mentioned in our "idea" chapter: examining the themes and people that strike her imagination and asking "what if?" Technique is, therefore, also knowing which questions to ask and when to ask them. Even if the Muse is off sulking somewhere, the playwright can answer such questions as: What should happen next, based on what just happened? Where do I want this story to go? What does this particular character feel at this moment? How do I integrate this bit of obvious exposition? These questions (and the hundreds like them that arise) can in and of themselves reawaken the writer's creativity. Technique is more than just a method of writing when you lack inspiration; it can prime the pump and usher in a new burst of inspiration.

THE TWO-SIDED BRAIN (THE CREATIVE AND THE CRITICAL)

As we mentioned above, once your creative juices are flowing, don't get in their way by allowing yourself to be too critical of your new ideas. Whether or not you believe that creative and critical thinking come from opposite sides of the brain, one thing is certainly true: Creative and critical thinking seldom operate at the same time. Like caring for young twins who never get along, if you try to listen to both yelling at the same time, you will only give yourself a headache. So, first send your little inner critic to his room and hear what your little poet has to say. Then, after the poet has nothing more to say, send him off with a hug and bring the critic out of detention to hear why everything you just wrote needs work.

People are more creative when they come up with many imaginative possible solutions and hold off judgment on them until later. One study placed a group of scientists in a think tank with a problem to solve. They were told that once they came up with a possible solution, they should all immediately analytically judge the idea. After a day of thinking and judging, they failed to solve the problem. The next day they were given an equally difficult problem to solve, but this time they spent the morning pitching possible solutions without critically judging them or even considering plausibility. That afternoon, the scientists returned and were asked to critically judge each solution they had come up with earlier. The division of labor worked. One of their morning pitches solved the problem. By turning off the critical side of the brain, they succeeded in increasing creativity.

How does this work for playwrights? By using your writing and brainstorming techniques. "What if?" is a powerful technique. So is doing a random character study. Let's say, for instance, you have no idea what your next play should be. But you sit down at your keyboard and start doing a quick character study of a homeless man you've seen who seems well-dressed, but spends his days washing windshields outside the convenience store. Why is he doing that if he's well-dressed? What might be the story behind that? What if he isn't really poor? What if he's a millionaire? What if he does this because he's working off some guilt about having all that money? Later on, you may decide that's not what interests you, and that's okay. But write it down anyway, don't analyze it. Then you have another thought—what if he inherited millions, but his family never told him about it and kept the money for themselves? What if his son makes sure he has enough for food and clothing, but is ashamed of what he considers his father's mental incapacity, and justifies his own greed by saying he doesn't want his father to squander wealth that will soon come to him, the son, anyway? What if the son's wife, in a jealous rage after discovering an affair, tells her father-in-law about the money? Then you realize you have a theme: Betrayal breeds betrayal—and maybe that's something you've been thinking about, because you've experienced it yourself. Maybe, subconsciously, that's why this character occurred to you. What other characters might work with this theme? And on you go. Later, you decide this is the direction you want to explore. So, using two simple techniques, you've eliminated your block and discovered your story, after all.

The next time you have a problem to solve, write down one possible solution after another, without being critical. Don't judge whether they will work or not. Let the "what ifs" fly, then winnow the answers down to what you're really interested in writing about. Soon you'll have a list of possible solutions.

SINGLE FILE, KIDS! (PROBLEM-SOLVING)

A creative roadblock can come from trying to solve too many problems at once. Just as a play is written one word at a time, the hundreds of small problems a play is made up of must be tackled individually. Your characters and story must be broken down into manageable components, so you have a chance to solve them one at a time. This is begun by specifying each problem in terms that are not vague. In his book *People in Quandaries*, Wendell Johnson recalls a psychiatrist who was often sent patients who were judged to be seriously maladjusted. He noticed that all of them showed one chief symptom: "They were unable to tell him clearly what was the matter." The solution depended first on their being helped to locate each precise problem. Wendell Johnson goes on to say, "Certainly any scientific worker of experience knows that by far the most important step toward the solution of the laboratory problem lies in stating the problem in such a way as to suggest a fruitful attack on it. Once that is accomplished, any ordinary assistant can usually turn the cranks and read the dials…There cannot be a precise answer to a vague question."

The process works even after your first draft (or second draft, or third) is written. If you're still confused about what's going on in your play, break the problems down into manageable components. Most problems are made up of dozens of smaller problems. Only when we unravel the big picture into its smaller parts can we begin to analyze. In fact, the word "analysis" comes from the ancient Greek word for "breaking down." After you've done this, and only after you've done this, it's time to brainstorm possible solutions. If you try to "be creative" before your problems are identified and broken into manageable components, the result may often degenerate into wild guesses. There's no need to depend on random inspiration; many techniques are available to solve your problems. Of course, some creativity is involved because one has to have moments of insight as each technique is applied, but right now you're not looking for the big flash of genius—you're looking to make what you've already created work better. Finally, test to see if the solution works. Have a reading of your play in front of a small audience—do they get it? Are they still confused or unmoved? Ask why—why, specifically—and go back and do it again.

SPILLED MILK (ACCEPTING FAILURE)

The vast majority of creative endeavors end in failure. When we pointed out that Thomas Edison conducted 2,004 experiments before finding the right filament, the real story was that he had 2,003 failures before he got it right. Picasso might have produced over 20,000 works of art over the course of his life, but much of it was mediocre, and he knew it. That didn't stop him. We don't have a record of Shakespeare's failures, but rest assured that he did us all a favor when he threw away the plays and sonnets that he'd spent weeks and months writing, but which came up short. Hans Bethe, winner of the Nobel Prize in physics, is quoted in *Creativity* by Mihaly Csikszentmihalyi as saying that two things are required for creativity: "One is a brain. And second is the willingness to spend long times in thinking, with a definite possibility that you come out with nothing." Failure is an important part of the creative process, so when a writing session ends in failure, don't beat yourself up. Having exercised your critical side, you now know what doesn't work (and what does), which you'd never have known it if you hadn't spent those hours or days or weeks going down the wrong path.

WHATEVER RINGS YOUR BELL (MOTIVATION)

Your motivation for wanting to be a writer can help and/or hurt your creativity. If your goal is to come up with an award-winning play that'll make you lots of money and win the critics' hearts, your motivation, "earning money and fame," will generally inhibit your creativity, because you'll constantly be making premature judgments about your work. Research and common sense have shown that beginning artists whose dream is primarily to make it big tend to drop out if they're not immediately successful. On the other hand, those artists who are focused on the creative process without worrying about tomorrow's success tend to stick with it for years, find more opportunities to be creative, and end up having greater chances of making it big (and even winning the critics' hearts and making money). Actor Stuart Ostrow summed it up nicely when he said to *The New York Times*, "So why are you on this journey? If you can answer the question without using the words money, glamour, fame, romance, or sex, you have the right to be taken seriously." The same is true in playwriting. If you focus prematurely on the end result, rather than the process, the journey, you'll sabotage both. Even for "successful" writers, life is full of rejection, failure, and disappointment. All you need to think about is *this* line, *this* moment, *this* page. As the Chinese philosopher Lao-Tze said, "A journey of a thousand miles must begin with a single step." If you're not enjoying your journey, you won't make it to the end.

CHARTING THE JOURNEY (SCENARIO)

One tool to help you write one page at a time is the scenario. A playwright's scenario is a blueprint, much like a screenwriter's scene cards or a film director's storyboard. A scenario includes the information from the front matter (a provisional title, cast of characters, and time/place/setting) and a step outline of the story (a lean, schematic list of your play's sequence of events). This outline should be full of reference points that can act as beacons, places to navigate toward within the dark void of an unwritten play. Alexandre Dumas (*The Count of Monte Cristo*, *The Three Musketeers*—the books, not the movies) opined, "You should not begin your work until you have your concluding scene, movement, and speech clear in your mind... You cannot very well know where you should come out when you don't know where you are going."

A scenario may help point out a play's faults and inconsistencies (e.g., a weak middle, or a lack of conflict, etc.) before you discover them the hard way, as you're writing. A scenario doesn't necessarily make writing easy, but it can free up your creativity so that you can deal with problems in a manageable and systematic way and not constantly ask yourself where your play is going.

The English dramatist Sir Arthur Pinero (*The Notorious Mrs. Ebbsmit*, *The Second Mrs. Tanqueray*) said, "Before beginning to write a play, I always make sure, by means of a definite scheme, that there is a way of doing it, but whether I ultimately follow that way is a totally different matter." A good scenario shouldn't be fixed in stone, but be designed to give you both direction and room to maneuver to find the right route. As you write, interesting possibilities will reveal themselves and new discoveries will change the story and characters, sometimes subtly, sometimes drastically. Often a writer will finish a play and look back at his scenario only to be amazed at how little of it was actually used. George Pierce Baker, Eugene O'Neill's professor at Harvard, wrote in his book *Dramatic Technique*, "He who steers by the compass knows how with safety to change his course. He who steers by dead reckoning is liable to error and delay." A playwright should never have an ironclad scenario, yet if the scenario has too many holes and leaps of faith and logic, the play isn't ready to be written.

The basic elements of a scenario are: working title, character names, and a basic outline that includes acts, scenes, and French scenes, as well as information on place, time, and setting. It might also include information on theme. (A sample scenario can be found later in this chapter.)

You don't need to write character descriptions when composing a scenario. Some playwrights like to, others don't. The reason for not doing it is that you might not want to set your characters in stone before you start writing. You want your characters to be free to grow, change, and reveal themselves to you as you write and discover their story. If that's the case, instead of writing detailed character descriptions, try including only a few character notes and possibilities. Note that skipping character descriptions can be dangerous for beginning writers, who can end up creating inconsistent characters; better to know your cast well if you're just starting out.

NOM DE GUERRE (YOUR WORKING TITLE)

The perfect title often doesn't occur to you until you've written your entire play; so, as you write, you only need a working title. You need some kind of title because it gives your play an identity, a focus, and a direction. You name your first few snatches of dialogue and notes on character and story in the hope that they will someday grow up into a full play. Tennessee Williams was famous for his evocative working titles: *The Glass Menagerie*'s working title was *The Gentleman*

Caller; *A Streetcar Named Desire* was originally titled *The Poker Party*. Titles can come from many areas:

The Little Foxes	A Quotation
Summer and Smoke	An Image
A Raisin in the Sun	A Poem
The Runner Stumbles	The Bible
Marty	A Character's Name
The Homecoming	An Action
Tobacco Road	A Place
The Tempest	An Event
Oh Dad, Poor Dad, Momma's Hung You in the Closet and I'm Feelin' So Sad	Humor

Your working title needs only to appeal to you, although your final title must communicate well to others. The first thing anyone knows about your play is its title. First impressions are so important that some playwrights test-market their titles, looking for that special title that piques curiosity while conveying the essence of the play.

You should keep a "titles file" of interesting phrases, poems, and word images that you hear through the years, things that strike you as meaningful and catchy. Hemingway and Faulkner found great titles for their novels in poems, Shakespeare, and the Bible: *For Whom the Bell Tolls*, *A Farewell to Arms*, *The Sound and the Fury*. However, beware of titles that are unnecessarily ponderous or obscure, or that don't communicate the tone and content of your play.

NAME THAT CHARACTER!

It's a good idea to name your characters as early in the process as possible. Naming your characters helps you think of them as people, rather than just types. For example, "The Father" or "The Boyfriend" are types, place-holders, not flesh and blood. You can enhance a character by finding a name that reflects (or contrasts with) the character's personality, geographical region, education, and ethnic background. In the movie *Gladiator*, for instance, the title character was originally named Narcissus, as was the real-life gladiator on whose life the film was loosely based. But Narcissus doesn't convey boldness, leadership, and courage, but rather, well, narcissism. So his name was changed to the manly Maximus. (More on naming your characters will be found in Chapter 5.)

THEM'S THE BREAKS (ACTS AND INTERMISSIONS)

The heart of your scenario will be the step outline of your story. To construct this, you'll need to break your plot into basic playwriting units: acts, scenes, and French scenes. You don't want to include individual beats (for more on beats, see Chapter 7), or too much detail. A scenario's step-outline is really just a plot-skeleton, the essence of your story's structure.

The largest unit in a play is an "Act." Acts are story sections divided by intermissions. The idea of acts and intermissions is relatively new in the long history of the theater. They only came into being about five hundred years ago. The ancient Greeks didn't use acts or intermissions, nor did Shakespeare. (The acts you find in his plays were added after his death.) They weren't introduced so the audience could take a bathroom break, either; acts are a result of the advent of indoor theaters in Renaissance Italy, whose stages were lit by candles that needed their wicks regularly changed and trimmed. The only way to do this without breaking into the performance was to add regularly spaced interruptions. They started with five acts (four wick-changing intermissions), but as candle technology improved and was later replaced with gas and then electric lighting, the number of acts dropped to four, three, two and then one.

Today, we still hold on to tradition and the convenience of acts and intermission. With today's shrinking attention span, they help keep an audience already accustomed to commercial breaks involved. Yet, as the great drama critic William Archer says in *Play Making*, "It is a grave error to suppose that the act is a mere division of convenience, imposed by the limited power of attention of the human mind, or by the need of the human body for occasional refreshment. A play with a well-marked, well-balanced act-structure is a higher artistic organism than a play with no act-structure, just as a vertebrate animal is higher than a mollusk." In other words, acts force a playwright to focus on structure, and on keeping the audience hooked.

A common way to end an act is with a "plot twist": a revelation or turn in the story that spikes the audience's interest and promises greater conflict and crisis in the next act. To quote Emmett Jacobs of the American College Theater Festival, "You have to get a pretty good inferno going in the first act to jump that firebreak of intermission."

In today's theater, playwrights use acts in several ways. Here are the most common ways to split a play into acts:

Three-Act Plays

The three-act format was common fifty years ago, but it's rarely used today. A double intermission makes the running time of the play longer than is audience-friendly today. Some modern plays, like Beth Henley's *Crimes of the Heart*, use three acts, but they're rare.

Two-Act Plays

This is the most common contemporary way to divide a full-length play. The act break is generally taken just after the middle of the story. Your audience will expect the first act to be slightly longer than the second.

Full-Length One-Act Play

This type of play has no intermission, so its beginning, middle, and end flow without interruption. The one-act was first tried in the modern theater by August Strindberg in 1888 when he removed the act breaks from his play *Miss Julie*.

If you're planning such a play, be concerned, as Strindberg was, about how long the audience can sit without the expected intermission. Our present-day attention span is certainly shorter than it was in 1888. The general theater-going public expects at least one intermission. However—perhaps growing on the realization that audiences can tolerate an intermissionless two-and-a-half-hour movie—there is a growing trend toward longer one-acts. (For example, *Art* by Christopher Hampton runs an hour and half.) Nonetheless, full-length one-act plays are generally shorter than two- or three-act plays and usually succeed at between 1 hour and 20 minutes and 1 hour 35 minutes.

Short One-Acts

Most beginning playwrights start with a one-act play. This can be anywhere from fifteen minutes to about an hour long. Although shorter than a full-length, it requires the same detailed work on structure and character. When writing a short one-act, you are working with time constraints, so your story shouldn't be as complex as it would for a full-length play. The scope must be limited, and generally without more than a single subplot. One-act plays generally revolve around one incident or occurrence in a character's life, often in a continuous time-frame.

Theaters seldom perform a single short one-act. More often, they'll produce an evening of one-acts. This means that your set must be modest so it can be quickly changed during the intermission between plays. It's also a good idea to limit the size of your cast. With the theater doing several one-acts in an evening, if too many actors are involved, it could place financial strains on the theater, and prevent your play from being included. Keep it simple, keep it small and you'll stand a better chance of being produced.

Sometimes a playwright will write several one-act plays as "companion pieces" designed to be performed on the same night. By doing this, the playwright doesn't have to share the evening with other one-acts. Companion pieces can have related or unrelated themes and stories. Examples of related one-acts are *Lone Star* and *Laundry & Bourbon* by James McLure. Examples of unrelated one-acts are Christopher Durang's *Sister Mary Ignatius Explains It All For You* and *The Actor's Nightmare*.

Ten-Minute Plays

For years, playwriting professors have assigned ten-minute plays as exercises. These are short (no more than ten pages) plays written to help the student understand dramatic techniques. Today, these exercises have become a popular form of playwriting, with more and more contests and theaters interested in showcasing them.

Such plays are extremely limited in scope, with sets so simple they can be changed in seconds. (You're often only allowed a generic chair and table.) The cast is usually limited to four or less.

The structure of a ten-minute play includes a very early point of attack, which commonly occurs at the bottom of the first page or top of the second. The play usually has only one conflict, which means that there is seldom time for more than one plot. Also, the tight structure allows for little exposition, so the entire story should fit within the frame of the play. The end of a ten-minute play falls very close to the climax, with room only for a line or two that hints at catharsis.

Theaters that produce ten-minute plays will stage as many as ten in one evening, so concentrate on one brief, exceptionally involving moment in your characters' lives, and your chances of being produced will increase. (For examples of ten-minute plays see Chapter 9.)

Once you've started writing, the structure of your play may change, and, as a result, so could the number of acts and intermissions. For example, playwrights have been known to start with the scenario for a short one-act, but before they're through, it has evolved into a full-length; or they intended to write a ten-minute, but it morphs into a one-act. This is all part of the process, but it shouldn't stop you from at least starting with an idea of which type of play you intend to write. And keep your original goal in mind, because, if your play expands, it may simply be due to lazy writing. Even long plays should be economical and include only essentials.

MAKING A SCENE

After the act, the next smallest unit in a play is a scene. Scenes, like acts and the play as a whole, have beginnings, middles, and ends. They contain most if not all of the elements making up the play as a whole: an event, a disturbance or inciting incident, conflict(s), and so on. A good way to think of scenes is as mini-acts without intermissions between them (although there may be a blackout in which the lights are dimmed).

One scene ends and a new one begins whenever there's a change of time and/or place. This means that a whole act that has no change in time or place has only one scene, while an act that contains five changes in place and/or time would have five scenes. Plays, unlike screenplays, generally don't have a lot of scenes, and the scenes are usually longer than those in screenplays. This isn't a hard and set rule—Shakespeare used a lot of scenes—but, generally speaking, modern plays will maintain action and keep the practical problems of cost and time-consuming set-changes down by using as few scenes as possible.

In playwriting, a change of scene is desirable only when absolutely necessary. This doesn't mean that all plays that have an abundance of scenes are poorly written. Many short scenes are fine, as long as the playwright makes this decision based on what's good for the play's plot-structure. If you have a play with many scenes, you should consider a couple of things:

First, are all the scenes (or blackouts) necessary? Scene changes and blackouts can pull the audience out of a play because the action continually starts and stops. If you need multiple scenes, try eliminating some or all of the blackouts, so the actors can walk from one scene directly into another. Also, be honest with yourself. If you're writing short scenes only because you haven't tried to maintain action for more than a few pages at a time, you are writing from a television/movie point of view in which short scenes are the norm. Try to group scenes together, and work at finding realistic transitions that can turn several short scenes into one powerful longer scene.

The second concern when writing many scenes is more pragmatic. When you change scenes, make sure any change in costume or set can be done quickly. One young playwright wrote an end of a scene that called for the main character to be wearing a three-piece suit. There was a blackout and the next scene began with this character wearing a funny horse outfit. (Imagine the audience yawning through that interruption.) The logistics of a scene transition aren't the director's or costumer's responsibility. The onus is on the playwright to write a play that can actually be staged. In the case of the funny horse outfit, the playwright was forced to write a "cover scene." This is a scene or bit of dialogue that continues the action onstage while the offstage actor is changing into a new outfit (in this case, the horse outfit). But a cover scene will only work if it and its dialogue move the characters and action forward. Otherwise it will feel like what it is—vamping for time.

THE REVOLVING DOOR (FRENCH SCENES)

The next smallest segments of a play (after scenes) are French scenes. A French scene begins whenever a character enters and/or exits, and continues until the next entrance and/or exit. For example, if a scene has John and Bob fighting and Mom comes in to ask Bob where the car is, Mom's entrance marks the beginning of a new French scene. Then, Bob storms off, leaving John and Mom to discuss where things went wrong with that boy, and we have another new French scene. The length of each French scene can vary greatly, as can the number of French scenes within a play, act, or scene. A farce may have dozens of French scenes, while a play with no entrances or exits obviously has only one.

Because French scenes are defined by entrances and exits—changes of character rather than changes of time or location—there is no formal curtain or dimming of the lights between them. Movement from one to the next should feel seamless, and the audience or reader is often unaware that one French scene has ended and another begun. French scenes are not marked in the script. They're just a technique to help the playwright structure the action. Neither audience nor readers need be aware of them.

The French scene originated, of course, in France, where hundreds of years ago the printing press was still a novelty and quite expensive. To cut costs, theaters would give an actor only those pages of the script that concerned his or her character, rather than the full script. The most cost-efficient way of dividing a play was from one entrance or exit to the next entrance or exit. While this did little to help the actors with character analysis and continuity, it did save a few precious pages.

This antiquated method of dividing a play would've been long forgotten had it not turned out to be so useful in playwriting. Because a French scene deals with only certain characters at a particular point, it's a natural way to divide a play into workable units. A playwright should treat each French scene as a mini-play, with all the structural elements (beginning, middle, end) of a full play. As each entrance or exit occurs, the play changes, characters' attitudes adjust, and the story moves forward. If, say, John and Bob are fighting about Mom's upcoming operation, and Mom enters (new French scene), John and Bob will react and, as a consequence, their argument will change. Perhaps they can't fight in front of Mom, or perhaps Bob now feels he can state the truth. When Bob storms off (new French scene),

John and Mom are left alone, and again attitudes and intentions change. In most cases, the most important bit of information (i.e., the revelation, the confrontation, the twist in the plot, the best line, the mini-climax, the capper) comes near the end of the French scene (just before the next entrance or exit).

One good playwriting trick is to interrupt a scene's action just before it hits its mini-climax. The entrance or exit of a character causes the conflict between hostile characters to remain unresolved and heightens the tension of the play. This is a technique borrowed by television—in this case, soap operas.

When building a scenario, a playwright might make a list that labels the action in each French scene, thereby pinpointing what that particular moment in the play is about. A hundred years ago, writers of Victorian melodramas used to give each act an alluring title. Although this is now outdated, a beginning playwright might consider titling (in their personal notes) each scene or French scene. This title is a mini-label that can pinpoint the conflicts and purposes the characters have at that particular moment. A playwright's list of French scenes might look like this:

French Scene	Characters Involved	Title	Action
#1	Beth & Henry	Awaiting the arrival	They plot how they will tell her mother (Sarah) that she lost the baby.
#2	Beth, Henry & Sarah	Baby shower gifts	Sarah arrives and first thing pushes Beth to open her baby shower gifts now. Beth opens one and breaks down in tears. She runs out.
#3	Henry & Sarah	Henry tells the truth	Henry tells Sarah that Beth was never pregnant in the first place. In fact, she lied to please her mother. Sarah storms out.
#4	Beth & Henry	Henry's decision	After Sarah leaves, Beth comes out. She's pissed at Henry for telling her mother the truth. Henry begs her to see a psychiatrist.

You Are Here (Place & Setting)

Place refers to the geographical location (real or imagined) where the action of the play takes place. Setting is what the audience sees on stage. So the place might be New England in 1850, but the setting is the exterior of the Cabot family farmhouse. The place might be present-day St. Louis, but the setting is Wingfield's apartment. Place and setting can greatly influence a play's characters and story. For example, can you imagine one of Tennessee Williams' steamy Southern plays set in Minnesota, or one of Noel Coward's sophisticated Manhattan comedies set in a Texas cowboy bar? Each location has different social orders, rules of etiquette, accents, and is populated by different types of people.

Always try to find a distinctive, interesting place and setting to locate your play that will directly reflect and affect your characters and story. For example, one of our students recently wrote a ten-minute play about a young boy asking a girl out on a date. Because he "couldn't come up with anything better," he set it in a café. It was a fine little play, but the setting did nothing to help the story or the characters. In his second draft, he changed the location to the back row of a church during a hellfire sermon. Suddenly the setting became an important part of the play, because it altered how the characters spoke, thought, and reacted. As a result, a rather bland ten-minute was turned into an interesting play. When you have the right place and setting, they can create a fun metaphor full of irony, a reflection of character, or an environment in direct conflict with the play's characters. Whatever you choose, make sure that it's a location that you know well or have researched extensively. For example, one beginning student wrote a play that took place at a television studio in Hollywood. The fact that she had never seen a television studio and knew nothing of how a television show was run didn't seem to bother her. She relied on her imagination (and what she'd seen on TV) and wasted her time writing a script that was full of errors, misconceptions, and stereotypes. Imagination is a wonderful thing, but when it comes to setting your scene, it loses out to truth.

Place and setting are the most important elements in creating your play's environment. Characters grow out of a specific environment, which defines and reveals their personalities. This is particularly true of a character's personal surroundings: their home, office, car, room, or any location directly related to that one particular personality. Characters' tastes, lifestyles, incomes, jobs, educations, and temperaments can be seen in their environments, the elements of which create indirect characterization: We know something of who they are because we see where and how they live. When writing a scenario, you should try to identify what makes its place and setting distinctive. What mood does it instill? How are your story and characters affected and reflected by this setting? On a practical level, can the set be built economically (is your environment stageable)? Recently, a student playwright wrote a one-act play that required a two-story set. Few theaters are rich enough to produce such a play, let alone such a one-act. Whether it's a one-act or a full-length, a play with a single, simple set has a better chance of being produced than one with many sets and effects. Almost all theaters are poor. You're shooting yourself in the figurative foot if you write a play that cannot be economically staged.

PREMISES, PREMISES (THEME)

As discussed in our "Idea" chapter, the theme is a play's primary statement, its overall message, the truth revealed by the story. Sometimes the theme can be stated in a simple sentence, such as, "A house divided against itself cannot stand" or "You can't keep a good woman down" or "Love conquers all." But more often, it's a complex maxim or a discovery the author has made about human nature. For example, try to state the theme of *A Streetcar Named Desire* in a simple sentence: "If you're an emotionally disturbed Southerner, don't visit your lowbrow brother-in-law?" We doubt it. Perhaps "Clinging to past, faded glories will only create heartache and disappointment in the present." But even that isn't quite sufficient. Lajos Egri insists that every good play has a single organizing premise, out of which everything else grows. This is true, generally speaking. But a full-length play can also have several interwoven sub-themes. For example, the ancient comedy *Lysistrata* has at least three major themes: 1) war is ridiculous; 2) men and women become silly and illogical when sex is involved; 3) it's infantile for men and women to act as if they don't need each other. Or these can be combined into a single, more complex thematic statement: "Women, being more sensible than men, can use men's brain-addling desire for sex as a weapon to keep their men from hurting each other in their equally brain-addled lust for war."

At the scenario stage, you don't have to have your theme fully worked out, though it's helpful to identify it as early on as possible. Seldom does a playwright start with a perfected take on her final theme. Theme often reveals itself during the writing of the play. One danger of getting locked into a particular theme from the start is that the writer may sacrifice character and story to "prove" that preliminary theme correct. This could result in a didactic or propaganda play in which the characters are only mouthpieces for the author's message and editorials. Whether it's a complex idea or a simple motif, the theme is subtextual, and should be deeply embedded in the action, *suggested* and not openly stated. You want to persuade your audience, not *indoctrinate* them. Therefore, it's best to avoid themes that sound like political slogans, personal mottoes, or life lectures.

Start with a clear, well-defined working theme, but be careful that you don't set it in stone, or use it to write a lecture disguised as a play. You want to illuminate and challenge; as everyone found out in high school, being lectured with truisms will only challenge your audience to stay awake. The writing process is full of delightful discovery, so allow your characters and story to reveal and improve your theme as your plot grows. However, if you find that your theme itself has changed, you will need to reexamine your characters and situations to make sure they still work, and that you're not straddling two inconsistent thematic statements.

SAMPLE SCENARIO

A finished scenario should not be long. It will have holes in the story, missing details, and areas left to be explored, but it will give you an idea of what the finished play is intended to be. Here is an example of what it might look like:

Working Title:
    Ace in a Hole

Place:
    New York City. Soho.

Setting:
    The William Henry Harrison, a transient hotel. The setting is Ace Campbell's old room. It's obvious from the faded clippings on the walls and the frayed upholstery that Ace has lived here many years.

Time:
    The present.

Cast of Characters:
    ACE - an old stand-up comedian. A total failure now, he once appeared on *The Ed Sullivan Show*.

    MR. LAGATUTTA - a senile Italian Roman Catholic. Divorced. Poor. Once a proud foreman for the American Thread Company, but now he has nothing: No retirement. No family. His only joy in life is bitching at and to Mrs. Konigsberg.

    MRS. KONIGSBERG - an ancient Russian Jew. Loves to cook. Loves life, loves Ace's old stand-up routines. Hates Mr. Lagatutta, but she can't live without him.

    WINK - a crazy transient who doesn't understand English, but he likes to pretend that he does. He's been there so long, no one questions why he's there or who he is. Always happy, but for no apparent reason.

    SHAPIRO - a lawyer. Good heart, bad intentions. Has

forgotten that not all people are as lucky as he. He's learned that it's easy to abandon people, including his wife.

SANDRA - an eviction officer. Hates her job, sees few options left to her, but deep down inside, she cares about people, or at least once did. She has lost sight of her goals.

MRS. ROLAND DEFOE - a wealthy woman. Loves her pedigree more than people, especially poor people.

Possible Acts, Scenes & French Scenes

ACT ONE

Scene & French Scene	Characters Involved	Action
Scene #1 French Scene #1	Ace Lagatutta Wink	It's another day of bickering and waiting to die at the transient hotel. Lagatutta feels old. Wink, who doesn't understand a word of English, actively participates. To break the monotony, Ace tries out a new stand-up routine. By "new," he means only twenty years old.
French Scene #2	Ace Lagatutta Wink Konigsberg	Mrs. Konigsberg enters with a letter telling Ace that he is to be evicted. Ace admits that his time is up. Both in this hotel and on this earth. He has so many regrets. If only it had worked out on *Ed Sullivan*.
French Scene #3	Ace Wink	Seeing that Ace is depressed, Konigsberg gets Mr. Lagatutta to come to her room, where they can fight in private. Ace is left with Wink. We learn about their special relationship - good friends who will miss each other. Note: What is the conflict?
French Scene #4	Ace Wink Shapiro	Shapiro enters. He's a public defender and has a plan to save Ace from eviction, but Ace says he's too old to fight anymore. He has a gun, he might just end it all.

Scene #1 **(cont.)** French Scene #5	Ace Lagatutta Konigsberg Shapiro	Konigsberg and Lagatutta bring Ace a big pot of soup to cheer him up. They're so old perhaps they think that Shapiro is Ace's son (or another transient). Lagatutta and Konigsberg pledge their support, but it's obvious that they'll be of no help.
French Scene #6	Ace Wink Shapiro	Shapiro gets rid of Konigsberg and Lagatutta. In private, he tells Ace that the building has been sold to new owners who want to make it into condos. He tells Ace that if he fails to stop his eviction, Konigsberg and Lagatutta will be next. Ace decides to put up a fight.
Scene #2 French Scene #1	Ace Wink	The next day. Ace tries out a stand-up routine on Wink. But Wink will laugh at anything. I mean, anything. Ace begins to realize that there will be no comeback.
French Scene #2	Ace Wink Sandra	Sandra, an eviction officer, arrives to evict Ace. He tries to stall by doing his standup routine. He fails totally. She's about to call the police and force him out when…
French Scene #3	Ace Sandra Lagatutta Konigsberg	Trick or Treat! Lagatutta and Konigsberg arrive wearing masks. They think it's Halloween. It's not even close. Sandra kicks them out.
French Scene #4	Ace Wink Sandra	Sandra starts packing Ace's stuff. She's really pissed. She's tired of her job, tired of the people she evicts. Tired of life. She nearly has a break-down.
French Scene #5	Ace Sandra Lagatutta Konigsberg	Lagatutta and Konigsberg come to the door for another round of Trick or Treat. They've forgotten which doors they've knocked on. Then, Lagatutta and Konigsberg decide it's time for a game of tag. Sandra loses it. She yells at all them. Accuses them of wasting their lives. She blames them for their situation. Lagatutta and Konigsberg leave in shame.
French Scene #6	Ace Sandra	The attack is too much for Ace, he takes out a gun and takes Sandra hostage.

ACT TWO

Scene & French Scene	Characters	Action
Scene #1 French Scene #1	Ace Wink Sandra Lagatutta Konigsberg	The hostage drama continues. They find out Shapiro is Sandra's ex-husband. Ace tells of his big break and how he became a failure. Sandra tries to make a compromise. They discover that Shapiro is really working for the landlord. Sandra is released and now wants to try to help them.
French Scene #2	Ace Wink Sandra Lagatutta Konigsberg Shapiro	Shapiro arrives and is forced to do a stand-up comedy act. Shapiro escapes.
French Scene #3	Ace Wink Sandra Lagatutta Konigsberg	Ace realizes that the gig is up. He jumps out the window.
French Scene #4	Roland Defoe Wink Sandra Lagatutta Konigsberg	Everyone is totally depressed. Mrs. Defoe enters. She's the new owner of the building and is looking for her designer.
French Scene #5	Ace Roland Defoe Wink Sandra Lagatutta Konigsberg	Ace returns. He has fallen on a window washer's platform and is still alive. Seeing the totally absurdity of life, Ace sets out to convinces the pretentious Mrs. Defoe that his crazy friend Wink is the famous designer she was suppose to meet here.
French Scene #6	Roland Defoe Wink	Mrs. Defoe goes over the design with the uncomprehending Wink. She thinks that his oddness is artistic temperament, that he is really a genius.
Scene #2 French Scene #1	Ace Wink Lagatutta Konigsberg Ace	The next day. The building is sold. They must leave. Everyone is packed. The old gang says goodbye to each other and the building they loved.
French Scene #2	Wink Sandra Lagatutta Konigsberg	Sandra stops by to help, I mean really help. She's found them housing, but what is their future?

```
Theme: Not sure yet, something about failure and being an
artist. Perhaps how to deal with failure. Living in the
moment? Not letting the failures of the past haunt the
present.

Notes: Must do more research into the world of the stand-
up comic.
```

BUTT MEETS CHAIR (TIME TO WRITE)

A lot of books and magazines advise you on how to be a writer. They offer daily affirmations, meditations, mantras, and exercises designed make you "feel" like a writer. We've even seen a how-to book on writing that offered a "mind-body" exercise in which you were supposed to skip and spin around and chant, "I'm a writer!" ten times. If this works for you, by all means give it a shot. But one thing we know for sure: You'll feel like a writer when you start writing. Having said that, here is a little advice. First, you need a place to write. This should be a permanent, private area, not something set up and torn down each time. The playwright who has to clear off the dining room table and set up the computer before writing won't accomplish as much as the writer who has a personal office dedicated to the task. And as for writing at your local coffee house…well, it looks good. It sounds romantic. But you're not trying to look good or sound romantic. You're trying to write a play. If you don't have room for an office, try to find a desk in the corner of the bedroom, a basement, someplace where you can close the door and create what the great Russian acting teacher Stanislavski called a circle of your own attention.

Next, you must set a writing schedule. Life is full of interruptions and problems that can limit the amount of time you have to create. If you have a second job, as 99.9% of all playwrights do, you need to set aside a part of each day that's only for writing. Start a daily writing routine and stick to it. Family members, lovers, and friends must understand that this is also your work time—it's your job to write, and just like someone who has to get to the office by nine, your job requires you to be at your desk at a certain time. Accept no excuses; whatever it takes, find the time, a quiet place, and write. If you don't feel like writing your play today, write a character study, take notes on another play or from this book. (The one thing how-to books are good for is to get you in the mood.) No matter how you do it, make sure that every day you spend some time as a playwright, which means *writing*. The best way to make sure you stick to a writing routine is to make it work with your nature. Do you work best at night? Do you like music playing? Do you need to take occasional walks? Figure out what will make it easier for you to get to work.

Once you've done this, take a moment to determine and accept what kind of writer you are. Do you write fast, leaving problems to be solved later, making many drafts, or are you more meticulous, making sure one scene is right before moving on to the next? Some writers find it helpful to write the first draft of a play quickly. Using their detailed scenario, they charge right in, forging the first rough draft in only a few days or weeks. If they can't write a section, they simply put "dialogue to come" or even "scene to come" and continue to rough out a first draft. This binge method of writing has some advantages, for it quickly gets a writer through a rough first draft. It allows the playwright to explore the whole play and make broad discoveries as the writing flows from the heat of the moment. The finished first draft is always lacking, but now more meticulous rewriting can begin. Other writers insist on making each page as perfect as possible before going to the next. This means that they go back and rewrite from page one each time a discovery is made. A change on page 30 means going back and rewriting pages 1 to 29. This is a tedious way to write, but can lead to a finished product in only a single draft (or rather a draft made up of many partial rewrites). This method doesn't work for most writers, but it might work for you (it works for Eric Roth, screenwriter of *Forrest Gump* and *The Insider*), and that's all that matters.

Some writers refuse to talk about their plays while they're still writing them. They worry that if you tell friends and relatives your story over and over, there's a good chance the desire to write the story will wane. (If you have already told your story a dozen times, why spend the time writing it?) Yet other writers find that by telling the story to a friend, they work out problems they never would've solved while sitting alone in front of the computer. Telling a story, like telling a joke, lets you know what's working and what isn't and where things sag or haven't been thought out properly. So experiment and see which works for you. Find both your best writing time and your best method and stick to them. Above all, remember, *a writer writes every day*. This means you.

Some of the best advice for anyone in the arts, including playwrights, is simply to start working, right now, and keep at it until you're done. As Anne Bogart, in *A Director Prepares*, says:

> Do not assume that you have to have some prescribed condition to do your best work. Do not wait. Do not wait for enough time or money to accomplish what you think you have in mind. Work with what you have RIGHT NOW... Do not wait for what you assume is the appropriate stress-free environment in which to generate expression. Do not wait for maturity or insight or wisdom. Do not wait till you are sure that you know what you are doing. Do not wait until you have enough technique. What you do NOW, what you make of your present circumstances, will determine the quality and scope of your future. And at the same time be patient.

5

Getting Into Character

****

No play can rise above the level of
its characterization.

George Pierce Baker

I yam what I yam.

Popeye

****

To paraphrase Juliet, what's in a character? Is it simply a "person" by another name, a faithful depiction of reality, perhaps modeled on someone you know whom you consider fascinating? Is it some fragment of your personality, an animus or shadow pulled from your own psyche? Or is a character in a drama more of a structural element, a function of the story—a "Hero" or "Ally" or "Mentor" or "Antagonist?" Or is a character an incarnation of some aspect of the theme—as with Juliet, a vehicle of ill-fated love whose sacrifice results in a greater good? All excellent questions, which have been asked and answered with various success and emphasis ever since Thespis strode the stage back in ancient Greece. The answer, of course, is that a good character is a mix of all these, and then some. Perhaps the most practical answer for a dramatist is that a character is someone who desperately wants something and then either acts upon that desire or actively represses it. That course of action or inaction is what will define your premise and your play. So let's start with—

"But wait!" you rudely interrupt, "hold on just a darned second! How do I even know who my characters are—why do I even need to know who my characters are—until I know my plot? Won't that tell me who my characters need to be? After all, didn't the great Aristotle himself insist that plot is more important than character, anyway?" Well, yes he did, professor. But, as discussed in Chapter 3 (regarding the plot-vs.-character, chicken-or-egg argument), Aristotle was only half right. And being half right, like having half an idea, will only get you so far. After all, remember that Aristotle also thought the earth was at the center of the solar system and that the sun went around it. So, for now, let's concentrate on how to analyze, create, and write great characters.

For the time being, keep in mind that a playwright has to be a student, and humanity is the teacher. If you attempt to invent a character to suit your plot without knowledge of what makes people tick, you're not likely to create someone who will have any resonance or reality. A character isn't a real person, but, like Frankenstein's monster, he or she is built from bits and pieces of real lives. So the more a playwright knows about the varieties of real human personalities, motivations, and emotions, the more she has to draw on and the richer her characters will be.

Of course, most characters are primarily aspects of the writer herself, and she certainly can't feel anyone else's emotions but her own. No matter how hard you try, when you develop a character, you're simply highlighting a particular side of your own thoughts and feelings. But this is no excuse for not studying others. It's a matter of empathy—you as the writer will grow and evolve more complexity through your better understanding of other people. Empathy, by the way, doesn't mean that to write about a father's death you must wait until your father dies or that you must face death to understand how a terminal patient feels or that you must murder in order to know your killer. But you must have something to base your knowledge on, so that you can imagine yourself in the place of another.

Two primary methods are used to create stage characters. More often than not, young playwrights treat their characters as static beings, whom they construct or deconstruct in an attempt to define and understand. This (de)construction method is a lot like dismembering a carcass on a dissection table, because it assumes that the parts equal the sum, and that individuals can be divided into fractions. These playwrights hope that if they mix the right ingredients in the right order, they'll create a living being and will be able to shout, like Dr. Frankenstein, "It's alive, it's alive!" The second method treats stage characters as moving targets. With this method, the only way to understand a character is to allow her to move, take action, and react to the various stimuli around her. The authors of this book are more in favor of the second method, or at least a combination of the two.

You need to know only just enough about who your characters are before trying to get them to take action. But how much is enough? Opinions differ, but we're against relying too heavily on the elaborate "character biographies" (sometimes called character studies) that are often assigned in writing classes (see below).

Building a play is the act of writing a character study, for it is the process by which the playwright discovers and creates the elements that makes a given character tick. The goal of the playwright facing the blank page, though, is neither to dive into a play with no idea at all of your characters' backgrounds and natures, nor to prepare novel-length histories of each character before turning to your story.

Keeping this in mind, you may nonetheless find some value in the (de)construction method (writing is an art, not a science, and our motto is "Whatever Gets You Through The Play"), so let's look at this approach, then move on to creating characters in action.

IT'S ALIVE! IT'S ALIVE! WAIT, NO IT'S NOT, MY MISTAKE (DISSECTING A CHARACTER)

When (de)constructing a character, the idea is to get inside your character's head and figure out the basic ingredients that make her tick, and make her unique. One way to gain this knowledge is to create a list of the character's traits. This is accomplished by asking a series of questions having to do with the character's physical, sociological, and psychological traits, as well as historical background information. Together, these traits begin to piece together the puzzle of your character.

PHYSICAL

What is the character's appearance?

What is the character's health?

What are the character's medical problems?

What does the character wear?

What is the character's age and sex?

SOCIOLOGY

What are the character's family relationships?

What is the character's nationality?

What is the character's religion?

What are the character's hopes?

What are the character's political views?

What is the character's class or status?

What is the character's occupation?

What is the character's career?

What is the character's financial situation?

PSYCHOLOGY

What are the character's superstitions?

What are the character's talents?

What are the character's ambitions?

What are the character's disappointments?

What are the character's inhibitions?

What are the character's obsessions?

What are the character's tastes?

What are the character's fears?

What are the character's phobias?

What is the character's philosophy?

What are the character's morals?

What is the character's temperament?

What are the character's mannerisms?

What are the character's hobbies?

BACKGROUND INFORMATION

What was the character's childhood like?

What was the character's education?

What was the character's relationship with his/her parents?

What was the character's first kiss like?

What was the character's war record?

What was the character's greatest moment of happiness?

What was the character's greatest moment of sadness?

Some teachers, including the great Lajos Egri, recommend building on this kind of list and writing long biographies of your characters that detail every experience all the way back to their birth. A problem with such biographies is that they can go on forever, each question leading to another, and another, and another…which is all wasted time if it doesn't affect what happens in your play. This kind of "background research" can not only be unhelpful, it can paralyze you. In theory, it sounds convincing to say, "If you know what your character did in preschool, you'll know why he'll do something now." But some theories are useless in practice, and this, in our opinion, is one of them. If your character was raped by a priest as a ten-year-old boy, that certainly might have some bearing, if your play is about his crisis of faith and this event affects his current state of mind. But knowing what he got for Christmas the year before won't. (If you really want to write a character biography, we've included a few samples in Appendix B.) Unlike a character in a novel, the sum total of any stage character's traits is too much for any playwright to completely detail or audience to comprehend within a play's time constraints. Dostoevsky, Proust, James Joyce, and Tolstoy all created incredibly detailed portraits of their characters. Not one of their novels has proved remotely adaptable to the stage.

A playwright doesn't try to reproduce a total living person, but to create a character who gives the impression that he's a living person, within the confines of a particular drama. So you must be selective. The relevance test is simple. If an element of a character's history affects the character's actions during the onstage course of the story—during the present—it is important and should be included. Everything onstage is present tense: It is happening, live, right now. If some past event haunts a character, it becomes present tense because it must affect him now, as revealed through his actions and dialogue. Also, if a part of the character's history—no matter how colorful—doesn't directly affect the here and now, it doesn't belong and must be cut. There's no point having your character soliloquize about the evils of smoking, which killed his father, his uncle, and his sister, if the play itself is about him trying to score with his boss's wife and has nothing to do with either mortality or illness. No matter how well-written, it won't affect the course of the story. So it's useless clutter.

"But wait!" you again heedlessly interject. "What about in *Hamlet*, when he goes on and on about how he knows the visiting actors, and then there's all that chatter with them about how to act, how they should 'speak it trippingly off the tongue,' and so on—what does all that have to do with 'To Be or Not To Be' and whether he should kill Claudius?" We're glad you asked. The point here is that Prince Hamlet is setting an emotional trap for the King, and so the play must be well-acted to produce the desired effect. But more, it shows that Hamlet is a cultivated, literate man for whom the crude action of murder is against his character—which in turn explains why it's so hard for him to just kill Claudius. But more, it helps explain why Hamlet is himself such a good actor, able to create the illusion of madness to confound his uncle and get closer to the truth. But more, it also creates a subtextual message: Played action must substitute for and delay real action until the truth is known, because once real action is taken, it's no longer play—once murder is committed, there's no going back. And there's the rub, so to speak.

So, if you as a writer can include a piece of backstory that might at first seem beside the point, but provides as many layers of application to a character's dilemma and course of action, by all means do so. Otherwise, exercise judgment and ask only those questions whose answers you suspect will show up in your script. The art of building a character, like all arts, is the art of selecting and arranging the important elements of life into a unified whole. Details are essential, but only those details that affect a character during the traffic of the play.

BUT WHAT IS SHE *LIKE*? (CHARACTER TRAITS)

One way to get around the character-biography trap is to concentrate on your character's dominant traits and emotions. Listen to people describe other people. Almost always, they will describe dominant traits and/or emotions:

"Joanne, the shy, fat woman in the office."

"Tybalt, the hothead who's always picking a fight."

"Tabitha, the nutcase who thinks she's being watched all the time."

"Hernan, the bitchy gardener who pretends he can't speak English."

"Wanda, the bleached blonde who can actually do advanced math in her head."

Each character will have traits that make him unique. These traits will make a particular character feel like the inevitable choice for the story. The character might be intellectual, foolish, wily, or obnoxious; subtly or astonishingly, their traits always differentiate one well-drawn character from all the others and define his function in the play. Look at any great play and you'll see that each character is unique, defined by distinct traits that make him perfectly suited for his particular story. Also, all good characters have a range of emotions, but a single emotion usually defines each character. A character's dominant emotion could be cheeriness, lust, anger, hate—take your pick. About the only dominant emotion that doesn't work well is self-pity. Characters—like real people—who feel sorry for themselves generally are too weak to take action, and therefore quickly become boring. An exception might be a comedic character, for instance, a long-suffering Jewish mother or jilted girlfriend whose function is to exasperate the protagonist. A main character might indulge in self-pity for a while, but must take action to snap out of it.

This simplified method of discovering character traits works only as a starting point. A deeper understanding is a must if your characters are to be anything more than simple stereotypes.

HEAR THE ONE ABOUT THE BLONDE, THE PRIEST AND THE RABBI? (STEREOTYPES)

F. Scott Fitzgerald observed, "Begin with an individual and you find that you have created a type; begin with a type, and you find that you have created—nothing." A stereotype is a character we know at sight, and who has little more to offer than what we've come to expect from past appearances in other plays. Stereotypes are the result of lazy writing, and often reflect a common prejudice or attitude towards a certain category of person. These "characters" are clichés based on stock conventions: the dumb blonde, the shady lawyer, the tall, dark, mysterious stranger, the hooker with the heart of gold, the spaghetti-eating mobster. While you can have some fun with these clichés, as Mel Brooks does in *The Producers*, in general, they're to be avoided. Even if you want to have a ditsy secretary in your play, you must ask yourself: How can I make her distinctive? How can I make her surprising? Maybe even, how can I turn this convention on its head? What makes this ditsy secretary different from the hundreds we've all seen before? You must acknowledge the difference between a character you've stolen and used without alteration and one you've reimagined to suit the specific needs of your play. Your existing model (i.e., stereotype) may satisfy the functions you are after in your play, but that doesn't mean you should copy her exactly. This is conceptual plagiarism, not borrowing. Always make it new, and make it yours.

YOU ARE WHAT YOU DO (CHARACTER IN ACTION)

HE SEEMED LIKE SUCH A NICE YOUNG MAN

Another reason not to rely exclusively on a detailed character-biography when building your character is that, as Robert McKee points out in his fine book, *Story*, a character is what he does, not how he appears. A character's true core may differ from or even contradict his observable characteristics. When pressed to his utmost extremity, forced to choose between two irreconcilably paths of a dilemma, his *true character* will emerge and may negate everything we see or think we know about him. Charles Dickens' character, Scrooge, is a loathsome, misanthropic miser—until, forced to confront the results of his life's actions, he reveals an unexpected core of generosity. King Claudius appears to be a model ruler—until Hamlet forces his uncle's true, perfidious nature to emerge. Nothing in Macbeth's character biography (except, perhaps, his choice of bride) predicts the murderous path he takes when faced with the dilemma presented by the witches' prophecy. Ted Bundy was a quiet, polite, well-educated young man who turned out to be a serial killer. So, creating a character with a true core hidden under a veneer of characteristics that may belie that truth—and then revealing that truth when your character is faced with his most life-changing decision—is one of a playwright's most valuable techniques, because it allows for the possibility of dramatic change, and dramatic surprise.

Characters will also differ according to the story form they're in. Novels, short stories, cartoons, sitcoms, operas—each form of storytelling has distinct parameters and approaches as to how their characters are created and revealed. The novelist can explore a character's background and inner thoughts through silent monologue and description. Opera reveals characters through their voices—tenor as hero, basso as villain—and all are allowed long expository arias. A play's characters must reveal themselves through action and dialogue, the outward manifestations of inner thoughts and desires. In short, plays are about people who *do* things. The word "drama" comes from the Greek words *dran*, to do, and *dromenon*, which means "something to be done, made or acted upon." Notice that they're called "actors" or "players," implying action. It's possible to write a great book, short story, poem, or movie that doesn't have a single person in it, but it's impossible to write a play without characters who take action.

Not all characters are good material for the stage. The Belgian poet Maurice Maeterlinck said, "An old man, seated in his armchair, waiting patiently, with his lamp beside him—submitting with bent head to the presence of his soul and his destiny—motionless as he is, yet lives in a reality—a deeper, more human, and more universal life—than the lover who strangles his mistress, the captain who conquers in battle, or the husband who avenges his honor." Yes, a person who takes no action can be just as deep as a character who sets out against a sea of troubles, but who'd want to watch him? Without action, there is no play; a bit of performance art from the early seventies, maybe, but no play. And so the lover who strangles his mistress or the husband who avenges his honor is a far better stage character than the old man sitting near the lamp. The great playwright (and member of the Hollywood Ten) John Howard Lawson (*Roger Bloomer*, *Loud Speaker*) said, "Drama cannot deal with people whose wills are atrophied, who are unable to make decisions which have even temporary meaning, who adopt no conscious attitude toward events, who make no effort to control their environment."

Action can be motivated by a desire, a want, a goal—anything that pushes characters to express themselves and take action to change their situation. This is what plays are about: change causing more change, in a word, *action*. As David Ball says in his wonderful little book *Backwards & Forwards: A Technical Manual for Reading Plays* (a must-read for all playwrights), "Action occurs when something happens that makes or permits something else to happen." Stage characters must do more than simply exist or contemplate—at least if they're major characters who should push the story forward. Even in Chekhov's plays, a refusal to take necessary action shouldn't be considered "inaction." It's a purposeful, if frustrating, response to the events taking place—the characters' inaction is the point of the drama. Actions are the characters' responses to the existing circumstances of the story, which, in turn, determine the future course of the story. Therefore, the character who does the most—or impedes action the most successfully—sets that course. This means that most real people would make lousy stage characters, because most real people seldom take action: We hardly vote, let alone set out against a sea of troubles to change our existence.

But action alone isn't enough: It must have a goal, and it must encounter opposition. As noted before, it must be dramatic action. Jeffrey Hatcher, in his excellent book, *The Art & Craft of Playwriting*, says, "It's easy to confuse effective dramatic action with activities. Activities are the dramatic equivalent of busywork. They may *look* like actions (a fistfight) and they *sound* like actions (a shouting match), but if they don't cause a reaction, then they're not actions." There must be conflict, true, but it must be conflict that affects the future course of the story—and important stakes must hang on its outcome. What is the point of watching two people fight if nothing changes as a result? The characters are active, but there are no stakes unless someone loses and decides to get revenge, or someone wins but ends up alienating the woman he longs for, or even comes to loathe himself, even in success (let's say, like Othello, he murders up his wife), in which case he's in conflict with himself. Hamlet is nothing if not in conflict with himself, half despising every action or hesitation in which he engages. Dramatic action is inner conflict's outward expression. Dramatic action can be overcoming one's own fears, or resisting other characters' goals or actions. Dramatic action can express defiance, taking a brave stance against authority or expressing an unpopular opinion, as in *An Enemy of the People*. It can be an armed encounter or a quiet kiss, as long as it conveys intention and as long as there is something at stake and consequences relevant to the character.

Dramatic action, then, occurs when a character decides to do something either because of or in spite of the consequences. This is one of the main problems with trying to base your characters on "real people." While everyone takes dramatic action now and then, most of us go about trying to avoid conflict. Conflict means pain, emotional or physical. It means effort and commitment. Most of us would rather just absorb the slings and arrows and turn on the TV. Until we're in enough distress that no alternative is possible, we don't want to contemplate change. Even when we want or feel deeply about something, we rarely do anything about it—because, in real life, it can mean real risk and real consequences. But this avoidance of conflict is deadly on stage, because until our characters do or say something that changes their circumstances, the audience simply won't care about them. Unlike real people—or rather, perhaps as Egri has it, *only* like real people who have reached an inescapable turning point in their lives—dramatic characters must force the issue, engage in conflict, take chances, and risk consequences. This is what we go to the theater to watch them do. They're metaphors. They do what we only dream, and succeed or suffer in our place. This is where the audience achieves catharsis, or spiritual cleansing, the Aristotelian goal of all drama. Characters are our surrogates, and sometimes our scapegoats, who are put out for sacrifice to carry away our sins, so we don't have to. Therefore, characters shouldn't necessarily reflect real people, but rather should feel real within the context of the theme, the desires, and the conflicts you've created for them. All characters are abstractions from reality, and exist within the play solely to serve its dramatic goals.

In his book, Jeffrey Hatcher offers a clean assessment as to why most characters fail. To summarize his argument: They haven't been given strong enough goals, difficult enough obstacles, or been provided with sufficient talents or opportunities to make action possible. Sounds simple enough, right? If only that were true. In fact, satisfying these three conditions requires a great deal of work.

ACTIONS SPEAK LOUDER...

In order for a character to take dramatic action, she must be in a situation in which more than one option is available to her, so she can make a choice. As noted above, the type of choice a character makes defines that character. The more important and difficult the choices, the higher the stakes, and the more important and interesting the character. A character facing—and acting upon—profound social, moral, or ethical choices can't help but be fascinating, even if those profound choices are made in a very subtle way. That is where Hamlet, for all his indecisiveness, remains the character all leading males aspire to play. The decisions he struggles with, and the stakes dependent upon them, are so complex and often so subtle that his character is taken through the entire gamut of human emotion. The key to all this is that *they are all difficult decisions*: to believe that his father's ghost actually exists; to betray a mother he loves by killing her new husband; to commit regicide; to turn away from the woman he loves because he can't divide his attention, even if his action drives her to madness and suicide, and so on. You want your characters to be torn—between love and duty, ambition and altruism, adventure and responsibility.

But let's aim a little lower. Let's look, for instance, at Bob, a character we've just made up. A forty-something high school teacher, he's middle-class and decent. He has a wife, a mortgage, a growing midsection, and is stuck in a rut. When he was younger, he wanted to play the saxophone, but reality and unpaid student loans eliminated that dream. Today, even though the loans are long paid off, Bob's routine is set and he lives with it. Bob is no Hamlet; he's not a tortured soul, just an accepting one. We can also say that Bob isn't a worthy stage character. Why? Because he just exists, he doesn't take action. But what if one day a beautiful, mature-beyond-her-years sophomore falls for Bob. She thinks his spare tire is adorable, and lets him know it. He calls her in and tries to reason with her, but she won't let it go. Worried to death, he calls in sick to avoid seeing her. Jilted, she tells the principal that Bob came on to her. To make things worse, the janitor saw the girl in Bob's office. But there is no proof; so, after a hushed-up cash "settlement," Bob's principal reads him the riot act and reassigns him to a new school (with a much longer commute). At the new school, rumors abound and the other teachers shun him. So, what does Bob do? He goes to his classroom, suppresses his anger, and teaches his class, glad that at least he didn't lose his job—or worse.

How about now? Is Bob a worthy stage character? The answer: "It depends." True, he takes action, he resists the girl's advances and keeps his job, but he makes no decision to take action that will change his circumstances. This kind of character only works if his refusal to take action is limited and later reversed (as with Nora in *A Doll's House*). Or, the refusal to take action over the course of the entire story might reflect the theme of the play, as with the characters in Chekhov's *The Cherry Orchard*, or the film *The Remains of the Day*, in which the butler's tragic inability to seize the opportunity for love condemns him to a life of loneliness.

Another possibility is that Bob, after being humiliated, abruptly quits. He tells the principal, the janitor, and his fellow teachers where to shove it, cleans out his pre-fab desk, and walks. What's more, when his wife doesn't believe his side of the story and leaves him, Bob decides to dig up dirt on the flirtatious girl and her family. He learns that she's pulled this stunt before: A biology teacher in the next school district lost his job and family because of her. Bob becomes obsessed by the girl's manipulativeness, as well as society's willingness to jump to conclusions and condemnation. He decides that the only thing he can do is publicly humiliate her—but not before he makes sure that she feels as threatened as he once did. As the curtain falls at the end of Act One, Bob invites her over for a "quiet dinner." How about now, is Bob a worthy stage character? Yes, because he's taken action— dramatic action that is bound to have powerful consequences. Notice that, in both stories, what Bob does (his action) defines his character far more than the fact that he's forty, a teacher with a mortgage and a potbelly, who once wanted to play the saxophone (his biograph). His core character trumps his characteristics. Yet, that seemingly inconsequential sax playing indicates he's a man with a touch of jazz in his soul. It lets us know he's capable of stepping outside of his box.

Effective dramatic action is character-initiated action that goes beyond a simple reaction to others or the environment. This action must cause circumstances to change or force other characters to take action. While characters may start out by reacting to what's going on around them, at some point they must turn the tables and act, confront their dilemmas, and either reap the rewards of their actions or suffer the negative consequences.

Why Do You Do That Thing You Do?

Characters who set out against a sea of troubles and suffer the consequences are certainly more interesting than those who play it safe, but these characters' big actions really aren't credible unless personal and understandable motivations stand behind them. Emerson said, "Cause and effect, means and end, seed and fruit, can't be severed; for the effect already blooms in the cause, the end pre-exists in the means, the fruit in the seed." Actions must grow out of the natures of your characters. They must not only seem possible and justifiable, but inevitable. You must look not only to the circumstances confronting your characters but to their own individual reasons for taking actions in the ways that they do. Characters' personalities, desires, and needs are the sources of motivations, that grow into dramatic actions when the situations are right.

Thinking up motivations is the easy part: revenge, injustice, ambition, haunting memories, sick relatives, whatever. You have to go behind all that to know why one character will act upon his motivation while another will not—why does one of two sisters avoid all contact with men, while the other is promiscuous? Why is one Stella and the other Blanche Dubois? If the writer doesn't know, her characters' actions won't appear natural or justified. A character who takes action for no compelling reason is just as pointless as a character with strong motivation who does nothing. (Unless you are intentionally drawing a character with those limitations, in which case you'll have either a hopeless scatterbrain or a resolutely passive-aggressive pain in the neck.) More often, characters do things without underlying reasons because the writer hasn't bothered to get to know them and set up these reasons.

In order to understand a character's motivation, the playwright must first understand the character's background information, the general, physical, sociological, and psychological traits listed earlier in this chapter (but again, *only* those traits that justify or explain the character's action). Next, the character must need or want something, so it follows that something must be missing from that character's life—something either taken away (a parent, job, security, honor) or not yet attained (love, happiness, equality), but greatly desired in either case. *The greater the missing element, the greater the need, the greater the motivation, the greater the resulting action.*

Now, there must be a catalyst that causes a particular motivation to come to the surface during the course of the play. This catalyst is an event that lifts all the roadblocks to taking action and sets the character free to act—or even forces him to act—on his motivation. The catalyst, the background information, the personality traits or needs, by themselves, are not motivation. Only when they combine do we create a fully motivated character.

Before we go any farther, let's deal with a common mistake playwrights often make when it comes to the catalyst (the event that causes a character to take action). It's important that you don't make your character's catalyst drunkenness, drug addiction, or any other twelve-step problem. Put another way, you shouldn't mistake the symptom for the cause. Say a man gets drunk and tells his boss off. If you think the catalyst is the alcohol, and therefore focus the play around that problem, you are missing the genuine catalyst, which is the unhappiness that has turned this character into a drunk and made him choose this particular night to tell his boss off. We're not saying that you can't have a character get drunk (or we'd have to say that Tennessee Williams had no business writing plays). But the reason behind a character's drinking is the true catalyst, not the act of drinking.

DO THE RIGHT THING

Looked at from his or her point of view, a character's motivation is always an attempt to turn a negative into a positive. This is known as a "positive motivation." Characters don't do things because they're "evil," insensitive, or emotionally unbalanced. (These are not motivations but conditions.) A character's motivation is always a need or desire to improve his situation, as he sees it (i.e., what will improve his situation is subjective and limited to his narrow take on things). The writer must look at motivation from the character's point of view, not her own—or rather she must make it her own while writing that character. This is especially important when writing an antagonist or other unsympathetic characters. You don't need to sympathize, but you must empathize—feel what they feel. From the perspective of empathy, a character can commit an "evil" act based on a strong "positive" motive. Say that a playwright writes the role of a father who abandons his child on the steps of a local church. If the playwright concludes that the father does so because the father is "hateful" and "uncaring," this shallow interpretation of the father's motivation will not lead to a well-written character. Instead, the playwright must find the father's positive motivation for abandoning the child. If you find this hard to do, you are probably still looking at the situation from your own point of view, not the father's. He justifies his actions in a number of ways: It's best for the child, because he can't provide for it or he sees himself as too emotionally unbalanced to care for it. He knows that if he sticks around, he'll do more harm than good—perhaps he's a pedophile, terrified of his own impulses. Whatever the case, it persuades him that abandonment is best for the child—a *positive* motivation.

No matter how objectively good or evil a character's actions may appear to others, he must think that what he's doing is the best option, the most positive action he can take, given the situation. A perfect example is found in *Death of a Salesman*. Willy Loman constantly acts on positive motivations, even when they're based on sheer delusion. He wants to be a good father and husband (positive motivations), but he's tormented and thwarted by memories of past infidelities—one of which traumatized his son—and by the shadow of his brother Ben, whose success is both a reproach and an irresistible mirage of brighter possibilities. Willy tries to get reassigned to a better office (again, a positive action), but is fired. When his neighbor offers help, Willy proudly refuses (a positive response, because accepting help would be admitting defeat and the loss of his American dream). In the end, he commits suicide for the insurance money, which he believes will help his sons attain the American dream (again, a positive). His actions might appear to others to be negative—certainly their effects are negative—but Willy Loman sees his actions as positives—and so must you if you're writing a similarly misguided character.

Another classic example comes from *Medea*. The title character of Euripides' tragedy murders her children because her husband, Jason, has abandoned her for a younger woman. It's perhaps the most horrible thing a person can do, but from Medea's point of view, she has several "positive" reasons for murdering her children: A quick death is better than letting her children starve to death in exile, so it's actually a loving act; their deaths will punish her husband, who deserves it; and she's better off without her children there as constant reminders of how their father treated her. What's more, her action is in character, because the one relevant part of her backstory that the Greek audience surely knew was that she'd previously killed and dismembered her own brother in order to help Jason escape with the Golden Fleece. So she had it in her to take this kind of action. Of course, such action usually ends badly. A character may believe that his destructive means will justify his hoped-for end, but he soon discovers that they create an ending more in keeping with his chosen means: He is himself destroyed. More recently (by 2,500 years or so), we find this kind of moral at work in plays such as *Deathtrap* and *Amadeus*.

To sum up, all well-written characters, at any given moment—even when they know they're doing something wrong—think their actions, given their situations, are justified or the only options open to them. They may be misguided, they may end up bringing destruction down upon themselves, but their impulses comes from a desire to turn what they perceive as a negative into what they perceive as a positive.

Paging Dr. Freud! (The Limits of Self-Knowledge)

Aristotle defines a character flaw as an "error," a "defect in judgment," or a "shortcoming in conduct," especially in the greatest (i.e., most tragic) characters. Similarly, dramas are not about perfect people with perfect awareness of themselves or others, or their situations. Like trying to see their own faces without a mirror, their range of self-awareness is limited and prejudiced by fears, hopes, and desires. They're too immersed in their own problems to be objective. This is what gives them room to grow and develop. For example, Hamlet is capable of killing, but he doesn't know this about himself at first; Blanche Dubois is deluded about what life has left to offer her, but she believes she's thinking clearly. In *Playwrights on Playwriting*, Arthur Miller pointed out that if Oedipus had had perfect self-awareness, he would have seen that "he was not really to blame for having cohabited with his mother, since neither he nor anyone else knew she was his mother. He would have decided to divorce her, provide for their children, firmly resolve to investigate the family background of his next wife, and thus deprive us of a very fine play." In each case, the character's mistakes are caused by a lack of self-knowledge, willful or accidental, the overcoming of which is at the heart of the story.

Limited self-knowledge may also mean that a character's personal view of himself is out of sync with others' view of him (as well as the playwright's view). This can be a productive source of conflict in a play. Everyone has a self-image. We think we're smart, dumb, handsome, homely, but often the way we see ourselves is very different from how others would describe us. Someone might see himself as a great lover, while his wife—contemplating an affair—has a very different opinion. One might see herself as someone who fears disapproval, is full of self-doubt, and rarely gets support, while others might view her as an irritating, hypercritical perfectionist. Either consciously or unconsciously, people want to persuade others that their own, particular self-image is correct. This is why we dress the way we do and buy cars that "express our personality." We're constantly saying to the world, "This is who I am, and you'd do me a big favor if you'd agree." When we instantly take a liking to someone, it's because they confirm our positive self-image. When we dislike them, it's often because they confirm our deepest doubts about ourselves, our negative self-image, and we either draw away from that person or spend a great deal of time trying to convince them that they're wrong about us. No character's true self is entirely obvious to him or her. We are all full of flaws and personal blindness, and these can make for wonderful characters—like Blanche Dubois, Willy Loman, King Lear, Macbeth, Orgon, etc. Shakespeare had great fun with the limits of self-knowledge (and its attendant dangers) in *A Midsummer Night's Dream*, in which his characters are drawn into a farcical web of misperceptions about themselves and each other, as did Oscar Wilde in *The Importance of Being Earnest*.

The key to creating this component of a character is to find his or her most appropriate flaw or blindness. For the protagonist, this flaw is an exception to or contradiction of the character's more dominant traits. Oedipus is a brilliant and caring leader; his flaw is a proud unwillingness to hear what Teiresias, the blind seer, is trying to tell him. Willy Loman is a caring, hardworking man. His flaw is a blindness to the emptiness of his work and the harm his "harmless" flings have caused. Orgon is blinded by a foolhardy confidence in his own judgment, leading to his conviction that the pious hypocrite, Tartuffe, is the answer to his prayers. With the antagonist, the flaw may be the most extreme example of his dominant traits and the source of his undoing: For instance, he may suffer from overwhelming pride that blinds him to the evil of his plan, or he may be insanely jealous, which compromises his judgment (as with Iago and Othello).

People—and characters—have limits: limited endurance, limited intelligence, limited morality. Although characters usually don't yet know their limitations (or secretly do, but are afraid to confront them), the playwright must know them, must know the characters better than they know themselves, in order to orchestrate the conflict and force them to confront their flaws.

If a flaw is great enough to destroy all hope of success, it is called a "tragic flaw." If it's a comical and/or harmless shortcoming, then it's called a "comic flaw." A character's journey is one of self-revelation, until he can finally know his own true nature—his core character—and expose what has been motivating, crippling, or nurturing him. Once this is known, the character is made whole, or, in the case of a tragedy or of an antagonist, the revelation may bring only defeat. In either case, wisdom is gained, catharsis is experienced, and the story is over.

JUST GHOST TO SHOW (UNFINISHED BUSINESS)

A common way to create a character flaw is to identify (and then bring to bear on the story) what "haunts" your character. This is known as the character's "*ghost*"—something from his or her past (perhaps guilt or unfinished business) that is so compelling that it cripples the character until it is put to rest. In *Hamlet*, of course, there is an actual ghost—the ghost of Hamlet's father—and the need to avenge his murder is what causes the action of the play. In modern dramas (including comedies), the ghost may be a failed career (*Death of a Salesman*, *Glengarry Glen Ross*), an unhappy marriage (*A Doll's House*), a lost opportunity for love (*Shakespeare's R&J*), trying to live up to a dead father's reputation (*A Few Good Men*), or any other issue from the past that will be resolved over the course of the story. Sometimes the ghost is revealed only through dialogue; sometimes there is a prologue in which we hear about it (as in *Richard III*). Usually the ghost influences or motivates your protagonist, but strong antagonists may also have ghosts, such as Iago's lost promotion or the prejudice that Shylock has suffered all his life or Captain Ahab's having lost his leg to Moby Dick or the Phantom of the Opera's loss of his music, physical appearance and lover. (Notice that loss is a common thread; what is a ghost but a lost life?) Such powerful spectres make an antagonist more complex, even sympathetic, to an audience—and an audience being able to see his side of the story is always a good thing. Whatever the character's ghost may be, it must be thematically related to the story's central conflict or it will not feel integral or necessary. If the central conflict is about your protagonist's failure as a salesman, his ghost had better not be that he lost a leg to a whale. Characters without a flaw and/or a ghost are unnaturally perfect and, therefore, as interesting as a Barbie Doll.

Do I Dare to Eat a Peach? (Internal Conflict)

Character flaws and unresolved issues often lead to an inner struggle with what may be your character's strongest opponent: himself. Internal conflicts arise from a moral struggle, an inner debate, anything that creates that most formidable obstacle: self-doubt. Your story will be strongest when your character faces two positive, compelling, but irreconcilable desires of nearly equal strength. He longs for both, but both can't be satisfied. For example, in *Hamlet*, the Prince of Denmark is driven to avenge his father, but he also wants to redeem his mother. In this case, the two desires are actually the same: to be a good son. But being a good son to one parent means creating grief for the other. Internal conflicts must be specific to your character, coming naturally from who he is and what he lacks most to be emotionally complete. If not, the conflict in his desires will not matter enough for him to take action. Faced with two incompatible and yet compelling desires, Hamlet is genuinely torn, on the horns of a dilemma, and therefore driven to seek a remedy.

Sometimes a character's flaw or ghost creates a negative desire, which comes into conflict with his specific need. In Aaron Sorkin's *A Few Good Men* (the play and the screenplay), the protagonist, Daniel Kaffee, is a talented but untested lawyer. He needs to become his own man: However, burdened by his dead father's daunting legacy, he desires to slide by and not face the challenge. This causes internal conflict: Will he rise to the occasion and risk it all for justice, or do only just enough not to embarrass himself? At one point he resorts to getting drunk—a negative action that, from his point of view, is actually a positive. He can't win, and he doesn't want to struggle with the sober truth, so why not get hammered and give up? It's a solution; not a good one, but one in keeping with his "ghost."

The antagonist faces a similar conflict: Col. Nathan Jessep wants total control in order to serve and protect his country; but what he needs is to realize that by breaking laws and ignoring human rights, he's actually betraying his country.

YOU CAN'T ALWAYS GET WHAT YOU WANT (NEED VS. DESIRE)

This last example brings us to the important distinction between need and desire. A main source of internal conflict (and growth) can come from the fact that what the protagonist consciously *desires* may be quite different from what he actually *needs*. Nora in *A Doll's House* wants to prove that she's a good wife. What she needs, however, is to leave her marriage altogether. King Lear wants all his daughters to flatter him. What he needs is to accept true love without adornment. Oedipus wants to save Thebes from the plague. What he needs is to realize that he himself is the cause of the plague. In *Amadeus*, Salieri wants to barter faithfulness to God in return for divine inspiration. What he needs is to recognize that God, who bestows His gifts according to His own mysterious plans, will not be bargained with.

A character's awakening to the truth—his epiphany—will often come after he has pursued the mirage of his desire into a desert of disillusionment. Only then can he see how foolish he's been, and what he really needs. Once his illusions have been stripped away, he's free to find true happiness in a comedy or true pity and terror in a tragedy.

The conflict of need and desire is one of your essential tools for constructing a character with psychological depth, but your use of this tool must always depend on the story you're telling. Sometimes need and desire coincide, as in *Inherit the Wind*, where Clarence Darrow's desire to bring an enlightened point of view into the courtroom coincides with his need to win the case. In contrast, in *Glengarry Glen Ross*, the salesmen want to make a sale at any cost. What they need is a way out of the grinding situation that has them at each others' throats.

NO STEPPING IN THE SAME RIVER TWICE

The Greek philosopher Herakleitos said that you can't step into the same river twice: Just as water that flows past the same point is always new water, the world is always changing, even when it seems the same. Human beings are no exception. We change from moment to moment, some more apparently than others, but we all change. Lovers marry and divorce; children grow up, age, and die. The change or growth in a character over the course of a play is called a "character arc." This growth dramatizes the writer's theme: from arrogance to humility, from poverty to wealth, whatever. Strong characters grow, learn, and "become," and in the process express some truth about human experience. Lajos Egri writes, "There is only one realm in which characters defy natural laws and remain the same—the realm of bad writing." (This is one reason why we're against an over-reliance on character-biographies, as they can create the sense that a character is a fixed being, incapable of change.)

People seldom change their thoughts or ways without being forced to, as when circumstances make them question themselves and their world. Situations that can force deep personal change are war, marriage, divorce, getting old, losing a loved one—in short, life. Life is a constant process of doing before dying. When you build a character, you must create not only who the character "is" at the start, but who the character will "become" after emerging from the crucible of conflict that is your story. And so great plays have characters like Nora in *A Doll's House* who starts as an incomplete girl who is controlled by the men in her life and ends as a women who is capable of taking the first steps toward independence.

Having said this, we must acknowledge that some characters resist change: They're the immovable rocks around which the irresistible forces of change must flow, altered by their presence. These characters are catalysts: They do not change, but their steadfast presence and the unbending morality they stand for changes or affects the world around them. Characters who do not change (well-written characters, anyway) must seem to be inevitable. They're somehow both less and more than humans, which is why they're often referred to as "traveling angels." Angels do not change. (Unless one counts that most human and approachable of angels, Lucifer.) They do not die. They appear and the world around them changes because they were there. They—and those human characters who share their qualities—live by an unshakable covenant, a set of beliefs or a code of honor that allows them to persist as rocks of stability in the face of a morally challenged and shifting universe. Sometimes these changeless characters have secondary roles, such as allies or mentors or threshold guardians (the blind Teiresias, for example) who cause the protagonist to grow. But, sometimes, the protagonist himself is an "angel" who changes little over the course of the play, as with Clarence Darrow in *Inherit the Wind*. Such characters tend to be icons more than people—they may go through hell, be beaten, have to watch their loved ones slaughtered, but, in the end, they remain steadfast, with their moral code intact, and the world is now changed thanks to their efforts. Such characters have a kind of contract with the audience: We know who they are, what they are, and what they will and will not do. And be warned, if you, as a writer, break this contract, you will alienate your audience. Again, it's a matter of appropriate character function: To change, or to be changed.

AW, HE LOOKS JUST LIKE YOU!
(CHARACTERS AS ASPECTS OF THE WRITER)

A well-written character is constructed from all of the above elements, but perhaps the character's most important quality is believability. Believability comes from the playwright's own make-up. You as the writer must invest a part of yourself in all your characters in order to make them real. Their lives come from yours, so you must recognize them as parts of yourself and find their voices, not only from listening to others, but from within yourself. No matter how different you think a character is from you, you wouldn't have thought of that character at all if something inside you hadn't resonated with him or her. Inside every writer are a hundred different fantasies or tendencies—memories or fantasies of power, sexual prowess, avenged humiliations, and so on—not all of which you'd boast about publicly, but all of which you can tap to create believable characters.

The great acting teacher Konstantin Stanislavski used an exercise to stimulate the imagination called "The Magic If." It involved one question: "*What would I do if I were this character under these circumstances?*" A playwright uses the "magic if" to find similarities between himself and his characters and to create honest, intimate emotions and thoughts. This is what we mean by writing from yourself. Your characters shouldn't just be you on your best behavior, but also the secret parts of you, the rich, diverse cast of inner characters who make up your complete identity. You must draw on those aspects of yourself that will bring the rough surface of reality to your characters, even if these aspects appall you—in fact, draw on them especially if that's the case, because those are aspects of your personality that contain the most emotional power. The shy writer must find his inner bold lover in order to write a Romeo. The peaceable writer must find the bully within herself in order to create a wife-beater. The arrogant writer must recall his humble childhood to write about the first day of grade school. No good character ever came from a writer who shut his inner life off from his character's creation.

As noted above, creating a character requires empathy (even with an antagonist). Sympathy is compassion, commiseration, even understanding, but empathy is more. It's walking in your characters' shoes. Empathy is substituting the emotions of another for your own, putting yourself in the place of another. It's as close as we can come to a shared experience.

Empathy happens when a playwright abandons external judgment in order to see things without prejudice. It allows a man to write a complex and believable woman, a woman to write a bold yet tormented soldier, a black writer to get inside the heart of a klansman, and a young writer to have some insight into the heartaches of a bitter octagenarian whose friends are dying or gone. It's popular today to say, "Only my kind can understand my feelings or background," but playwrights need to transcend these barriers and find the common ground between races, genders, and ages. Producer/director Arthur Hopkins summed it up nicely by saying, "Heartaches are heartaches in the Avenue or the Bowery, and love and trouble and weakness and strength are pretty much common to all kinds of people." Research gives you the details you need to create external accuracy; empathy is what brings those details to life.

Writers often say that after hours of struggling to find the right voice for their characters, the characters seem to begin speaking all by themselves, creating their own dialogue, as if the writer were merely channeling or taking dictation—as if someone else has taken control of the keyboard. This is the magic moment when the characters come alive. Of course, it's still the writer who creates that life, but this is the moment of true connection with one of those inner voices.

This magic moment, however, carries its own dangers. You must realize that in spite of your strong connection, you are not the character, and vice versa. Each character needs to acquire an identity distinct from yours, just as children must become their own people. If a playwright identifies too strongly with a character, she starts to become a diarist. Diary entries may be valuable as a record of the day, as fodder for characters and stories, but they must be transformed to suit a drama or they will bore the audience. Write what you know and who you are, but don't slavishly depend on it. No one cares about your life and problems unless they're really, really interesting. Use your experience, but use it to create a story a wide audience would care to see.

A corollary of this problem is that time and again, young playwrights create secondary characters who are more interesting than their protagonists. This is because the playwrights too closely identify with their protagonists. The protagonist becomes a surrogate for the writer, and since, from the writer's perspective, he or she is normal, the protagonist becomes blandly normal as well. It's easier to develop secondary characters who are less like ourselves because we can more easily see them from an outside perspective. You must try to achieve an outside perspective on your protagonists, so you can see them more clearly. If you find that one of your secondary characters is not only more interesting but also better equipped to carry the theme of your story, you might consider making this other character your protagonist.

WHAT'S IN A NAME?

As noted in Chapter 4, characters' names can shed light on their nature and function. They can reflect attitude, class, and heritage. A name gives a first impression that influences the reader's attitude about a character. "Adolph" will immediately conjure up Adolph Hitler; "Jackie," for those of a certain age, will bring up associations with Jacqueline Kennedy Onassis. And there are other ways names give us information. "Willy Loman" tells us a lot. He adopts a weakened form of a strong name, William, and he's the "low man" on the totem pole. "Blanche Dubois" suggests pallor and pretension. "Mercutio" is perfect for a mercurial character; "Benvolio" literally means "well-intentioned." "John Proctor" suggests upright rectitude. Irony or contrast also work well in naming your characters; for instance, a sadistic killer might be named "Smiley." Look to pop-song titles, people in the news, anything that summons up an appropriate association. Phone books, graveyards, and baby-name books are all good sources of inspiration.

One caution: do not ever—EVER—give two characters names that are so similar that the reader gets them confused with each other, like Garry and Barry, or Jim and Tim, or even Harriet and Hazel. (Unless you're after a comic "Tweedle Dum, Tweedle Dee" effect.) Although you may have valid artistic reasons for using such combinations as Harry & Hazel, Sam & Sid, or Jerry & Berry, they can cause confusion. Most readers and directors don't take the time to go back and reread; once lost, they stay lost and the script is tossed on the rejection pile. Whenever Shakespeare puts an Edward and an Edmund in the same play, eyes glaze over in classrooms across the nation. So try to create some variety.

WHAT ART THOU, THAT USURP'ST THIS TIME OF NIGHT? (CHARACTER FUNCTIONS)

It's not enough to come up with a bunch of characters to populate your story. You must decide *why* each of them is in your play. Who are they? What are they? How do they serve and advance your premise? Are they the right characters to generate essential actions and conflicts? Why are they the perfect, indeed, the only imaginable, characters to enact this particular drama? *A character without an essential function does not belong in your play.* Each must serve a unique and necessary purpose and add a unique and necessary quality, without which the story would not only be less effective, but would collapse. Plays are, above all, about urgent necessity. Nowhere is this truer than in your dramatis personae.

THAT IS SO (ARCHE)TYPICAL!

Building on the work of Carl Jung and Joseph Campbell, whose *Hero with a Thousand Faces* revolutionized the study of mythology, Chris Vogler has written an equally influential book, *The Writer's Journey*, which analyzes the mythic archetypes inherent in many of the world's great stories. Chief among these archetypes who inhabit our dreams, myths, and stories is the central character, the conveyor of the theme, the pursuer of the quest, and perhaps the hardest of all characters to write, because he's the closest to our image of ourselves: The Hero.

A FIGHTER BY HIS TRADE (THE PROTAGONIST)

The Hero in dramatic terms is the protagonist, the figure around whom the play is written and whose story the audience is principally following. The word "protagonist" comes from ancient Greek and referred to the first actor to engage in dialogue or action (literally, the "first" or "forward combatant," which shows how central conflict is to his identity). It eventually came to mean the principle player, who might appear somewhat later in the story but still carried its weight. Some plays now start with the antagonist instead (see below) to set up the stakes and the problem the protagonist must face. Some plays keep the audience waiting on purpose, to create suspense: When will we finally meet the guy everyone's been talking about? In such cases, even though absent physically, the protagonist may be present in the form of the anticipation his impending appearance inspires in others.

The majority of plays have a single protagonist. In movies, there is a sub-genre, known as "buddy movies," in which two protagonists work in tandem. Buddy protagonists are less common on the stage (largely because the success of buddy movies tends to depend on raucous, cinematic physicality), although there are stage examples such as *The Maids*, *Waiting for Godot*, and *Rosencrantz and Guildenstern Are Dead*. (Interestingly, none of these are Realist plays. These plays deal less with the jocularity of the buddy movie and more with using a joint protagonist to explore the idea of a divided mind, a single personality split between two characters.)

More common on the stage are "ensemble plays" such as Lisa Loomer's *The Waiting Room* and Shakespeare's *A Midsummer Night's Dream*, in which the premise is worked out through the actions of multiple protagonists. But even these generally have one protagonist who is more prominent or dominant than the others. For example, in *A Midsummer Night's Dream*, one could argue that Pyramis, as the main human lover, is the protagonist. But his role tends to feel perfunctory among the antics of Bottom, Puck, and the others, who truly own the play. Multi-protagonist plays can be difficult to write, so if you are writing your first play, you may want to start simple, with a single protagonist story.

Some author/actors—especially those coming from performance art and stand-up comedy, such as John Leguizamo (*Freakazoid*) or Julia Sweeney (*God Said "Ha!"*) or Eve Ensler (*Vagina Monologues*)—not only keep it to one protagonist but to one actor (usually themselves), through whose dialogue a cast of subsidiary characters are conjured.

The protagonist's primary function is to embody a play's premise and drive its main conflict. As we said, sometimes the antagonist will initiate the conflict, and the protagonist may (and often does) have second thoughts about taking action. He or she may even be reactive or passive for a short time (think of

Nora in *A Doll's House*); but once she does get involved, she's the one who makes things happen. Other characters may make the situation intolerable, they may abuse or prod, but the main action and the main conflict is the protagonist's. In other words, the protagonist shouldn't just be running away from something, but running toward something. Look all the way back to the plays of Sophocles or Aeschylus: In *Oedipus Rex*, Oedipus is fleeing from his fate of being doomed to kill his father and marry his mother. Yet he's also moving toward something: the kingship of Thebes and his role as its savior. In *The Eumenides*, Orestes is fleeing from the Furies, who are after him for killing his mother. But he's also running toward Athens and justice to present his case in a court of law and reason. No one is interested in a protagonist who is nothing but a victim or a coward. A protagonist may be a victim or an underdog—in fact, he usually is, as this creates a sense of identification and sympathy in the audience. But the whole point of the dramatic story is for the protagonist to fight back or move toward a definite goal, so that the audience is empowered by vicariously partaking in the protagonist's success or given a gut-wrenchingly sad lesson by his failure.

The audience need not like or even empathize with the protagonist. No one— at least no one we know—would want to invite over the likes of most of Tennessee Williams' or Sam Shepherd's protagonists. Care to share a meat pie dinner with Sweeney Todd? We thought not. Rather, it's more accurate to say that the audience must be fascinated by the protagonist and drawn into his course of action. But this is easier if the audience likes him. If the protagonist is too headstrong, obnoxious, self-pitying, or self-absorbed, the audience may turn off unless you give them a good reason to remain engaged. If you do, then even such despicable protagonists such as Richard III or Tartuffe will hold the audience's interest, and it will want to see what becomes of them.

Even if—especially if—you are writing about an extraordinary hero, you must include something to which ordinary people can relate. To do this, your protagonist must in some way seem vulnerable, an underdog in his contest with the antagonist. This may reveal itself as a comic or character flaw, or through the protagonist's difficulty in attaining his goal.

When we speak of the stakes and goals that motivate the protagonist's dramatic action, there must of course be consequences for the protagonist, but also for other characters. Your protagonist should have more to lose or to gain than anyone else in your play—except for those around her whose fate depends on her success or failure. A protagonist may fight only for her life or well-being, but these are low stakes unless you're writing a light comedy or the character is alone in her jeopardy or you are writing about a selfish or despicable character. If not, your protagonist should also fight, wittingly or not, on behalf of others who will suffer unless she takes action. Obviously, these others have as much to lose as she does, but the responsibility is the protagonist's alone, whose success or failure proportionately increases by the stakes the other characters represent. Oedipus seeks to save all Thebes—not just himself—from the plague, even at the cost of his throne and his mother's life. Willy Loman's success or failure will affect his entire family. Othello's failure to trust the right person will cost not only his own life but Desdemona's as well. Even in light comedies like Alan Ayckbourn's *The Norman Conquests* or farces like Oscar Wilde's *The Importance of Being Earnest*, the protagonists' stakes are multiplied by the effects their actions have on the happiness of others. Conversely, the protagonist who takes dramatic action but has nothing personally at stake in the outcome is both unbelievable and less interesting than the one who stands to lose his life, love, or honor.

The audience must feel the same emotional investment in the protagonist's success or failure as the protagonist does. This comes from understanding and approving (or disapproving) of the protagonist's goals and the stakes involved. The plausibility of the goals isn't really important—Don Quixote's goals are by definition quixotic, but we still want to see him dream the impossible dream. The audience should be able to say, "If I were the protagonist in this situation, I would have similar feelings and hope I would have the courage, strength, or motivation to take the same actions." This is true with evil protagonists, too. In their shoes, we would still feel as they do. This brings us to someone else who, from his point of view, is not only right but the true hero of the story: the antagonist.

WERE I THE MOOR, I WOULD NOT BE IAGO (THE ANTAGONIST)

According to Chris Vogler, there is a figure who represents the dark side, who works to oppose the premise's hopeful outcome, who lurks wherever light shines upon the Hero: the Shadow. This is generally personified in the character of the antagonist—the person, place, or thing that stands in the way of the protagonist achieving her goal or is perhaps bent on her destruction. Furthermore, there must be no room for compromise between them. Each must, by their very nature and the stakes of the outcome, be incapable of backing away from the confrontation. The antagonist can be a human, an animal, an act of nature, or even something supernatural. It can also be the protagonist's own dark side, her inner conflict or character flaw, such as jealousy or self-doubt.

A common mistake young writers make is not fully developing the character of the antagonist. An undeveloped antagonist is not only boring, but indicates that the writer has not understood his protagonist's dilemma, either. For one thing, if the antagonist is weak, the conflict will also be weak—and the protagonist's potential victory will seem obvious and hollow from the beginning, so there will be little interest in seeing him go about winning it.

The antagonist must be the perfect, indeed, the inevitable, opponent for the protagonist—a dark reflection of the protagonist, his shadow. When we have a conflicted protagonist, the antagonist often makes real and external that which the protagonist most deeply fears or resents in himself. When Iago says to Cassio, "Were I the Moor, I would not be Iago," he's foreshadowing a transformation in Othello—who will ultimately come under Iago's spell and act like Iago, mistrustful and filled with rage and jealousy. Hamlet, Macbeth, Othello, Salieri, all are their own worst enemies. Their antagonists reflect or embody their inner failures.

In good plays, the antagonist is as complex and more powerful than the protagonist—more powerful, because he's a *magnified aspect of the protagonist's shadow* as well. Professor Moriarty is more than the equal of Sherlock Holmes, and more multifarious in his motives. Hamlet should be king—but Claudius is the king. Hamlet is capable of secretive and premeditated violence—but Claudius has already acted upon such urges. Hamlet has an unhealthy sexual fascination with his mother—but Claudius has already quasi-incestually bedded her. Othello is Iago's superior—but he isn't master of his own passions or a capable reader of people's motives. Iago is. In *Amadeus*, Salieri is Mozart's boss, so to speak. But Mozart is Salieri's shadow in that he's the vehicle for God's voice through music, a goal that Salieri has fruitlessly devoted his life to achieving, while moralistically suppressing all those carnal, visceral enjoyments that Mozart so heedlessly enjoys.

The playwright must find the antagonist's character arcs, dominant emotions, history, traits, and "positive" motivations (the rationale by which he or she justifies his or her actions)—and make sure they match up to those of the protagonist. The antagonist may be the one character who is least like you, the writer, and therefore the most difficult to create—unless you can look to your own unpleasant impulses—to your shadow. Go into the dark side your own heart and mind, find those aspects least like your noble hero—or most likely to painfully remind him of his failures—and then have fun.

Always remember, as the old radio series intoned, "The Shadow knows"—from his point of view, it's *his* story. If you don't find the understandable motivations behind your antagonist's actions, that character will be a cheap, dull stereotype. Screenwriter David Rintels (*Not Without My Daughter*) casts it in another light: "Presenting one side of the story is not drama. One side is polemic or propaganda. The best drama comes when you let both sides make their best case—winner take all. It's not drama to have only one side of an issue."

Friends, Romans, Countrymen, Lend Me Your... (Supporting Roles)

Supporting roles are exactly that: characters who support the main characters. They're necessary to the story, but are not as fully explored as the protagonist or antagonist. However, time should be spent in developing them. Although their motivations and actions may be more obvious and less complex, the same steps taken to develop a protagonist or antagonist must be taken with the main supporting roles—which, if created properly, can become among the most memorable of your characters. Lear's Fool, Polonius, Jacques, Diamond Jim, and Emperor Franz Joseph, are all supporting roles whose presences feel essential to their plays because they have been so well crafted.

Often, supporting roles act within a subplot that reflects or contradicts the main plot. For instance, Laertes' headstrong willingness to take immediate action to avenge the death of his father contrasts with Hamlet's dithering. A good example of characters who create a subplot that mirrors the main story is found in Alan Ayckbourn's *The Norman Conquests*, where Norman's philandering advances toward Ruth, Annie, and Sarah are echoed by Annie's frustrated attempts to inspire romantic energy in the diffident Tom. Following Chris Vogler's model, supporting characters often wear a variety of what he calls masks: the mask of the Shape-Shifter or Trickster or Mentor or Gate-Keeper. Ariel in *The Tempest* is a Shape-Shifter, the Porter in *Macbeth* is clearly a Gate-Keeper. These masks may also apply to a play's main characters. Hamlet adopts the role of Trickster, feigning madness, to trap the king. Polonius is a rather self-conscious if ineffectual Mentor, while Salieri starts as a Mentor to Mozart and then becomes a Shadow and Shape-Shifter as he goes about destroying the boy genius.

Double Trouble

The term "double gesture" describes an actor's simultaneous gesturing with both hands in exactly the same way: both hands pointing, pleading, accusing, etc. This gesture is considered weak because both hands are expressing the same emotion. Rather than reinforcing the moment, they overplay and undermine it. So actors are taught that a single gesture or two contrasting gestures are more powerful than a double gesture. The same is true in writing. If two characters have similar functions and personalities, a good case can be made for eliminating one, combining them into a single character, or figuring out how to differentiate them. (Unless you're creating a specific group, like a Greek Chorus, or the comic, nattering biddies in *The Music Man*. But this group is really one character divided to allow dialogue within itself.) For example, suppose you're writing a family drama.

You've got two teenage brothers, both troublemakers. Both are selfish and rude to their parents. If they're too similar in what they're given to do, chances are you could eliminate one and, in the process, make both the remaining character and the drama stronger. Or you could give each a different temperament and a different function. Make one brother the ringleader, who bullies his less-aggressive sibling into defying their parents. But say the younger brother finally has had enough and defies the older brother—or even commits suicide to get out of this situation. Either choice propels the story and generates *conflict that is about something*.

Another important reason why no two characters should be too similar is that they're less likely to clash, so there will be less potential for conflict between them—and all major characters need to have competing motives and hence conflicts. So make sure that you never create two characters who consistently sympathize or agree. Most importantly, however, such conflict shouldn't be arbitrarily imposed upon characters, but grow out of their natural differences and the purposes they serve in the drama.

The differences and functions of your characters both determine and are determined by what actions they take to move the story forward. Is the character a Mentor, a Wise Old Man who provides advice and wisdom to your Hero (or to the audience), as he guides him through the drama? Is she an ally who helps carry out the protagonist's (or antagonist's) plan? Is she a Trickster or Shape-Shifter, a false ally who appears to act on the protagonist's behalf, but in fact betrays him to the antagonist? Is she a Threshold Guardian, there to warn the Hero away from his course of action, or even impede it? Does the character drive a subplot? Or is the character a surrogate for us, the audience, a "fly on the wall," watching and interpreting the actions of the protagonist? Again, for an excellent and much more complete analysis of character functions in a "hero's journey" or quest story, see Chris Vogler's *The Writer's Journey*.

KNOW THY CHARACTERS AS THYSELF

All we know about characters is limited by the context of the stories they're in. We don't *really* know them. What would Willy Loman do on vacation with his family? Or even your childhood neighbor, whom you've used as a model? Do we know? Probably we can imagine it, but that requires bringing something new to the character—a new piece of information that offers new insight. But, suddenly, it's become a new character.

One student writer created a rather two-dimensional, stereotypically nasty character. When asked if he really knew the character, he answered, "Oh sure, he was my mom's boyfriend when I was in high school." But all he really remembered were the boyfriend's appearance, mannerisms, and habits, and the things he didn't like about the man. Knowing your characters is more than recalling their outer attributes. It means getting inside them, creating a foundation for their personality and desires so you do not have to stop and think about what they will do or say in a given situation; you have no doubt about their next action, because the characters are acting as you would *if you were them in that situation*. To do this, you have to deeply empathize with the people you've studied, including yourself, and all the inner cast of characters that you, the playwright, are made of.

6

Dialogue in Action

Let those that play your clowns speak
no more than is set down for them.

Hamlet

When it comes right down to it, we're all actors and constantly engage in dialogue. So why is writing dialogue is so difficult? We speak to each other every day; shouldn't it be easy to record and recreate it? Arthur Miller (*Death of a Salesman*) pointed out in *Harper's Magazine* that one of the oddest things about our lives is that, as never before in human history, we're constantly surrounded by acting—from actors reading the evening news to everyday conversations, we spend our time watching performances and doing a great deal of acting ourselves. He said that it seems "that when one is surrounded by such a roiling mass of consciously contrived performances, it gets harder and harder to locate reality." Perhaps this is why, when we write dialogue, it often sounds so unnatural, for the contrived performances of real life don't always work well in the honest world of the stage. Or maybe it's the reverse: Real life, however much we try to orchestrate it, remains messy, and so does the way we speak. We begin a thought, let it go, stammer, pick up another thought, resort to clichés ("Hot enough for you?"), and generally grope our way toward communication like blindfolded kids trying to pin the tail on the donkey. Good dialogue is precise and purposeful. It's a distillation of the normal chaos of everyday speech. Perhaps the very act of writing dialogue forces us to analyze ourselves, understand how and why we speak, and admit that we're engaged in a contrived performance called life. In many ways, writing dialogue is like trying to find the letter "Q" on the keyboard. While typing, our fingers find it automatically, but when we must single it out, we're forced to lift our fingers and search the keyboard as if we'd never typed before. Writing dialogue is much the same—for it forces us to lift our minds, analyze our cluttered voices, and choose one letter at a time.

For playwrights, writing dialogue is what it's all about. Through dialogue we reveal our characters, tell the story, push our points of view—and say what we would've said, if we'd been fast enough and clever enough to think of it when we had the chance. How often have you come up with the perfect punchline, insult, declaration, or witticism after the fact? In a play, you can have your characters succeed where you failed. For the playwright, it's never too late to find the right words. As American novelist and poet Rosellen Brown (*Tender Mercies*) said to *The New York Times*, "I still write for the same reason I wrote when I was nine years old: to speak more perfectly than I really can, to a listener more perfect than any I know." Playwrights find perfection and freedom through dialogue. Novelists have the resources of description and explanation at their disposal, as well as the ability to go silently inside their characters' minds. Not playwrights—our resources are our characters' actions and, primarily, what they say out loud.

THE BUILDING BLOCKS OF DIALOGUE

Dialogue is not everyday speech, it's speech that has been heightened, edited, clarified, and perfected—yet it must feel like everyday speech (at least within the world of a given play). The most important thing to remember is that dialogue doesn't begin with talking; it begins with your *characters' need to speak*, how they listen, the shades of underlying meaning that colors what they say and how they react to what's said by others. Good dialogue is the result of well-defined characters in a well-structured story that puts them into situations where they're not only compelled to speak (or avoid speaking), but have something specific to say (or reason for not saying it). It's a combination of what characters are consciously thinking at the moment, and how those thoughts are modified by their subconscious desires. It should feel like simple communication, yet be colored by the characters' environments, histories, emotions, and desires.

I Can't Shut Up About This (The Need to Speak)

Why do we talk? Generally, because we want something. If we want nothing, we say nothing. Talking is the most fundamentally human way of conveying our needs and desires to ourselves and to others around us. Babies cry when they're hungry or wet. As we grow, our approaches to verbalizing desires get more complicated: adults cry, yell, plead, cajole, joke, threaten, murmur, pontificate, and apologize. We explain, teach, defend, seduce, evade, pout, and challenge. In the privacy of our own rooms, we may even talk to ourselves, exhorting, scolding, coaching, reminding—making vague thoughts more concrete or weakening inner demons by exposing them to the light. In short, our dialogue comes to define our moment-by-moment existence. Dialogue is action: action taken to satisfy a want or desire. What each character wants defines why and how he is moved to speak. Any line that is not a motivated action will fail.

When we fail to get what we want by direct communication, we may become tongue-tied or learn to hide our agendas and manipulate our speech in order to satisfy our wants. We do this because sometimes direct communication ("I despise you and intend to steal your wife") can defeat our goals, if not get us into real trouble. So we disguise our desires and create indirect verbal strategies to get what we want. Sometimes, we don't even know we're doing it, but our subconscious does, coloring our speech with secondary meanings and unrealized desires. This is the origin of *subtext*, of saying one thing while meaning another, which is the most sophisticated kind of dialogue.

ARE YOU LISTENING TO ME? (HOW CHARACTERS HEAR EACH OTHER)

One of the problems beginning writers often have is that they focus exclusively on what characters say. But one of the most important aspects of dialogue (which is a two-way street) is how characters listen and react. No two characters listen the same way. As in real life, everything a character hears is filtered through his psyche, emotions, and experiences. Characters interpret, misinterpret, and read special (even unintended) meanings into everything that is said to them. A young, inexperienced girl may hear and react to her boyfriend's "I love you" in a very different way than a woman who's been wounded by a series of cads. We may also hear what we want to hear rather than what is actually being said, and in doing so we reveal a lot about who we are, our frame of mind, as well as our prejudices and personality. This opens up responsive dialogue to include layers of subtext. (For more on subtext, see below.) For example, I say, "Bob just bought a brand new BMW." Now, if you like BMWs and care about Bob, you might hear me say, "For once in his life, Bob thought of himself first, took his hard-earned cash, and got himself a well-deserved cool car." In which case, you might respond, "Way to go, Bob!" On the other hand, if you think Bob is a moron who only wants to flaunt his wealth, you might hear me say, "What a stupid show-off! If he doesn't know what to do with his money, why doesn't he give it to charity or something worthwhile?" If this is Bob's third new car in three years and you don't really care (or are secretly jealous), you might answer, "So what else is new?" Your response reveals more about you than it does about Bob and his new car. *How* a character hears is more important than *what* a character hears.

In the following exchange, the characters simply listen and respond. They hear exactly what the other is saying, and, as a result, the dialogue is flat and reveals nothing about the characters.

> JULIE
> I bought a new dress today — look.

> MAC
> At the department store?

> JULIE
> They were having a sale.

> MAC
> I like the color. But I thought you already had a blue dress.

> JULIE
> It's not quite the same shade, and it's getting worn out, anyway.

Because this dialogue is not affected by the characters' imperfect abilities to listen, their emotional states or their personal takes on things, it tells us nothing about them. Let's see what happens if we give Mac more of an attitude about Julie's purchase:

> JULIE
> I bought a new dress today — look.

> MAC
> Again?

> JULIE
> They were having a sale.

> MAC
> That doesn't mean you have to buy! You already have a blue dress, for Christsake.

> JULIE
> (*starting to cry*) I haven't had that dress for two years!

When we adjust it again, this time to reveal what Julie hears, the result is even more interesting dialogue:

> JULIE
> I bought a new dress today — look.

> MAC
>
> Again?

> JULIE
>
> You don't think I'm worth it, do you?

> MAC
>
> I wasn't saying that — but you already have a blue dress.

> JULIE
>
> Other men might think I look good in it, you know.

If you're having trouble knowing what the character is hearing, you can always write it out. In the following sample, the playwright has written not only what the characters are saying (**in bold**), but he then follows it with what the character hears (*in italics*). Of course, before the playwright shows it to anyone, he would cut out all the italics.

> **BOB**
>
> **I love you.**

> *WHAT SALLY HEARS*
>
> *(I'm desperate.)*

> **SALLY**
>
> **I'm not ready to settle down.**

> *WHAT BOB HEARS*
>
> *(I'm not ready to settle down until you do something about your nose.)*

> **BOB**
>
> **I can get a nose job.**

> *WHAT SALLY HEARS*
>
> *(I can become anything you want. I will follow you anywhere. I will be like a nose…or a noose around your neck.)*

> **SALLY**
>
> **I need a little air.**

> *WHAT BOB HEARS*
>
> *(I bet you can get a lot of air in that nose.)*

> **BOB**
>
> **That hurts. Love is about more than just physical beauty. Beauty fades, love lasts forever.**

> *WHAT SALLY HEARS*
> *(Marry me and you'll be looking at this nose forever and*
> *ever and ever.)*

> **SALLY**
> **I think I'm going to be sick.**

> *WHAT BOB HEARS*
> *(I need time to think about it.)*

> **BOB**
> **That's all right. It's a big step. But I know you love me.**

> *WHAT SALLY HEARS*
> *(I'm not going to take "no" for an answer.)*

> **SALLY**
> **Are you stalking me?**

> *WHAT BOB HEARS*
> *(I am incapable of commitment because men have always hurt*
> *me in the past.)*

> **BOB**
> **Trust me. I'm different. I would never hurt you.**

> *WHAT SALLY HEARS*
> *(I'm the same as all the rest.)*

> **SALLY**
> **Leave me alone.**

All powerful dialogue is a dance of interpretation and misinterpretation. If your characters' conversations are merely conveying literal information, they aren't carrying the essential freight of theme and characterization. Characters hear subjectively what their own awareness, insights, moods, and beliefs permit them to hear. Take this into account and you'll write better dialogue. You will also avoid writing unnecessary or obvious lines and get directly to the important thoughts and emotions.

YOU'VE HIT IT ON THE NOSE (SUBTEXT)

Another aspect of dialogue is that just as we don't necessarily hear what is being said, we often don't quite say what we mean or mean what we say (or know what we mean to say). We may speak in a kind of code, conveying what we mean without saying it directly: "I'll make him an offer he can't refuse" or "I am too much i' the sun." When a character says exactly what's on her mind, it's called "on-the-nose" dialogue. It's on the nose because the character is actually speaking her subtext.

Subtext is a second layer of meaning (often the most significant layer) lying beneath a line of dialogue. It's the hidden message behind the words, the real reason a character chooses to speak. It tells us a character's underlying emotions, thoughts, and ideas without her spelling them out in so many words. Good dialogue is like an iceberg—only part of the meaning appears above the waterline. And so a line like "You're my best friend" may appear to be simple and have few interpretations. But when a playwright adds a character's subtext and the context of the situation, it can take on hundreds of possible meanings. "You're my best friend" could mean "I don't want to have sex with you" or "Please help me" or "I am about to betray you." Writing from the perspective of subtext is also known as "writing between the lines," because what is not said is often more important than what is.

One way to avoid on-the-nose dialogue and create subtext is to have your characters speak about a different subject than the subject at hand. For example, a woman who's wondering if she's going to get a raise might mention to her boss the fact that her car is in bad shape and she's thinking about trading it in. This way, she tests her boss to see if he'll spill the beans, without revealing her true purpose. The dialogue concerns getting a new car, but the subtext is, "Hey, boss, am I going to be able to afford it?"

One of the most famous subtext scenes is the marriage proposal from Anton Chekhov's *The Cherry Orchard*. In this scene, Lopakhin (a new millionaire) contemplates marriage to Varya (the adopted daughter Lyubov, who is bankrupt). Varya and her family have been waiting for years for Lopakhin to propose, but Lopakhin isn't so sure he wants to. Here is the proposal:

> VARYA
> (*looking at the luggage*) I can't seem to find it…
>
> LOPAKHIN
> What are you looking for?
>
> VARYA
> I packed it myself and I don't remember.
>
> LOPAKHIN
> Where are you going to now?
>
> VARYA
> I? To the Ragulins…I've agreed to go and look after their house…as housekeeper or something.
>
> LOPAKHIN
> That's in Yashnevo? It's about fifty miles. (*pause*) So life in this house is finished now…

> VARYA
>
> (*looking at the luggage*) Where is it?…Perhaps I've put it away in the trunk… Yes, there'll be no more life in this house.

> LOPAKHIN
>
> And I'm off to Kharkov at once… by this train. I've a lot of business…I'm leaving Epikhodov here…I've taken him on.

> VARYA
>
> Well, well.

> LOPAKHIN
>
> Last year at this time the snow was already falling, if you remember, and now it's nice and sunny. Only it's rather cold… There's three degrees of frost.

> VARYA
>
> I didn't look. Our thermometer's broken…

The subject of marriage never comes up, but it colors every moment of the scene. In the end, Lopakhin walks away, the marriage proposal never takes place, but the subtext makes a scene about luggage, thermometers, and jobs become very interesting because we know that Lopakhin is thinking about proposing and Varya is expecting a proposal. Neither of them, however, can bring themselves to confront the issue in a straightforward way.

SPEECH THERAPY (THE STRUCTURE OF DIALOGUE)

There's no such thing as small talk in a play. Every word has a purpose, every line drives the story forward. To ensure this, playwrights often (consciously or unconsciously) work in structural building blocks known as beats. A "beat" is a single unit of thought. It's a small section of dialogue that's accented by a particular emotion, action, subject, or idea. A change in emotion, action, subject, or idea means the beginning of a new beat. Fiction writers have paragraphs, playwrights have beats. Now you might ask, Why do playwrights (as well as actors and directors) use the word "beat," which seems to suggest a rhythmical unit of time, cadence, or pause, rather than a word like "unit" or "section," which would make a lot more sense? Some say that this musical term came to its nonmusical, dramatic meaning when the disciples of the great acting guru Konstantin Stanislavski (the head of the Moscow Art Theatre and often called the father of modern acting) came to the United States to enlighten us about Method Acting. The story goes that the Americans were confused by the Russians' thick accents and mistook the word "bit" for "beat." If you say the line, "First you must split the play into little bits," with a Russian accent, you'll find the possibility of truth in this theatrical urban legend. True or not, looking at "beats" as "bits" makes a lot of sense. A playwright divides dialogue into bits in order to clarify the progression of a character's actions and motivations, moment by moment. For example, the following dialogue sample is divided into beats. (Please note, beats are never indicated in the script, as they are here. This is only for example.)

BEAT #1

> DARLA
> You're feelin' better.

> HENRY
> Me? I feel like shit.

> DARLA
> Where the blazes is a double hernia anyway?

> HENRY
> I'd show you but I'd be arrested.

BEAT #2

> DARLA
> You ready to go to the hospital?

> HENRY
> I cancelled the papers and I'm havin' the mail forwarded
> to you. Your mother will just lose it. Besides I think she
> opens my mail. Tries to find out if I got a lover. I can't
> prove anything, but my Sears bill is missin'.

> DARLA
> I'll be staying for a while so I can pick up your mail.

> HENRY
> I already told that idiot mailman. Told him three times,
> so maybe it'll stick. Last time I was gone, he sent it to
> your mother. I spelled it out. Whatever you do, don't send
> it to your mother. Sent it to her anyway. And of course
> she had to come to the hospital and read it to me.

>> (*She notices the boxes.*)

BEAT #3

> DARLA
> What you got here? Your new book?

> HENRY
> Just junk. Thought I'd donate it. Throw it out. What the
> hell.

                    (She lightly kicks the boxes
                    with the tip of her shoe.)

          DARLA
They're heavy. How'd you get'em up here?

                    (She starts to open a box but
                    HENRY stops her.)

BEAT #4

          HENRY
Your mama had her cataract surgery.

          DARLA
What? When?

          HENRY
She wants you to dial up the minute you get in. Like now,
Heifer.

          DARLA
Why didn't you tell me?

                         (DARLA quickly dials the phone
                         and waits while it rings.)

          HENRY
She didn't want me to. Said you'd just fret. Now remember,
you didn't fly, you--

          DARLA & HENRY
Took a train.

          HENRY
I told her not to dilly-dally. Told her, one eye at a
time. Did she listen? Course not.

          DARLA
She never lets it ring more than twice.

          HENRY
Waited too long, so she had to get both eyes done at once.
Got some nurse with her twenty-four hours a day.

          DARLA
Did you send flowers?

          HENRY
Why should I? She can't see 'em.

In order for a beat to work, each character must have a motivation (a need) that drives the beat forward, causes conflict, and provokes the next beat. When beats are working, the actions and the motivations of the characters can be charted, beat by beat. For example, the previous scene may be charted like this:

BEAT	DARLA	HENRY
#1	She must find out about her father's health.	He doesn't want her to know that he doesn't have a hernia. In fact, he has cancer.
#2	Tired of his smart-ass answers, she suggests that they head for the hospital. At least there, once she checks him in, she can ask the doctor about his condition.	Henry knows that he's probably not coming back, so he delays. He doesn't want to leave his home.
#3	She sees the box, thinks it might be copies of the new book he's been writing.	It is the new book, but no one would publish it. He's ashamed of the fact that he had to self-publish it. Must stop her from seeing it.
#4	She's worried about her mother, but also feels guilty because she hasn't called her.	He's thrilled that the focus is off him. He's happy that his ex-wife is as unhappy as he is.

Of course, playwrights seldom make such charts; this process happens naturally in their heads while they're writing. But if you have a scene that's not working, charting out its beats can be a great way to pinpoint the exact moment the dialogue fails because it's either unmotivated or leads nowhere. This can also be a great way to clarify the conflicts that drive a scene forward. Again, all dialogue is about *want*. If, in any beat, the characters want nothing, they will say nothing—or nothing meaningful, at any rate. And what a character wants must be in conflict with what the other characters want, or you don't have a play.

NEEDLESS TO SAY (AVOIDING OBVIOUS EXPOSITION)

All plays take place within a limited frame. That frame contains only those things the audience can see and hear while they're in the theater. Yet, not all stories easily fit within such a confined structure. Often, a story requires background information or exposition (i.e., "backstory"), which explains or justifies the characters' actions.

Exposition is how a playwright covers what happens offstage, in the past, or at any other point outside the geographical and temporal frame of the play. The playwright's problem is how to reveal the expository material without making it obvious or tedious. For example, the following dialogue is packed with obvious exposition.

                              BOB
How's Mom?

                              JOHN
Considering the fact that she's nearly seventy, our mother
is doing just fine.

                              BOB
If only she hadn't had that heart attack last year.

                              JOHN
That was a bad one. Left her in the hospital for three
months.

                              BOB
I took care of her, remember? I was here every night till
the nurse kicked me out.

                              JOHN
What about me? I was there every morning.

                              BOB
You were. She's been a good mother. Remember the time she
lied about your age so that you could join Little League?

                              JOHN
How could I forget? I'd never be a Big League pitcher if
it wasn't for her.

                              BOB
And I'd never be a barber if she didn't let me experiment
on her head.

Unless they're both complete idiots, these brothers would never have this conversation: They're telling each other things they both already know. This horrible dialogue is an extreme example, but it reflects a common problem—dialogue that does nothing to move a story forward, but is there simply for exposition. It's not conversation, it's filling in the audience on the characters' backstories. If the only purpose of a scene or bit of dialogue is to "fill the audience in," it will always fail because the action (and dialogue is a form of action) has nothing to do with the needs of the characters—who don't need or want to hear this information.

But what if the story can't move forward until the audience is aware of some background information? Exposition is a necessary part of most plays—but the trick is to expose the needed information as efficiently as possible without the audience realizing you're doing it. This may appear to some playwrights as a Catch-22, but can be done by using techniques that hide the exposition. These methods include *conflict*, *linking*, and *confidants*.

MISTEMPER'D WEAPONS (EXPOSITION AND CONFLICT)

The simplest and most often-used method to conceal exposition is through conflict. Robert McKee has a catchy phrase for this technique: "Turn exposition into ammunition." If characters are arguing or having even a mild disagreement, their dispute or squabble allows the audience to hook onto the emotion of the conflict without being conscious of being fed exposition. The writer may even get away with having one character tell another something they both already know, if that character is using the exposition as a weapon: "You think you're so great just because you went to Harvard! Well, you're not, you're just a drunken bum, like dad was!" Use of conflict is a natural solution because a play is never about people who agree with one another, so conflict should be there anyway. In the following dialogue, see how much backstory is covered, yet is never the subject of the scene:

SCENE 1
(NURSE enters putting on her coat. ART runs in wearing a birthday party hat.)

ART
Would it help if I said I was sorry?

NURSE
I'm sick of your excuses! I know you writer-types can't take criticism, but you're leaving jobs half finished! You're leaving residue. Residue that I have to deal with.

ART
Perhaps we should get out of here and have a quiet dialogue about how we're going to work together. You know, face the challenges--.

NURSE
He can't be left alone.

ART
When my sister gets here--.

NURSE
She's two hours late! The party's off! No one came!

ART
Could you at least sing "Happy Birthday" with me?

> NURSE
> Why should I? Your father fired me not ten minutes ago.
>
> ART
> But they're going to be here any moment — grand kids with toys and, and, and sticky hands!
>
> NURSE
> I gave him his Dr. Pepper and linguine. That made him happy for about two seconds. You'll find his medications on the television--.
>
> ART
> Perhaps you could wait until the agency sends over another nurse--.
>
> NURSE
> Mr. Lagattuta, check him back in. You want to prove you're a good son? You've done it. Tell Dr. Darrel you want him in for, for, hell, "observation." Why you want a smelly, dying old man around escapes me. Yes, he is your father, but he's a hateful bastard.
>
> ART
> He's not that bad. He taught high school English for thirty years. That tends to make you bitter.
>
> (The nurse gives ART the finger
> and exits.)

From this short exchange we learn that Art is some sort of writer and that there was supposed to have been a birthday party for his dying father, but that Art's sister and her kids never showed up. We also learn that Art's father is not a nice person, at least as far as the nurse is concerned, and that he taught high school English for thirty years. Yet, at no point are any of these the subjects of direct discussion in the scene; they're alluded to as part of a larger conflict involving the son trying to get the nurse to stick around. This conflict, not the exposition, drives the scene. The audience is drawn into the drama, all while they're given a great deal of information about what happened offstage before this scene began. Conflict is at the core of all drama, so, if conflict drives your scene, you can easily hide, in plain sight, all the exposition you need in order for your story to move forward.

THE PAST IS ALWAYS WITH US

One serious mistake beginning playwrights often make is that they treat exposition as something that happened offstage or in the past, when they should approach it as something that directly affects the present situation and as a result is an essential part of the present conflict. Onstage, there's no such thing as the past: Everything is in the present, because every character (and real person, for that matter) is the sum total of everything that's ever happened to them. For example, in the previous sample, Art's need to defend his father against the nurse's charge that he is a "hateful bastard" compels Art to point out that his father taught high school English for thirty years, which explains why he's a bitter person. Art's present need to defend his father forces him to come up with a justification. As a result, the past and present are wed, and his current argument grows directly from past events.

Another way to think of it is that *exposition should be revealed on a need-to-know basis*. Don't just throw it in. Make sure you've chosen the right place and time for this information to come out, or it will be forgotten or slow down the scene or feel forced and out of place. If a conflict is related to why this information needs to come out here and now, the exposition will blend seamlessly into the scene— becoming part of the natural action of the scene.

What you need to do as you reveal past information is to discover the *link* between the present situation and relevant issues from the past. For example, you're sitting in traffic waiting for the light when a vintage 1957 Chevy pulls up beside you. Suddenly, you remember, as if it were yesterday, your first kiss, which just happened to take place in the back seat of a '57 Chevy. The same natural link should occur with dialogue in a play. Something happening in the present must compel a character to recall the past—or anything outside the actual present-tense context of the conversation. So, if a certain bit of exposition needs to be revealed before the story can move forward, something must happen in the story in the present that motivates, even forces, the characters to offer up that bit of exposition.

Exposition should also do more than just explain the past. It should, as David Ball says in his wonderful book *Backwards & Forwards*, *propel* the present action. Let's go back to our example of the '57 Chevy: If this were a scene onstage, having the character remember that her first kiss happened in a '57 Chevy wouldn't be enough. How does this memory affect her current behavior? Does her memory of past passion lead her to conclude that all the romance has fallen out of her marriage? Or does it move her to find out what happened to that greasy mechanic who kissed her so many years ago? Is it the beginning of an affair? Whatever it is, the exposition should prove critical to the action of the play. Think of how Blanche Dubois' rosy, pathetic memories color her current attitudes and actions in *A Streetcar Named Desire* or how Stanley Kowalski's exposition about the Napoleonic Code provides fuel for his dominating behavior. If your exposition does not cause, or at least reflect, your characters' motivations and actions in the present, then it's not important to the story and must be cut or reworked until it does.

YOU TALKING TO ME? ARE YOU TALKING TO ME?! (THE PROBLEM SOLILOQUY)

Today's playwrights are at a disadvantage. For thousands of years, exposition wasn't such a problem: If a playwright needed to cover some bit of backstory, he simply had a character turn to the audience and explain it in the form of a monologue or soliloquy. But then, during the Renaissance, critics (mostly in France and Italy) began calling for greater verisimilitude. (Verisimilitude is a French word that means "the quality or appearance of truth or reality.") The truth and reality they were calling for had little to do with truth or reality by today's standards, but it did usher in some playwriting techniques that made for more authentic stage depictions. For example, some Renaissance critics said that it was quite ridiculous to have a character give a soliloquy to an empty stage. Really now, when was the last time you heard a sane person (not counting playwrights) walk into an empty room and start verbalizing into thin air about his deep personal problems or what happened before he walked into the room (unless he's on a hands-free cell phone)? These critics also said that "asides" (a theatrical conceit that allows characters to talk to the audience without other characters being able to hear them) were completely phony. This left playwrights with a problem: Soliloquies and asides were easy ways to let characters not only reveal their deep personal feelings, but to quickly set out the required exposition. Playwrights had to come up with a way to solve the problem without incurring the wrath of the critics.

HAVE SOME CONFIDANTS IN YOUR STORY

The Renaissance playwright's quick fix was the introduction of "the confidant." *Confidants* are minor characters (usually a servant, a maid, a best friend, or some other appropriately receptive character) who were placed within a scene simply to give the main character someone to talk to. Instead of making pronouncements to thin air, the protagonist would confide in a trusted maid, who would listen and then disappear from the story, but not before providing a soliloquy a sense of greater verisimilitude. A perfect example of the confidant is Siro, the servant in Machiavelli's *Mandragola*. Callimaco, the protagonist, goes so far as to begin his exposition with: "I believe you've heard me say a thousand times, so one more time won't matter, that I lost my family when I was only ten years old..." After hearing this long solo recital, Siro essentially disappears from the play, other than to do errands.

Today, on a purely practical basis, using disappearing confidants would be just too expensive. Actors cost money and the theater is too poor to pay for an actor who does nothing but listen to exposition. All characters must advance the story and be essential to it, but this doesn't mean that you can't have at least one character who must be filled in about past events. Thousands of plays have been written in which a fiancée is introduced to the family for the first time, old friends meet up again after not seeing each other for years, strangers meet on a park bench or a train, or some character is new to the situation, around new people or in a new environment where they must be informed of the other characters' backstory. From Edward Albee's *Who's Afraid of Virginia Woolf?* to Henrik Ibsen's *A Doll's House*, playwrights constantly write plays in which some member of the cast is an outsider to whom past events must be related, which helps convey the exposition to the audience. But this only works if the confidant's reason for being in the story is more than just being a sympathetic ear, and that the exposition not only links the past to the present but affects the central conflict.

Dancing by Yourself (More on Monologues and Soliloquies)

Of course, soliloquies and monologues are still a part of contemporary drama—Salieri's sardonic monologues and asides are the backbone of Peter Shaffer's *Amadeus*—but they're a far smaller part than when Shakespeare could have a character simply walk out, welcome the audience, and tell them the backstory of what they were about to see. Today, unless you're writing some sort of romantic, absurdist, or nonrealistic play, soliloquies can all too easily seem old-fashioned, contrived, even goofy. So don't write them until you have some real mastery of the form. Some playwrights try to muster greater verisimilitude by having a character speak into a tape recorder, make diary entries that are then read aloud, or use a cell phone. These are only thinly disguised soliloquies and seldom work because they're so clearly forced. The only people who speak into tape recorders are either businesspeople making "notes to self" about to-do lists or writers working on plays. And not even teenage girls read their diaries out loud—unless perhaps it's to a confidant. (Maybe here's where you could get away with that cell phone.) In short, for verisimilitude, characters need to play off other characters.

Given all this, the first thing to ask about writing a monologue: "Is it needed?" A monologue is a moment in a play when a character has so much to say, so many feelings to communicate, that she cannot be interrupted. In *One Writer's Beginnings*, Eudora Welty tells a story about her mother talking on the phone. Sometimes her mother would just sit and listen for long periods, punctuated by an occasional "Well, I declare" or "You don't say." After one of these single-sided conversations, Eudora asked what it was all about. Her mother answered that it was the woman from down the road who "was just ready to talk." The same is true for a monologue. It requires a character to be compelled to choose this particular moment to break into a speech—she must be ready to talk. If you've determined you have such a character and such a moment, write your monologue, then cut it in half, and then cut it in half again. If you do this, you might just have something. By your second draft, you'll often discover that you didn't need that monologue after all (unless you're writing a play like *Vagina Monologues*, which is all monologue, and falls into a different category of biographical or autobiographical narrative).

If you flip through your script and see a monologue on every other page, you're most likely in trouble, for monologues can force characters to turn inward and feed off themselves, rather than relate to other characters. Soliloquy can become solipsism. Such inwardness can drag characters into "false monologues" in which their speeches, even if supposedly to one another, are really completely solo entities. In other words, the characters are no longer interacting with each other but simply sharing the stage, like candidates at a "debate" who never really talk to one another but instead wait their turn to give prepared statements.

In the following example, two lawyers argue over evidence. Notice that they do not interact, but give speeches that have little to do with the other character.

                    BURGER
    That was twenty years ago. People change. What's the truth
    today? Where is the proof? In any event, you can't blame
    someone today for how they acted twenty years ago.

                    MASON
    Thank you for telling me how to do my job, but we adjourned
    before I could do so. They asked the question. A question
    I couldn't answer because I'm afraid the prosecution has
    exactly what I have. Proof! One divorce decree. I stole it
    from the county records when the trial began. Was being a
    good little lawyer-man, coverin' my client's ass. I'm good
    at that.

Now here is the same scene, broken into dialogue. Notice that the elimination of false monologues allows the characters to play off each other rather than feed off themselves. The result is a scene with more conflict and energy.

                    BURGER
    That was twenty years ago. People change. What is the truth
    today? You should've said something--

                    MASON
    Thank you for tellin' me how to do my job--

                    BURGER
    You should have demanded proof.

> MASON
> We adjourned before I--
>
> BURGER
> You can't blame someone today for how they acted twenty
> years ago... Why didn't you object?
>
> MASON
> I couldn't! I'm afraid the prosecution has exactly what I
> have. Proof! One divorce decree.
>
> BURGER
> Where did you get that?
>
> MASON
> I stole it from the county records when the trial began.
> Was being a good little lawyer, coverin' my client's ass.
> I'm good at that.

Finally, if you *must* have a monologue, make sure that it doesn't sound rehearsed. Your character shouldn't know he's about to give a speech, or even exactly where the speech is going. Just as in life, your characters must find their way and work out their words as they go. The best monologues are those in which the character isn't sure, when he starts his speech, where the speech is going or what conclusion he will reach by the end. To be, or not to be—that is the question... Hamlet never reaches his answer. To make your dialogue feel authentic, don't have your characters always speak in complete, thought-out sentences with proper grammar and paragraph structure. Let them stumble, feel their way, and only during brief moments of enlightenment or when torn by deep emotional conflict let them become poetic.

OTHER EXPOSITION NO-NOS

If you're writing your first play, using a narrator is probably not a good idea. Granted, some great plays—such as Thorton Wilder's *Our Town* and Tennessee Williams' *The Glass Menagerie*—have narrators, but these were written by masters. The basic problem with narrators is that a character talking to the audience (or themselves) is often contemplative, thoughtful, and reminiscent—in other words, the story has stopped dead in its tracks in order to trot out exposition. So, unless you're a damn fine writer (i.e., a lot of people, other than your mother, have told you that you write well), you're not going to pull it off. If you absolutely must have a narrator or a soliloquy, be sure that the character giving the speech is also an integral part of your story and that he too has a conflict that must be resolved. Oh, while you're at it, it wouldn't hurt to make the speeches short.

It All Started When I Was a Zygote in My Mother's Womb...

The most common mistake new playwrights make is having too much exposition. Any information about characters that fails to move a story forward must be cut. For example: How many children does Lady Macbeth have? Shakespeare doesn't say. That's because this information doesn't advance his overall plot. All we need to know is that she had at least one child, and that having "given suck," she knows "how tender 'tis to love the babe that milks me," and that she "would, while it was smiling in my face, have pluck'd my nipple from his boneless gums, and dash'd the brains out" in order to make her husband king. Now that's motivation. And what are the Capulet and Montague families feuding about in *Romeo and Juliet*, anyway? It's never mentioned, because it's not important to the action of the love story. What does Willy Loman sell in *Death of a Salesman*? Again, it's never specified, because it's that he sells, not what he sells, that is important to the character. Most of the time, a playwright needs to only hint at what happened in the past; letting the audience use their imaginations to fill in some of the gaps for themselves can make a backstory more, not less, intriguing. A bit of mystery is always more seductive than the harsh light of complete exposure; that's why lacy underwear exists. In some ways, playwrights are like attorneys (or Victoria's Secret models), for they must reveal just enough to win over their audience, and no more. Law professor Kenney F. Hegland writes in his book *Trial and Practice Skills*, "The discipline is to force yourself to say—and prove—what is relevant. Not to say—and prove—everything; if you do, you have said nothing."

I've Said It Before and I'll Say It Again: Once Is Enough

Another common mistake young playwrights often make is repeating exposition. An old-fashioned dictum is that everything in a play should be stated at least three times in order to make sure the entire audience gets it. Audiences today, conditioned by movies, TV, and ubiquitous sound bites, are much quicker on the uptake. If the play is well-written and its exposition clear, a playwright seldom needs to repeat the information—unless she's bringing something new to the telling, as in a mystery play in which things are not necessarily as they seem to be. *Tell your audience clearly and tell them once.* The second time, you'll bore them. The third time, you'll lose them.

Another good way to avoid obvious exposition is to scatter exposition throughout a play; this goes back to letting the audience in on the backstory only on a need-to-know basis. Good exposition should be swiftly absorbed and woven into the dramatic events and dialogue of your play, and never laboriously explained.

HIS ACCENTS MILD TOOK UP THE TALE
(THE CHARACTER'S VOICE)

Words are a playwright's paint palette. Your choice of words is like a painter's choice of colors. When mixed correctly, not only are the inner colors of a character's mind revealed, but the shadings of his education, upbringing, beliefs, personality, prejudices, soul, ego, as well as conscious and unconscious hopes, desires, and morals. How you choose and mix your words affects your whole picture. For example, a character who says, "I'm innocent" usually has a very different personality from the one who says, "I'm not a crook." The character who says, "You're shittin' me" usually has a different level of education from one who says, "You, sir, are attempting to deceive me." The character who says, "Blow, wind, and crack your cheeks" has a different nature and a different state of mind from the character who says, "Damn, but it's breezy today." A universal problem for beginning playwrights is that all their characters tend to sound exactly the same.

CASTING CALL

It's another old adage—a true one this time—that the reader should be able to cover up a character's name and know exactly which character is speaking, just by the speech patterns and choice of words. One way to get your characters to pass this litmus test is to cast your play before (or as) you write it. In other words, imagine that a distinctive actor, personality, celebrity, public figure, relative, or friend is playing each part, and then write each character's dialogue as if that particular personality were playing the role. This only works, of course, if you first have a firm idea as to your character model's nature and function, which in turn leads you to that character's unique voice. You have to be able to hear each character in your mind's ear. (By the way, make sure that you never tell anyone that you're stealing their voice.)

But this "casting" method for writing dialogue will only take you so far. For even when a character's voice is inside your head, you must still find the right words and rhythms. When it comes right down to it, people don't choose their words carefully—they're too busy just talking—but playwrights have to.

SOUNDS

Every consonance and assonance has a sound that can help reveal a character and tone of the moment. For example:

The right word in the right place.
The perfect word, perfectly placed.
An accurate word, in its correct location.
A proper expression placed with perfection.

They all say the same thing, but are accented by different sounds and what poets call scansion, which is the rhythmic cadence of the line. For example, the first line repeats the hard "R" three times. The rigidity of the line suggests perhaps an officer who must demand attention and authority as he *grrrr*owls at his soldiers. The second line, "The perfect word, perfectly placed," is dominated by soft "Ps" and gives the sentence comfortable feminine sounds, so we envision a young maiden playfully flattering a suitor. The third, "An accurate word, in its correct location," has hard, precise sounds that bring to mind a businessman instructing a subordinate. While the fourth, "A proper expression placed with perfection," is populated by rhythmic "Ps" and luxurious "Sh" sounds that remind us of a matronly lady impressing friends at a tea with her perfect pronouncements. Notice that in each case, the character and situation were revealed not only by the choice of words, but also by the choice of sounds and rhythms.

Some playwrights have become famous for their sounds. Tennessee Williams was a master at not only finding the right word but the right sound. For example, in *Cat on a Hot Tin Roof*, he has Maggie describe her sister-in-law—and rival for Big Daddy's estate—as a former "Cotton Carnival Queen." Notice that the alliteration of hard consonants reveals the character's jealousy, derision, and coarseness, even though none of the words by themselves automatically imply jealousy, derision, or coarseness. Shakespeare also used such techniques exquisitely in all his plays, which were, of course, largely written in verse, accentuating the rhythms of the language. For example, in *Much Ado About Nothing*, when Claudio disgraces Hero at the marriage altar over a supposed infidelity:

```
Sweet Prince, you learn me noble thankfulness.
There, Leonato, take her back again.
Give not this rotten orange to your friend.
She's but the sign and semblance of her honor.
Behold how like a maid she blushes here!
O, what authority and show of truth
Can cunning sin cover itself withal!
Comes not that blood as modest evidence
To witness simple virtue? Would you not swear,
All you that see her, that she were a maid,
By these exterior shows? But she is none;
She knows the heat of a luxurious bed;
Her blush is guiltiness, not modesty.
```

You can hear the hissing sounds of the sibilant "S" recur; in this way, Shakespeare enables Claudio to call his highborn bride a "slut" and "snake" without having to speak these words. Or take Macbeth's lament:

```
Tomorrow, and tomorrow, and tomorrow
Creeps in this petty pace from day to day
To the last syllable of recorded time;
And all our yesterdays have lighted fools
The way to dusty death. Out, out, brief candle!
Life's but a walking shadow, a poor player
That struts and frets his hour upon the stage
And then is heard no more. It is a tale
Told by an idiot, full of sound and fury,
Signifying nothing.
```

The repetition of "tomorrow" perfectly expresses the dragging futility Macbeth is feeling. The reliance on alliterative pairs of words emphasizes them, hammers them home: "petty pace," "dusty death," "poor player." The inversion of "Ts" and "Ds" in "tale told by an idiot" suggests the sense of being trapped in an endless loop. And notice the hard, pointless pomposity evoked by "struts and frets his hour upon the stage." More than just timing, rhythm is a verbal construction that creates an emotionally charged pattern. Each individual character has his or her own rhythms, which manifest themselves and make themselves felt in a play's dialogue. It doesn't have to be the firm rhythm of poetry; the rhythm of dialogue can be much more subtle and flexible. It's a gentle adjusting of sounds, stresses, and tempo that reveals the character and the emotion of a given moment.

Hup-Two-Three-Four! (Tempo)

Dialogue is designed to be spoken at a particular speed (fast, slow, erratic, and so on). This is its tempo. Perhaps tempo is the heart beating inside of us, or the rate of our breathing. Tempo can convey emotions as strongly as the words being spoken. A playwright can't notate his script as music composers do to tell the actor at what rate to talk. Instead, a good line of dialogue suggests its own tempo. It has an internal clock that should be unmistakable to the reader or actor. Some playwrights, such as David Mamet, have made distinctive tempo a signature element of their dialogue.

More often than not, a playwright doesn't look specifically to tempo unless something's wrong with a scene or character. If something isn't working, she goes back to examine a character's tempo to see if it's inconsistent with the mood or moment. Here is an example of a speech in which the tempo is out of sync with the action and character:

```
                              (BOB approaches BETH. She
                              backs toward the bed.)

                    BETH
Stay away from me! You aren't getting near me again, or
I'll have to tell your father, and your mother, and anyone
```

```
else who will listen to my story. Get your hands off me
now, because I will not put up with you, or any other man
again as long as I live.
```

This is obviously a frantic moment, yet Beth speaks in long, complete sentences, complete with pauses, which makes for a slow tempo. To solve this problem, a playwright might break up the lines into shorter sentences, creating punchier lines. A scene in which two characters exchange many short, incomplete sentences will tend to have a fast tempo, whereas longer lines will slow it down. This is by no means a rule. Longer lines, if written as run-on, unpunctuated dialogue, may speed up a speech, and short, completed-thought lines will make it read slower. Read the following similar speeches and notice how the first seems to read slower than the second.

```
                    SPEECH ONE
What's your problem? Don't tell me. You don't have any.
Yeah, right. I know you do. So does everyone on the block.
You're not Mr. Sociable. Give up the pride. Call her. You
won't regret it.
```

```
                    SPEECH TWO
What's your problem and don't tell me that you don't have
any because I know you do and so does everyone on the
block. You're not exactly Mr. Sociable, so give up the
pride and call her or you'll regret it.
```

If a playwright has a strong understanding of her characters and their emotional states before she writes, a character's speech rhythm and tempo will come naturally. A true understanding of rhythm, tempo, and sounds can't be taught; it comes from years of writing—and listening. If you're a good listener, the natural sounds and tempo of those around you will invade the characters you write, so when writing realistic dialogue, it's a good idea to listen to real people, people you know. When you finish a draft, the best way to know if the tempos and sounds are working is to have the play read aloud. So, gather some friends and do it.

I Do Declare: Avoid Conclusionary Statements

Stanislavski said that "in general" is the death of drama. In other words, characters who talk in broad generalities lean toward being stereotypes rather than specific, dramatic, interesting characters—unless, as with a character like Polonius in *Hamlet*, the playwright's point is to create such a dull character. For example, the following line of dialogue is lifeless because the character delivering it is making general statements rather than giving specific details:

> BETH
> Your mother was over today. She's so nosy. We have to do
> something. She's driving me nuts.

Specifically, the words "nosy" and "nuts" are broad generalizations. They fail to communicate the particulars of the mother's visit, and so Beth's line is ordinary, on the nose, and boring. Beth has described a stereotype. Her lines say nothing memorable about the mother-in-law or Beth because they lack the remarkable, noteworthy, precise, unique details that would reveal Beth and her mother-in-law's personalities and situation. But, if the playwright replaces the generalities with specifics, the audience will know that the mother is "nosy" and driving Beth "nuts" without the character having to say so in such obvious terms.

> BETH
> Your mother was over today. It didn't take her ten minutes
> to try to potty-train Ben, tell me I was using the wrong
> bleach, and drill me on what type of birth control we use.
> We have to do something!

In general, we can state categorically that, without exception, the best way to avoid broad generalizations is to steer clear of conclusionary statements. These are speeches, lines, and/or words that express a character's particular deduction, sum up his feelings, or clearly psychoanalyze the moment. For example, if a character says, "I'm so depressed," that's a conclusion. The character has weighed the facts, analyzed their meaning, and come to the conclusion that he's depressed. This is boring because it tells us what to think, rather than giving us the basic details that would allow us to draw our own conclusions. If you allow your characters to explore the details of their conditions, you will have no need to state their conclusions out loud.

Here are several examples of conclusionary statements and how they might be rewritten to make for more interesting dialogue and characters. The conclusionary words, phrases, and lines have been underlined.

Conclusionary	Non-Conclusionary
My life is just too <u>complicated</u> right now. The children <u>take all my time</u>. I don't even have <u>a moment to think</u>. And you want me to spend the afternoon in the park with you? <u>You're crazy!</u>	Bobby cracked his head open. Seven stitches. Sally can't get over the fact that her dog died on Christmas morning. We found him under the tree. Merry Christmas! And you want me to spend the afternoon in the park with you?

This man is <u>guilty</u>. Look at him. <u>It's written all over his face</u>! And what's more, he obviously <u>feels no remorse</u>.

Look at him. Those beady little eyes, tight lips, sweaty forehead. He knows he did it, and so do I.

I love you.

I can't seem to swallow when I'm near you.

You've always <u>hated</u> my writing, Pop. And I've always <u>resented</u> you for it. <u>And yet I've always known in my heart that you were right</u>. <u>I'm not a writer</u>. <u>I've been kidding myself</u>.

"It is the function of all art to give us some perception of an order in life, by imposing order upon it." T.S. Eliot. That was one of the first things you taught us, senior year in high school. And then you flunked me. I've spent my life trying to change that grade in your eyes. But Pop, I can't find the order. It eludes me. All I seem to do is make notes in the margins of life. "The margins of life." That's a great title. A good writer would write it down.

I SEE WHAT YOU MEAN—IMAGERY

Most characters, whether they're kings or hicks, use imagery when they speak. Imagery may be poetic metaphors that stimulate the audience's imagination and memories as a romantic heroine articulates her love ("A rose by any other name…") or simple similes that express how an earthy farmer feels after a hard day on the tractor ("I feel like an old nag ready to be put down"). Playwrights, like poets, make detailed observations that create mental images for the audience. Like a certain smell that wakens a long-forgotten memory, these images are the fastest and most profound method of communication, for they turn an idea, a concept, or an emotion into a shared or symbolic experience. To create verbal imagery and symbols, a playwright replaces conclusionary statements with exciting facts, observations, and comparisons that lead us to the desired conclusion. Detailed imagery can save what might be a mundane speech or scene. A classic example comes from Eugene O'Neill's *Long Day's Journey Into Night*:

EDMUND

```
I was on the Squarehead square-rigger, bound for Buenos
Aires. Full moon in the trades. The old hooker driving
fourteen knots. I lay on the bowsprit, facing astern, with
the water foaming into spume under me, the masts with every
sail white in the moonlight, towering high above me. I
became drunk with the beauty and singing rhythm of it, and
for a moment I lost myself - actually lost my life. I was
set free! I dissolved in the sea, became white sails and
flying spray, became beauty and rhythm, became moonlight
and the ship and the high dim-starred sky! I belonged,
without past or future, within peace and unity and a wild
joy, within something greater than my own life, or the
life of Man, to Life itself! To God, if you want to put it
that way. Then another time, on the American Line, when I
was lookout on the crow's nest in the dawn watch. A calm
sea, that time. Only a lazy ground swell and a slow drowsy
roll of the ship. The passengers asleep and none of the
crew in sight. No sound of man. Black smoke pouring from
the funnels behind and beheath me. Dreaming, not keeping
lookout, feeling alone, and above, and apart, watching the
dawn creep like a painted dream over the sky and sea which
slept together. Then the moment of ecstatic freedom came.
The peace, the end of the quest, the last harbor, the joy
of belonging to a fulfillment beyond men's lousy, pitiful,
greedy fears and hopes and dreams!
```

Edmund's speech ends with a statement that joy means being fulfilled beyond man's lousy, pitiful, and greedy fears and hopes and dreams. This is a conclusionary statement, but the verbal imagery before it gives it power by providing it with specific, visual details that allow the audience to enter into Edmund's world and see why he drew his particular conclusion.

However, imagery for imagery's sake can drag a play down, like any other digression that doesn't advance a story. A poet might be able to get away with this, but a playwright must tie all images into character and plot. A recent reading of a new play provided us with a good example. It was packed with evocative verbal images: references to Indians holding toasters, blood pouring from an elephant's eyes, and sweet lakes in the sun. These piqued some audience members' interest for a while, but soon had them yawning because, while the images were evocative, what they evoked had little to do with the action of the story. In theater, imagery (and symbols) must contribute to the story, theme, and characters, or they're wasted.

Y'ALL LISSEN UP, NOW (DIALECTS)

Nowadays, in deference to their actor's intelligence, playwrights no longer pho-netically spell out a character's dialect. The following speech in a Southern accent is shown as it might have been written fifty years ago (with some exaggeration to make the point):

BURMA JEAN
That's cawse meyun don' train boys to be meyun, mamas
do. And whither you lahke it owuh not, a fathuh trains a
gull to be a woman, but they neveuh finish. They leave us
incomplete. Wah? I don't know, mebbe theyur scayud of us.
Mebbe the minute we staht growin' boobs they back awf. Owur
mebbe they need us and if they finished the jahb we'd be
too indepindint. Straynge how they nevuh set us free and
yet fawlt us for owuh depindince.

Today, the same speech would be written with only the words of the dialect (and their implied rhythms and tempos), leaving the exact sounds for the actor to find through dialect (phonetic) work. A character description would indicate that Burma Jean speaks with a Southern twang, and might even specify which region of the South she comes from, but it wouldn't go into such phonetic detail. Today, the same speech would read:

BURMA JEAN
(*speaking with a soft Alabama drawl*) That's because men
don't train boys to be men, mamas do. And whether you
like it or not, a father trains a girl to be a woman, but
they seldom finish. They leave us incomplete. Why? I don't
know, maybe they're scared of us. Maybe the minute we start
growin' boobs they back off. Or maybe they need us and if
they finished the job we'd be too independent. Strange how
they never set us free and yet fault us for our dependence.

Dialect is about more than just giving a character an accent. Like "dia-logue," "dia-lect" implies an interaction, it doesn't exist in a vacuum. You must take into account the socioeconomic, religious, and historical forces that shape a character and result in an accent. For example, let's take the well-known American dia-lect of New York/Brooklynese. To understand it, you must identify the outside forces that shaped its tempo and rhythms. In doing research, you'll find that the tempo we know today directly descends from the flood of Irish immigrants in the late nineteenth and early twentieth century, who, while assimilating, neverthe-less brought with them their lilting speech patterns and penchant for changing the initial *th* in words such as "these," "them," "those" into "Ds," making the familiar "dese," "dem," "dose." The Irish sensibilities toward forced deprivation, independence, and the deep desire for roots might come to play into your modern New Yorker's character. You may also factor in that the New Yorker's reputation for being loud results from his environment, for he competes with the constant din of crowded streets and city noise. As a whole, these may account for the husky, insistent, and singularly assertive New York/Brooklyn dialect.

Writing a dialect well involves research. Never assume that you know how one part of the country speaks. Find out for yourself, and find out why. Above all, don't rely on what you hear on television. Secondhand dialect is just another form of stereotype.

YOU DON'T SAY (DIALOGUE TO AVOID)

Certain lines of dialogue just don't work. No rule states that you can't use them, but, generally, their very existence is a warning that something is wrong. For example, such lines as, "I can't believe that you're moving to Wyoming" or, "So, what do you think?" are often there simply to start a conversation. If your scene is full of action and characters with definite needs (as it should be), conversations should start spontaneously without such false prompting. Lines like "What do you mean by that?" or, "What're you trying to tell me?" seldom advance a story and act only as filler between real thoughts. If you have such phrases as, "As you know" or, "As I told you" or the word "remember" attached at the beginning or end of a line, chances are pretty good that *obvious* exposition is lurking nearby.

Introductions such as, "Sit down and let me tell you about it" let the audience know that a long, boring speech is about to begin, and this is their cue to take a nap. First drafts are often filled with lines that begin with "So," or "Well," or "You know." By the second draft, you'll discover that most of them can be eliminated, as this example illustrates:

                         JOE
        So, are you going to the funeral?

                        ALLEN
        Well, I don't know. I need time.

                         JOE
        You know, I think you should.

                        ALLEN
        So, are you telling me or asking me?

All of these filler words can be cut without affecting the sense or spirit of your lines. Another thing to avoid is name-calling, the use of the name of the character being spoken to in every line:

                    JOE
Allen, how are you?

                    ALLEN
Joe, boy, it's good to see you.

                    JOE
I was just thinking that, *Allen*.

                    ALLEN
How long has it been? Gosh, *Joe*, what? Three years?

It goes without saying, no doubt about it, clichés must also be avoided like the plague—and you can say that again. A cliché is a worn-out or commonplace phrase that has become trite. Clichés are like a debased currency: They're worthless and have little value. Passing them off as dialogue insults the intelligence of the audience. Phrases such as "beyond the shadow of a doubt," "beat swords into plow shares," "it'll all come out in the wash," "it's water under the bridge," or "as alike as peas in a pod" are just plain lazy writing. People do talk in clichés, but a play deals with *heightened* language, so a playwright should come up with new ways for characters to state old truisms—unless such clichés are an intentional aspect of your character.

LIFE STUDIES

Years ago, an old Parisian street artist who was delicately adding the final touches to one of his creations was asked what was the most common mistake made by beginning painters. He answered, "They look at the canvas too much." The same is true of beginning playwrights. They spend too much time looking at the page and not enough time studying the people they're writing about. If you simply attempt to invent dialogue, you're spending too much time looking at the canvas and not enough studying real people. A playwright must take the time to study human beings, for they're the stuff on which strong, believable dialogue is based. A playwright is a student, life is the teacher. A character is built from bits and pieces of human lives, so a playwright's ability to create characters and write dialogue is based on her ability to examine and understand the motivations and emotions of human beings. Listen to people talk, learn how different types communicate, and then *imitate*. Attentive imitation and study, combined with the principles laid out in this chapter, will lead you to the distillation of everyday speech called dialogue.

7

Looking Good

****

You shall see them on a beautiful quarto page,
where a neat rivulet of text shall meander
through a meadow of margin.

R.B. Sheridan

****

Imagine yourself a judge for a playwriting contest. The three-foot pile of submitted manuscripts is daunting. At first you try to give every play a chance, forcing yourself to read without judging by appearance. But soon you discover that every poorly formatted play is, without exception, poorly written as well. After days of reading, you begin rejecting scripts simply by their appearance. Guess what? This is what really happens. You may not be able to judge a book by its cover, but producers, directors, and play-contest judges do. If your play doesn't follow proper format, you've shot yourself in the foot before you've even begun. Put yourself in the reader's shoes. You've got to plow through half a dozen scripts tonight. The last ten were hard to follow, boring, had long "diary-entry" speeches, fuzzy fonts and typos. And, you've procrastinated reading until the last moment. Now, late at night, you face the pile. The first play is 145 pages—much too long. The next is a mass of loose pages—too messy. Two of the last three have formats you've never seen before—these playwrights haven't taken the time to learn the right format. So you grab the last script and hope for the best. At least it appears professional, it follows the proper format, and it begins with a great title and an attention-grabbing event. You settle in, suddenly not so weary or wary—and this playwright has won the first of many battles to come. A new play should always look as if it's going to be an easy (or at any rate, well-presented) read, which means it follows the proper format. It's a simple courtesy to the reader.

There are two things you must know about formatting. First, unpublished plays follow a format that's different from what you find published in Samuel French, anthologies, or magazines. Though these formats may look good, they were probably developed to compress the play and save paper on publication. In any event, they're wrong for a spec or submission script, so if you use a published play as a format guide, you'll look like an amateur. Several computer programs will automatically give you the proper format, but you don't have to spend a lot of money on software. You can create a proper submission script format quickly and easily with Microsoft Word or almost any other word processing program. Let's go over the basic rules.

THE LOOK

Use a laser, inkjet, or other high-quality printer. Don't even think about that old fashioned dot-matrix you've had since Reagan was president. If you still own one, trash it immediately. No one wants to read a script that doesn't look like it was written in this century. They expect crisp, bright letters. Choose a standard font (i.e., not a fancy one) that is easy to read: Courier, Bookman, or Times New Roman (11 or 12 point—whichever is more readable without looking like the big letters in a children's book). If you still use a typewriter, use Pica (ten letters per inch). Elite is too small. Whichever font you choose, make sure you use the same one throughout. Changing fonts might make your script look jazzy, but theaters aren't interested in jazzy. They simply want it to look professional and be easy on the eyes.

PAPER

Twenty-pound, 8.5x11-inch, white (and only white) paper is the standard. Don't spend your money on fancy stock. You're going to be sending out a lot of scripts, so use whatever's cheap, as long as it works in your printer.

BINDING

Theaters and playwriting contests require that your script be firmly bound. The best way is to use spiral or strip (also known as "Velo") bindings. These require a special device to punch holes in the margin and thread in plastic combs that hold the script together. Most copy shops will bind your script for a nominal charge, but if you're sending out a lot of scripts (and you should be), it's time to invest in your own binder. They can be found at most office supply stores. The three-hole punch and metal brad method used for binding feature film scripts is unacceptable for binding a play, as are staples, folders, three-ring covers, glue, rivets, spit, snot, or anything else you can think of.

FRONT MATTER

TITLE AND TITLE PAGE

Your title page is the first thing a reader sees, so make the title engaging, something that'll grab the reader's eye. Lew Hunter, Distinguished Professor of Screenwriting at UCLA, recalls when he once had a huge load of scripts to read in one night. He opened his briefcase, dumped them on his coffee table, and started sorting. Most had titles like *Memories, Impressions,* and *Frank's Story.* Without thinking, the first script he grabbed was *Love Stinks. Memories* might've been a better script, but *Love Stinks* was the first one he cracked, simply because of its title. Of course, a title needs to grab the reader, but it also must accurately reflect the play's subject matter, genre, feeling, and theme, or the reader will feel misled and let down. The master of titles was Tennessee Williams. *A Streetcar Named Desire* and *Cat on a Hot Tin Roof* evoke strong, multi-layered images in the reader's mind and suggest powerful ideas. These lead one to think, "If the playwright can say all this in just the title, the play that follows must be great."

Print or copy your title page on a heavy piece of colorful paper or card stock (thirty- or forty-pound paper works just fine), and use that as the cover. Don't waste your money on vinyl or clear plastic covers or those fancy report covers you buy at Staples and Office Max. Heavy, colored paper will do. The title is the only place in your script where you can use a larger or more distinctive font, but don't get carried away. Avoid sophomoric fonts like those horror-flick "bleeding" letters, even if they seem appropriate to the story. Center your title about one-quarter-inch to the right of true center (that quarter-inch will make it look centered when the script is bound) and about one-third down the page. In a smaller font (smaller than the title), place your name directly below the title, also centered one-quarter-inch right of true center. Before your name (or just above it) place the word "by." Some playwrights prefer, "A New Play By" or "A New Comedy By," which are also perfectly acceptable. Some like to point out the obvious by stating, "An Original Play By."

In the lower right-hand corner of the page (using a small but legible font), put your contact information, including phone number(s), street, and e-mail address. If you have a playwright's homepage, you'll want to include your www address. But don't include this if it's only a personal page, with pictures of your family and dog Spot. (For more on creating a playwright's homepage, see Chapter 10.) If you have an agent, include his or her name, agency, e-mail and street address, and phone number. If you don't have an agent, don't worry about it. The vast majority of playwrights don't have agents. Under this information you may also include a copyright notice. This should read, "Copyright 2005" or "© 2005." Some writers put their names after the copyright notice: "© 2005 Bob Jones." This isn't necessary. Your name is under the title, so it's assumed that you're the author and holder of the copyright. (For information on how to copyright your script see Chapter 8.) If you include a copyright notice, do not include redundant information such as "All Rights Reserved" or "Property of Bob Jones." If your title page is cluttered with repetitious information, what does that say about your script? And keep the copyright notice in the same small font as your contact info. A page with prominent copyright dates and three variations on the theme that the script is the exclusive property of the author won't keep someone from stealing your play, but it may keep him from reading it, because it reeks of amateurish insecurity. The chances of someone plagiarizing you are small, and if someone really wants to plunder your work, nothing you put on the cover will stop them, anyway.

TITLE PAGE NO-NOS

Some playwrights list on the title page the name of a production company that supposedly owns the script. They think this makes their scripts appear more "legit." Don't do it! Nothing screams "amateur!" more than a script written by Tommy K. Smithy and owned by "Tommy K. Smithy and Associates." Your title page should also not mention which draft the manuscript represents. Directors, producers, and readers aren't impressed this is *only* "Draft One." If you put "Draft One" on the title page, they'll more than likely be concerned that you haven't taken the time to send them a well-developed script. On the other hand, "Final Draft" can indicate that you believe the play is finished and can no longer be improved. No play is truly finished until it's been through the rehearsal process. So, if you need to indicate the draft for your own personal use, then record the date you finished the draft in tiny font under the copyright. This way you can quickly tell the draft without the reader's knowledge. The only exceptions to this are if you are in rehearsal and are doing rewrites—then it's perfectly acceptable to indicate the draft so that the director, designers, and actors won't be confused. Draft numbers can also be used when you've been commissioned to write a play. One clever playwright who felt he needed the draft number on each script put the date of the draft to the far left-hand side of the page, so far to the left that it was under the binding. This way he could find out the draft, but no one else would know it was there.

YOU BE DEDICATED, NOT YOUR PLAY

You don't want a dedication page. If you want to thank a spouse, teacher, or friend, do it in person. The only exception is if you think thanking someone will help get your play produced or if you are required to because you got a grant to write the play. For example, on a separate page you might say, "Developed through a grant from the Chicago Foundation for Abused Women." If you really feel you need to dedicate a script to an individual, then bind a special script with the dedication page and give it to that person, but leave that page out when you send to theaters, directors, and contests.

Some playwrights like to include a page with the poem that inspired them or words that attempt to set the mood. Again, just don't. No one reads these poems, no one cares what inspired you. Readers aren't taking your play, curling up in a big chair by a warm fire with cup of mocha-mint-quiet-time coffee as they might with a novel. Quite the opposite. They're in a hurry. They just want to know if your play will attract an audience, if they can pay their bills with it, if it's any good. Once the play is in production, you might want to show the poem to the director, but before that time, keep it to yourself.

With all the elements in place, the title page should look something like Fig. 1.

CAST OF CHARACTERS, TIME, PLACE, AND SETTING

The title page/cover is followed by the Cast of Characters page. This page lists each character's name, age, and a *very brief* description. Although one can find counter-examples, especially in older plays, nowadays, long, detailed character descriptions aren't considered necessary here (or anywhere else in a play, for that matter). The reader needs just enough pertinent information to launch her into the story. A character's personality, desires, wants, background, and philosophy of life should be clear from your play's dialogue and action and need not be explained before the play begins. The audience won't get the benefit of character descriptions, they'll have to rely on what's happening on stage. The most you need to explain is the character's age, race (if it's important to the story), sex (if it's not clear from the name), and a few simple words of introduction, such as "A woman on welfare," "Kim's niece," or "A priest." If your play uses double-casting (using one actor to play more than one role), you will want to indicate this on the Cast of Characters page. The Latin "Dramatis Personae" is sometimes still used instead of "Cast of Characters." It's a little pompous, but acceptable.

The cast of characters is followed by an indication of the play's time, place, and setting. If the cast list is short, the time, place, and setting information should be placed on the bottom of the same page. If the cast list is long, put the time, place and setting information on a separate page.

Time is when the play happens, for example, "Time: Early evening - the present," or "Time: Morning - December 7th, 1941."

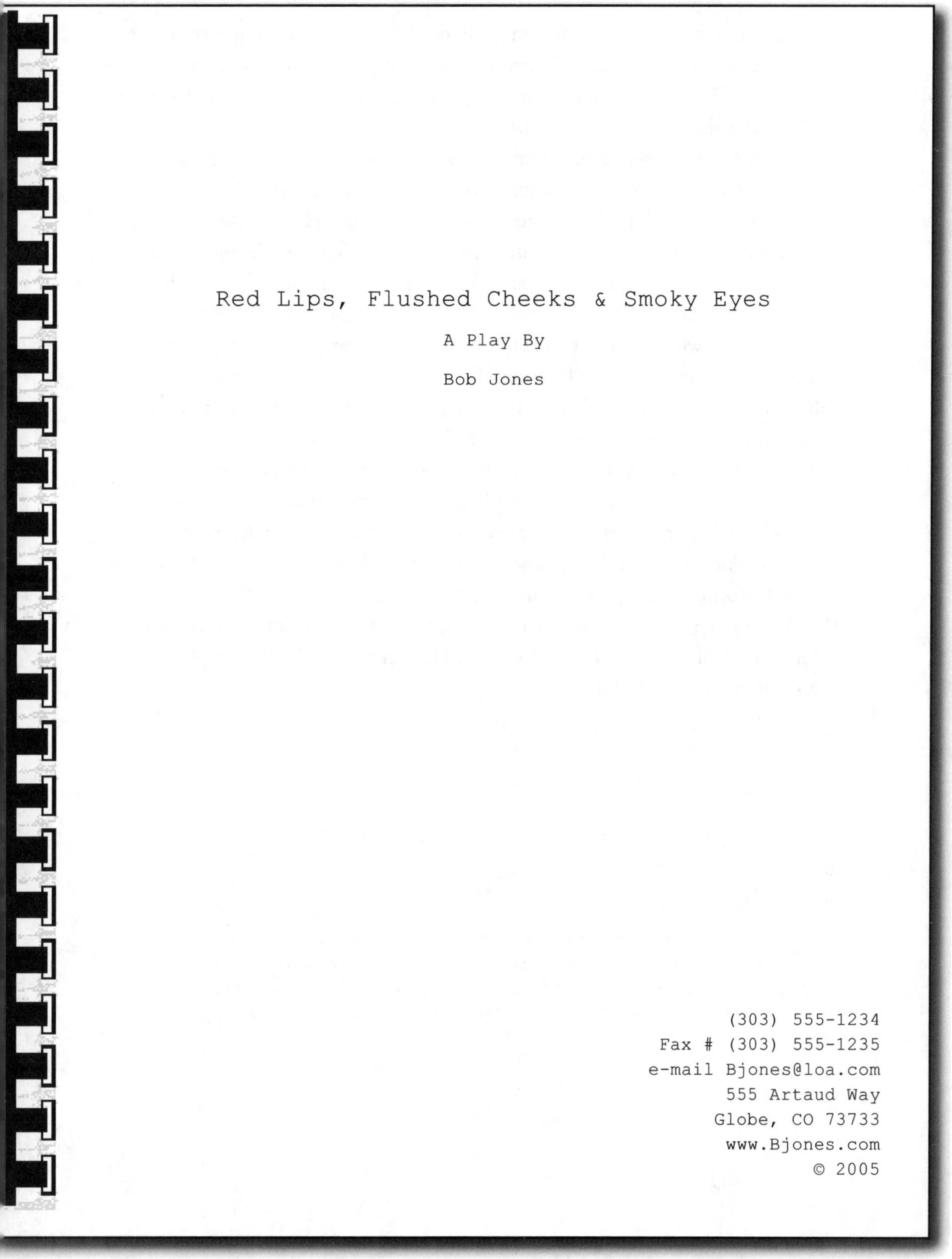

Red Lips, Flushed Cheeks & Smoky Eyes

A Play By

Bob Jones

(303) 555-1234
Fax # (303) 555-1235
e-mail Bjones@loa.com
555 Artaud Way
Globe, CO 73733
www.Bjones.com
© 2005

Fig. 1

Place is the location of the play. It might include the name of a city, a country, or a more general location. For example, one might write "Place: New York's Lower East Side," or "Place: A small Midwestern Farm Town," or "Place: A Space Station."

The Setting or "set description" is what the audience will see on stage. This information should be clear, simple, and to the point. Describe only what will have actual relevance to the characters or action of your play. Chekhov, the great Russian playwright, said "[If you] describe a gun hanging over the fireplace of the set, by the end of the play, that gun had better be used." In other words, don't describe anything that doesn't advance the story or characters. Your set designer will come up with plenty of stuff on her own, so your job is only to reveal the essence and essentials of the location, the mood, and crucial elements, as you lead the reader's eye around the set. Also, unless absolutely necessary to the sense of the scene, avoid terms such as "stage right" or "down stage left" to direct the placement of props, furniture, windows, or doors. Published plays might do this, but that's only because they want to help high school and amateur productions that seldom have experienced designers. The set for your play will be different for every production, so let the designers design. The playwright's setting description should inform, suggest, and inspire, not dictate.

While some manuals insist on centering the time, place, and setting information, there really isn't a standard format. Here are a couple of examples of how this information might be presented:

```
TIME: Early evening — the present

PLACE: Atlanta

SETTING: A plain jury room, government-issue,
industrial gray, somewhere in an aging municipal
building. A large table and chairs used for jury
negotiations dominate the setting. In the corner
is a water cooler, candy machine, and Mr. Coffee.
Yellowing framed pictures of George Washington and
Abraham Lincoln look down on a faded American flag
stiff from years of hanging in the same position.
```

Or:

```
                    TIME:
Late afternoon in May - 1975

                    PLACE:
Galveston, Texas
```

SETTING:

A neutral playing area that can become several
places. Most of the time it suggests various rooms
in the house of Norman Sr. and Belle Burnand, whose
minds were shaped by The Depression, so nothing is
too fancy or without purpose. Two playing areas are
more permanent. One is the front porch, where Indian
summer hangs a skyline of bullion-tinted leaves over
the rusted deck chairs and the entrance to the house.
The other is a tiny section of basement. There we
find bare light bulbs, wet block walls, and an ancient
coal furnace that has been converted to oil. Its
tentacle-like heating ducts make it look like an
upside-down octopus.

Your cast of characters and set description page should look something like
Fig. 2.

Some playwrights add a fourth bit of information to this page: <u>Staging</u>. This is
added when the play needs to be staged in a particular style in order to work. For
example, the playwright might write, "<u>STAGING</u>: The actors sit in full view of
the audience and watch the play as they wait for their entrances. They will also
help make quick scene changes." Or he might write, "<u>STAGING</u>: The action
is continuous. There are no blackouts between scenes." Staging instructions are
perfectly acceptable as long as they're concise and critical to the intended effect
of the play.

If your play has many scenes, you may want to include a list of the scenes and
locations. Put this on the cast of characters page (if there's room) or on a page
following the Cast of Characters and Time/Place/Setting page(s). It should look
something like this:

ACT I

Scene 1 — A rooming house, Chicago, 1973
Scene 2 — Ben's living room, New York, 1994
Scene 3 — A hospital waiting room
Scene 4 — Ben's living room
Scene 5 — A church, the next day

ACT II

Scene 1 — Ben's boyhood home, Chicago, 1973
Scene 2 — School room, Chicago, 1974
Scene 3 — Ben's living room, 1994
Scene 4 — Church, two weeks later

CAST OF CHARACTERS

EMMA(*Dr. Mann*) .... A Vassar English Professor (late-50s)

JILL WORTH .... A former student (30ish)

DAISY .... A Woman in a Wheelchair (35ish)

STARR .... A freshman at Vassar (18)

Time: The present. October. Late afternoon

Place: Emma's Office at Vassar in Poughkeepsie, New York.

The Set: The office of Professor Emma McCunn. She's had the same office for thirty years and it looks it. There are hundreds of books, some untouched for a decade. It's the perfect place to read "The New York Times Book Review." The office is large enough to have a couch and two writing desks with old typewriters. In the corner is a painter's easel with nearly blank canvas.

Fig. 2

THE PLAY ITSELF

After the Cast of Characters, Time/Place/Setting, and optional Scene List page(s) comes the first page of the script. This is how typical unpublished play manuscripts are formatted in the U.S. and Canada:

MARGINS

Dialogue, stage directions, and character names each have different margins (see below), but a play generally uses standard margins of one inch on the top, bottom, and right sides of the page and 1³/₈ inches to 1½ inches on the left side to allow extra room for binding.

PAGE ONE

On your script's first page, you'll want to repeat the play's title and then space down a bit before you start the actual text.

PAGE NUMBERS

The title, cast of characters, as well as any pages that come before the first page of the play itself are not numbered. Page numbers then appear in a small font in each page's upper right corner. If your play has more than one act, indicate the act number by spelling out "Act One" or with Roman numerals: "Act II." Do not use modern numerals. Any of the following are acceptable:

```
                                    (Act One) 12.
                                 Act One. Pg. 12.
                                    Act II - 12
                                          I - 12
                                             12.
```

We recommend *not* placing your name beside the page number, as in this example:

```
                                        Jonson 13.
```

Some playwrights do this so that if a page should fall out, the theater will know to which script it belongs. Others say it reinforces name recognition, acting to subtly but constantly remind the reader. The fact is that most theaters hate it when a playwright places his name near the page number because it prevents them from reading the script "blind," in other words, *without* knowing the author's name. In order to avoid any prejudice or favoritism, some theaters (and playwriting contests) will remove the title page before they give the script to a reader, providing an ID number instead. If the script earns a favorable review, this number will allow them to look up the playwright's name. If your John Hancock is on every page, you prevent them from doing this, and many theaters and playwriting contests automatically disqualify any script that has the playwright's name on every page. Put your name only on the title page. If the script is properly bound, there's little chance of pages falling out, and even less chance that the reader's opinion will be in any way affected by the constant repetition of your name.

CHARACTER NAMES

Every play has three basic parts: dialogue, character names, and stage directions. Each element has its own formatting rules. The easiest are character names. They should be capitalized and tabbed in four inches from the left side of the page: If you fold a sheet of 8½x11-inch paper in half lengthwise, the character names should start about a quarter-inch to the left of the fold. Don't double-space after a character name: The dialogue should come on the very next line. (Note: Character names used in stage directions are also always capitalized.)

DIALOGUE

Unlike a screenplay, a play's dialogue dominates the page. The left-hand margin should be approximately 1¼ inches, and the right margin 1 inch. Dialogue should not be justified or hyphenated at the breaks. Dialogue is single-spaced, followed by a double-space when the line of dialogue is finished. (See below for examples and Appendix C for a template.)

CAPITALS, Bold Lettering, Underlining, and *Italics*

Sometimes a playwright will use capitals, bold letters, underlining or italics to help the actor or reader understand how a line should be spoken. For example, a line might read,

```
                    SAM
Put down the knife! Please, I'm begging you! HELP! HELP!
HELP!!"
```

Depending on whom you talk to, some find this obnoxious (including most actors and directors), while others don't seem to mind. Today's trend is toward simplicity, however, and most playwrights realize that actors and directors want to be free to try out their own choices. If you really feel you must alter your font to provide emphasis, do it sparingly (if you do it on every page, you're not) and only when it's critical to the understanding of the line. The line above is perfectly clear without the capitals, bold lettering, underlines, and italics. They simply aren't necessary, and that ought to be the case with all of your dialogue. Playwrights provide the words. Intonation, pitch, and emphasis are the responsibility of the actor and director. All the standard practices concerning punctuation apply to dialogue, but a few are unique to playwriting.

Double Dash (--)

The double dash is used to indicate when a speech or line has been interrupted. It usually signals a lively or even heated exchange. For example:

> ANTON
> If you ever talk to Kathy again, if you so much as look at her, I'll break every bone in--

> LUIGI
> Shut up and get out!

A character can even interrupt himself:

> DAVID
> She said she was tired, so I took her home, she kissed me goodnight and I went back to the-- Wait a minute. Are you saying she lied to me?

Ellipsis (...)

An ellipsis indicates the omission of a word or phrase, or the point where a character loses his train of thought, drifts off, hesitates, or fades to another subject. Ellipses tend to lend dialogue a slower pace:

> GEORGE BERNARD
> I was once so in love… but what's love? Love is…I mean, you can't hold it. You can't sell it. You can't… Hey, you hungry? I'm starving…what was I talking about?

During a phone conversation, an ellipsis marks the moments when the other, off-stage, party is speaking:

> LANFORD
> No, you're lying. He really asked you to marry him…? When…? You're joking…! But you have to tell Fred… You don't mean that.

You wouldn't normally use double-dashes here because, while they do indicate interruptions, they don't imply the pauses where the actor is listening to the voice on the other end.

Exclamation Point (!)

Of course we all know that an exclamation point (!) indicates that a character is yelling or expressing intense emotions. It can also be used to end a declarative (and, of course, exclamatory) statement such as, "He's a genius!" Exclamation points are more common in play dialogue than in formal prose, but use them only when it's really necessary to clarify the delivery of a line. Reading a play with an exclamation point—or a double (!!) or even triple (!!!)—at the end of every sentence gets old fast—not everything they're saying can be that exciting, emphatic, or amazing!!!!! If a character is yelling a question, it is acceptable to use a question mark and exclamation mark together (?!), but how often do characters yell questions at each other? Really, HOW OFTEN?! So use it rarely.

Comma (,)

In dialogue, the humble comma is used just as it is in prose, but it can also be employed to indicate a slight hesitation. Hesitations occur naturally in speech, affecting its meaning, so indicating them may be important at times. The following lines differ greatly in meaning with and without commas.

```
                    TENNESSEE
        My baby, my baby, my baby.
```

And

```
                    TENNESSEE
        My baby my baby my baby.
```

The first indicates that each "my baby" is followed by a slight hesitation. This might mean that each word could be given a different weight, or perhaps the line is said slowly. The second line shows the playwright intended not even the slightest gap between words and so they run rapidly together and are given equal stress. By adjusting commas, the playwright can help actors understand the tempo of a given line of dialogue without making them feel dictated to from the page. (Note: If you don't intend a hesitation in the dialogue, you needn't use a comma simply for grammar's sake.)

Hyphen (-)

In dialogue, as in prose, the hyphen is used to link compound words such as twenty-five or forget-me-not. A hyphen appears in dialogue when the playwright inserts interjections into related sentences or thoughts, often for comic effect:

```
                    OSCAR
        I've read your script five times - almost all of it
        each time - and all I know for sure is that it's a play
        populated by fools, pop philosophers, and enervating
        inactivity.
```

ABBREVIATIONS

Abbreviations are used in dialogue only if the character pronounces the abbreviation. For example, if you want the character actually to say "TV" instead of "television" or "POV" instead of "point of view," then the abbreviation is OK. Abbreviations used as shorthand are not. For example, don't write "Dr. Jones." Use "Doctor Jones." The same is true of numbers. Instead of writing "15," write "fifteen." The only exception is if the number requires more than a few words, like "1,492," in which case the number doesn't need to be spelled out.

DUAL DIALOGUE/OVERLAPPING DIALOGUE

Although it doesn't happen often, if two characters need to speak at the same time, you should split the page in half and allow each character's lines to sit side by side on the paper:

```
          JOHN                      MARCIA
Would you get your life    You never listen to me —
together? You make me sick, all you do is talk about
lying around the house.    yourself--
Doing nothing!
```

PARENTHETICALS ( )

Parentheticals are adverbs or verbs or phrases that suggest how a particular line of dialogue should be delivered or describe an action that clarifies why a character says something. Unlike stage directions (see below), parentheticals are placed either after the character's name or into the dialogue, and each refers only to its immediately following line of dialogue. To clarify that these are not words the actor is supposed to speak, they're enclosed in parentheses and italicized. As with capitalization and underlining, actors and directors tend to resent parentheticals as intrusions onto their turf, so they must be used economically, and they must be short (usually only one or two words long). The best time to use a parenthetical is when a line has a great deal of subtext and you must ensure a clear interpretation:

<pre>
                    EUGENE
                   (grimacing)
        I love you more than life itself.
</pre>

Or when a line is short and needs clarification:

<pre>
                    LORRAINE
                   (lovingly)
        Oh?
</pre>

As noted, parentheticals can be put within a dialogue passage:

<pre>
                    LORRAINE
        I've had about enough of this. You've got to take some
        responsibility. (JOHN holds out flowers) See what I mean?
        You can't afford those…oh my God — tulips? (her heart
        melting) Oh, John… I love you.
</pre>

Some standard playwriting/acting terms and abbreviations used in parentheticals are: pause, beat, off, and O.S. "Pause" is a temporary lull in the dialogue, but not a stop in the action. The characters may need a moment to consider a major revelation, or perhaps an important change of subject can only be motivated if the character has time to work things through. "Beat" is used in dialogue to indicate a hesitation slightly longer than a period but shorter than a pause. (In playwriting the word "beat" has several meanings; see Chapter 6.) "O.S." means Off Stage. This is used when a character is yelling a line from off stage. One old-fashioned parenthetical that is pretty rare these days is "Off" (short for "playing off"), to indicate that a line of dialogue is motivated by something the character is seeing or touching. This is used only when clarity is in doubt. The following exchange of dialogue uses all of these:

<pre>
                    HAROLD
                   (off the dead body)
        Are you trying to tell me this has been here for two days?

                    ANTONIN
                   (O.S.)
        Wait, don't touch it!

                    HAROLD
        He's expired, what's the harm? (beat) Wait. Oh no. It's
        Jean-Paul!

                    HENRIK
        I think I'm going to be sick. (pause) We were lovers.
</pre>

The problem with parentheticals is that they slow down the read. The above example, with four parentheticals in four lines of dialogue, is only to show how they're used. If you use them this much in your play, you'll bore your reader. As noted above, whenever possible, the interpretation of the dialogue should be inherent in the lines. If you average more than one parenthetical per page, then more than likely you have a problem with—or are not confident of—your dialogue. Here's an example of what you want to avoid:

```
              BETH
Perhaps. (beat) Perhaps you should write a play about
real life. (pause) I mean, in real life people don't fly
around in anthropomorphic spaceships. We don't spend every
minute shooting proton lasers or making confessions of
love. (sadly) We're more occupied with eating, drinking,
flirting, and talking stupidities. (upbeat) You should
write a play in which people arrive, go away, have dinner,
watch TV, talk about the weather, and play cards. (hopeful)
Let everything be just as complicated and, at the same
time, just as simple as it is in life.
```

Also avoid parentheticals that don't directly affect a line's delivery or interpretation:

```
              BETH
People eat their dinner, just eat dinner (walking to
the window), and all the time their happiness is being
established or their lives broken up.
```

Unless Beth's walking to the window is critical to the understanding of her line (in this case it's not), it should be left out. And avoid parentheticals that are obvious from the dialogue or context:

```
              BETH
         (looking out the window)
Isn't the view wonderful from here?
```

STAGE DIRECTIONS

Stage directions deal with the physical elements of the play and help guide the characters' sayings and doings. They can convey the blocking (movement of the actors on stage), a character's reaction if unspoken, or how a character looks. Stage directions start four inches from the left side of the page, just like character names. They're single-spaced and enclosed in parentheses (but <u>not</u> italicized, as is done with parentheticals). If a character's name appears in the stage directions, it is ALWAYS capitalized to help the actor quickly find the stage directions for his character. Stage directions look something like this:

```
              (HENRIK grabs the bag of
              macaroons from the coffee table.
              MAURA dives across the couch to
              retrieve them. She misses and
              lands sprawled at his feet.)
```

The keys to good stage directions: First, make them short and sparse. Your script should be dominated by dialogue, not stage directions. If you have a stage direction that's three sentences long, try to cut it down to two. You want to try for no more than two stage directions per page. Second, they should not go into details unless those details are significant to the story or characters. You are not the director, so don't try to be one through stage-directing. Include only the most important directions. A stage direction like "(SAM points the gun at LAN-FORD)" probably is important and should be included, while "(LANFORD takes a long drag from his cigarette)" is probably not important and should be left out unless there's a bomb in that cigarette or an important point to the action. Some-times it's a matter of context: "(SAM points the gun at LANFORD. LANFORD takes a long drag from his cigarette.)" You can also eliminate any stage directions that are obvious from the dialogue. For example, if a character says, "Please sit down" and the character does sit down, you don't need the stage direction "(She sits.)" Also, avoid directions like "(WILLIAM crosses down stage right.)" The set design will be different for every production of your play, so stating "down stage right" will be meaningless. Better something specific and important to the action, like "(WILLIAM moves to intercept JERRY)." You want a Jack Webb, "just the facts ma'am" exactness about your directions. George Bernard Shaw's habit of expanding his stage directions into essays was fine for him, but not a good idea for a modern, beginning playwright. Be more like Shakespeare, who kept his stage directions simple. In *The Winter's Tale*, Shakespeare wrote perhaps the most famously understated stage direction ever:

(Exit, pursued by a bear.)

A good rule of thumb for your stage directions is that they should take no more time to read than it will take for the corresponding actions to occur on stage. In other words, if Bob exits pursued by a bear, all you have to do is write, "(BOB exits pursued by a bear)," or "(Terrified, BOB runs out chased by a bear)," or "(The bear runs out after BOB)." (Note: It may be advisable to capitalize the word "bear"—unless you're set on using real animals—as this implies an actor dressed in a bear suit.) If you go into a blow-by-blow description of Bob's terri-fying, gruesome, desperate, death-defying, headlong dash for safety—if you load your stage direction with lots of verbiage—it'll take longer to read about Bob's exit than it will take for the actor playing Bob actually to exit. Plays happen in real time on the stage—and on the page.

Remember, your unpublished manuscript will look very different from most published plays, which often have detailed stage directions. Publishers such as Samuel French and Dramatists Play Service will greatly amplify stage directions (and even include exact blocking) to help high school and amateur directors who may have little experience in directing. These amplifications are often drawn from the first production and were not in the playwright's original script. This has upset many directors, whose blocking has been "borrowed" without permission.

Real directors hate to be told how to exactly stage a play. This goes for actors and designers as well, and so stage directions should invite collaboration rather than telling anyone unequivocally how to stage, design, or act your play. As a matter of fact, many directors claim that they don't even bother to read stage directions. This is unfortunate because they really ought to. The stage directions should be as important as any line of dialogue. The reason directors skip them is because for years, playwrights have been including unimportant, long-winded descriptions that do little but interrupt the story. You can avoid this by keeping your stage directions short, sweet, infrequent, and to the point.

DESCRIBING YOUR CHARACTERS

When introducing a character in the stage directions, keep it brief and precise. You don't want to stop the read with a long delineation. The description is a stepping-off point, a first impression, just as the audience will get when the character enters. Any further character information should come from the dialogue and action. An excellent example of character description is found in *A Streetcar Named Desire* in which Tennessee Williams compares Blanche to a "moth." In a single word the playwright allows the reader to picture the character, the actor to understand the rhythm of Blanche's movement, and the costumer an interesting place to begin the design. Here are several samples of character description:

```
(BELLE, a flaky fifty-year-old,
always in a quiet, personal hurry,
rushes in.)

(GEORGE enters. He's the General
Patton of fathers. Intense. Seemingly
unhappy.)

(They come face to face with JERRY
SWANN, a sleazy young executive with
an ever-present ass-kissing smile on
his face.)
```

DIALOGUE INTERRUPTED BY A STAGE DIRECTION

When a line of dialogue is interrupted by a stage direction, you should place "(*Cont'd*)" next to a character's name. Example:

>   WENDY
> When I was your age I let another five years go by before
> it occurred to me that first marriages are always failures.
> They were never meant to succeed.
>
>   (WENDY grabs a DRUNK and throws
>   him out of the bar.)
>
>   WENDY (*Cont'd*)
> If they really wanted first marriages to succeed, they'd
> put a moratorium on marriage until the age of thirty or
> thirty-two.

STAGE DIRECTIONS TO AVOID

Stage directions should not include comments like "(MARTHA is a charming woman with frank insights)," or "(BETH is fun to be around when she's had some wine)." These characteristics should be clear from the action and dialogue. Stage directions also shouldn't include anything that can't be seen or played by an actor on stage. For example, you shouldn't write, "(BETH enters, she is Oscar's long-lost sister)," or "(ELMER and LILLIAN were once roommates. They have remained close friends since college days)." If Beth is Oscar's long-lost sister, that information should come out in the dialogue and not be openly stated in the stage directions. Without words, no actor in the world could possibly play that Elmer and Lillian were once roommates. If Elmer and Lillian are best friends, you might say they hug and treat each other like old chums, but the fact that they were roommates and have remained close since college should come out in the dialogue. In short, stage directions can clarify a character's reaction, but they do not tell what a character is thinking. For example, it would be unacceptable to write, "(JAMES thinks he should apologize for killing KIRKWOOD'S cat, so he mopes near the door for a moment)." But it is acceptable to state: "(Confused, JAMES mopes near the door for a moment)." This is acceptable because both being confused and moping can be played by an actor. What James is thinking can't be revealed except through dialogue. The audience can't read exactly what a character is thinking, but they can see the character's reaction to his or her thoughts. (The reaction in this case is that James mopes.) Just like dialogue, stage directions must work on two levels: the *page* and the *stage*. Working on the page means that the stage directions are lean enough that a reader, designer, director, and actor get the needed information without being distracted from the dialogue. Working for the stage means that whatever the stage direction calls for must be physically stageable by the actors and financially stageable by the theater.

Here is how your script should look. A play format template is located in Appendix C.

Paraphrasing Chekhov

Act I

(The lights rise on the main room of
the Dantchenko Colony for Artists and
Creative Inquiry. Once an ornate
summer mansion, it's seen better days.)

(We find two Chekhovian actors:
CONSTANTINE, a vehement, young, and
sensitive screenwriter and his UNCLE
BORIS, an older, oversized, self-
important screenwriter with numerous
ailments, including rheumatism. They set
up a makeshift writer's workstation.)

                    BORIS
Wastepaper basket?

                    CONSTANTINE
Check.

                    BORIS
Dictionary?

                    CONSTANTINE
Check.

                    BORIS
Roget's Thesaurus?

(BORIS throws the thesaurus out the
window.)

                    CONSTANTINE
Check--. Wait. No thesaurus.

Fig. 3 (continued on next page)

I -2

> BORIS
>
> Here! In my noggin. Give a word - any word!
>
> CONSTANTINE
>
> You mean--.
>
> BORIS
>
> Yes, any word!
>
> CONSTANTINE
>
> Like, off the top of my--?
>
> BORIS
>
> Surprise me.
>
> CONSTANTINE
>
> Okay. "Obnoxious."
>
> BORIS
>
> Repulsive, disagreeable, repugnant, annoying! I tell you, I'm a
> walking, talking… *(trying to find the right word)* Repository.
>
> CONSTANTINE
>
> *(unimpressed)* That's just amazing.
>
> BORIS
>
> Remarkable, wonderful, stupendous, staggering.
>
> CONSTANTINE
>
> Quite a talent, Uncle Boris--.
>
> BORIS
>
> Ability, gift, skill, proficiency, handiwork! Did I ever tell you about
> the time I rewrote <u>Butch Cassidy and the Sundance Kid</u>--!
>
> CONSTANTINE
>
> I thought that was written by William Goldman.
>
> BORIS
>
> I didn't get credit - no, but, yes, I did a lot of little improvements,
> character tweaking, important modifications--. Oh! I changed the line,
> "Who are those fellows" to "Who are those *guys*."

Fig. 3 (continued from previous page)

ODDS AND ENDS

BLEEPING WIDOWS

A widow is a character name or speech that is cut off at the bottom of a page and continued on the next. Widows make a script look unprofessional. Always check your script's pagination. If a bit of dialogue is cut off by the end of a page, write "(continued)" and at the top of the next page, place the character's name again, and continue the speech. If a character's name falls at the bottom of a page and his or her dialogue on the next, move the character name to the next page.

THE END

The last page of a scene should have the words "(END OF SCENE)" in parentheses, and the end of an act should include the words "(END OF ACT)." The end of the play should state (THE END) or the more formal (CURTAIN).

GET WITH THE PROGRAM—DIGITAL FORMATTING

Many software programs (like FinalDraft) help screenwriters format screenplays. These programs almost always have an option that allows for play formatting too. But, buying an expensive formatting software isn't necessary. All modern word-processing programs have *templates* or *style sheets* that can be programmed to suit any formatting needs, including those of a play. The following will show how to do this on the most common word processing program, Microsoft Word. (Of course, depending on your version and whether you're on a Mac or PC there will be slight differences.) Other word processing programs use a similar method.

A template is a formatting document that serves as the basis for new Word documents. Once you've set the style of the template, it's a breeze to write plays and format as you go. To set up your template, start by opening a new document ("New" is under the file menu). A box like this will open:

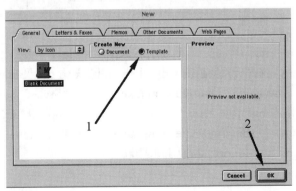

Fig. 4

First, click on the button that says "Template" and then click "OK." A new document will come up called "Template 1." Next, from the "Format" menu choose "Style." A box like this will come up.

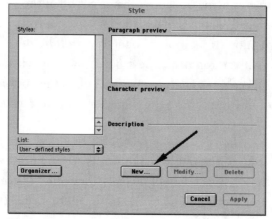

Fig. 5

Click on "New" and you'll get a box like this:

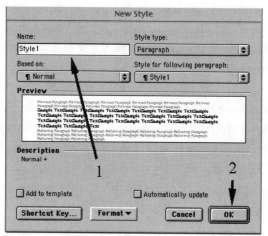

Fig. 6

In the "Name" box (where it currently says "Style 1") type the word "Dialogue." Then click on "OK." This will take you back to the "Styles" box (Fig. 5), but notice that the word "Dialogue" appears in the "Styles" box. Now repeat. Click on "New." This time type "Stage Directions" and hit "OK." Repeat this step once more, only this time type "Character Name" and click on "OK." Now your "Styles" box should look something like this:

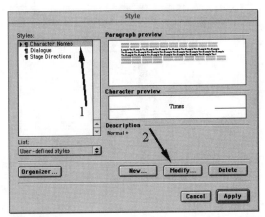

Fig. 7

You have just created three styles and are ready to define their qualities (such as caps, margins, and such). You do this by highlighting the style (1) and clicking the "Modify" button (2). You're back to the "Modify Style" box.

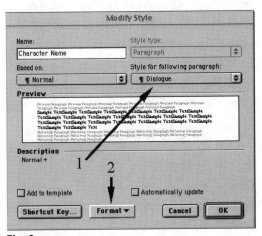

Fig. 8

You are now ready to define "Character Name." First go to the "Style for following paragraph:" pull-down menu and make sure the next style is "Dialogue." (By doing this you make it so that after you type a character's name, when you hit return, it will automatically go into dialogue settings.) Next, click on the "Format" button. This will give you several options. The two you are concerned with are "Fonts" and "Paragraphs." Highlight "Fonts" and a box like this will come up:

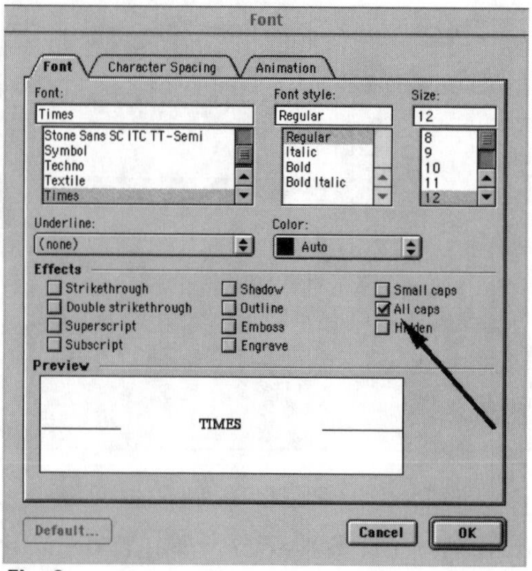

Fig. 9

From here you can define the font, font style, and font size. (As you define each style, be sure to give them the same font and size.) In Fig. 9 the playwright has chosen "Times," "Regular" and size 12. This works, but it can be any very readable font. Next checkmark the "All caps" box. Click on "OK." You'll be back to the "Modify Styles" box (Fig. 8). Go back to the "Modify" button but this time select "Paragraph." A box like this will come up:

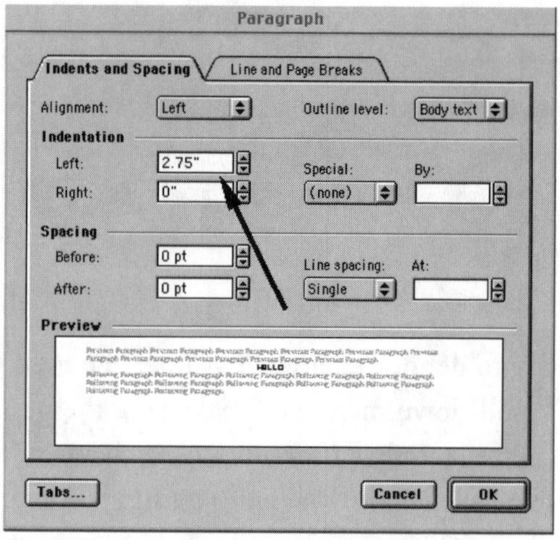

Fig. 10

Type into the "Indentation Left" box "2.75" and click on "OK." (This indentation, combined with the preset 1.25-inch left margin, will bring your character name indentation to the required 4.0 inches from the edge of the page.) Congratulations! You have now defined the font and formatting for your character names.

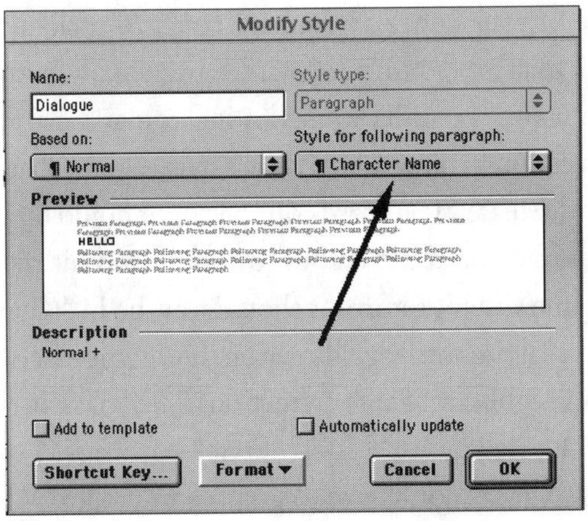

Fig. 11

All you need to do to now is to define your styles for dialogue and stage directions; simply repeat the process, only this time from the "Styles" box (Fig. 7) you'll highlight "Dialogue" and again click on "Modify." In the "Modify Style" box, you'll highlight "Character Name" for the "Style for following paragraph:" because when you finish writing a line of dialogue and hit return, more than likely the next style you're going to want is "Character Name."

Next click on "Format" and bring up the Font box. In font (Fig. 9), click on the same style and size of font that you chose for "Character Name," but *do not* check mark the "All caps" box. Click on "OK." There's no need to go to the "Paragraph" box, because dialogue doesn't need any special indentation.

Next, do the same for "Stage Directions." "Stage Directions" are exactly the same as "Character Name." (Unless you've gone a step farther under the "Format" submenu and selected "All caps" for the "Character Name" function; if you've done this, you'll need to undo it for "Stage Directions.") In the "Modify Style" box be sure to click on "Character Name" for the "Style for following paragraph:" because when you finish a stage direction, again the style you'll probably want next is "Character Name." In the "Font" box make sure the "Font" and "Font Size" are the same and once again, do not check mark the "All caps" box in the font box (Fig. 9). When you click on "OK" it will take you back to the "Style" box (Fig. 7). From here click on "Apply." Close the document. It will ask you to save it. Call it "Playwriting Template" and save.

You've done it! You saved yourself a template, and a lot of time. Now let's take it for a test drive. If you're on a PC, open a new Word file. In the section called "New from Template," click on Playwriting template. Word will open using that template. If you don't have such a box, just open the playwriting template file and click on "Save As."

Give the file the name of your new play. You are ready to rock and roll. In the menu bar will be a little box that says "Normal" with a tiny arrow beside it. Click on the arrow and you'll see a list of the different styles including "Character Name," "Dialogue," and "Stage Directions." Type a character's name, go to that box and pull down "Character Name," and release. The words on the page should be perfectly formatted for character. Place your cursor at the end of the name and hit return. It should now be in dialogue. Type a line and hit return. It should now be in "Character." In order to go to "Stage Directions," write the stage direction, highlight what you've written, and go to that little box and highlight "Stage Directions." To make it even easier, you can use the "short cut key" located in the "Modify Style" box (Fig. 11) to assign a function key to each style. This way you don't have to go back to the little "Style" box, you can just highlight the text, hit whatever function key or key combination you've assigned, and you're done.

Finishing a Play

8

Copyrights, Rewriting, and Development

****

People have asked me, "Why don't we have more good plays?" I said,
"Why don't you ask why we don't have more bad plays, because if you have
more bad plays you'll have more good plays, because that feeds the ground."
That's the manure that makes things grow. It's very valuable manure, as manure
is valuable to growth. We need activity, we need action, we need trial, we need error."

Harold Clurman

****

Playwrights should never place the words "Final Draft" on their scripts. There's no such thing as a final draft. Ben Jonson (author of *Everyman in His Humour* and *Volpone*), in his book *Timber; Or, Discoveries Made upon Men and Matters*, said about Shakespeare, "Whatsoever he penned, he never blotted out a line." If this were true, then Shakespeare was a rarity among playwrights, for all playwrights rewrite. Rewriting on your own can be a lonely and perplexing process without a plan of attack and feedback, and so most plays go through a development process that includes a series of cold readings, rehearsed readings, script-in-hand performances, and/or small workshop productions, which give playwrights the feedback they need in order to rewrite productively. In this chapter, we'll look at rewriting and development, but first, before you go any farther: Once you've finished a draft it's time to protect it.

MINE, ALL MINE (COPYRIGHTS)

Before you have a public reading or participate in development of your first solid draft, you'll want to copyright your work. Copyright affirms your exclusive right to and ownership of your particular words (i.e., intellectual property). A copyright gives the playwright and the playwright alone the right to change, reproduce, distribute, perform, and profit from his or her creation (or control who will reproduce, distribute, or perform it). If your play is copyrighted, others will break the law if they attempt in any way to exploit your play without your permission.

Some people think they can perform a copyrighted play without permission as long as they don't charge admission. This is not true: Copyright applies whether money changes hands or not.

In order to copyright something, it must exist in a tangible form. In other words, you can't copyright a thought, concept, or an idea: It must be written down, painted, carved, or in someway recorded. So, if you have a wonderful idea for a play, you can't copyright that alone, you must write the play. You can copyright plays, books, articles, screenplays, pantomimes, choreography, and music, but you can't copyright titles, character names, short phrases, or bits of dialogue (though trademark laws can be applied here). So, if you want to call your play *Angels in America*, you can legally do so (even though it would be a really stupid idea), but you can't use the stories, characters, or any part of Tony Kushner's Pulitzer Prize-winning and copyrighted play. You also can't copyright subject matter. For example, it's perfectly acceptable to write a play about a salesman who kills himself, as long as you don't use any part of *Death of a Salesman*. Arthur Miller's play is copyrighted, but the subject matter, salesmen who kill themselves, is not. In short, copyright protects the expression of an idea, not the idea.

A copyright lasts for the author's lifetime plus seventy years. In the case of a co-authored work, the term lasts for seventy years after the last surviving author's death. The term used to be fifty years after the author's death, but the Sonny Bono Copyright Term Extension Act increased the period of protection by an additional twenty years. This act was passed because Disney Corporation was about to lose the copyright on Mickey Mouse, so they put pressure on Congress to change the law, because they didn't want Mickey falling into public domain.

Copyright gets a bit murky, and sometimes complicated after that, because estates of the author have occasionally won the right to maintain a copyright beyond even this extended term, as was the case with Winnie The Pooh. However, in general, after a copyright expires the protected rights pass into "public domain," which means that the play, music, book, or Mickey Mouse for that matter, is then owned by the general public, and all of us have the right to use, reproduce, or change the play, music, book, or Mouse without permission or payment. For example, the plays of the great French comic playwright Molière (*The Imaginary Invalid*, *Tartuffe*), who died in 1673, are now in the public domain and can be produced or adapted without permission or charge—although the translations of his plays, if the translator is still alive or died within the last seventy years, are still copyrighted.

How To Copyright Your Play

Technically, all plays are automatically copyrighted from the moment of their creation, but to best protect yourself, you should formally copyright your plays through the Copyright Office of the Library of Congress. It's easy. All you need to do is go to the United States Copyright office website at http://lcweb.loc.gov/copyright/ and click on "Forms." Next, select "Form PA" (for performing arts). This will automatically download to your computer a PDF file containing the full application form. If this is your first copyright, you can also download instructions. Once you've filled out the application form, you'll need to snail-mail it to the address on the form, along with your script and a non-refundable filing fee of $30.00 (as of this writing).

The moment your application arrives at the copyright office, your *official* legal protection begins, though it may take four to five months for you to receive your certificate of registration, which is your official record of copyright. File away that certificate and forget it, until you need it, which will most likely be never. Once you have your copyright, you need not re-copyright your play every time you make changes. Only when your script has been significantly altered should you shell out the cash to re-copyright it. Don't be tempted to save money by doing what is called the "poor man's copyright." This unofficial attempt at copyrighting has the playwright mail his script to himself. The playwright then puts the unopened envelope into storage. This way, or the thought goes, he can prove he wrote the script by that particular postmarked date. A poor man's copyright is not legal, defensible, or recommended. We know of no substitute for shelling out the cash and getting an official copyright from the government.

Why Is Copyright So Important?

It's critical that you copyright your script because theater and development of new plays are full of collaboration. Yet, once in a great while, those who collaborate, make suggestions, contribute ideas, and/or brainstorm with the playwright feel that their contribution entitles them to be listed as a co-writer and/or to receive a portion of the playwright's royalty. Sometimes the playwright has no objection to this. For example, Tony Kushner shares 15% of his royalty for *Angels in America* with two dramaturgs who helped with the development of his play. (For more on dramaturgs see below.) This isn't a problem if the playwright contractually agreed to such an arrangement, but there have been several famous cases of late in which directors, actors, and dramaturgs have sued a playwright because they helped with a play's development by giving suggestions or contributing ideas and, therefore, felt entitled to be listed as co-writers and/or receive a portion of the royalties without the playwright's consent.

One of the most famous cases was brought about by dramaturg Lynn Thompson, who sued to claim a portion of the royalties of the Pulitzer and Tony Award-winning rock musical *Rent*. Written by Jonathan Larson (who unfortunately passed away before it opened), *Rent* is one of the most successful Broadway musicals of late. Some have estimated that it could bring in hundreds of millions of dollars before its worldwide run is over. Lynn Thompson's case was complicated because she and Larson did not have a written contract spelling out their working relationship (for more on contracts, see Chapter 11), but their creative relationship was also complex because Thompson was involved in the script's early development. In her lawsuit, Thompson claimed authorship of nearly half of the musical's book and 9% of its lyrics. The lawsuit split the theater world: The Dramatists Guild (see Chapters 10 and 11) took the side of the playwright's estate, while such famous playwrights as Tony Kushner took the side of the dramaturg. The result was a series of lawsuits, counter-suits, and appeals, which led to an out-of-court settlement. All of this might've been avoided if the writer had had a written contract and copyrighted his work before he entered the development process.

You don't have to have a multi-million-dollar musical for copyright to come into play. In another famous case, playwright Karen Erickson had to go to court to stop the Trinity Theatre in Chicago from performing three of her children's plays. Trinity Theatre claimed that several of its members were joint authors with Ms. Erickson because the plays had been developed at the theater, with company members acting as part of the development process. Collaboration and development are important parts of theater, but they are not the same as being a play's author. Unfortunately, it doesn't take much for some people to think that they are co-authors. In the Trinity Theatre case, one actress wrote a suggestion on a napkin (which Erickson incorporated into her play *Time Machine*), and that alone made the actress feel that she was a co-author. Another actor claimed that because he came up with a better title for the play *Much Ado*, he too was a co-author. But because Ms. Erickson had copyrighted the plays in advance, she had an airtight case. For someone to claim joint authorship, two elements are needed according to the case of Childress v. Taylor, a case which many courts cite as a precedent. First, the contribution of each joint author must be copyrightable. Second, the parties must have intended to be joint authors at the time the work was created. In this case, the actors' contributions, a title and an idea, were not independently copyrightable, but Erickson's script was. Add this to the fact that the various parties had no contract stating that they were co-authors, so Erickson easily won her case.

The third play in Trinity's multi-play lawsuit, *Prairie Voices*, was more problematic because it was developed using Trinity Theatre actors who improvised scenes that Erickson recorded and on which she loosely based her script. But Erickson had also provided the stories on which the improvisations were based, and she alone decided which of the actor's lines and/or suggestions were to be incorporated into her script. As a result, the court determined that it was Erickson who created a tangible, copyrightable script, and so she won this case as well.

Playwrights and theater people must understand that, in order to qualify as an author, one must supply more than ideas, lines, refinements, and suggestions. An author is the one who actually "creates the 'work,' that is, the person who translates an idea into a fixed, tangible expression entitled to copyright protection" (Community for Creative Non-Violence v. Read).

The ownership of a play, unlike a produced screenplay, remains with the playwright. No one is allowed to make changes, omissions, or alterations without the consent of the playwright. What's more, any changes or alterations made with the playwright's consent become the property of the playwright. Even if those changes or alterations are someone else's idea, they still belong to the playwright, for it's the playwright who owns the underlying work and decides what changes and alterations will be incorporated. So, if a director, producer, actor, or anyone makes suggestions on how to improve your script and you choose to incorporate these suggestions, those other parties cannot come back at a later date and demand joint authorship. Your work is your work, and you should never share authorship simply because someone makes a few good suggestions. Conflicts, such as those mentioned above, don't arise often, but if an unscrupulous or ignorant member of a theater should confront you regarding sharing credit because of a suggestion (even if the individual's suggestion turned your play around and made it a great hit), stand your ground. The law is on your side—but be sure to protect yourself by copyrighting your play before you ask for other people's help, have a staged reading, or enter into any development process. Erickson's advice to all playwrights is, "Always have a written contract" and, "Don't think that just because you've copyrighted your script that you can't change it. It doesn't have to be perfect. Once you do copyright it, you're the only person who can change it." We agree; protect yourself. It takes only a few moments and a few bucks, but it is well worth it.

BASING YOUR PLAY ON COPYRIGHTED MATERIAL AND/OR REAL PEOPLE

Not only is a copyright an important protection for a playwright, it also comes into play if a playwright is thinking of doing an adaptation. For example, if you want to adapt a novel, poem, or short story into a play, you must first wait for the work to pass into the public domain or secure the underlying rights (i.e., get written permission) from the living author or, if the author has died within the last seventy years, written permission from the author's estate (or other copyright owners). So, for example, when Tom Stoppard based his play *Rosencrantz and Guildenstern Are Dead* on characters and ideas in Shakespeare's *Hamlet*, he didn't have to get anyone's permission, because Shakespeare was long dead and his plays are in the public domain. But if you wanted to base your play on Tom Stoppard's *Rosencrantz and Guildenstern Are Dead*, you'd better get his permission, or wait until seventy years after his passing, or you'll be face to face with a lawsuit. This applies whether the work you wish to adapt is published or not. For example, if you base your play on someone else's unpublished diaries, letters, and/or personal interviews, you'll need a signed release giving you permission from the original creator (or his/her estate, if the material is not in the public domain) that shows that you have permission to use his or her words.

RIPPED FROM THE HEADLINES...

If you are going to write a play based on real people, the copyright laws get murky and can change from state to state. Most people have the right to control their personal identity (including voice, likeness, and "style"), so your "based-on" play can easily become an invasion of privacy and subject to lawsuits. We say "most people" because people who are recognized as "public figures"—such as politicians and media stars—give up some of these rights by the very fact that they are public figures. When it comes to dramatizing historical events and public figures the rules can be more relaxed. In *Nixon's Nixon*, playwright Russell Lees presents conversations that might have happened between President Nixon and Henry Kissinger before Nixon's resignation. The play is a damning condemnation of both men, and yet it is permissible because both men are/were public figures. But our advice is to play it safe and consult an attorney before you proceed with a story based on the life of a real person.

POKING FUN

The legal rules also change when it comes to parody. A parody is a literary work that imitates the characteristic, style, story, or characters of an existing person or existing creative work for "comic effect" (a term open to judicial interpretation). Parodies, which are not copies, borrowings, or imitations, are protected speech and fall under that part of the copyright laws known as "fair use." For instance, a comedian on *Saturday Night Live* might do a skit in which he parodies a movie star, exaggerating that star's foibles and mannerisms. Or a political cartoonist might use the image of Mickey Mouse (not a person, but a copyrighted image nonetheless) in a cartoon lampooning a "Mickey Mouse" politician. So if you have a satiric aim to your parody, then more than likely you will be safe, but there is a thin line between parody and copyright infringement (and there've been many lawsuits that have gone both ways), so some playwrights refuse to tread there.

If the possibility exists that someone other than a public figure (say your next-door neighbor) will recognize himself in your play, limit identifying traits and make sure there's little similarity between events and names. When a character is based on a living person, some writers try to add one trait that is so unbecoming that there is very little chance that that person would be willing to come forward and claim that the character is based on himself. This is known as the "small penis" rule. A playwright does this by basing a character on a real person, but giving that character a really small penis (or similar unbecoming trait), which will make it less likely that the real person would be willing to come forward and say, "I'm suing because you based that character on me!" Other writers will include a disclaimer stating that their play is purely fictional or that it's based on true incidents, but that the names, persons, and characters have been fictionalized. This doesn't always help, but it might. The important thing to remember is that when you're writing a play about actual events or real people, be sure to check with an attorney before you go too far.

MORE THAN YOU EVER WANTED TO KNOW ABOUT COPYRIGHTS

For more information on copyrights, check the Library of Congress' Webpage at http://www.copyright.gov/circs/circ1.html. This site will answer every question you can think of, from "Could I be sued for using quotes or samples?" to "Somebody infringed my copyright: What can I do?" to "How do I protect my sighting of Elvis?" (Seriously, the answer is there.)

Other great websites with copyright information are Friends of Active Copyright Education (F.A.C.E.) located at http://www.csusa.org/face/index.htm and Ten Big Copyright Myths Explained at http://www.templetons.com/brad/copymyths.html.

For copyright laws that pertain directly to playwriting, you might also contact the Dramatists Guild (see Chapter 10); they have several helpful pamphlets on the subject.

GETTING DRAFTY IN HERE (REWRITING)

Once you've copyrighted your play, it's time to begin the development process. "Development" is just another way of saying rewriting. Rewriting is always under the control and power of the playwright (because you have the copyright). When your first draft is finished, you should look objectively at what you've written in the heat of passion. Rewriting is repair work, so, before beginning a new draft, first be clear on what needs to be repaired. Only when you have a good sense of your script's problems and possible solutions should you begin your next draft.

Rewriting is much like writing—it requires a plan of attack. The problem is, after weeks, months, or years of work on the same story and characters, a playwright's vision can become cloudy and the creative answers hard to see through the mist. There is a story about three Hollywood screenwriters who were doing a rewrite of a children's movie. They'd been working on it for weeks, the deadline was looming, but they just couldn't make the story work. The problem was that the original draft contained a horse, and they couldn't integrate the animal into the story. They were pulling another all-nighter. It was getting near dawn when one of the writers said, "What damn horse?" It suddenly occurred to them that they were trying to adhere to an element that didn't fit anymore. The story had grown; the damn horse was no longer needed. The lesson is, when rewriting, be willing to change and ready to explore new possibilities.

Sometimes a playwright knows her script isn't ready, yet she can't figure out what's wrong. When this happens, the playwright needs *new eyes*, in other words, the ability to look at a script as if for the first time. The best way to acquire new eyes is to spend time away from your play. Some writers work on another project, others simply take a vacation. It seldom takes more than a week or two, but the playwright should take whatever time it takes to totally divorce herself from her play—lock it up, don't think about it, don't even touch it. After a few weeks, take the script out of hiding, find a comfortable chair, get a nice hot cup of coffee and one mean, long, red correction pencil, and start reading. Almost immediately, faults will reveal themselves and hidden problems will become obvious. You'll wonder what the hell you were thinking when you wrote it. And you'll also see much more clearly what you meant to write instead.

HEAR, HEAR!! (READINGS)

Probably the best method of acquiring new eyes is to have a reading of the script. Plays are written to be acted and heard, not silently read, and so this is the fastest way to see what works, what doesn't, and to launch into rewrite mode. A reading may be staged in several ways. Most writers start with a private reading without an audience and move up to a fully staged reading for an invited audience.

FRIENDLY CRITICISM (PRIVATE READINGS)

Once you think your script is ready, make copies, invite a few friends over (preferably actors, but at least people who can read clearly and intelligently out loud), assign the roles, including someone to read stage directions, and then sit back and listen to your play. Because the participants will be reading cold (without rehearsal), they may stumble and misinterpret lines. That's fine; the reading is for you, not to impress your friends. During the reading, don't be tempted to read a role yourself; in fact, *do not read along at all.* You'll get lost in your own reading and not really hear what's happening. Just listen, take notes, and judge honestly. Look for dialogue that doesn't work, plot points and motivations that aren't clear, and story logic problems. After the reading, take a break and then openly discuss the play with the reading's participants. Get everyone's opinions. Friends will want to be kind, but don't let them. Don't allow them to merely praise the script. Empty praise won't help you rewrite. Ask everyone to be kind but *honest*—if there's a problem, you want to know about it. If you're thrilled about how things went and wouldn't change a thing, then you're most likely kidding yourself or not ready to be a playwright. Nobody writes a perfect first draft—nobody. When the reading session is done, you should be armed with pages of notes and ready to roll on a new draft.

PUTTING IT OUT THERE (PUBLIC READINGS)

Many theaters offer a play-reading series in which new plays are read aloud to a small and/or invited audience. You can find these theaters in books and magazines like *Insight for Playwrights*, *Dramatists Sourcebook*, and Dramatists Guild's *Resource Directory*. (See Chapter 10 for more about these sources.) Not only is this an opportunity for you to hear your script, but it can also be your audition if the theater holding the reading considers new work. This is why you need a private reading first. You don't want to discover basic flaws in public.

A cold reading might be fine when it's just you and a few friends sitting around your living room, but a cold reading can be a disaster in public. If a theater insists that a cold reading is all they can do, politely say that you're not interested. A playwright should try to work with other artists, but this is one situation where you must kindly insist that the theater have at least one rehearsal of your play before it's read in public.

You can take several steps to help ensure a successful public reading. First, make sure that you or the director "casts to type." This means that the chosen actors are playing characters close to their own age, race, and temperament. You don't want a nineteen-year-old kid playing a seventy-year-old or an easygoing gentleman reading the part of a bar-fighting cowboy. Second, the actors should get the script a few days before the reading, so that they have a chance to read it, and, at the very least, one rehearsal should be held so that the actors can read the script through together and have a chance to ask questions. In their book *Scriptwork: A Director's Approach to New Play Development*, Donna Breed and David Kahn state, "If actors have the script a day or two in advance, they can begin to formulate the broad outlines of character and relationships; they will also bring to the reading a sense of what they have already found in the script. If the actors read the script cold, they generally go with their instincts and their moment-to-moment discoveries." An actor's moment-to-moment discoveries can be wonderful, but they can also be very wrong, so, during the rehearsal, don't be afraid to tell an actor what your intentions are. Unlike rehearsal, where you want to step lightly on the actor's creativity (see "Working with Actors" in Chapter 11), a stage reading is done for your benefit, and you should hear the play the way you meant it to be done. Third, during the reading, have the stage manager read only those stage directions affecting the clarity of the play. Long, dry passages of stage directions will bore the audience and unnaturally interrupt the flow of the performance. If you can, cut at least fifty percent of your stage directions. You don't want the actors constantly interrupted with "She walks to the window" or "He takes a pause." Above all, cut parenthetical remarks such as "sadly" and "proudly." Let the actors play the emotions instead of reading them to the audience.

During the reading, the playwright should not only listen to the play, but also watch the audience's reactions. Those reactions may be subtle. If audience members shift or wiggle in their chairs, it can mean they're bored. Audience members may cough or even close their eyes for a rest as they lose interest. Don't get too deeply into your play: Give yourself a great deal of aesthetic distance. Once, we attended the reading of a new comedy in which no one in the audience laughed except the playwright, who enjoyed himself immensely. After a while, the playwright's guffaws infected the audience and they began laughing at the playwright, which he interpreted to mean that his play was a great success—so he laughed even harder. A reading is an event at which a playwright should be quiet and objective. Sit in back, where your note-taking won't bother anyone, and be objective. You may want to have a copy of the script in front of you so you can make notations.

If you can't find a theater in your area that hosts such readings, there's nothing wrong with renting a space, putting up flyers, finding actors and doing it all yourself.

THE DISSECTION (POST-READING DISCUSSIONS)

More often than not, a theater company will follow a reading with an open forum led by a moderator. At this time, the audience, cast members, and the theater's staff will be asked to discuss and critique your play. Be warned: These discussions usually contain half-thought-out ideas, unhelpful comments, and such worthless phrases as, "I liked it" or "I think the second act could be bumped up by five percent." They can, in short, be brutal.

Many years ago, the Circle Rep in New York held a post-reading discussion that was particularly noteworthy. The reading had gone well and, as the discussions and critique began, the audience agreed that it was a very good play. The first comment to the playwright was, "Thank you. Because of your play, I'm going to call my mother and tell her how much she means to me." The next comment was, "Your play was brilliant. Thank you." This was followed by another five minutes of positive and upbeat comments. Then, the other shoe dropped: "There was a very minor problem in the second act," and the audience member went on to expound to the group on some small structural flaw. The next person suddenly jumped in and said, "You're right! There is a problem in the second act!" The next note built on that thought, and the next critic agreed with him, and so on. (The group dynamic is a powerful and mysterious thing.) Suddenly the feeding frenzy had begun. One hour later, the majority of the audience had convinced themselves that the playwright had major rewrites ahead of her and that the play did not "speak to anyone" in its present form. The audience had circled themselves into the opinion that the play, which they loved only an hour before, was a total failure.

When this happens, it is largely the fault of a moderator who does not know how to guide the discussion; and that's not uncommon. After several such note sessions, playwrights learn that the general public doesn't know much about the intricacies of playwriting, yet they have no hesitation when it comes to telling you how to fix your play. They thrill at the opportunity to give a critique, but their priorities often get mixed up. Their first concern is not to sound foolish, their second is to say something constructive—and the majority will sacrifice number two in order to fulfill number one. You'll also find that most theater companies don't understand that these open, "democratic" play discussions/critiques are often of little use to the playwright. From the reading alone, most playwrights (if they are actively listening) know exactly what's wrong with their script and what needs to be rewritten. Having said this, if you opt out of these post-reading discussions, most people will consider you arrogant, egotistical, and overconfident. And what's more, out of all the irrelevant or even hurtful comments that may arise during the post-reading discussions, there may be some that are invaluable. So grow a thick skin and a discerning ear, and stick around.

You can improve your chances of having useful post-reading discussions/ critiques by taking a few basic steps. First, after the reading and before the

discussion, under the pretense of thanking everyone for attending, make a statement about what you've learned from the reading and what changes you're
considering. This can save precious time, for it allows the audience to move
past the obvious problems quickly, rather than re-stating what you already know.
Although this will frustrate some people—you have denied them their chance to
enlighten you—most get the hint. Second, if the moderator hasn't already done
so, make up a list of questions you have about the plot, characters, story, and
theme and ask your audience for specific answers; in other words, give the discussion some structure and a direction to go in. Third, never become defensive! If
they didn't like your play, there's absolutely nothing that you can say during the
post-reading discussion that'll change their minds. Even if you totally disagree,
even if your writing is being ruthlessly attacked, you can't try to redirect the discussion with justifications.

Years ago, the same Circle Rep had a policy that did not allow playwrights to
speak during the post-play discussions (unless a question was directly asked of them).
The idea was that the play should defend itself and not need justifications, explana-
tions, or comments from the playwright. This policy never worked. If your theater
has such a policy, see if they will at least let you make a statement about what you've
learned and ask questions. If they won't allow that, then know that you're with a theater that isn't really interested in a post-reading "discussion" but a post-reading note
session, which may become a meaningless exercise you'll have to endure in order to
get the reading. Fourth, the audience has done you a favor by coming to the reading,
so be certain you let them know you think their point of view is valuable (whether it
is or not). When an audience member repeats their point of view or tries to dominate the discussion, it's usually because they believe their opinion was glossed over.
Give them a positive response, thoughtfully nod a lot, make little sounds that indicate that you're interested, take notes (or at least pretend to), and let them know that
you'll give it a great deal of thought. Then do exactly that; what may sound stupid at
first may be the springboard to a genuine insight.

If all of this sounds unnatural, it is. During the post-reading discussion, the playwright must become an actor. All playwrights are to some degree defensive, insecure,
and misunderstood. We are also contemplative, creative, and have a deep desire to
communicate. Let that latter part of your personality come out during a post-reading
discussion and you'll find that it'll go much more smoothly. But know that the real
notes come the next day, after the performance (by performance, we mean both
the reading and your performance during the post-reading discussion), when you
allow yourself to cool off and get a little distance. Sit down with yourself and/or the
director, dramaturg, literary manager, or a friend and go over your notes, thoughts,

and reflections. Distance (even the lapse of just one evening) will allow the best ideas to bubble to the top. This is a time when precise analysis will dominate impromptu, subjective opinions. But above all remember that positive feedback may be great for the ego, but negative feedback is needed in order to re-write.

If you attend the reading of another playwright's work and want to give notes, try to be concise as well as considerate of the playwright's intention. In other words, give notes the way you would want to get them for a play of yours. Your typical post-reading note-giver falls into one of two types: people who love to hear themselves talk and people who try to tell the playwright how they would write the play, if they had the time and talent to do so (both of which, of course, they believe they have). One thing's for sure: Post-reading discussions seldom utilize a strict critical or playwriting vocabulary. Yet, there are those rare note-givers who really make a difference. (This is you, of course.) These people give exact notes on structure and character that are followed by precise examples. Their appraisal of the script goes far beyond "I liked it" or "I didn't like it."

Instead, they often follow the ideas of the German romantic playwright, philosopher, and critic Johann Wolfgang von Goethe, who offered a simple formula for play analysis that has been used for hundreds of years. He felt that we may not like what an artist says and we may not care for her style, but these dislikes are not as important as the answers to the following critical questions: What is the artist *trying* to do? This question is often forgotten at post-play discussions. Too often people just state their own likes and dislikes without first identifying the playwright's purpose. The note-giver must try to understand the playwright's intention. What is the play trying to say? What is the playwright's goal? Without bringing your own prejudices into the equation, can you clearly identify why the playwright brought these particular characters, actions, and story into being? Then you can more helpfully address how well the artist has done it; judge the degree of success or failure the playwright has achieved in relation to her goal. Be as specific as possible. Where are the playwright's techniques, methods, and talents helping or hurting her attempt to achieve her goal? How effective was the play in fulfilling the playwright's intention? The final step is to ask if the finished play was worth the time and effort on the part of the playwright as well as the viewer: Does the play have valuable, interesting ideas or does it merely rehash old ideas with no new perception? Does the play help anyone understand life, society, or the world? If it didn't communicate to you, did it communicate to anyone else? Was the end result worth the effort? Using Goethe's methods can lead to a well-structured, clear, intelligent assessment of a play that is always useful to the playwright, particularly if your answers to these questions contain relevant examples.

IT'S GREAT, LET'S FIX IT (PLAY DEVELOPMENT)

In the last fifty years, the rise of the regional theater movement has sparked a growth in hundreds of theaters, programs, workshops, and festivals that devote themselves to new-play development. Some of the most celebrated are the Bay Area Playwrights Festival, The Mark Taper Forum's New Work Festival in Los Angeles, The Midwest Play-Labs in Minneapolis, Sundance in Utah, the National Festival of New Canadian plays at the Alberta Theatre Project and, most famous of all, the O'Neill Playwrights Conference in Connecticut. These organizations, and more than a hundred smaller ones, have profoundly influenced how plays are written. Where once playwrights took their work directly to a producer or director, who (if they liked the play) would then work with the playwright toward production, now playwrights often attend new-play development programs, where they are given—depending on the organization—everything from a series of rehearsed readings followed by note sessions to weeks of daily rehearsals with the benefit of professional and/or nationally known actors and directors. Some of the most famous and well-funded development organizations offer playwrights travel and housing expenses and even a stipend, while the poorer and smaller ones are often forced to make the playwrights pay their own way.

The intention of these new-play development programs is to help playwrights test, rewrite, and improve their play. The development process often terminates not with a production, but in a small staged reading. This is almost like a mini-production, although the actors are seldom off-book (i.e., they don't memorize their lines).

Sometimes a theater will then option a play (see Chapter 11) and consider it for a real production; but more often, after the development process is over, the playwright is free to shop her play around to other theaters, producers, and directors, noting that it was developed by such-and-such an organization. New-play development is now embedded in our theatrical culture and often celebrated. For example, Moises Kaufman's *The Laramie Project* and the Pulitzer Prize-winning play *Wit* by Margaret Edson both benefited from extensive development before they were first produced.

Developed to Death

New-play development organizations have also been a source of debate and complaint from playwrights who feel that their plays have been, as playwright Steven Dietz (author of *God's Country, Lonely Planet*) said, "developed to death." Edward Albee (*Who's Afraid of Virginia Woolf?, A Delicate Balance*) went even further when he said to *The Dramatist*: "There's a very, very good reason for [the play development process]: It is to de-ball the plays; to castrate them; to smooth down all the rough edges so they can't cut, can't hurt. It's to make them commercially tolerable to a smug audience. It's not to make plays any better." Many playwrights feel that the development process at most organizations is judged a success only if the play is changed, not necessarily improved—otherwise, what was the point of it all? As a result, playwrights who don't heavily rewrite their plays during development are sometimes labeled non-cooperative (or at least, assumed not to have gotten much out of the process).

Some playwrights feel that the only way they can succeed is to placate the actors, director, and audiences so that everyone is happy. This (which is normally the screenwriter's headache and source of so many bad movies) leads to plays that are designed by majority rather than plays that celebrate a playwright's unique voice. Lillian Hellman (*The Children's Hour*, *Little Foxes*) is reputed to have said, "Decision by democratic majority vote is a fine form of government, but it's a stinking way to create." Many playwrights feel that the development process is well-intentioned but that what we need is less development and more productions. Steven Dietz, in an often-quoted article in *American Theatre* magazine, articulated the problems with play development:

> Our playwrights have, with the adaptability of cockroaches, learned to write brilliantly to fit the form—and in today's theater, more often than not, the given form is not production, it is the staged reading. We have a wealth of these well-made plays because we have a wealth of staged-reading writers.

He went on to say,

> The demands of a full dramatic event and the text that galvanizes it will never be codified to fit a workshop and will never be reduced to fit a staged reading. We must empower our playwrights to challenge, not placate, directors. We must enable our playwrights to educate, not emulate, dramaturgs. The stage most certainly has its limits, but our writers should be grappling with the limits of production, not of development.

And,

> If we do not recognize that by using a formula to develop plays we will get formula-plays; if we settle for a theater of cause instead of a theater of effect; if we continue to treat our playwrights as trespassers who write program notes instead of prodigal sons/daughters who write plays; if we use workshops and staged readings not as a rehearsal tactic, but as a hurdle to production—if we do those things, we will get the theater we deserve. We will never get a *Hamlet*. And that will be not only our loss, but our legacy.

Okay, now that we have totally depressed you about the development process, let's look at how you can make it work for you, despite its problems—for the majority of playwrights say that their experience in play development at most theaters is positive.

WHEN IT WORKS

Before you even submit a script to a development theater or organization, you must first question if the development process is right for you and your play. Most development organizations have a statement in their listing that reads something like, "We want playwrights who have a strong interest in participating in development and who desire to share in a process of growth and discovery." In other words, if you think your script is perfect or even damn near perfect, there isn't much sense in applying to a development program, because they'll consider your writing to be a "work-in-progress" and in need of rewriting according to their own version of what works.

Once you've had a script accepted into a development program (the details on how to submit scripts to theaters, producers, agents, and development organizations are covered in the next chapter), you need two talents: first, the ability to win friends and influence people, and second, the ability to remain true to your script. As Polonius would say to Hamlet if he were a playwright, "This above all, to thine own script be true." The problem is that while these two statements may sound easy, they're often in direct conflict with each other. Playwrights have a fabled paranoia and suspicion of those who want to "improve" their script, while people who want to "improve" your script seldom give you credit for the fact that you've been working on it for a year and your closeness doesn't necessarily mean blindness.

When you enter into the development process you'll be working with actors, directors, literary managers, and dramaturgs. (Working with actors and directors is covered in Chapter 11.) The line between literary managers and dramaturgs can be fuzzy, as almost all theaters define their respective duties in a different way. Generally speaking, a literary manager is someone who supervises a theater's basic literary needs. This person will do everything from reading new scripts to helping the artistic director select scripts to preparing materials for visiting school groups to leading post-play audience discussions. A "dramaturg" is more. She is the theater's literary adviser. A dramaturg is often an expert in a particular area of theater history, literature, and/or criticism. She helps directors by assembling appropriate background materials on a given script and/or by advising directors on a particular theatrical style or historical period. She can act as a playwright when she edits or adapts old scripts. She also often helps develop new scripts by staging readings, heading playwriting contests, and helping with development workshops. (But people who call themselves literary managers will do many of the same things. As we said, it's confusing.) For our purposes here, we'll just use the word "dramaturg" to refer to the person responsible for all the aforementioned duties. The dramaturg during the development process can be (as is often the case) the director of your script or an altogether separate individual.

A good dramaturg knows that the copyright belongs to the playwright and that his job is to offer—and not demand—changes. The dramaturg should be a colleague who assists the playwright by making suggestions and giving advice, but should never be a taskmaster who treats the playwright like little more than a Hollywood writer-for-hire. In a sense, the dramaturg should be the ideal audience for the playwright.

For the playwright working with a dramaturg, the key is to make sure that the dramaturg has an understanding of your script and that his suggestions help you take your script where you, the playwright, want it to go. When it comes right down to it, as Bert Cardullo and Peter Lang say in their book, *What Is Dramaturgy?*, "The only person who can 'develop' a play is its playwright. Director, dramaturg, actors, and designers are resources for this process, but do not control it." Know that you have control, but be sure to be open to new ideas and willing to experiment and even fail. Mihaly Csikszentmihalyi in his book *Creativity* quotes Hans Bethe, winner of the Nobel Prize in physics, who says that two things are required for creativity: "One is a brain. And second is the willingness to spend long times in thinking, with a definite possibility that you come out with nothing." Don't be afraid if you spend long hours in the development process and come up with nothing. If failure is not an option, then creativity is not an option.

WHEN IT DOESN'T QUITE WORK

Unfortunately, development doesn't always work for the playwright. A noteworthy instance of play development gone wrong happened in the summer of 1986 to Clifton Campbell and his play *Emerald Tree Boa*. Campbell's script was one of three selected out of nearly 200 submitted to the Mark Taper Forum's new-play workshop. By being chosen, Campbell won five weeks of development, which included working with a professional cast of actors and a Tony Award-winning playwright/director. It was every playwright's dream but, according to a *Los Angeles Times* reporter who observed the entire process, things went wrong almost immediately. Before the first reading, the director warned Campbell, "Prepare to be violated." By the second day of development, the actors were already questioning Campbell's dialogue and improvising their own. By the end of the first week, some actors were advising the playwright to add more "sex" because "sex sells," while others were talking about what a thrill it is to be able to "duke it out with the writer." All during this process, Campbell was going home each night and rewriting in an attempt to accommodate the criticisms. Two weeks in, writing-by-committee had taken over to the point where Campbell jokingly changed the title page to read *Emerald Tree Boa: A Play by Eight People*. After five weeks of notes, experimentation, improvisation, and rewriting, the play had fourteen new scenes and was no longer about two men who are in love with the same woman, but was now about a woman who is trying to find herself in a masculine world. At the conclusion of the development process, when the play was finally given a public reading, the playwright was so embarrassed that he left the building rather than attend. After all this, the Mark Taper Forum never produced the play. For its subsequent production in Chicago, several months later, Campbell went back to his original draft and used only a small percentage of what he got from the Taper development process.

Years later, Campbell—who went on to become a successful playwright, screenwriter, producer, and Emmy-nominated television writer—reflected on what happened. He said it was a good experience and a horrible experience. "It was boot camp in a lot of ways. I came out of it alive and a lot stronger. I didn't die and, in the end, I still had my original play." Campbell's advice to playwrights about the development process:

> You've been given a very unique tool, which consists of people and personalities and creative energies that are at your disposal. The playwright's first responsibility is to take advantage of that the best he can and still remain loyal to the material. Second, the playwright's responsibility is to learn from the experience. Whether this play or the next, the playwright can carry through a lot of things that come during the development process and apply it to your work and your voice in general.

Above all, Campbell warns, don't let the development process kill your voice:

> Today, because of all the film, television, and all the forms of entertainment that are being shoved at us, if you don't have a distinct voice, you're never going to get produced. Because if an audience wants a story, they'll go to the movies, they'll read a book. Theater is not just the story you tell, it's got to be a distinctive voice.

Finally Campbell said, "Just because a theater develops a play, that doesn't mean they're going to produce it." There are two types of new-play development organizations: those that just develop new plays but never produce them (Sundance and O'Neill) and those that develop a play with the possibility of future production (the majority of development programs, including the Mark Taper Forum). But the sad fact is that new-play development seldom leads a theater to commit to a real production. It's not uncommon to find a playwright's résumé full of readings and/or development workshops, but few productions. As a result, many playwrights feel they're not writing for the stage anymore, but writing for staged readings that are no substitute for real productions. Why would theaters spend all that time and money developing new plays and then not produce them? We believe it's because development and workshop productions often dissipate the desire to do real productions. In many ways, development and rehearsal are the same thing, so once the process is over, the theater's actors, directors, and producers feel that they've already been through the process and that actually staging the play would only be repeating what they've already done. As a result, the vast majority of theaters that develop new plays do not end up producing those plays, so if you spend the development process only trying to please the director and the producing organization, hoping that you'll land yourself a full production, you'll simply turn yourself into a writer-for-hire. Worse, you'll be a writer-for-hire who does the work, but doesn't get paid. Take Clifton Campbell's advice, learn and grow from the experience, take advantage of a wonderful opportunity, but remain loyal to your play and your voice.

How to Find a Play-Development Program

You can find hundreds of play-development programs in such books and magazines as *Insight for Playwrights*, *Dramatists Sourcebook*, and The Dramatists Guild's *Resource Directory* (see Chapter 10 for more about these sources), but you can also find them by simply typing the words "new play development" into an Internet search engine. Don't put in just "play development" or you'll get a ton of extra sites on developing your child's ability to play with other children. But "new play development" will land you dozens of sites about theaters that offer development, including a lot of smaller theaters that have regular development programs (some of which might be in your area).

FERTILE GROUND

Readings and the development process are not for ego gratification. Though they can be gratifying when they go well, their primary purpose is to test and improve a script. Too often, the playwright calls a reading or workshop production a failure because the script fails. This need not be the case because, as Harold Clurman (co-founder of the Group Theatre) says in the quotation that started this chapter, "Even manure is valuable." So even if the development process doesn't go well, it can be considered a success if it can help you rewrite or, as in the case of Clifton Campbell, makes you a better writer.

9

Two Ten-Minute Student Plays
Dissected and Discussed

****

All the world's a stage, and most of us
are desperately unrehearsed.

Sean O'Casey

****

It's important for playwrights to read plays. Published, professional plays are obvious choices, but sometimes reading plays by struggling playwrights just like you can be helpful. In this chapter, we'll take a look at two student-written ten-minute plays. Both of them were good enough to win the regional American College Theater Festival Ten-Minute Play Contest. The judges for this annual contest select eight regional winners out of thousands of scripts submitted by college- and university-level playwrights across the United States. The eight finalist plays are then performed during the American College Theater Festival at the Kennedy Center for the Performing Arts in Washington, DC. There they can win various national awards. (For more on the American College Theater Festival check out their website: www.cwu.edu/~nwdc/kc/index.htm.)

Both of the following plays won their regional contests, but failed to win any of the national awards. Why? The truth is that we'll never know. The judges each had their own opinions, preferences, and prejudices. But we can study what some other professionals think of these scripts. So, after each play, we'll include short critiques written by a variety of playwriting professors, judges, playwrights and readers. When you're done reading the plays and the critics' thoughts, ask yourself with which opinions you agree or disagree and why. Also ask yourself how you might improve the scripts if they were yours to improve.

Our thanks go to the brave playwrights, Thomas Michael Campbell and Todd McCullough, who volunteered their scripts for dissection.

RESPONDENTS

KAREN L. ERICKSON began her directing career in educational theater directing more than fifty productions with teenagers and children. She then went on to work for fifteen years in many Chicago Equity and non-Equity theaters directing, producing, performing, and writing productions. Today, Karen continues to write and direct and also works with the Kennedy Center in Washington, DC, travels around the world speaking on the value of arts education, writes books on teaching drama, and teaches at Columbia College in Chicago.

JOEL MURRAY has written, directed, and acted in more than 150 stage, film, and primetime and daytime television productions, including national commercials. He is Chair of the University Division for the Southwest Theatre Association, Co-Chair of Playwriting for the MidAmerica Theatre Conference, and Vice-Chair of Playwriting for the Kennedy Center American College Theater Festival, Region VI.

GORDON REINHART has worked as a professional actor and director all across the country, including the Attic Theater in Detroit, L.A.'s Theatre 40, Northlight Theatre, the Idaho Repertory, and the Idaho Shakespeare Festival. He is the former Artistic Director of the Snowmass/Aspen Repertory Theatre.

Blind Date

A Ten-Minute Play

By

Thomas Michael Campbell

Cast of Characters

JAMES -------- a confidant, cynical man, early-30s

SALLY -------- a confidant, intelligent woman, late-20s

PLACE: A city

TIME: the present, maybe the past

SETTING: the scene takes place in front of a restaurant at night.

Blind Date

>   (JAMES enters to find SALLY
>   waiting for him)

                         JAMES
Found one.

                         SALLY
One what?

                         JAMES
A parking spot. Good one too. Right there.

                         SALLY
Oh… Great.

                         JAMES
Right… How long's the wait?

                         SALLY
Ten to twenty minutes.

                         JAMES
That's not so bad.

                         SALLY
I suppose you're right.

                         JAMES
I try to be.

                         SALLY
What?

                         JAMES
Right. I try to be right.

                         SALLY
Oh. I guess that's a good goal to have.

                         JAMES
(*beat*) You don't think that's okay?

                         SALLY
No, I do. I just don't know if I would brag about it.

                         JAMES
I'm not bragging, I'm just making a statement.

                        SALLY
Whatever.

                        JAMES
(*beat*) You don't want to be here, do you?

                        SALLY
I'm not a big fan of blind dates.

                        JAMES
I can take you back if you want.

                        SALLY
No. No, I… Do you want to go back?

                        JAMES
I really don't have anything else to do.

                        SALLY
Me neither.

                        JAMES
Then I guess we're stuck together.

                        SALLY
Yep!

                    (Long pause.)

                        JAMES
You're exactly the way Sam described you.

                        SALLY
You too. I guess that's a good thing.

                        JAMES
Very good.

                        SALLY
Are you saying that you're the kind of guy that's into
physical beauty?

                        JAMES
All guys are into physical beauty. The ones that pretend
they aren't are just using it as a ploy to get into your
pants.

                        SALLY
I'm not wearing pants.

                         JAMES
Metaphorically.

                         SALLY
My metaphorical pants?

                         JAMES
In a way.

                         SALLY
You certainly seem to think you know what you're talking
about.

                         JAMES
Maybe it's just clairvoyance.

                         SALLY
I doubt that.

                         JAMES
You're saying that I can't be a clairvoyant person?

                         SALLY
No, I'm saying that you don't have the courage to show me
that you are!

                         JAMES
Ouch. You know it's not a very nice thing to call a man a
coward.

                         SALLY
I didn't say that you were. But that doesn't mean that I
automatically think I owe you something just because you
have external genitalia.

                         JAMES
Wow…

                         SALLY
What?

                         JAMES
I just think it's great when beautiful women say words like
genitalia.

                         SALLY
You think I'm beautiful?

                    JAMES
Did I say beautiful? I meant ballsy. I should've said
ballsy.

                    SALLY
And yet you said beautiful. Freudian slip maybe?

                    JAMES
Possibly. But Freud said a lot of crazy of shit that is
pretty bogus.

                    SALLY
So you don't believe in mind over matter?

                    JAMES
I believe that the mind is supposed to enhance matter.

                    SALLY
Enhance matter?

                    JAMES
Translate what the body is feeling in a way that makes it
intellectual and easy to comprehend.

                    SALLY
It's never easy to comprehend what the body is feeling.

                    JAMES
Oh right, so that means we shouldn't even try. (*beat*) Do
you wanna dance?

                    SALLY
You want to dance. In line. With all of these people
watching us?

                    JAMES
Why do you care about what they think? Besides, I don't
really know what we're doing here if we're not willing to
take a chance.

                    SALLY
I am taking a chance.

                    JAMES
So you wanna dance?

                    SALLY
No.

                              JAMES
Well I guess that answers the chance-taking… thing.

                              SALLY
(*beat*) You know James, I'm not sure if I can really handle
you.

                              JAMES
That's all right. I'm sure you have very talented hands.

                              SALLY
Sam said you were a smooth-talker. Should I be on my guard?

                              JAMES
For what?

                              SALLY
I have a lot of experience with guys who say the right
things when they want to, but then they end up like all
the rest.

                              JAMES
All the rest?

                              SALLY
Full of shit.

                              JAMES
Well… I don't think I'm full of shit. I just like to talk.
I like words.

                              SALLY
What's your favorite word?

                              JAMES
Okay, but I don't want you to read to much into this.

                              SALLY
What is it?

                              JAMES
I'll tell you but you can't freak out.

                              SALLY
I won't.

                              JAMES
Promise?

                              SALLY
Promise.

                              JAMES
Fornication. (*beat*) I just made things weird, didn't I?

                              SALLY
Well you say your favorite word is fornication and I'm just
supposed to be okay with that?

                              JAMES
Just because it's my favorite word doesn't mean it's all I
think about.

                              SALLY
Oh come on. How stupid do I look?

                              JAMES
You don't look stupid at all but maybe, just maybe, you're
letting the meaning of the word get in the way of the fact
that it's just a fun word.

                              SALLY
Are you serious?

                              JAMES
Yeah. C'mon, say it with me. Fornication. It really is a
fun word to say. C'mon. Fornication. Just say it.

                              SALLY
For… fornication…

                              JAMES
That was weak. You have to say it like you're actually
enjoying it. Not physically. Just verbally. Fornication.

                              SALLY
Fornication.

                              JAMES
Better. Again.

                              SALLY
Fornication.

                              JAMES
Good, now you're getting it. One more time.

                              SALLY
Fornication! (*she notices somebody looking at her*) That was
loud.

                              JAMES
See, you just have to be open to other realms outside of
your own perceptions. (*beat*) So what's your favorite word?

                              SALLY
Fuck!

                    (They laugh. Long pause.)

                              JAMES
Still think I'm full of shit?

                              SALLY
I just don't want to get hurt anymore.

                              JAMES
(*beat*) I dated a girl once that thought it was funny to
make me feel stupid. She would say something and then I
would reply to it, and then she would make some sort of
half-assed attempt to make me feel shallow. But it was okay
because she always laughed about it.

                              SALLY
See… I just don't understand it, James.

                              JAMES
What do you mean?

                              SALLY
Why is there this overwhelming need for companionship when
far too often it makes the companions miserable?

                              JAMES
Well isn't it better to feel miserable when somebody is
there to be miserable with you?

                              SALLY
No. Because what's wrong with just being together?

                              JAMES
For better or worse. Till the end of time.

                              SALLY
(*beat*) I have to admit that you are like nobody I've ever
met before.

JAMES
I agree. It's like it's almost a dream.

SALLY
So I'm your dream girl.

JAMES
But then I would have to be the man of your dreams. And I
can't imagine being the man of anybody's dreams.

SALLY
Why's that?

JAMES
I have faults.

SALLY
Everyone does. It's a prerequisite of being human.

JAMES
I have a temper.

SALLY
I snore.

JAMES
I have a wart cluster on my right foot.

SALLY
I only shower every other day.

JAMES
My ass is unusually hairy.

SALLY
My boobs aren't as good as this bra makes them look.

JAMES
I have heart disease in my family.

SALLY
My family has a high case for alcoholism.

JAMES
I don't make enough money to support a family.

SALLY
I do.

                    JAMES
Why are you doing this?

                    SALLY
Doing what?

                    JAMES
This isn't supposed to be easy! It's supposed to be hard.
And irritating and frustrating and…

                    SALLY
I'm taking a chance. I thought we both were.

                    JAMES
And what if we're wrong?

                    SALLY
At least I know that I'm not playing some game.

                    JAMES
Neither am I.

                    SALLY
And we obviously connect. Right?

                    JAMES
It's weird, okay? It's like, what if this is that moment
where I'm just supposed to know that you're the one?

                    SALLY
Like the search is over?

                    JAMES
I don't think I want to keep searching.

                    SALLY
Then what do we do?

                    JAMES
I think I should kiss you.

                    SALLY
That's big.

                    JAMES
It depends on the kiss.

                    SALLY
There's no taking back a kiss if you mean it. Like
                    (continued)

> SALLY (Cont'd)
>
> electricity. It's not the potential that kills you, it's the current. (*beat*) But I will dance with you.
>
> (They slowly move together.)
>
> JAMES
>
> (*beat*) That guy is waving at you.
>
> SALLY
>
> Oh, our table must be ready. (*beat*) Shall we?
>
> JAMES
>
> I think we should.
>
> (The lights fade to black.)

The End

COMMENTS BY KAREN ERICKSON

This playwright has chosen a universal concept, "the blind date," which touches many with feelings of dread or tension. This is a worthy choice as an entry point for a play of such short duration, where you want the audience to identify quickly. There are snappy lines illuminating tension between the characters. The play comes to a final "period" and presents the director with the opportunity to build upon the manner of the exit.

This scene, however, is not yet a full-fledged play of any length. Missing are essential story and dramatic elements. First is the lack of attention to the setting. Where are these characters exactly? Why was this place chosen as the locale? Is this the best spot on earth to illuminate the tensions associated with a first date? Why?

Next is the mystery of the action in context. There had to have been a moment before the scene's introductory action because we can infer that James picked Sally up and dropped her off before parking the car. What conversation or events in the "moment before" lead to all of this hostility and bantering that seems so artificial for a first date? A context could have added verisimilitude.

Next, who are these people? Could better names have been chosen to communicate stronger identities? The character's voices are lost in the effort of the playwright to be humorous and witty. Because there is virtually no character development supporting the lines, we soon lose interest and find the conversation tedious. What do these characters want? Why can't they get it? What obstacles must be overcome?

The only obvious obstacle in the play is the wait to get a table. There is little dramatic action or character activity that might illuminate conflict or theme. To have the characters stand and simply spar at each other, doing nothing, puts a great onus on dialogue. And the dialogue here cannot sustain this play because of the missing essential elements noted above.

There is no mystery in this play, nothing to be revealed. There are no surprises. Here is a scene with no story. There was no trust in the characters to reveal their own story through events. Characters must be three-dimensional and authors must trust them to speak.

COMMENTS BY JOEL MURRAY

A playful, albeit awkward, young man and a somewhat icy young woman who have had difficulty finding love verbally duel on their blind date as they wait to be seated for dinner at a restaurant. Although much of their banter is superficial, they ultimately discover that they might tentatively make a go at a relationship, with the suggestion that it might be a long-term relationship. It seems both characters have been so damaged in past relationships that James has been driven to a devil-may-care attitude bordering on the obnoxious, and Sally has adopted the opposite approach—that of a defensive, guarded pessimist. When their façades drop around what may very loosely be called the main turning point, we find them to be vulnerable and needy; yet it stretches probability to accept them beginning any sort of meaningful relationship.

Partly because they do not share any history and partly because they have no obvious strong intentions and obstacles, there doesn't seem to be much at stake. Although she makes it clear that she doesn't care for him, she decides to stay for dinner, as neither has anything else better to do. He plays the "annoyer," while she plays the "annoyed." Although the dialogue and their relationship do escalate to something more personal, I never feel that either one must accomplish something through the other. Therefore, the conflict is limited to arbitrary, pedestrian banter. Both characters certainly have much to get off their chests, so they energetically try to top the other with callous remarks, unintentionally bad logic, and revelations of personal flaws.

Ironically, both are described as "confidant" (watch your spelling!), but neither is confident. In fact, both have low self-esteem. Sally fishes for compliments (e.g., "So I'm your dream girl") and James is self-loathing (e.g., "And I can't imagine being the man of anybody's dreams"). These vulnerable qualities might be developed in ways that might make for more of an engaging struggle, especially if done earlier in the play, as the characters might be revealed more sympathetically. This is critical, as the author seems to be telling us that there is the potential for romance in the world between disparate, desperate souls if they just keep themselves open. Yes, there is hope for all of us! A beautiful message. Thus, at the risk of sounding prescriptive, I really wanted to see James and Sally dance together slowly as the lights faded, ignoring the waiter's call for dinner, which might depict their inner need more clearly. This final image could be simple, powerful, and telling; and still allow them to be cautiously optimistic about their future together, which is a strong, sensible point the author is clearly sensitive to. However, it's getting to this final statement that is most problematic.

Due to the arbitrary nature of their dialogue, the play seems to meander almost formlessly without one character forcing the other into a "probable and necessary" outcome. I need some critical handles. I like mystery and surprise and the absence of any obvious, verbal or visual, exposition; but I am perplexed by why these characters have been brought together and what happens to force them into a complimentary relationship. I like to see and/or hear, however subtle that might be, what makes characters change. Certainly there is some dialogue alluding to their desire for romance and their subsequent disappointments, but I don't believe I know anything essential about them to care what happens to them. Perhaps that is still in the playwright's mind, and perhaps he chooses to keep it there. It's often a tough call regarding what to include and what to cut. But it does seem that they become interested in one another and tentatively hopeful about the future (e.g., "And we obviously connect. Right?") based primarily on a few rapid-fire declamations of personal flaws (e.g., "I only shower every other day.").

I always like to know what drives a playwright to write a particular piece, and what she is trying to reveal, and why she must reveal it. Perhaps if the author of this script tuned into these questions, he might become more precise and specific. Certainly there are technical aspects the author must perfect in this piece, but it might help to start from the primitive reflex that draws him to write about this subject. He should consider listening very closely to what his characters have to say and let them say it through his heart. Don't be afraid of their raw nerves, clumsiness, and desperation in place of superficiality. There are many people out there who will want to watch and listen to what he must say.

COMMENTS BY GORDON REINHART

This is a delightful play—and that is both the good news and the bad news. What's working and what is the challenge here is the same—the writer's damn cleverness!

It is working well on three levels. First, it's an effective situation because it's simple and pressurized: blind date, time limit as they wait for a table, public place, expectations of sex or rejection, etc. Second, Thomas has a good ear for dialogue—what this means specifically is that actors will want to play the scene, and this is a very good thing. Actors will intuitively know that they have a good shot at being truthful in the play. Finally, he's bleepin' funny. That whole beat about "fornication" and how to say it and then she gets to say her favorite word with deadpan simplicity—big laugh. As a side note, I appreciate how he uses the word "fuck" once and for effect. This is not a moral stance here; too often student playwrights use this language in the name of gritty reality when in the reality of the theater it becomes just another substitute for action and the impact is actually boredom.

Let's look at where the play can move: The potential for moments—events that would change the course of the action—is often squelched. The reason for this is a disease that actors and directors also suffer from—the dreaded "please don't let me be boring" syndrome. The result, though, is not an avoidance of boredom, but if not its creation, then certainly lower stakes. If we sense the playwright is not going to let us dive vertically into a moment but instead keep us on the horizontal track, it becomes easy to tune out. For example: SALLY has poked him a number of times—*I just don't know if I would brag about it.* And *I'm not a big fan of blind dates.* And *Are you saying that you're the kind of guy that's into physical beauty?* And *I'm not wearing pants.* And then, *No, I'm saying that you don't have the courage to show me that you are!* Now of course this is realistic dialogue but, dramatically they are missed opportunities. I feel these moments land on an audience as invitations to delve deeper into what is going on with her. We can see something is up; why can't he? The invitations are not, seemingly, responded to. JAMES just offers up snappy dialogue rather than stopping and dealing with her. Consequently, the beat never shifts and we stay on the horizontal track. This is a long-winded way of saying the play is a bit over-written. Ironic, huh? I suggest a little elbowroom for the actors to create some moments, sans dialogue.

Finally, I get the sense that Thomas is aware on some level that things need to shift—and so it happens with: *(beat) Do you wanna dance?* Again, I'm not saying it's not truthful, but it does keep the play on the surface of things. They do something (semi) outrageous to shift the action and bring us to the end—but, funny enough, it's actually an easier out than staying in the potential of some of those earlier moments and seeing where they might lead. In the first half, it seems the two (especially JAMES) are passing up chances to truly explore the relationship and the current situation, and then in the second half they seem to have traveled light years and now are dancing and discussing (implicitly) marriage! I understand in the ten-minute play format you have to move fast to an ending, but that doesn't necessitate an exclusively surface or sentimental treatment. The long pause after the "Fuck" is, on the other hand, very effective and does invite some non-dialogue moments.

Overall—it is a good piece of work. I suspect that if it were staged and worked a bit, the playwright would soon see what he could let go and what avenues he might explore deeper, and what he had that is working, which is quite a bit.

COMMENTS BY ROBIN RUSSIN

This is an agreeable little play, with some fun and funny interplay. However, it suffers from a number of problems. On a minor level, we find a misspelling on the first (cast of characters) page, "confidant" instead of "confident." Not a huge thing, but not good way to create a first impression.

However, there are more significant problems. For one thing, there is very little genuine conflict, even comic conflict. The characters express some small reservations about the date and about each other, but they did both show up, and both seem unwilling to leave, so there's not much tension between them. This is because their characters are too similar and the obstacles the writer has placed in their way are either nonexistent or too small. Both are attractive and witty, so what's not to like?

In fact, both sound almost exactly alike, with a back-and-forth cadence that offers little to separate them as distinct personalities. If they're basically the same person, where can the conflict come from? As for their past poor experiences, we only hear about those in the most generic terms, and neither seems overly burdened by them. And then, in the space of ten minutes—before they're even seated for dinner—they go from coy antagonism to imagining the rest of their lives together! This is an enormous leap in logic and sense for two people who have just expressed reservations about even being there in the first place. Nothing they've said or done has given us any sense that they've experienced love at first sight. They simply have acknowledged that neither finds the other loathsome. What's more, neither of them seems particularly needful of this kind of long-term commitment.

These leaps in sense are reflected in the dialogue. When James asks why he might not be clairvoyant, Sally retorts, "…you don't have the courage to show me that you are!" She doesn't know him at all, and therefore this comment comes out of left field. The banter about Freud is off the mark, as Freud was not known for insisting that mind controlled matter, unless you stretch "matter" to mean hypochondriac behavior. And James' further thought that we should try to intellectually understand our feelings goes nowhere in the context of the play. Also, when Sally asks James if she should be on her guard, this makes no sense because she's telling him she herself already has lots of experience with fast-talking time-wasters. This implies that asking him would be pointless; for one thing, if he were one, he wouldn't admit it, but in any event her professed worldliness begs the question. She also contradicts herself when, after asking why we bother with relationships, she then asks what's wrong with just being together. It's either one or the other.

One other problem stands out—there is almost no use of props, which means that the actors are given nothing to do but talk. In fact, there are only four minimal stage directions, and two of these are parentheticals. Even when the characters finally dance, it's only for a few seconds, and we're given little idea as to how this contact affects them "(They slowly move together.)" It might be more effective to shift some of their dialogue to occur while they're dancing, so their physical interaction could play off what they are saying and give some badly lacking subtext. In short, the writer simply hasn't paid any attention to his staging (what Aristotle called "spectacle"). This reinforces a sense that there isn't much more to this pair than yakking.

For a play like this to work, we must sense much stronger and differing personalities, much deeper attractions, and more compelling reservations, which can spark a satisfying conflict and resolution. Think of the characters in Jessica Goldberg's *Refuge*: Amy is a young woman abandoned by her parents, while the amiable drifter, Sam, goes from being a one-night stand for her to the one thing she can count on. Admittedly a longer play, but even in its setup there is a far greater range of character and possibility.

Forever Blue
or,
The Pregnancy Test

A Ten-Minute Play By

Todd McCullough

CAST OF CHARACTERS

NEIL, late-20s

SUSAN, late-20s early-30s

* * *

TIME:
A spring afternoon

PLACE:
A big city

SETTING:
The bedroom in Susan's apartment.
There's a bed, a nightstand, maybe a chair.
Also, the door leading to the bathroom.

Forever Blue
or,
The Pregnancy Test

> (*LIGHTS UP*. The door to the
> bathroom is closed. NEIL enters
> in gym clothes, a jacket, with a
> racquetball racquet in a duffel
> bag.)

NEIL

Hello? Honey?

SUSAN
(O.S., from bathroom)

Just a minute!

> (NEIL takes off his jacket, opens
> the bag, pulls out another pair of
> shoes, sits on the bed, and starts
> changing.)

NEIL

So I was at the gym--

SUSAN
(O.S.)

What?

NEIL

I said I was at the gym, and I ran into Ken--

SUSAN
(O.S.)

Oh yeah?

NEIL

Yeah, and he and Connie just got back from Barbados and
I guess it's really beautiful and he got a great package
deal, so I was thinking we should--

> (NEIL comes across the pregnancy test
> box on the nightstand. Pause.)

NEIL

Honey?

                    SUSAN
                    (O.S.)
Yeah?

                    NEIL
What, uh... what's this?

                    SUSAN
                    (O.S.)
What's what?

                    NEIL
This. Is this a...?

                    SUSAN
                    (O.S.)
I can't hear you, I'll be out in a second.

                    NEIL
                    (sitting on bed)
Holy shit.

                    (Long pause.)

                    NEIL
                    (knocks on the door)
Hello? What is it, a written exam?

                         (No answer. After a moment, the
                         door to the bathroom opens and Susan
                         enters. Pause.)

                    NEIL
What, um...

                    SUSAN
Do not overreact.

                    NEIL
I, uh... is this... are, um...

                    SUSAN
Oh God.

                         (Susan goes back into the bathroom,
                         closes the door.)

                    NEIL
Hey! Susan? Susan? We need to... is it blue? (*looking
at the box*) 'Cause the box says it's blue if it's... if
you're... if I'm doomed. (*pause*) You know, they should
make these so that if you're pregnant, a little skull and
                         (continued)

                              NEIL (Cont'd)
crossbones appears, you know, or maybe the words "You're
Fucked" show up in baby blue lettering, you know? (*pause*)
Hey, I'm sorry, I didn't mean to... shit. Susan? Are you
coming out?

                         SUSAN
                         (*O.S.*)
No.

                         NEIL
No? What do you mean--

                         SUSAN
                         (*O.S.*)
I mean no.

                         NEIL
So it's blue.

                         SUSAN
                         (*O.S.*)
No.

                         NEIL
So it's not blue.

                         SUSAN
                         (*O.S.*)
No.

                         NEIL
What the hell? It's not multiple-choice! You are or you
aren't! Let me see this... (*looks at the box, to Susan*)
It's 99.5 percent accurate! (*beat*) Jesus Christ! 99.5
percent?! What kind of fucked-up science is this? A woman
pisses on a stick and BAM! You're a daddy! (*pause*) Okay,
calm down, calm down. It can still be negative. (*beat*) Oh
God... you said you were late... you said you were late!
Four days! Four days late!

                         (He's about to leave when we hear the
                         sound of the toilet flushing. NOTE:
                         If a toilet flush is unavailable, skip
                         NEIL's next line and move right into
                         SUSAN's entrance.)

                         NEIL
The death knell....

                         (SUSAN enters, hands behind her
                         back.)

                    NEIL
Let me see it.

                    SUSAN
Wait. Neil. Before I, before you look at this, I think we
need to have a discussion.

                    NEIL
Discussion? There's gonna be a discussion? What is this,
pregnancy by committee? Let me see it!

                    SUSAN
Okay.

                    NEIL
No, don't. Don't let me see it. I don't wanna know. Oh
God, I'm screwed.

                    SUSAN
Screwed?

                    NEIL
Yeah. You're pregnant, aren't you? I mean Jesus, four days
late?

                    SUSAN
Sometimes women can be late.

                    NEIL
Four days?! What other signs do you need? Does the sky
have to turn red? Do mountains have to crumble? I mean
Jesus Christ, does a goddamn stork have to fly through the
window and peck my eyes out?!

                    SUSAN
It's a pregnancy test, not the apocalypse!

                    NEIL
What's the difference? They're both the end of the world
as I know it!

                    SUSAN
Well, I take it you don't wanna have kids.

                    NEIL
Hey, look, we've been dating for a while, about nine
months, ironically enough, and it's great, and I love you--

SUSAN

But.

NEIL

But I don't know if I'm prepared to be a father.

SUSAN

Neil, I'm not saying I necessarily want children either.
But if it happens, it happens, and it would be nice to know
that our love is strong enough that we could stay together.

NEIL

Love? Love?! What does love have to do with anything? We're
talking about BABIES! Love has nothing to do with babies!
It's all about, you know, it's Pampers and slobber and,
and spreading white powder on tiny asses! I can't do that!
I can't dispose of someone else's crap! I mean, I don't
even pump my own gas and all of a sudden I'm crocheting
booties?! Booties, for Christ's sake?!

SUSAN

No one's asking you to crochet booties, Neil! But we need
to talk.

NEIL

My God, how did this happen? One time. One time without
protection and all of a sudden I'm a progenitor, I'm
virile. Oh Jesus. Just let me see it, why prolong the
suspense?

SUSAN

I need to know first. I need to know if you love me. You've
said you do, but I need to know beyond any shadow of a
doubt.

NEIL

I... you know, I don't know what to say. (*pause*) I love
you, I really do, but... if that thing is blue, I... I
can't be with you. I can't do it.

(Long pause.)

And I mean, I want you to know that I won't be a deadbeat
dad, I'll support whatever you decide, I'll pay child
support--

SUSAN

Neil, you wouldn't have to pay child support. I make three
times what you do.

                    NEIL
Yeah, well, whatever, but I'm not ready for this kind of
commitment.

                    SUSAN
So you don't love me.

                         (Pause.)

                    NEIL
I really care about you a lot, but if love means becoming
a father, then I guess... I guess no. (*pause*) There are
still a lot of things I wanna do....

                              (Long pause. Susan looks ready to
                              cry, but she doesn't.)

                    SUSAN
Well, you can go do them now.

                    NEIL
What?

                    SUSAN
I'm setting you free.

                    NEIL
But what about the...?

                    SUSAN
Hmm? Oh, here.

                              (She hands him the test. Pause as he
                              looks at it.)

                    NEIL
It's not blue. Hey. Hey, it's not blue. Susan, it's not
blue! The box said that--

                    SUSAN
I know.

                    NEIL
So you're not pregnant!

                    SUSAN
I know.

                    NEIL
But that's great! That's fantastic! But wait a minute, you
were four days--

                          SUSAN
No I wasn't.

                          NEIL
But you--

                          SUSAN
Neil. I'm not pregnant. I can't be. I got my tubes tied
two years ago.

                          NEIL
Your tubes, what... You're saying you can't get--

                          SUSAN
Pregnant? Nope.

                          NEIL
And you weren't gonna tell me this?

                          SUSAN
What's the point?

                          NEIL
What's the *point*?!

                          SUSAN
Yeah? What's the point? I needed to know if you loved me,
if you wanted to be with me, and I found out. It's as
simple as that.
                   (Pause.)
                          NEIL
You...

                          SUSAN
Could we please not make this any more awful a moment than
it already is?

                          NEIL
You liar! You've lied to me for the past nine months?

                          SUSAN
And you to me.

                          NEIL
How?!

                        SUSAN
You said you were in love with me, wanted to be with me,
wanted to marry me.

                        NEIL
Look, we just talked about marriage, okay--

                        SUSAN
Oh what does it matter? What does it even matter anymore?
I lied to you, you lied to me, who cares?

                        NEIL
You went to all the trouble of buying the pregnancy test,
keeping me in agony--

                        SUSAN
Agony? You should be relieved, you won't have to crochet
any booties now. And the test? Well, $9.99 is a small price
to pay for a little peace of mind.
                    (Pause.)

                        NEIL
I don't believe this! I can't believe you! You're like
Medea minus the dragons!

                        SUSAN
You're right. It was a terrible thing to do.

                        NEIL
You're goddamn right it was!
                        (NEIL puts his jacket on, starts to
                        leave.)
                        SUSAN
I'm sorry. Please--

                        NEIL
I don't want to see you ever again.
                        (NEIL exits. Pause. SUSAN reaches
                        into her back pocket, pulls out
                        another test, this one blue.)
                        SUSAN
                        (*patting her stomach*)
Baby blue. Looks like it's just you and me.
                        (*LIGHTS OUT.*)

                        (THE END.)

COMMENTS BY KAREN ERICKSON

There is much to like about this play. First and foremost, the playwright has a story to tell and brings us into the action through his characters rather than forcing events upon us as the author. Each of the characters in this short play has a distinctive voice that communicates personality, background, and relationship. We are left wondering and eager to know more about them, which is always a desirable quality. In addition, many selections of text generate mood and *reveal* information without *telling* us. For instance, when Neil says, "…look, we've been dating for a while, about nine months, ironically enough…," this provides information on the nature of the relationship while giving the character a clever turn of thought directly related to the conflict.

The playwright has employed the use of literary (irony, foreshadowing) as well as theatrical (offstage voice, door as symbol) devices to engage the audience and create dramatic tension and suspense. The metaphorical use of the pregnancy test as "relationship test," the beginning that starts so dramatically with a discovery, and the surprise twists and turns growing logically from the conflict keeps the audience advancing to the outcome. These are all vital elements in supporting and creating dramatic action.

To heighten this work, the next draft might include more specific details that impart reflective insight overtly or subliminally. One element of story I find neglected here is the setting. A lack of details left me with many questions: Whose apartment is this? Hers? His? Theirs? What decorative elements in the apartment reveal character status, age, or values? Neil enters, so he obviously has a key, but he doesn't take anything with him at the end except his jacket. Why does he leave the bag and racquet? Entrances are important but so are exits. The abrupt exit in this play left unanswered questions that could have been easily addressed through a moment of action or the addition of selected text. The beginning also presented a wonderful opportunity to amplify and communicate more about Neil's character before he makes the play's essential discovery.

There are many unfinished moments in the play that a word, a gesture, a turn of phrase could have clarified. For example, later in the play Neil makes the statement, "I can't dispose of someone else's crap! I mean I don't even pump my own gas and all of a sudden I'm crocheting booties?!" What does this mean? It appears to be a reference to status and wealth. Does he take a limousine everywhere? Can he afford to always have his gas pumped for him by an attendant? Does he travel mainly by air? There is no previous reference to ground and connect this comment.

Lastly, what defines the relationship of these two characters? They have lived together for nine months, but must play games to communicate essential values? The moment of most distress is when Neil says, "You know, they should make these so that if you're pregnant, a little skull and crossbones appears, you know, or maybe the words 'You're Fucked' show up in baby blue lettering, you know?" Why does he shout these lines in such a manner that Susan can overhear? This seems crass and out of place for the relationship, flying in the face of verisimilitude. The revelation of Neil's character flaws are central to the play, but his overt and intense reactions make it hard to believe that Susan was this unaware of his feelings and/or would live with such a man. A more finely tuned subtle disclosure would have strengthened the play.

COMMENTS BY JOEL MURRAY

The author smartly gets the action moving quickly by setting up the main conflict with Neil's discovery of the pregnancy test on page one. Overall, there is much to recommend about this script where structure is concerned: The stakes are set up early, the conflict increases gradually and fairly consistently, and a couple of clever plot twists are spun, especially at the end, where the reader is left contemplating the what and the why of the turn of events.

Given these merits, it also seems that the script falls prey to its own cleverness. In short, the rich themes of betrayal, love, and responsibility are sacrificed for the sake of the plot and its twists. Moreover, these powerful themes are too often treated in a television sitcom manner. Humor is great in these situations if it is motivated by the circumstances, but there is too often the feeling that the author is begging for jokes for the sake of the jokes. This tends to kill momentum and suspense, as well as the characters' integrity—especially where Neil is concerned.

The characters contrast well, but I was curious about why they were together. It seems that the bar could be raised and each character could bring more of a sense of ethics and dignity to the table. Both characters are understandably upset by the play's end, but along the way, Neil comes off as callous, dimwitted, and selfish. Also, I question why he was not already anxious, as he was told that Susan was "four days late." Susan is Machiavellian, insensitive, and selfish. The characters' qualities may be engaging in another imagined world, but they don't fit here. In moments of extreme crisis, people reveal who they truly are, and hopefully that lands them on higher ground. In short, I would like to know more about Susan's plan of action, as I think I need to understand her better, if not be sympathetic with her position. She is the central character, the most intriguing and grounded of the two, and I'd like to know more about her. I don't want things spelled out, but I think it's critical here to flesh her out more. Granted, this is a short script with the potential for significant dramatic interest, and to follow any standard, linear development while fleshing the characters out thoroughly is not probable.

Briefly, I would recheck some of the formatting choices. Also, in realistic plays, it's difficult to believe characters who talk to themselves, unless it is driven by the circumstances and character need, as this often leads to stilted exposition and/or a weak attempt at humor. In addition, I'd like to see the author pick one title, as two titles weaken the strength of the issue and themes. Be bold and choose one. I think both are fine, but not on the same title page. Further, characters generally shouldn't discuss facts that they already hold to be true ("…we've been dating for a while, about nine months…"). Some of the dialogue crackles and has some very nice rhythms, but overall, I would really like to hear the characters "speak for themselves": Briefly put, I'd like to hear the author's voice. For sure this takes time, but this playwright has potential.

COMMENTS BY GORDON REINHART

Subtext does not equal lying and "dramatic" topics do not necessarily add up to drama.

This play uses the "short story" trick of a sharp reversal that shocks us. I have two problems here: One is that the playwright dips into that well about two times too often and, two, it works in prose, but (and despite the rash of films that do this trick) I don't feel it works as well with drama. In the end it seems a pretty small bang for your buck. We come to the drama with the inherent understanding that things are not as they seem. So these revelations of information is like hitting us (in this case repeatedly) over the head with what we already know—"See! You don't know everything that is going on here, HAH!" We come to the theater as detectives to a crime scene—that is the fun of it. A character can say, "I love you," but in the theater we relish it when it becomes clear they mean the opposite! If information is revealed out of a place where we have NO CHANCE to know it, then I begin to feel more like a victim of a practical joke. Practical jokes can be fun but by their nature they keep the victim in the dark. As an audience member, I hope to be a participant rather than a dupe. The characters, NEIL and SUSAN, would seem to agree with me.

                    SUSAN
        You're right. It was a terrible thing to do.

                    NEIL
        You're goddamn right it was!

The biggest problem in the relationship is not whether NEIL really loves SUSAN but the fact that the relationship is built on lies. We seem to travel from one jerk to another. In the first half, NEIL's fear of being a father, though understandable, allows us to easily dismiss him because he is aimed out the door.

He doesn't fight his fear for the sake of loving SUSAN, he bails. We sense this and can't invest in him because he's clearly about to exit! So our "money" goes to SUSAN only to find out she is a lie wrapped in a deception with sprinkles of half-truths. Where are we to put our money? NEIL is self-obsessed and has little problem with taking a hike, and SUSAN is a manipulative "Medea." It all adds up to very low stakes. I mean, do they break up? Do they stay together? As SUSAN says, "Oh what does it matter? What does it even matter anymore? I lied to you, you lied to me, who cares?"

Do people behave this way? Of course, but in the theater we need characters (however flawed) with integrity. Iago has integrity in that he is moving in one clear direction with consistency. His tactics may be varied, but his direction remains consistent, he is "true" to his action. This play has a great setup—guy comes home to find his lover in the bathroom and the box for a pregnancy test by the bed. I'm there! At the end, however, I'm left with nothing but the desire to get out of these people's lives. They lie and they are cruel—and though people are like that—I don't, as a rule, spend much time in their company. I look for drama to be more than accurate.

I'm left with a final thought: I've been pretty harsh in my response. Why is that? As teacher, I know this happens only with the most promising of students. But also, Todd's work has provoked some strong feelings in me and I'm intrigued. If only he could use his power for good instead of evil! Todd's writing is wicked. It does have power. I feel he just has a slightly skewed definition of drama. It does not mean "dramatic" topics and bad behavior—it is a thing done, an action taken and responded to with nothing withheld and something at stake, and at some level we have to give a damn.

COMMENTS BY ROBIN RUSSIN

This play does a good job of setting up the stakes of a conflict, and how two very different personalities attack the problem at hand. The characters have very distinct voices and actions, and the obstacles they face are big enough to generate a serious set of stakes. The writer has also managed a number of surprising and well-done reversals, particularly the zinger at the end. There is an effective use of the main prop as a metaphor for the relationship—though one might object that a pregnancy test is too small to be clearly made out on the stage by the audience.

The main critique might be that, although distinct from one another, the characters nonetheless lack a degree of internal consistency. NEIL is presented as smart and literate—but if he's that terrified of fatherhood, why wouldn't he have used protection? What's more, SUSAN isn't exactly blameless here, as the writer seems to want us to feel. The same question arises: Why didn't she use protection—unless she was trying to trap him into marriage? It doesn't seem the playwright's intention to portray her as a stupid or self-destructively needy woman, but she is clearly the engineer of this little psycho-drama. When NEIL accuses her of sadistically playing out a game to see how serious he is, she leads him to believe this is not the case. However, in fact it turns out that it is the case, and this game-playing makes her much less sympathetic than the play clearly intends.

Even given these problematic character issues, it's difficult to see how these two might have ended up together—particularly SUSAN with NEIL. NEIL comes across, from the very first run of dialogue after he discovers the pregnancy test, as a complete jerk: "…if I'm doomed." So what did she ever see in this guy? In trying to get to the conflict, the writer has jumped the gun. It might be more effective for NEIL to at least attempt to be a nice guy and equivocate a bit while trying to dig the results of the test out of SUSAN, and then begin to get panicky and unpleasant when she won't answer.

One might say that this play displays the problems that arise when a playwright first develops a plot and then tries to inject characters into it without really doing the homework of fully developing those characters to make sure they're the right characters for this particular plot. In a rewrite I would suggest that the writer take a step back and re-examine the characters and come up with internally consistent personalities, so that they can drive the situation with greater believability (and leave us with a clearer sense of the intended theme).

Marketing a Play

10

I'm Finished, Now What Do I Do?

Growth as a writer for the stage depends on
seeing your work on stage.

Tony Kushner

We hate to break it to you, but Broadway is dead. Critics have been saying it for years; now it's true, at least as far as new playwrights are concerned. In 1965, forty new plays opened on Broadway. In 1995, there were fewer than ten. At one point in the 2000 season, there wasn't a single recently written comedy or drama running on Broadway. Broadway is now dominated by huge corporations; as an example, Disney uses its immense, two-thousand-seat houses to promote staged versions of its children's movies. Other big houses put on retreads of proven crowd-pleasers. Recycled spectacles dominate Broadway today, not new plays. This is a real problem for new playwrights, because even the A-list playwrights whose plays used to dominate the Great White Way must now look to regional theaters. This drives B-list playwrights down to the smaller theaters and the unknown playwrights out of the picture entirely. It's a domino effect, and the loser is the beginning playwright, for few theaters are willing to take a chance on an untested play. So, if your life's goal is to be produced on Broadway, the odds are that you are out of luck, no matter how talented you are.

Now that we've depressed the hell out of you, we must say that getting your play produced by a local or regional theater is not a pipe dream. The key to success is aggressive self-promotion. Playwriting is not just an art, but a business. Even playwrights who have agents must manage and build their careers. This means that you should attend theater conferences, join several theater companies, attend readings, invite people to readings of your work, build a clientele, and keep a database of directors, actors, and producers who are willing to read your work. In this chapter, we'll look at how to get produced and win playwriting contests, with and without an agent. But first, you've finished a play: So it's time to join the Dramatists Guild.

DRAMATISTS GUILD

The Dramatists Guild of America, Inc. (DGA—not to be confused with the Directors Guild of America, which uses the same acronym), functions as the playwrights' union. It helps playwrights with contracts, royalty disputes, legal battles, government issues, and advice. The Dramatists Guild is an "open-shop" union. This means that membership is optional: You don't have to join the Guild in order to get produced (even on Broadway). Open-shop unions are not as powerful as union shops (sometimes called "closed-shop unions"), of which you must be a member as a condition of employment. For example, the Writers Guild of America (WGA), representing television writers and screenwriters, is a union shop. This means that you have to be a member of the WGA if you are going to write for any Hollywood studio or television show, who conversely have agreed to work only with WGA members. As a result, the WGA can and has called strikes and has the power to keep wages high and agreements reasonably fair. The DGA, because membership is optional, cannot call a meaningful work stoppage, so wages are generally lower. The disparity of power between these two unions is a result of how screenwriters and playwrights market their work. As the Supreme Court sees it, screenwriters are considered writers for hire—that is, they sell not only their words but their copyright. This makes screenwriters employees, and employees are allowed to form an airtight, powerful union shop. Playwrights, on the other hand, keep their copyrights and only rent their words to a theater, so they're considered part of management. Managers, in the United States, are not allowed to form closed-shop unions, so playwrights are left with a helpful and supportive—but fairly weak—guild.

The Dramatist Guild is trying to change this with a new bill that has been introduced in the U.S. Senate. Sponsored by Senators Ted Kennedy (D-Mass) and Orrin Hatch (R-Utah), The Playwrights Licensing Antitrust Initiative would give playwrights the right to bargain collectively for everything from royalties to creative control. This legislation, if enacted, would give playwrights the same power as screen and television writers, but, at this writing, no one knows if the bill will ever pass, let alone be considered by the full congress.

This doesn't mean you shouldn't join, however, for there is always strength in numbers, and the Guild offers many valuable services, publications, and workshops (although workshops are limited to major cities). The Guild's bimonthly magazine, *The Dramatist*, is packed with information and interesting interviews with theater professionals. The Guild also offers its members a toll-free hotline to answer business and legal questions and obtain advice concerning contracts and copyrights. Members can get reduced rates on theater tickets and can even purchase group-rate health insurance. There are three levels of Dramatists Guild membership: *Student* members are given full access to the DGA's services at special affordable dues. *Associate* membership is for anyone who has ever a written play (even if that play has never been produced). *Active* membership is for those playwrights who have had a major production on Broadway, off Broadway, or at a professional regional theater. Only active members are allowed to vote in DGA elections. To join, call (212) 398-9366 or visit their website: www.dramaguild.com. You can also write them at:

The Dramatists Guild
1501 Broadway Suite #701
New York, NY 10036

GETTING PRODUCED & WINNING CONTESTS WITHOUT AN AGENT

To get produced or win a contest, all you need is a great script, a contest or producer to mail it to, postage, and fortitude. It's that easy. If it's so easy, why do so many playwrights fail? Failure is often just being unlucky; however, a playwright can do certain things to improve her chances. First, never send out a play until it's ready—after you've spent months or even years of writing, rewriting, attending staged readings (see Chapter 8), and polishing to make it as good as you can possibly make it. Also, the script's format should be impeccable (see Chapter 7). Second, you'll need to find the right contest or theater for your script, so you don't waste your time mailing it to people who aren't interested in it. Third, you need to know proper mailing etiquette: how to write a cover letter and what to include with your submission. Fourth, you need determination and a thick skin.

THE RIGHT PLAYS AT THE RIGHT TIME

There are several resources to help playwrights find the right theater or contest.

Insight for Playwrights is a newsletter that you can have snail-mailed or e-mailed to you every month. Founded by Patrick Gabridge and edited by Karin Williams, *Insight for Playwrights* contains information on playwriting contests, development programs, theaters interested in new work, and articles designed to help fledgling and more experienced playwrights alike. What makes this newsletter indispensable is that it has detailed information about exactly what a given theater is looking for, making it easy for playwrights to find perfect matches for their plays. You can get *Insight for Playwrights* by writing:

Insight for Playwrights
2206 Washington St.
Merrick, NY 11566-3543

You can also subscribe at the publication's website: www.writersinsight.com. (You'll save a few bucks and a bit of the rain forest if you have the issues e-mailed to you rather than subscribing to the hard copy.)

The best book for information on contests and theaters is the *Dramatists Sourcebook*, published by Theatre Communications Group (TCG). Available at most good bookstores, Amazon.com, or at TCG's website (www.tcg.org), the *Dramatists Sourcebook* is published annually and contains more than three hundred pages of facts on agents, contests, theaters, grants, workshops, and publishing opportunities. It also has a helpful "special interests index" that lists exactly what type of play each theater is looking for (adaptations, children's, African-American, gay and lesbian, etc.). It also has a submission calendar to remind you of various contest deadlines. The *Dramatists Sourcebook* is an absolute must for all playwrights. It generally comes out in late summer.

Another great source of information is The Dramatists Guild's *Resource Directory*. Published annually, this book lists playwriting conferences and festivals as well as contests, producers, publishers, agents, attorneys, grants, and service organizations. *The Resource Directory* is not sold in stores or over the web. The only way to get it is to join the Dramatists Guild.

You might also try *Writer's Market*, published by Writers Digest Books, and the monthly magazine *The Writer*. Although these publications focus on fiction and short stories, they do occasionally list a few playwriting contests. If you've got the money, buy them; if not, just get *Insight for Playwrights*, *Dramatists Sourcebook*, and Dramatists Guild's *Resource Directory* and you'll have most of the information you need to know.

You can also find theaters and contests simply by searching the web. Type "playwriting contests" into a search engine and you'll get many hits. You can search a given city's theaters by typing in the name of the city followed by the word "theater." For example, type in "Chicago theater" and you'll find lots of theaters. (Hint: be sure to try both spellings: "theater" and "theatre.") Then investigate each theater's website. This can be time-consuming, but you just might find new and interesting theaters that are not listed in the standard publications and, as a result, are not receiving as many scripts.

To Send or Not to Send, That Is the Question

Once you've compiled a list of possible theaters and/or contests, you'll want to narrow that list by researching each theater's and each contest's likes, dislikes, and limitations. For example, it's a waste of time and money to send your brilliant comedy about four guys who abandon their wives to attend a wiener roast to a theater that's only interested in serious lesbian plays. It's also a mistake to send your mega-musical, with a cast of twenty-four and a second act that takes place on the flight deck of an aircraft carrier, to a theater that has ninety-nine seats and no wing space. Most contest and theater listings will give some indication of what they're interested in, but often you need to do more research. One way to look up information about a theater is through *Theatre Profiles* from Theatre Communications Group (TCG). This pamphlet has information about more than four hundred different theaters, including their house size, stage type, and their artistic mission statement. You can find out more about *Theatre Profiles* at TCG's website at www.tcg.org.

So how do you find a theater's website? The Dramatists Guild's *Resource Directory*, *Dramatists Sourcebook*, and *Insight for Playwrights* will (almost always) list a theater's Internet address. A theater's website may not clearly state its preferences, but the site will often list its season. If you find that a theater just produced *Guys and Dolls*, it's a safe bet that your aircraft-carrier musical will not be immediately rejected. If they've recently produced a string of light comedies, perhaps your wiener-roast play is worth trying. Another thing to check is the artistic director's bio. A theater's website will often give bios for its staff, from which you can find a pattern and know if your play is to their liking. But be warned, you'll sometimes find theaters that say one thing and do another. For example, the listing in the *Dramatists Sourcebook* may say that a theater is into "cutting edge material," yet their season consists of Neil Simon and the musical *I Do! I Do!* There is nothing to be done in these cases except give it a shot, if you've got the postage and the patience. Otherwise let that one go. There are plenty of others.

What Does the Theater Want? (Script? Query? To Be Left Alone?)

When you submit a full script, not only should it look professional and follow the proper format, it must be neat and clean. You don't want to submit a script that looks as though it's been read and rejected by a dozen other theaters. When a script is returned from a theater, check it for pencil marks, bent pages, and general appearance. If you use a spiral binder, you can improve the look of a used script by replacing the title/cover page.

Before you submit a full script to a theater, you'll also want to make sure that that theater accepts unsolicited scripts. A "solicited" script is one that the theater requests from a particular playwright; an "unsolicited" script is one that a playwright sends without first getting the theater's permission. Check the *Dramatists Sourcebook* and/ or *Insight for Playwrights*. Both will usually state which theaters accept unsolicited scripts. Or give the theater a call. If you send an unsolicited script to a theater that doesn't accept them, it will be automatically rejected (that means they won't even read it). Theaters that accept unsolicited scripts want you to include a cover letter (see below) and a self-addressed return envelope with proper postage, so that they can send the script back, along with their rejection letter. (As if the cost to the playwright isn't great enough, you must also pay for rejection.) If you don't want your script back, then state that in the cover letter. (Better yet, ask for the script to be recycled.) But you'll still want to include a small self-addressed, stamped envelope (SASE) so that you can experience the joy of reading your rejection letters.

Most theaters won't accept unsolicited scripts. They don't have the time, space, or staff to read them. Instead, they'll want a query, which includes a cover letter, a short résumé or bio, a brief plot synopsis, a dialogue sample, and a self-addressed, stamped postcard (SASP) that the theater can send back, rejecting or requesting your full script. A query is like an actor's audition, and just like auditioning, it must be done well or the theater will shout, "Next!"

YOU'VE GOT IT COVERED

Cover letters must be short and sweet. Theaters get hundreds, if not thousands, of such letters every year and they don't have time to read tomes. They want the essentials and they want them fast. Your cover letter should include a brief pitch of what your play is about and any information that might spark the particular theater's interest.

A pitch is not a deep examination or step-by-step recounting of the play, but a quick, two- or three-sentence summary designed to make the reader say, "What an interesting situation, conflict, and/or character(s)." (Well, they might not say exactly that, but you get the idea.) The pitch is in the cover letter for one reason: to get the theater to request your script. It's not meant to be literature. However, it must represent your qualities as writer—the pitch line must be interesting and show you have talent. We know a writer who had a hilarious comedy, but whose pitch was as dry as a legal brief. No one responded, because he hadn't shown in the letter that he was actually funny. But don't overdo it or hard-sell the script (or they'll think that the writer doth protest too much). We once saw a cover letter in which the playwright wrote, "This is a wonderful play, which you must read. If you're the type of producer who loves to please an audience, don't let this script go by." This not only sounded desperate, but wasted space because it said nothing about the play itself. A playwright is not a used-car salesperson. A well-written sentence or two that creates interest will do.

In Hollywood, pitching film stories is an art. Screenwriters are always pitching movie and television ideas to producers, agents, or anyone who will listen. There are even classes offered on how to pitch. Yet pitching doesn't always work well for playwrights. Can you imagine writing a two-sentence pitch of Edward Albee's *Who's*

Afraid of Virginia Woolf? "My play is about a bitter college professor and his verbally abusive wife who get their kicks by socially torturing a younger couple. They also discuss an imaginary child." Not all plays fit into a two-sentence pitch; nonetheless, you have to try. One way to write a pitch is to state who the protagonist is, what he wants, and what conflict(s) result. For example, you might write something like this: "*Jewish Sports Heroes and Texas Intellectuals* is a comedy about a daughter who comes home to Texas to confront the dogma of her sexist-egotistical-homophobic-cowboy-philosopher-father. And, if she has time, she's going to tell him that she's living with a woman, has been artificially inseminated, and intends to name the kid after him." One thing you generally want to avoid is overtly stating your play's theme or subtext at the expense of character and story. For example, "*Night Journey* is about the freedom, love, and happiness that all people desire, but so few obtain. Why? Because we spend too much time in pursuit of possessions and money." Notice that after reading this, you have no idea about the character(s) or story; what's worse, everything is described in such generalized and, therefore, meaningless terms that it's impossible for it to generate much interest. Another important distinction between the above two examples is the title. The first is intriguing and provocative. The second is soporific. So, remember, in the limited space of your written pitch, a good title becomes even more important. If you can't write a decent short pitch, it's a warning that you may not have a clean take on your story: Your play may not be clearly written, and therefore is not ready to be sent out. (For more information on pitching, read *Screenplay: Writing the Picture* by Robin Russin and William Missouri Downs.)

Also, your cover letter should include any information that might help get your script read. For example, you might mention any awards it's won or that you know someone at the theater to which you're writing, or that such-and-such respected playwright recommended that you submit it to the theater. (Only if this is true, of course—all it takes is a phone call to expose a lie.) You might also mention where it was developed, read, and/or (if the theater is interested in previously produced plays) where it has been produced. If the play has been produced and has received good reviews, throw in a few for good measure. If a theater has rejected your work before, but asked you to send your next script, mention the name of that previous script and who invited you to submit your next one. You'll also want to point out how your script fits the theater's needs or artistic mission, or that it may be perfect for the theater because it has a small cast and simple set. You might also try a little brown-nosing, saying that you've been to their theater and enjoyed their productions. (Again, do this only if its true.)

At the end of the letter you'll want to state any final bits of information. You might point out if an SASE is or is not included (because you do or don't need the script back). If you're sending a query, you'll want to mention that there is an SASP enclosed. Close by stating that you are looking forward to their reaction and leave it at that. On the following page is an example of what a cover letter might look like:

Tom O'Hock
1870 9th St.
Clarksdale, MS 10203
(***) 555-8879 • Fax # (***) 555-2197 • e-mail: Tenwilliam@aol.com

July 12, 2005

William Congreve
Artistic Director
Teatro Olimpico
389 N. Whizzer
Chicago, IL 60609

Dear Mr. Congreve:

I read in *Market Insight for Playwrights* that you are looking for new comedies.

Jewish Sports Heroes and Texas Intellectuals is about a daughter who comes home to Texas to confront the dogma of her sexist-egotistical-homophobic-cowboy-philosopher-father. And if she has time, she's going to tell him that she's living with a woman, has been artificially inseminated and intends to name the kid after him.

This play has only three characters and a simple set. It took first place out of 500 scripts at the "Festival of New Works" at the Mill Mountain Theatre in Roanoke, Virginia.

Enclosed are sample pages, a synopsis, bio, and an SASP.

Thank you for your time and consideration. I look forward to hearing from you.

Sincerely,

Tom O'Hock

Homepage: www.TomOH.com

Fig. 1

A query includes a short résumé or a bio with information about the plays you've written, where they've been produced, and awards you've won. You might also include information about your education or special writing classes you've attended. But just like with everything else in a query, your résumé or bio should be kept short and include only what is relevant. If you used to be a cardiologist but your play has nothing to do with medicine, it really won't help you to mention that bit of background; in fact, it might make you sound like a dilettante. If this is your first play and you don't have any worthwhile writing credits, don't include a résumé or bio, just let the play speak for you.

A query contains a dialogue sample, to give the theater an idea of your writing. Listings in The Dramatists Guild's *Resource Directory*, *Dramatists Sourcebook*, and *Insight for Playwrights* will usually tell you how many sample pages a theater wants to see. Most theaters request five to ten pages, though there are some that want as few as three or as many as twenty. The question is, which pages from your script should you send? Usually, it's best to include the very beginning of your play. If your play is ready to be submitted, the first five to ten pages should be a perfect sample, making the reader want to read more. If you feel that the first five to ten pages aren't that strong, then that means, more than likely, that your script is not ready to be sent out. If you do want to send a dialogue sample from later in the play, you'll need to write a brief introduction to set up the submitted scene and characters.

A brief synopsis of your play should be attached to the dialogue sample. You don't need to detail the whole plot; you simply want to whet a reader's appetite. In two or three short paragraphs tell your play's story, concentrating on character and conflict and not its theme or a philosophical statement you want it to make. Avoid generalizations. With your synopsis, you want to identify your play's genre, cast size, and staging requirements. You'll increase your chances of getting read, let alone produced, if the cast size is small and the staging requirements minimal.

Your synopsis is critical because if you don't hook the reader here, she won't read your dialogue sample, so don't whip this out at the last minute. Write several drafts and "test market" them. Have a few friends read them and critically tell you which, if any, have piqued their interest. Here's an example of what a synopsis page might look like:

A VIEW FROM THE LIGHT BOOTH
A farce by Moss Growen

CAST OF CHARACTERS

HAMNET......................The Stepson
CLAUD......................The Stepfather
SHANNON....................Assistant Stage Manager
GARRY COOPER................An Actor
PATROLMAN SHUBERT ....A Policeman

PLACE: The Wayfarer Theatre, Chicago.

SETTING: A light booth located in the balcony of this small
off-loop theatre. Unused light gels and fresnels lie about.
On the back wall is a large poster announcing The-Chicago-
Ensemble-Repertory-Group-Theatre's production of *HAMLET*; the
requisite picture of Shakespeare has been augmented with a
blurb reading, "I rolleth in my grave!" Beside the poster is
the exit, a ladder leading to the grid, and a large fire axe.
In front of the light booth runs the balcony railing.

TIME: Saturday Evening - The final performance of the season.

SYNOPSIS: A VIEW FROM THE LIGHT BOOTH is the NOISES OFF of
technical theatre. The entire play takes place in the light
booth of the Chicago-Ensemble-Repertory-Group-Theatre on the
final night of the company's questionable production of HAMLET.

The story of HAMLET is mirrored inside the light booth as
Hamnet, the technical director, comes face to face with the
new board operator, Claud, his ex-stepfather. It's not a happy
reunion; there are too many ghosts. Claud married Hamnet's
mother right after Hamnet's father died and then left her
to pursue his first love, the theatre. Claud's presence is
the last thing Hamnet wants to deal with, for he has become
disillusioned and decided that tonight will be his swan song.
He's leaving the theatre to become a dental hygienist.

As stepfather and stepson attempt to work out their troubled
relationship, they must deal with the one crisis after another
that befalls the production of HAMLET: The cast comes down with
food poisoning; Yorick's skull turns up missing; the police
want to shut them down; and worst of all, the critic from the
Chicago Tribune chooses this night to review the show. The
techies decide there is only one way to prevent disaster: The
critic must die. As they plot to kill the critic, by dropping
a fresnel on him, Hamnet and Claud learn to love each other and
theatre again. This time HAMLET has a happy ending.

Fig. 2

A reminder: You'll want to include a self-addressed stamped postcard (SASP) so that the theater can let you know if they want you to send the full script or not. SASPs can be hand-written if you have nice handwriting, but playwrights often print them. The problem with printing them is that most printers won't handle the small postcards you get at the post office, so do it yourself, using the postcard sheets available at most office supply stores that are designed to go through your printer, each sheet containing two or three punch-out postcards. (Microsoft Word has an "Envelopes and Labels" feature that makes using these sheets easy. It's located in the "Tools" menu.) Some playwrights save money by purchasing heavy paper (which is cheaper than postcard sheets) and a cutter and making their own postcards. If you do this, take the paper you plan to use to the post office to make sure it meets their thickness requirements. On the front of the postcard you'll place a stamp, address it to yourself, and give as the return address the name and address of the theater to which you're submitting your play. On the back, put a simple question, like: "Do you want to see my script?" Then place a "Yes" and "No" so they can simply circle one or the other. The front and back of your SASP should look something like this:

```
William Congreve
Artistic Director
Teatro Olimpico
389 N. Whizzer
Chicago, IL 60609
```

Stamp

```
                    Tom O'Hock
                    1870 9th St.
                    Clarksdale, MS 10203
```

Would You Like To Read A Copy Of

DEAD WHITE MALES
(A new comedy)

YES?   NO?

Fig. 3

Some playwrights like to get fancy with their postcards. This is also acceptable:

Would You Like To Read A Copy Of The Dark Comedy

"*Dead White Males* has a lot more to say about the educational system - and, by reflection, our society as a whole."
- *Orange County Register*

"a catalyst for change"
- *Las Vegas Journal*

YES?   NO?

Fig. 4

Some playwrights include in their queries a brief (notice how that word comes up again and again?) pitch of other plays they've written: Their hope is that, if the theater doesn't like their main play, it might be intrigued by another and request that script instead. Their postcards would look like this:

Would You Like To Read A Copy Of The Dark Comedy

DEAD WHITE MALES
YES?   NO?

I've enclosed a brief synopsis of several other plays I've written. Would you like to see a copy of:

_____ ALL THE THINGS I SHOULD HAVE SAID

_____ COMMA HAPPY

_____ SMALL SACRIFICES

Fig. 5

Queries can be good for both the theater and the playwright: The theater has fewer scripts to read, while the playwright saves on copying and postage. If you're sending out a lot of queries—and you should be—you'll want to keep postage costs down by playing with the number of pages you send as well as the weight of the paper you use. You might want to include only an eight-page dialogue sample instead of a ten-pager, or you might want to find 16-pound paper instead of 20-pound, thereby saving a precious ounce. This might not seem like a lot, but over time, if you're sending out hundreds of queries, postage savings can add up.

Above all, your query must be clean, well-written, and well-organized so that it can be quickly read. Just as with an actor's audition, presentation is critical. Above all, remember that the reader will judge your ability to write by your cover letter and synopsis. A poorly written query can keep a well-written script from being read.

CASTING YOUR NET (E-MAIL QUERIES)

Each year, more and more theaters accept e-mail queries. A handful of theaters have gone so far as to accept *only* e-mail queries, and reject the old-fashioned method. E-mail queries can be very helpful to a playwright because they eliminate postage, speed up the theater's response time, and save a few trees. But they can also make it easier for the theater to say "no" with a simple click. For now, however, it's best not to send an e-mail query unless you know for sure that a theater accepts them. *Insight for Playwrights*, *Dramatists Sourcebook*, and Dramatists Guild's *Resource Directory* will often tell you which theaters are open to or prefer e-mail queries. If the listing doesn't mention anything about e-mail queries, assume that that theater doesn't accept them. You don't want to tick off an artistic director by tying up his personal e-mail with your files.

An e-mail query contains the same information as the snail mail type, only you'll have no need to include a postcard. Just cut and paste your cover letter into the e-mail's body text and attach your sample of dialogue, your synopsis, and your bio. Don't use the ease and cost-efficiency of the net as an excuse to send a longer dialogue sample. If you haven't hooked them by page ten, you won't. Also, based on the possibility that either you or the recipient theater have an ancient computer or use some obsolete word-processing program, you might want to think twice before sending an attachment because the theater's computer may not be able to open it.

COMINGS AND GOINGS (SUBMISSION RECORD)

Now that you're sending out scripts and queries, you'll want to keep a careful record of whom you're sending them to. This should include the play's title, date sent, date returned, response, contact person, artistic director's name, theater's name, www address, e-mail address, phone number, and street address. You'll also want space to put detailed notes about the theater and their response. If you're pursuing your career as you need to, over a period of months and years you're going to send out hundreds of queries and scripts, so you may even want to use a database program like Microsoft Excel or Claris Filemaker to keep your submissions in order. Such programs will allow you to sort theaters into "favorites" or "avoid" lists, so when you finish your next play, you'll already know which theaters, agents, and directors to contact. It's fine, by the way, to submit your play to more than one theater or contest at a time. Well-known playwrights often have productions of a single play being staged simultaneously at different theaters around the country (or the world). Life is short, and the acceptance/rejection process is long.

THUMBS UP, THUMBS DOWN (HOW THEY EVALUATE A PLAY)

Every theater evaluates differently, and no two readers will view your play the same way. The following are examples of evaluation forms currently used by the Utah Playfest Contest and the Mill Mountain Theatre New Play Competition. Both are typical of forms used across the country. Put yourself in the reader's shoes and take the time to fill in these forms. Does your play pass the test? Would *you* recommend it?

```
                        UTAH PLAYFEST
                    READER'S RESPONSE FORM

Short Play _____    Full Length _____

Title of play _____

Name of Author _____

Name of Reader _____

Date Assigned _____    Date Due _____

Recommended for Consideration _____

Not Recommended for Consideration _____

Here is an evaluation form you may consider using in reviewing
the play you have been asked to read. Please check items that
you see as problem areas.
```

Fig. 6 (continued on next page)

Fig. 6 (continued from previous page)

THOUGHT/PREMISE:
    ____ is not clear
    ____ is too obvious, stated openly
    ____ play centers on more than one thought
    ____ characters do not suit it well
    ____ plot does not suit it well

CHARACTERS:
    ____ read like unadulterated stereotypes
    ____ do not grow or "discover" anything
    ____ are not opposed to each other
    ____ are unrealistic
    ____ do not demonstrate conflict well

LANGUAGE/DICTION:
    ____ is unrealistic (stiff/poetic)
    ____ is not suited to characters/mood
    ____ exhibits little variety among characters
    ____ some speeches are too long
    ____ lacks foreshadowing/plants

CONFLICT:
    ____ is static
    ____ no concrete objectives
    ____ is unclear/unfocused
    ____ focus of conflict changes during the play
    ____ jumps

FORMAT:
    ____ actor or stage directions
    ____ title page
    ____ character names (capitalized, "con't")
    ____ spacing (single/double)
    ____ pagination

PLOT:
    ____ has no sense of urgency
    ____ is cinematic (too much freedom with unities)
    ____ is not coherent or logical
    ____ is predictable/unoriginal (no twists)
    ____ scenes are too long/short
    ____ needs equilibrium/denouemont

PRESENTATION:
    ____ not typed or poorly typed
    ____ not neat (for example, smudges, correction by hand)
    ____ typos, misspellings, bad grammar
    ____ improperly stapled or bound
    ____ length of play (too short/long)

COMMENTS:

MILL MOUNTAIN THEATRE NEW PLAY COMPETITION

Reader Critique Report (Page 1)

Recommend to selection committee YES NO
Appropriate idea/treatment for MMT? YES NO
Ready "to go" YES NO
Good idea but needs work YES NO
TITLE _____
AUTHOR _____
ADDRESS _____
TELEPHONE NO. _____
History of Play _____

_____
Agent _____
Address _____
Phone _____
Rights _____

Play number _____
Date Processed _____
Reader _____
On a scale of 1-10 what
is your rank of this play?

_____
Received _____
SASE: YES NO
PC YES NO
Returned _____
Standard refusal YES NO
Other _____
Forwarded to judges _____
NOTES:_____
_____

Type of play:

Farce	Sitcom	Melodrama	Satire
Tragedy	Musical	Religious	Drama
Memory	Monologue	Pseudo-Historical	Historical

No. of Acts _____ Pages _____ Historical Period _____

No. of Women _____ Ages _____ No. of Men _____ Ages _____

Special Characteristics _____

Costumes:

Many	Few	Pull	Designer	Simple
Construct	Rent	Street Wear	Transformational	Possible Period

Setting: _____

No. of Scene Changes _____

I did (or did not) like this play. State opinions and give
concrete examples.

_____

_____

In general the characters are:

Stereotype	Prototype	Unbelievable	Unusual	Interesting
Well-Developed	Undefined	Flat	Biographical	

Fig. 7 (continued on next page)

Fig. 7 (continued from previous page)

MILL MOUNTAIN THEATRE NEW PLAY COMPETITION
Reader Critique Report (Page 2)

On a scale of 1-10, does this play have

Astonishment (immediate interest)	1 2 3 4 5 6 7 8 9 10
Suspense	1 2 3 4 5 6 7 8 9 10
Satisfaction	1 2 3 4 5 6 7 8 9 10
Conflict	1 2 3 4 5 6 7 8 9 10
Counterconflict	1 2 3 4 5 6 7 8 9 10
Do I believe?	1 2 3 4 5 6 7 8 9 10
Do I care?	1 2 3 4 5 6 7 8 9 10
Am I interested?	1 2 3 4 5 6 7 8 9 10

Main Idea or Theme (Author's Intent) _____

_____

Imagery _____

_____

Plot line _____

_____

Is there a permanent change in one or more characters? _____

_____

What is unusual about this play (different?) _____

_____

What is exceptionally good about this play? _____

_____

What is exceptionally poor about this play? _____

_____

I feel that this play would be sent to the selection committee
because? _____

I feel that this play needs further work because? _____

_____

I feel this play is worth the extra work because? _____

_____

Printed with permission of the Mill Mountain Theatre
Copyright Mill Mountain Theatre

SCORE! (INCREASE YOUR CHANCES)

Like everyone else, readers, producers, dramaturgs, and artistic directors play favorites. When a pile of scripts comes in, they'll first read the scripts that come from hot agents. Next, they'll read the scripts that come from less-than-hot agents (we'll cover how to get at least an uncomfortably warm agent later in this chapter), followed by scripts that have been recommended by a friend of the artistic director and those written by playwrights whose work they know. First-time scripts by unknown playwrights will be read dead last. Everything is stacked against you—the unknown playwright—so don't do anything to make a bad situation worse. (For a lively example of life from the reader's point of view, check out Appendix A.)

Linda Eisenstein, an award-winning playwright who for a decade was the director of the Cleveland Public Theatre's Festival of New Plays, came up with this list of *Seventeen Surefire Ways to Get Your Script Rejected* (which we reprint with her permission):

> 1) Write a play with nothing but unpleasant characters. This is an age of antiheroes, after all. Make sure no one is onstage whom an audience could possibly like or want to spend time with. If audience members wanted to be comfortable or happy, they should have stayed home.
>
> 2) Choose a topic that you think is marketable but you don't really care much about; after all, a playwright should be able to crank out something mildly entertaining without a strong point of view. Something like an episode of your favorite sitcom should go over well, don't you think?
>
> 3) Write a play that requires a realistic set change every three or four minutes. Or that has at least two or three insurmountable props, perhaps a driveable car that goes on- and off-stage. Or lots of cool special effects. If *Miss Saigon* can have a helicopter that hovers and lands onstage, why can't you?
>
> 4) Don't include a cast list at the front with the names and number of characters; after all, you wouldn't want the theater to be intimidated by the cast size right away. Let them discover the vast army of characters by reading the play. Make sure to include plenty of characters that have only one or two lines. After all, actors need work.
>
> 5) Don't number the pages, either. Let the theater guess how long it'll take by hefting it. Anyway, 160 pages isn't all THAT long, is it? Especially when the play is in five acts and twenty-three scenes.
>
> 6) Leave the pages loose or stuck together with a paper clip that easily falls off. (This is especially effective when you've been diligent about Rule 5 above.)

7) While you're at it, invent your own play format; the one from Samuel French or *Dramatists Sourcebook* is sure to be too confining. Be creative with your spelling and grammar, too. All of this will show an irrepressible, original mind at work.

8) Open your play with several pages of stage directions, in long, impenetrable blocks. Describe the sets and furnishings in such numbing detail that the set designer will know exactly where to buy the priceless antiques you need for scrupulous authenticity.

9) Make sure that the first ten or fifteen pages are nothing but exposition or trivia by minor characters. Most audiences don't settle in or stop rustling their programs until fifteen minutes into the play. Don't give them anything meaty until their bottoms have conformed to their chairs.

10) Put in lots of stage directions for every speech, indicating exactly how you think an actor should say the line. Example:

JANE
(*coyly*)

No.

JOHN
(*very angry, but holding it in*)

Why not?

JANE
(*flirting more hesitantly now*)

Because.

JOHN
(*swept away with passion*)

All right, then.

11) Be sure to include at least one three-page monologue, per character in every scene. And do keep all the characters onstage whether they have anything to do or say in the scene or not; after all, the actors need to practice concentrating on listening intently for a half hour without dialogue or stage business.

12) Make the dialogue as generic as possible. You might, for instance, write an absurdist play where all the characters are named MAN and WOMAN 1, 2, 3, and so on, and they all spout general philosophical abstractions until it's hard to tell their characters and dialogue apart. That way your play will be intellectually deep and universal, and everyone will be able to identify with it.

13) Alternatively, base your play on your own life, particularly your frustrations and how no one understands and appreciates you. Don't change ANYTHING; people need to experience unvarnished reality.

14) Print your script on a dot-matrix printer in which you haven't changed the ribbon in years. Use a "creative" font, such as all italics or cursive. Then photocopy it on the lightest possible setting to conserve toner. Even better, write your script in longhand. Anything to make it stand out from all the others.

15) Send your script to every theater you ever heard of. Don't bother finding out what kinds of plays they usually do; they're bound to love your masterpiece, no matter what. After all, everyone, from a radical experimental company to a Shakespeare festival to a community theater that only does musicals, NEEDS to experience your gripping fifty-three-character historical play about Civil War amputees.

16) Diligently follow up by calling the theater every week or so until you're sure your script has been received and read. That way the staff will be sure to remember your name.

17) Leave your address and phone number off your script, and don't include an SASE (self-addressed stamped envelope, manuscript-sized) for return of your script either. That way, you'll never have to face rejection—because the theater won't be able to find you.

SKIN-THICKENERS (FOLLOWING UP, REJECTIONS, AND HALF-REJECTIONS)

You send a script or query to a theater and you wait, and you wait, and you wait. How long should you wait? If a theater asked you to send them a script (i.e., you first sent them a query and they asked you to send the script), it's acceptable to make a polite follow-up phone call (or letter) after getting no response for two months. On the other hand, it's wrong to call or write a theater if they haven't responded to your query—other than to find out if they received it; it's possible it got mislaid among the many letters they've received. If they did receive your query but don't respond to it, take their silence as a rejection. A follow-up phone call (or letter) won't help and will more than likely do harm. You'll be shocked at the number of query postcards that are never returned. At least fifty percent will disappear into the great space/time continuum never to be seen again. This is because all theaters are understaffed and they get hundreds of queries every year. The United States is near the bottom of major industrialized countries when it comes to funding for the arts, so don't expect any theater, no matter how famous, to have bays full of eager readers opening queries and reading scripts. The process takes time. Lots of time. And stuff gets lost or falls between the cracks.

If—hoorah!—you do get a "yes" to a query, send your script as soon as possible. Include a brief cover letter reminding them of their invitation to send your script and thanking them for taking the time to read it. You might want to put the words "Requested Material" in block letters on the envelope. This lets whoever is handling the theater's mail know that your script is actually one they *want* to see. Also be sure to toss in an SASE so they can send back a rejection letter, if your play doesn't pass go.

Rejection letters differ little from one theater or contest to the next. Most are short form-letters that seldom state why your script was rejected. The standard line is some variation of, "Your play isn't right for our theater at this time." Needless to say, this doesn't give a playwright much to go on. It's tempting to call a theater and ask for an explanation, but this will only burn bridges. Theaters get so many scripts, they won't remember yours, let alone why they rejected it. One way of getting feedback without the reader knowing is using glue: place a pin-drop of glue on certain pages (for example, pages 5, 10, 25, and 50). Place it close to the binding where it won't interfere. When the reader opens to that particular page, the tiny drop of glue breaks. Later, when the script is returned, the playwright can quickly see if the glue is broken. If it is, the writer knows that the reader made it at least that far into the script. If not, she knows the reader became bored and stopped reading. This way you'll at least get an idea of where you lost the reader. You'll also discover that quite a few scripts are returned unread. Some theaters get so backlogged that they simply have to return whole piles of *requested* scripts without consideration. We know of a theater that rejected a six-foot-high stack of plays simply to make room for a new office copier. This is nothing but a waste of the playwright's time and money, but it happens. Gluing pages will let you know if a theater has such a practice, so you can avoid sending it your next effort.

Occasionally, a theater will send a half-rejection letter in which they say that they aren't interested in this particular script, but they are interested in your writing and would like you to send your next script. Take this very seriously. Theaters don't invite you to send another script unless they're seriously interested. If you have another play, send it immediately; if not, send a thank you letter, make a note of their response in your submission record, and, as soon as you have a new script, send it off with a letter reminding them of who you are, the title of the script you wrote that they liked before, and who invited you to send your new script.

MAKING FRIENDS AND INFLUENCING THEATERS (NETWORKING AND SELF-PROMOTION)

Networking is more than schmoozing, it's the art of meeting people and being in the right place at the right time. If you're in a big city that's home to lots of theaters, attend opening-night parties, join a theater company, volunteer at a theater, attend workshops sponsored by local theaters, and, if a theater is doing a reading of a new play, be there. Be courteous, but be dogged. Do whatever it takes to get your name out there. Name-recognition is important. Artistic directors, readers, producers, and agents are far more willing to consider scripts written by people they've heard of or met than the stacks by "unknowns" that arrive daily.

You should always be ready to verbally pitch your play should the situation arise. Hollywood screenwriters are experts at the art of the quick verbal pitch, and playwrights should be too. This isn't to say that you should go to theater parties and do nothing but pitch your plays, but if the conversation comes around to playwriting and you're talking to someone who can help get your play produced, there's nothing wrong with saying, "I'm working on a new play. It's about..."

Among the newer ways to help get your name out there is with a webpage. Your playwright's webpage should include your contact information, bio, and/or résumé. You might also include information about your upcoming productions as well as synopses and sample pages of your scripts. This is a business site, so leave off those pictures of your beloved pet and your family vacation to Dollywood. When you send out your query letters, be sure to include your www address and invite the reader to look you up.

NECESSARY EVILS (GETTING AN AGENT)

"What's the difference between a bantam rooster and an agent? A rooster clucks defiance..." The relationship between writers and their agents has always been a difficult one. Agents are notorious for not paying attention to writers they represent—unless, of course, that writer has a script they think they can make money from. It's a fact of life and you should know it up front—agents are salespeople. They're interested in making money—period. In playwriting, this can be a real problem, because, unfortunately, there's so little money to be made.

Beginning writers often concentrate too much energy on trying to find an agent. If you're just starting out, you don't need an agent and probably couldn't get one even if you tried. When it comes right down to it, most playwrights don't have and don't need agents. Unlike Hollywood movie producers, the vast majority of theater producers and artistic directors will accept scripts submitted directly from the writer. Only about ten percent of all theaters demand agented submissions. Add to this the fact that The Dramatists Guild will help beginners (if they're members) with contracts, and it's easy to see why most beginning (and intermediate) playwrights do not have agents. So, if you're just starting out, instead of pursuing an agent, spend your time writing great plays, winning a few contests, and getting a few productions under your belt—then agents will take notice and pursue you. As a matter of fact, most agents won't look at your work *unless* you've won an important playwriting competition or are a graduate of a major MFA playwriting program.

After you have won an important playwriting contest and have a few successful productions under your belt, the easiest way to get an agent is by referral from a director, a writer, or a producer who loves your writing and is willing to recommend you to their agent or a friend who just happens to be an agent. This is why networking is so important; you need people like this to know your work. If you can't get a referral, you're going to have to do it the hard way. Start by getting an up-to-date list of agents. You want a *playwriting agent*, and most screenwriting and television agents aren't interested in playwrights. You can find lists of playwriting agents in the *Dramatists Sourcebook* and The Dramatists Guild's *Resource Directory*.

Contact an agent the same way you look for a production: by sending a query with cover letter, résumé, synopsis, dialogue sample, and a self-addressed, stamped envelope or postcard. Your letter should concisely state something about you and your play. Don't be too formal; you can let them know you're human and perhaps have a sense of humor. Any information on awards, productions, and reviews should be included in a short résumé. If you have no awards and few productions, then you aren't ready for an agent. Never send a full script to any agent or agency before they've requested it. Be warned: Some agents don't even want a query, all they want is a letter telling them about your play, awards, and reviews. The only way to know whether an agent wants a query or a letter is to call the agency and ask the office assistant.

With agents, simultaneous submissions are perfectly acceptable. In other words, you can mail queries and/or letters to a handful of agents at a time. If they fail to respond, take that as a rejection. If you've written a good letter and your synopsis and dialogue are excellent, perhaps one or two agents will request your script. After sending the script, if you haven't received a response in a few months, it's perfectly acceptable to call. More than likely, you'll speak with the office assistant. Be polite. Assistants have been known to help polite beginning playwrights. They can move your script to the top of the reading pile or remind the agent about you.

If an agent asks you to sign, it's time to do your homework. Call The Dramatists Guild, ask around, try to find as much information about that agent as possible. What's his reputation? Is she respected? Ask the agent who else she represents. Any big names? What successes has she had? When you decide to sign with an agent, be sure to read her contract carefully. A playwriting agent's standard fee is ten percent (though some may take as much as twenty percent for amateur productions). Larger agencies will copy your script for you, smaller ones will ask you to send them copies. If your agent answers her own phone, you know you're with a small operation. There's nothing wrong with that. A small agent is better than no agent. Make sure the agent wants to represent you as a playwright and doesn't just want to represent one or two plays you've written. Finally, never sign with an agent who demands an up-front fee. Some unscrupulous agents have been known to ask for a "signing fee" with the promise to refund the money when the script is produced. This is a scam. Agents get paid only when they succeed in getting you a production: In other words, after you get paid.

REJECTION DEJECTION

Rejection is part of a playwright's job description. One reader will call you brilliant; the next will label you an amateur. You have to learn to deal with it and keep going. Set a goal: Enter one contest a week or send a query to two theaters a week or whatever your budget and time will allow. If you win one contest for every fifty you enter, if one out of every ten returning SASPs asks you to send a script, you're doing well. And remember, even if you get an agent, it's your career, so it's still up to you to promote it.

11

Getting Real:
Production and Contracts

****

To be a playwright you not only have to be a writer,
you have to be an alligator... a playwright lives in an occupied country.
He's the enemy. And if you can't live that way, you don't stay.

Arthur Miller

****

In his excellent book, *Mis-Directing the Play*, Terry McCabe cites an oft-repeated director's witticism: "From now on, I'm working only with dead playwrights." He goes on to point out that playwrights don't have an equally good witticism about directors. We would like to correct this oversight. Here goes: "From now on, any director who doesn't work to understand, appreciate, and remain faithful to our play is going to be dead." (Okay, that may not be entirely ethical, or even witty, but it does express the general frustration most playwrights feel during a production. Besides, we're writers, we can rewrite.)

Todd London, the artist director of New Dramatists Theatre, said to *The Dramatist* magazine, "Two things I know: (1) For writers to understand a theater's community, they must be made part of it; and (2) the fusion of individual talent and collective energy fuels great theater. Twenty-five hundred years of theater history tells us this, but too few have been listening." Staging a play depends on collaboration—yet collaboration is often a playwright's downfall. In their lonely, painful, solo struggle with the page (or computer screen), playwrights seldom learn the techniques needed to participate in an ensemble. In short, they're lousy socializers. And most members of the ensemble (actors, designers, and the director) aren't used to having the playwright's input. Let's face it, the playwright is the only member of the ensemble who can be dead—and, in most productions, who is. In fact, most members of the ensemble prefer it that way. Dead playwrights don't mind being paraphrased, edited, and rewritten; they aren't judgmental, and (if they've been dead long enough) they don't even demand payment. (For more information on copyright laws, see Chapter 8.)

In today's theater, living playwrights too often are treated as if they were dead, or at least not quite living. Their copyright is ignored, their requirements forgotten, and their hard work unappreciated, when the playwright has most likely lavished more time (and perhaps more creativity) on the finished product than all the rest of the team—actors, designers, and director—combined. The playwright, however, is always the "primary artist," so-called because she conceives the original idea, creates the characters, and builds the story. The rest of the team (directors, actors, and designers) are secondary or "interpretive artists" because they take the playwright's original thoughts, characters, and story and show the audience what they think the playwright's creation looks and sounds like. This chapter, then, is about how to navigate this transition from the primary to the interpretive side of the theater, the processes that happen after the playwright leaves the confines of his lonely study and enters the world of interpretive artists; for no matter how significant the playwright's contribution, the play is not complete without the work of the full ensemble.

First of all, a playwright needs to understand the chain of command within the theater ensemble and how to participate. In turn, the ensemble must accept and encourage the playwright's participation. To make this happen, the playwright walks a tightrope: She must make sure her voice is heard while stepping on as few creative toes as possible. And all creative people have gigantic toes. As playwright Robert Anderson (author of *Tea and Sympathy* and *I Never Sang for My Father*) said, "When I taught playwriting, I told my students that half the job was learning how to write a play; half was learning how to get along with other people." One way to make sure you can all get along is to start out with a written contract.

THE DOTTED LINE (LEGAL PROTECTIONS)

Never allow your play to be produced on a handshake. (Or even an air-kiss.) No matter who's producing it—a close friend, a college buddy, or your mother—always demand a written contract. We're not going to spend much time on this, however, because there's already a great reference book on the subject: *Stage Writers Handbook* (published by Theatre Communications Group) is a complete business guide for playwrights (as well as composers, lyricists, and librettists). Written by Dana Singer, a lawyer and the former executive director of The Dramatists Guild, this book gives exhaustive information on contracts, copyrights, author's rights, underlying rights, and much, much more. Every playwright, from first-timer to seasoned professional, should own this invaluable book. Having said this, here are some useful bits of basic information on contracts, options, subsidiary rights, and royalties.

THE TIE THAT BINDS (CONTRACTS)

Beginning playwrights who don't have agents often think they have to negotiate their own contracts or hire an expensive lawyer. This is not the case. The Dramatists Guild has dozens of pre-approved standard contracts that cover all the bases. These contracts are available to members for a nominal charge. (To join The Dramatists Guild, see Chapter 10.) The Guild has contracts for small theaters and showcase productions, as well as for major professional productions and collaborations. Should you encounter any problems, the Guild also has lawyers who will answer your questions at no extra charge.

A standard contract lists the number of performances, the production dates, and also has detailed information on the author's rights, billing credits, subsidiary rights, and royalties.

GETTING PAID (ROYALTIES)

Hundreds of years ago, plays were bought outright. This is no longer the case. Playwrights never give up their rights or control of their scripts; they now rent them. That rental fee is the royalty, which can be either a share of the proceeds or a set fee paid to the playwright for the right to perform her play. Royalties can vary widely from one type of theater to the next. The smallest productions (colleges, high schools, and community theaters) often pay the playwright a small set fee for each performance (fifty to one hundred dollars is not uncommon—but for up-to-date figures contact The Dramatists Guild). With larger, professional productions, the playwright's royalty is often a percentage of gross. Gross means the total amount of money the theater takes in at the box office *before* paying its bills or actors or anyone else. Therefore, writers are in first position for payment. Five to ten percent of gross is not an uncommon royalty. Occasionally, the producer will offer the writer a flat dollar amount. This allows the writer to be paid per performance, per week, or per run of the show and not have to gamble on the box-office receipts.

AUTHOR'S RIGHTS

The contract should state the playwright's rights. This includes an acknowledgment that the playwright is the exclusive owner of the copyright; that changes, alterations, and/or omissions to the script cannot be done without the playwright's approval; and that any revisions that are made become the sole property of the playwright. The contact should also state that no one involved with the production (director, producer, or other person) can make any claim of co-authorship. It may also contain the provision that the playwright is willing to work with the producers or director to rewrite the script (all new scripts are rewritten during rehearsals), but there should be no statement requiring the playwright to make changes demanded by the director or producer. In other words, a clause that states that the playwright is *willing* to make revisions is acceptable, but not that the playwright *has* to do so. The contract should also have a clause that states that the playwright has the right to attend rehearsals and approve the director and casting. Even if you're not going to attend rehearsals, the contract should give you the right to participate. Finally, the contract should state that the playwright's name must be prominently placed above the director's name in all advertisements. (This is the exact opposite of movie credits, for which the director's name is given the most prominent position.) For more on author's rights, be sure to pick up a copy of *Stage Writers Handbook* (see above), which has a detailed chapter on production contracts. Or you can check with a copyright or entertainment lawyer and/or use an approved contract from The Dramatists Guild.

Subsidiary Rights

If a professional theater company is staging your play's world premiere, they may ask for subsidiary rights. This means that they want to have legal claims that continue well after the production has ended. Sometimes their demands are simple. For example, a theater might include in the contract a clause requiring that all future productions must have an announcement in the program stating that the play was originally produced by their organization. This is a sort of free plug for them. Other theaters or producers may also want a percentage of the profits should your play be produced again. That's right, they want a royalty paid to *them* every time your play is produced. This is common but also very complicated. If a theater has such a clause in its contract, be sure to check with your agent (if you have one), The Dramatists Guild, and a lawyer before you sign. Such a payment may be worthwhile if the theater is prestigious and will likely assure your play being reviewed by important critics. It may not, if all it will mean in the future is an ongoing bookkeeping headache.

Options

Occasionally a producer or a theater will want to option your play. There are two types of options: exclusive and nonexclusive.

An exclusive option gives that producer or theater sole rights to produce your play for a given length of time (usually a few months, perhaps a year). A playwright who grants a theater an exclusive option is agreeing not to allow any other theater to produce the play for that set period of time. In return, the writer receives an advance payment as insurance that the production will take place, due regardless of what profits the theater may or may not make from the production. If the set option period expires and the theater or producer hasn't staged the play, the playwright keeps the money and is free to market the script elsewhere. The payment to the playwright may be small if the option is for a short period, or much larger if the option time is longer. To get a ballpark figure of how much money should change hands, call The Dramatists Guild. If the producer or theater does produce your play during the option period, the advance payment is sometimes an advance against the playwright's royalties (not always, though) and is deducted from them.

A nonexclusive option does not grant the theater or producer sole rights to the script. For example, a nonexclusive option may cover only one city or geographic area for a set amount of time.

If you are offered an option, treat it just like any other contract; seek advice from your agent, lawyer, The Dramatists Guild, or *Stage Writers Handbook* (or all four). Don't allow a theater or producer to sweet-talk you into optioning your play without some sort of payment. Demand payment, demand a contract that states the length of the option, exact effective dates, how much money you'll be paid up front, and how much your royalties will be once they produce your play.

Contract Hell

Many years ago when I (Bill) was just starting out, I was visiting New York City when a friend from graduate school told me that he wanted to do an Equity-waiver production of my first play. (Equity-waiver meant it was a small enough theater that he didn't have to pay union wages to the actors.) He met me at a restaurant on the East Side and hauled out a contract: seven pages of single-spaced legalese. To be honest, I didn't know better, so I didn't think anything of it when the contract stated that he, the producer, was going to get sixty percent of the royalties for the next five years. It also stated that he owned the rights to any television or movie version for the next ten years. In return, he promised me twelve performances of the play somewhere in one of New York's many small black-box theaters sometime within the next two years, but the contract also stated that, if for some reason he failed to fulfill his side of the bargain, the contract would still be valid. My option fee for all this was to be twenty-five dollars. He told me, "It's a tough contract, but if you want to be produced in New York, you really have to give up any rights the first time around." Not exactly sweet talk...

He hauled out a pen for me to sign. I stalled. I suspected something was wrong when I had to pay for my own lunch. After the meeting, I walked over to the Dramatists Guild and dropped off a copy for the legal department to review. When I arrived home, the phone was ringing. It was the president of the Guild. He didn't even say hello, but shouted, "Have you signed this contract?" I told him I hadn't. "Thank God," he said. "This is the worst contract I have ever seen. I'm thinking of asking Stephen Sondheim to write music for it so I can sing it at our annual Christmas party." In the end, I called my "friend" and told him no deal. I lost a friend (or someone I'd thought was a friend), but gained self-respect. Never be so desperate for production that you're willing to sell your soul. Stand up for your rights, get paid, and always check with your agent, a lawyer, or The Dramatists Guild before you sign. And, above all else, educate yourself; get a copy of Dana Singer's *Stage Writers Handbook* and read it cover to cover.

GROUP DYNAMICS (THE ENSEMBLE)

Once you've got your contract, you're ready to become a member of the ensemble. A theater's ensemble can be divided into four categories: producing/administration, creative, construction, and production. Producing/administration include accountants, box-office staff, secretaries, fund-raisers, publicity managers, grant writers, artistic directors, and producers who run the business aspects of any theater. The creative side includes the director, actors, designers, and, to some extent, the artistic directors, and producer(s) who stage the production. The construction crew includes the technical director(s) and crew chief(s) who supervise a company of seamstresses, contractors, and laborers who hang the lights, build the sets, fabricate the props, and stitch the costumes. The production team includes stage manager(s), house manager(s), and ushers, as well as the light, set, and costume crews who work behind the scenes during a play. (Fig. 1 is a chart showing the chain of command for these various groups.) At larger theaters, all these jobs are divided among numerous artists, administrators, and laborers. At smaller theaters, there's quite a bit of doubling up. For example, the set designer will also be technical director and even perhaps part of the set construction crew; the costume designer may also be the seamstress, while the producer might also be artistic director. Playwrights generally deal with only a small part of this ensemble. Here are the parts the playwright deals with the most:

Producer - The producer can be an individual or individuals who put up their own money to finance a production, an individual who controls an investor's money, and/or an individual in charge of an institution, university, community organization, or theater company. In short, the producer is the one who controls the business side of the production, and is the one with whom you will negotiate your contract. Because the producer controls the money, he often wants a say in the creative process and will give the playwright and director suggestions on how to improve the script and production. If a producer's suggestions are good, by all means take them. If the suggestions are worthless, feign great interest until the producer has left the room, and then get down to business.

Artistic Director - Most theater companies have an artistic director who is in charge of the overall vision or goal of the company. The artistic director will often choose which plays are to be produced, as well as which directors will direct. Even with all this power, the artistic director does not have the right to force a particular director on a playwright without the playwright's permission (see more below). A director is in charge of a single play, while an artistic director is in charge of an entire season of plays. At smaller theaters, the artistic director and producer are often the same person. (This person may also be the dramaturg.) If you have a problem with your director, see the artistic director.

Director - The director, of course, is the one who directs the play. She can be a permanent member of the theater company or hired to direct a particular play. The director is the primary member of the ensemble as far as a playwright is concerned. (We'll talk about the director in detail below.)

Stage Manager - Sometimes called the S.M., this person is responsible for everything from scheduling rehearsals and rehearsal spaces to assisting casting and enforcing discipline. The stage manager also conducts technical rehearsals, keeps the prompt book, takes rehearsal reports, authorizes the opening of the house to let the audience in, authorizes when an understudy goes on, and calls brush-up rehearsals. The assistant stage manager (A.S.M.) is often responsible for smaller things, like getting coffee. If you want to know where and when a rehearsal is scheduled, are having problems finding parking, or need to tell someone that you are going to be late for rehearsal, call the stage manager.

Dramaturg – Most large theaters and university theaters have someone who fulfills the responsibilities of the dramaturg, although in smaller theaters these tasks may be divided between the other members of the production staff. Generally speaking, the dramaturg's job is to provide information to the rest of the cast and crew with a play's history, context, and special demands. This includes writing a textual analysis of the play; researching the play's history of any prior productions; providing the director with notes on the play's language and/or issues of poetic meter; and writing introductory materials for the play's program. The dramaturg usually attends rehearsals and provides general collaboration with the director, producer, and actors. He may also be involved in marketing and advertising the production.

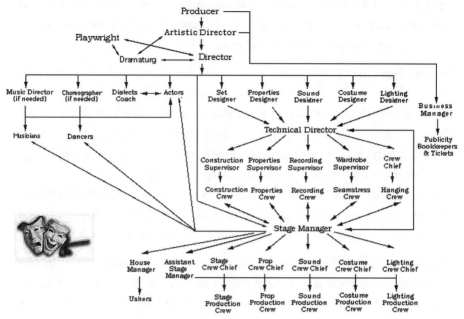

Fig. 1

FIRST AMONG EQUALS (DIRECTORS)

For thousands of years, playwrights directed their own works. In ancient Greece, twenty-five-hundred years ago, it was the playwright's duty to stage his play and instruct the actors. Playwrights also often played the lead roles themselves. Thespis was the first known actor in the Western tradition, from whom we get the word Thespian. We know his name because in 534 B.C. he won the Festival of Dionysus, the first playwriting contest. He may be remembered as an actor, but he was also the first known Western playwright/director.

Only about a hundred and fifty years ago did directors, as we know them today, come into being. Modern directors are responsible for interpreting the play, developing its production concept, staging the play, and supervising the work of actors and designers. In the Hollywood film industry, directors have almost total control and can and often do tell the writer(s) what to write or rewrite. In television (sitcoms and hour-length shows), the directors go almost unnoticed and are often subservient to the writers, who are often also producers on the show. In the theater, technically, the playwright and the director are supposed to be equals. We say "technically" because every production is different, so each playwright/director relationship must be clearly defined before the rehearsal process begins.

CHOOSING AND APPROVING A DIRECTOR

The first thing all playwrights must know is that it's their right to choose and/or approve who will direct their plays. If you don't like the director, if you feel he doesn't understand your play, even if he doesn't look at you right, you have the power and right to say no. But you must say "no" before you sign the contract and/or before the director is officially on board. Once you've signed the contract and/or agreed to the director, the playwright doesn't have the power to fire the director. Now, the consequences of saying "no" might be that the theater will not produce your play, but that's okay, because the wrong director will not only make the playwright's life hell, he may also ruin the play. As playwright Terrence McNally says, "Work with good directors. Without them your play is doomed." A good director is one who understands and likes your play. A great director is one who's gone through a similar journey as the playwright. These directors have empathy for (or as least sympathy with) what the playwright is trying to say.

The phone rings, it's the Food and Footlights Dinner Theatre calling. They want to produce your play. You do a little dance, thank the god Dionysus, and yell, "Okay!" Wrong. Your first response should be, "Who's the director?" Next, you should request that this director give you a call so you can meet. (Don't call them, have them call you.) Professional theaters won't have a problem with this, but occasionally you'll run into smaller, non-professional theaters that will find this rather suspicious. These theaters think that the playwright should be overjoyed and never make demands, and if you do, you're some sort of defensive jerk. But, if you are calm and matter-of-fact about your request, their suspicions can be tamed (though they won't disappear entirely). You simply want to meet the director (and see his résumé) before you give approval. Once you get the name of the director, get on the web and do a little research. If the director has directed a lot of Neil Simon and your play is an experimental surrealist piece about Nazis, this might give you pause. This is not to say that he isn't the right director, it's just that you want to be sure that your director has directed plays comparable to yours. If you've written a dark comedy, you want a director who's done a little Chekhov or Feiffer. If you've written an absurdist comedy, then you want a director who's staged Ionesco or Durang. If your play is realistic, you'll want a director who knows a little about Ibsen or Shaw.

Next, you need to understand what type of director you're dealing with. Directors generally fall into two categories: interpretive and creative. An interpretive director has a deep respect for the playwright's words and uses his imagination and talents to serve the playwright's vision and accurately stage the original intention of the script. A creative director changes the playwright's play in order to come up with a "refreshingly original production." Creative directors feel that the script is a nice starting place, but that the production must find its own voice—often, startlingly, coinciding with their own voice and not the playwright's. Needless to say, most living playwrights would rather work with an interpretive director. (Dead playwrights don't have much say in the matter, which is why they're a favorite of creative directors.)

It's the director's job to work with you, to understand, develop, and stage your play as you see it. This is not to say that the director is there to serve the playwright—both are there to *serve the production.* Think of it this way: You own the blueprint, so make that sure the contractor sees the project as you see it, understands it as you do, and has creative, interesting ideas on how to construct it. If, during your interview, the director says that he can "save" or "fix" your play, he is most likely the wrong director. For one thing, why would he want to direct a broken play? If the play really needs repair, it's not ready for production and you have no need for a director, at least not yet.

During your director interview, try to build a relationship. Be relaxed and confident (but not over-confident). Build bridges, find common areas of interest, and keep it light. Here are some questions a playwright might want to ask a prospective director:

1. Does the director like the script?
2. I mean really, does the director like the script?
3. Does the director have a clear concept that's consistent with your intentions?
4. Is the director interested in your opinion?
5. Are the director's concepts and ideas flexible?
6. After talking with you, do the director's concepts and ideas change?
7. Did the director choose to direct your play, or did the artistic director assign it to him?
8. How many new plays has the director directed?
9. Has the director worked with a living playwright before?
10. Does the director understand the playwright's rights?

Finally, get to know a little about the director: Where is he from? What's his life experience? What do you have in common? The playwright-director relationship has been called a marriage, and we all know that arranged marriages can be problematic.

One way the playwright can get to know the director is to sit down and read the script to each other. Playwright David Hwang did this with his director during *M. Butterfly*. By doing this, Hwang said, "We were able to see whether the approaches to the characters seemed to be similar." Finding a like-minded director is critical. Robert Anderson said, "It is important that the playwright and director are doing the same play. Sounds strange? It often happens if the play hasn't been talked out beforehand that they are *not* doing the same play."

If you are comfortable with the director's answers to your questions, if you feel that you and the director are doing the same play, then, hopefully, you have found your director and can agree to have your play produced (or at least start contract negotiations). But, always remember, at this stage you have the right to say no. You're handing over your baby, so make sure its guardian is someone you trust.

THE DIRECTOR AND REWRITES

Directors can put a great deal of pressure on playwrights to rewrite. After all, they must exert influence and control or they can't do their job. If the playwright/ director roles are not well-defined, a passive playwright will almost certainly be manipulated, while a demanding playwright will alienate the director and creative ensemble. The playwright should be eager to take good suggestions and correct flaws, but there is a big difference between the playwright's obligation to improve the play and an obligation to make specific revisions demanded by director, producer, or actors. You are not a writer-for-hire; you own the copyright and don't have to make changes unless you believe they will improve your play.

Many times, a playwright has had to step in and use the copyright laws to stop directors. For example, Edward Albee took legal action to end a production of *Who's Afraid of Virginia Woolf?* in which the director had put the cast in drag. Samuel Beckett stopped a production of *Waiting for Godot* that had an all-female cast. Arthur Miller had to threaten legal action to end production of a significantly modified, experimental version of *The Crucible*. There are, however, also many famous instances of directors "saving" and "ruining" a play. The most famous concerns the great director and co-founder of the Moscow Art Theatre, Stanislavski, who insisted that Chekhov's play *The Cherry Orchard* was not a comedy nor a farce, so he staged it as a tragedy. By most accounts the production was a failure as it played to half-empty houses. Chekhov didn't even bother to attend. Only when it was restaged as a dark comedy, as Chekhov intended, was the play a success. Another famous case of playwright/director conflicts concerns the original production of Tennessee Williams' *Cat on a Hot Tin Roof*. Director Elia Kazan insisted that Williams rewrite the third act before he would direct the play. Williams did the rewrite but later published the play with his original third act. He included the rewritten "Kazan" version as an appendix. A similar thing happened with Archibald MacLeish, who published two versions of his play *J.B.*, as did William Inge with *Picnic*. Why did these playwrights rewrite? To please the director? To produce a hit? Perhaps, but they must have still felt that their original scripts were better, truer to their voice, or they wouldn't have made sure their versions were passed on to posterity.

Once, the American theatre was called "the playwright's theater," but today, director/playwright conflicts seem to be becoming more common. In his autobiography, *Timebends*, Arthur Miller writes that, in the theater, there was a time when "the playwright was king of the hill, not the star actor or director, and certainly not the producer or theater owner, as would later be the case." In today's theater, directors have stolen the spotlight. This change in focus came about primarily as a reflection of Hollywood, where the director is considered the principal artist, while screenwriters are merely disposable employees whose only purpose is to serve the director.

Today, the playwright is still the author of the script, but more and more directors see themselves as the author of the production. (Some even copyright their blocking.) This has resulted in a concerted effort to marginalize the playwright, an attitude now showing up in the approach of graduates of MFA directing programs and also in books on directing. For example, Richard Schechner writes in his book *Performance Theory*, "The work of those doing the production is to re-scene the play not as the writer might have envisioned it but as immediate circumstances reveal it… I don't think that even the first production of a drama is privileged in this regard—unless the author stages the play himself, and that privilege dies with the author." Certainly this marks a dramatic change from the days when the playwright was considered to be the primary artist. Where once screenwriters were envious of the playwright's artistic control, now playwrights and screenwriters are starting to feel a kinship.

What these directors don't understand is that most playwrights are more than willing to rewrite as long as the changes don't transform their voices—in other words, as long as they feel their plays still represent their takes on things. Harold Clurman, who worked with many great playwrights (including Lillian Hellman, Clifford Odets, and Eugene O'Neill), said, "A playwright doesn't want his play 'improved' if the improvement leads to making a different play from his own. He wants his voice to be heard, unless he thinks of himself as a journeyman prepared to provide a commodity that might somehow prove profitable. But not many playwrights think of themselves in that light." Novelist James M. Cain said when imagination is not free, when imagination serves the medium instead of the medium serving it, "that is the end of pride, of joy in getting things down on paper." No rehearsal process should curtail the joy of getting things down on paper. No director should make a playwright just a writer-for-hire. If you are writing only to please the director or the actors or anyone other than yourself, there's a good chance that the rehearsal process, the director, and ultimately you yourself, have failed you.

However, power of ownership can be self-defeating, too. Although it's true that The Dramatists Guild and copyright laws prohibit anyone from changing even a letter of a playwright's play without permission, a playwright must be inherently aware of which battles are worth fighting. The original vision is yours, but you can't have so much control that you turn the director, designers, and actors into puppets. As director Terry McCabe says, "When the actors have been reduced to cogs in the director's machine, something is amiss." The same is true for playwrights: If the playwright is only a cog in the director's machine, or the director a cog in the playwright's, something's amiss. Playwrights who have all the answers, who won't compromise, who are constantly reluctant to rewrite, who believe that their creative power is being challenged every time someone makes a simple suggestion, are not interested in producing the best play possible.

BEING PART OF THE PROCESS

After contract considerations, the next thing you much decide is whether or not you're going to be able to attend rehearsals. Unless you live around the corner from the theater, the fact is that most small theaters can't afford to bring you in for the rehearsal process. Just like the now-disappearing music programs at local high schools, the playwright's presence is often the first expendable when budget cuts are made. Also, playwrights have a reputation of being a pain in the butt, so many directors prefer to not have them around. This is sad, because having the playwright present is one of the best ways to guarantee a creative and productive rehearsal process.

The first time a new play is produced, the playwright ought to be present for the entire process. According to The Dramatists Guild, the playwright has the right to attend all rehearsals and production meetings and to approve casting, whether it's the first, twentieth, or hundredth production of the play. If a theater says that it's their policy not to allow the playwright to attend, make it your policy not to allow them to do your play. But, just because you have the right to attend doesn't mean you should be there at every moment. There are some rehearsals where the playwright's presence is not needed, and at times it's nice to give the director and actors a little breathing space. Also, just because the playwright is allowed to attend doesn't mean that the playwright is in charge. Let's look at how the playwright should participate in production meetings and casting before we go into the rehearsal process.

MEETING, MEETINGS, AND MORE MEETINGS...

Production meetings can take several forms. There are publicity meetings, where the main topic of conversation is how to promote the play and sell seats. Artistic meetings are those in which the director, designers, and dramaturg (if there is one) come up with the play's production concept. Production meetings are those in which schedules, details, and problems concerning the design and construction of the set, costumes, and lights are worked out. It's rare for the playwright to attend publicity meetings, but if you do, be helpful and allow the publicist to lead. Artistic meetings are more likely to be useful for you to attend, as they are concerned with the production concept: its central metaphor, thematic idea, symbol, or allegory that will be reflected in the staging and design. This is something that you and the director should already have talked over before this meeting. During the meeting, the director may present a complete production concept, or the designers, dramaturg, and director may work out the concept as a team. If you attend, make suggestions, but also listen and know that, as playwright, your expertise is characters and story. Let the designers design. A good playwright tries to inspire the team, not dictate to it. (See more below under Working with Designers.)

CASTING ABOUT

During casting, a good director will be interested in the playwright's ideas. If you're there, though, you should remain in the background. Let the director run the audition. As you consider each actor, consider the following: Does the actor have the vocal clarity, intelligence, technique, energy, and stage presence the part requires? What's your first impression? Is the actor the right type for the role? After the audition, meet with your director and let her know your preferences, in specific terms, as to why you think a particular actor is right or wrong. Then go away. Let the director do the casting, but make sure that she gets your approval before any cast list is posted. Some directors will view this as an invasion of their authority, so be sure *before* the process begins that they know you'll be following Dramatists Guild rules. You should get the cast you want, but be willing to compromise.

During rehearsals, the playwright/director relationship may be different with every production. Some directors will talk to the playwright during rehearsals, while others concentrate on the actors and want to meet with the playwright only afterward. Directors who are uncomfortable with you being there often feel that playwrights tend to cramp their style. You can make these directors feel at ease by being upbeat and supportive. Whatever the situation, you and the director should talk about the rehearsal process long before rehearsals begin. Invite your director to lunch and let her know what you expect, listen to what she expects, and agree to certain ground rules before you set foot in the rehearsal hall. Here are a few ideas on how to make it work:

Don't Attend Every Rehearsal

Give your actors and director a little breathing room. Watching them grapple with every tedious step of the process isn't necessary, and sometimes your presence can inhibit them. As Elia Kazan said, "I didn't watch you make your mistakes. I'd rather you didn't watch me make mine." Decide with your director which rehearsals you will attend and be ready to change your plans should the director feel your presence is needed or not. Allow the ensemble to show you the discoveries they've made during your absence.

Allow Everyone to Fail

It's important that the playwright allow every member of the ensemble to try new things, to experiment and fail. When you wrote the script, you tried new things, experimented and failed, so let everyone have the freedom you allowed yourself.

Don't Fix It Right Away

Just because a particular line, moment, or scene isn't going well, don't be tempted to rush in and rewrite. Actors and directors need time to make it work.

Don't Fix It Right Away (Part 2)

On the same side of the coin, if the director asks you to change a line after only one or two read-throughs (and you feel the line works), don't rush to change it, but kindly ask that the line, moment, or scene be given more rehearsal time.

Talk to the Director

Questions and artistic differences should be discussed away from the actors. Many directors are more than willing to compromise, accommodate, and even admit they're wrong, if it's done *in private*. A playwright who publicly disagrees or fights for power with a director will cause division within the ensemble.

Let the Director Do the Talking

Unless you and the director have decided otherwise, don't give notes to the actors or designers without the director's knowledge. Even if the playwright and director are in total agreement, let the director be the note-giver.

Don't Make the Rest of the Team Your Lackeys

Be a team member. Allow everyone's voice to be heard and every member of the team to add to the process and finished product. This means that the finished product may not be exactly what you imagined, but better.

Don't Be a Problem Playwright

If you are giving notes like, "Wait, she's not supposed to take a drag on her cigarette on that line!" more than likely you are a problem playwright. Your job is not to micromanage or direct the play, but to help each member of the ensemble to make discoveries, additions, and corrections that improve your play. You own the script, but you don't own the production.

Don't Be a Problem Playwright! Part 2

We mean it, don't be a problem playwright! It gives us all bad rap. Learn to work with the people who bring your words to life.

A common problem that playwrights run into when working with a new director is that many directors haven't got the foggiest idea of how to work with a playwright. Most books on directing don't talk about the playwright/director relationship, and some MFA directing programs never bother to teach it. If you're dealing with a theater that specializes in new work, you generally won't have this problem, but with other theaters, you'll discover directors who are totally blank when it comes to working with living playwrights. Sometimes they'll view you as a threat to their power. Seldom do they understand that the playwright and the director are equals. You can correct this situation by calmly and professionally educating your director. Agree on the rules of your working relationship early and stick to them. But don't be surprised if everyone, not just the director, tells you how to rewrite your play, while, in turn, being closed to your suggestions. Get used to it and calmly roll with the punches—it's just part of being a playwright.

WHEN YOU CAN'T ATTEND REHEARSALS

There's no substitute for attending rehearsals. If you're dealing with a big, professional theater, this won't be a problem, because they'll generally have the funds to bring you in. But, if you're dealing with a small, impoverished theater (like most beginning playwrights do) that can't afford to, then make sure that you're available to the director. Let the director know that you expect to talk on the phone at least every other day during the rehearsal process and that you'll need regular updates on design, casting, and directorial choices. The director should even be able to call you during the rehearsal if necessary. Before the rehearsals begin, the playwright should be sent copies of the set and costume designs and his opinion of them taken into account. If the theater does regular rehearsal reports, then ask to have them faxed or sent to you. Often, stage managers send daily e-mail rehearsal reports to all the designers and actors, as well as the theater's management. Make sure you're included.

If a theater can only bring you in for a short period of time, don't ask to be flown in for the final rehearsals, previews, and opening night. By then it's often too late to make significant changes. Instead, ask to join rehearsal about a week into the process. The great Russian director Meyerhold suggested that play rehearsal was much like the stages of a rocket. The first stage is the playwright, then the playwright falls off and second stage (the director) takes the play; then the director falls off, and the third stage (the cast) takes the play. Finally, the actors fall off and the play belongs to the audience. There is some truth to this, so it's important that the playwright be at rehearsal when she has the most power and influence to launch the play in the right direction. This may mean that you'll miss opening night, but the opening night is a finished product, and being a playwright is about creating that product. It will be a better product if you are there for the process.

MINE, ALL MINE—DIRECTING YOUR OWN WORK

As we said at the beginning of this chapter, playwrights have been directing their own plays for thousands of years, but if you're just starting out, directing your own play is not advisable. Unless you've been trained in directing and/or have directed several plays, it's a mistake. The common reason given for not letting playwrights direct their own work is that they lack "objectivity." But as playwright Steven Deitz (who has directed many of his own plays) points out, just as many directors lack objectivity as playwrights. Others say that playwrights shouldn't direct their own work because they're too close to their words. Well, aren't directors too close to their directing and actors too close to their acting? Go down that road and nothing will get done.

A lack of perspective can be a problem (for all concerned). But there are ways a playwright can achieve perspective. First, try to direct one of your plays that you didn't finish just last week. Just as with rewrites, time is a great way to achieve distance. If you wrote it several years ago rather than several months ago, even better. Another way to achieve perspective is to direct one of your plays that you've already seen others direct. If the play has one or two productions under its belt, you'll have a greater chance at success, because you've learned a few things from the other directors' successes and mistakes.

The real problem with directing your own play is a lack of directing technique. Playwrights who do not have experience in directing are less likely to compromise. They seldom take into account the unique point of view and insights each member of the ensemble brings to the production. Instead, they try to stage the play exactly as they imagined it while writing it. The result is a rehearsal process spent "bringing everyone up to speed" with the playwright/director's vision, rather than making discoveries. One solution is to find a mentor to help you, an experienced, understanding director who has passion and respect for your play and is willing to help you avoid mistakes. If you can't find such a mentor, then you must at least realize that you are now wearing two hats: those of the playwright and the director. Don't let the playwright inside you take over; that stage of the rocket has fallen away. Now you're dealing with actors and sets. Your world is no longer the page, but the stage. Now you're a director.

WORKING WITH ACTORS

No two productions of a play are identical, and no two actors will play a role exactly the same way. Thousands of actors have played Hamlet, and every one of them was unique in his interpretation. Compare Sir John Gielgud's with Mel Gibson's: Their performances were completely different, yet they were saying the same words and playing the same character. This variation is possible because a character that appears onstage is a combination of the playwright's creation and the actor's personality and talents. Each actor will bring to a role his own life experiences, point of view, and interpretation. This is not something you should oppose, but welcome. Let yourself be surprised—within limits, of course.

During the rehearsal processes, actors need one consistent voice to guide them. So, again, if you are not directing and you have a problem with an actor or want to give a note, go through the director. On those occasions when the director thinks the playwright can or should give notes directly to the actors, then talk to the actors on their level. Actors don't want to hear about a play's theme, philosophical motifs or political overviews. They want to know what they're supposed to be doing and why, in the motivations, actions, and words that help them play the moment. Above all, do not give them "line readings," where you demonstrate exactly how to play or say a particular action or line. This is an actor's nightmare, because it takes away his creativity and turns him into a marionette. It doesn't let him find those choices by which he can bring a character to life. Give him your take on the motivations for and goals of his character's actions, but let him do the acting, let him explore, experiment, try, fail, and try again.

Actors can be a wonderful source for rewrites. During rehearsal, listen to where they stumble on a word or phrase, as well as where they struggle to find the moment. These are possible places for cuts and/or rewrites. Pay attention to where they unconsciously paraphrase or add or subtract a word, and ask yourself if the way they're saying it is better, more natural, or truer to the character than the way you wrote it. During rehearsal, allow the actors to add or cut an occasional line. If the director uses improvisation as part of the rehearsal process, be there with pen and paper so you can record any good lines that may come out of it. By the end of the rehearsal process, the actors should be experts on their characters; and who better to listen to than an expert? Terrence McNally said to *The Dramatist* magazine, "A good actor hears the way you (and no one else) write. A good actor makes rewrites easy. A good actor tells you things about your play you didn't know. A good actor is your only friend when the audience is out there on an opening night." Of course, on occasion you'll have to deal with a bad actor, perhaps one who demands that you rewrite simply to fit his needs. On these occasions, always enlist the support of the director. Be polite, but insist that the actor take up his concerns with the director present—and always remember you are there to serve the play, not the actors.

TYPES OF REHEARSAL

Rehearsal processes can vary, so the playwright must be ready to adapt her style to the needs of the situation. Let's look at the different types of rehearsals and what your responsibilities as playwright are for each. The one note that applies to all rehearsals is that the director and playwright should meet immediately following each rehearsal to discuss changes and improvements. These meetings should happen often during the early parts of rehearsal, for you'll discover that as rehearsal continues, the playwright can do less and less to correct problems. By the end of the process, the play belongs to the actors, and all a playwright (or a director for that matter) can do is hope you've made the right decisions. A list of the basic types of rehearsal includes:

Table Work - Many directors start by seating the actors at a table and having them read the play though. After the reading (or sometimes during), the director and actors discuss their thoughts about the characters, motivations, and meanings, and discuss the play in general. Table work is usually a time when the playwright can freely talk to the actors, but shouldn't say too much. Let the director do most of the talking. Answer questions, but don't dominate or lead the rehearsal. This will be the first time you hear the cast read the script, so spend most of your time taking notes on what works and what doesn't. After the rehearsal, meet with the director and go over any possible changes.

Blocking Rehearsal - This is a series of rehearsals during which the director and actors work out the basic movements onstage. In some cases, the director has all the movements worked out before rehearsals begin (this is known as pre-blocking), but more often than not the director (often with the help of the actors) works out the blocking during a series of rehearsals that can take several days. During blocking rehearsals, the playwright should sit quietly in the house and take notes. Interrupt the rehearsal only if you feel the director is missing something important. This shouldn't happen often because you have described all the important blocking in the script.

Working Rehearsals - During these rehearsals, the director works on individual scenes. At some working rehearsals, improvisation might be used, allowing the actors to explore things that are hinted at in the script. Other working rehearsals are dedicated to discussions of motivation, character analysis, and creative exercises. Early working rehearsals are filled with pauses as the play is worked, changed, and reworked. Later working rehearsals are more about fine-tuning. Once again, the playwright should sit and let the director direct. Give any notes or comments to the director, in private, and not to the company as a whole.

Special Rehearsals - If a play has fight scenes, musical numbers, dance numbers, or regional or foreign accents, the director can call special rehearsals for each. There is seldom a need for the playwright to be present during special rehearsals. Check with the director to see if she wants you there.

Off Book - This is the rehearsal where the actors first have their lines (supposedly) memorized. It's called "off book" because the actors will no longer have the script (the book) with them during rehearsal. If they forget their lines, they'll call, "Line!" and the stage manager will read the line aloud for them. This is a boring rehearsal. The playwright seldom needs to attend.

Run-Through - Here, the entire play or all the acts are run from beginning to end with as few interruptions as possible. A run-through gives the actors a feeling for how the play works as a whole. During run-throughs, the playwright should sit and take notes. Limit the number of acting and line notes so that you can quickly meet with the director before the director gives notes to the actors.

Speed-Through (sometimes called a Line-Through) - In this type of rehearsal, the dialogue is said as quickly as possible in order to help the actors learn their lines. The playwright need not attend.

Tech Rehearsals - By this point, rehearsals have moved from the rehearsal hall to the stage. During tech (technical) rehearsals, the lights, sound, props, and set are added. The first tech rehearsal can be a very slow process. The actors often have to stop and go back over a particular moment so that the light-board operator and other assistants can time their cues (the line or event on stage that prompts a change in lights, sound effect, etc.).

Cue-To-Cue Rehearsals - During this rehearsal, the majority of the play is skipped and the actors only perform those moments that have light, sound, or other tech cues. During these, the playwright should remain in the background and stay out of the way. Give your notes on set, lights, costumes, and acting to the director.

Dress Rehearsals - These are the final rehearsals, only a few days before the play opens, when costumes and makeup are added. The dress rehearsal can be a hectic time, so if you do have notes, wait for the director to decide when the time is right to give them.

Final Dress Rehearsal - This is the last rehearsal before an audience is invited. Ideally, the play runs without stopping, as if it were a real performance. The playwright should attend, but you are there more for moral support than anything else.

Previews - During previews you have an audience, but they pay only half price for their tickets. Critics are not allowed to attend, because the play has not officially opened. During each preview, the director takes notes and calls special rehearsals to correct problems. If the director agrees, the playwright might also rewrite bits and pieces of the play that don't work. This can be a tough time for playwrights, full of late nights, as bits of the play are rewritten. By now, the script should be pretty much set, but if there is a major rewrite, be sure to do it right after the rehearsal, so that actors can get their changes first thing in the morning. (Smaller theaters and college productions seldom have previews.)

Opening Night - The official opening of the play. The playwright should sit in the back and try not to be too sick, or at least too vocal about it.

SET OPINIONS (WORKING WITH DESIGNERS)

During rehearsals, treat the designers like actors: Your notes on the set, costumes, and lights should be conveyed through the director. During design meetings, let the designers interpret your thoughts rather than telling them exactly what the stage must look like. For example, here is Eugene O'Neill's set description for *Desire Under the Elms*:

> The action of the entire play takes place in, and immediately outside of, the Cabot farmhouse in New England, in the year 1850. The south end of the house faces front to a stone wall with a wooden gate at center opening on a country road. The house is in good condition but in need of paint. Its walls are a sickly grayish, the green of the shutters faded. Two enormous elms are on each side of the house. They bend their trailing branches down over the roof. They appear to protect and at the same time subdue. There is a sinister maternity in their aspect, a crushing, jealous absorption. They have developed from their intimate contact with the life of man in the house an appalling humaneness. They brood oppressively over the house. They are like exhausted women resting their sagging breasts and hands and hair on its roof, and when it rains their tears trickle down monotonously and rot on the shingles.

Notice that O'Neill gives only his impressions, feelings, and images, leaving room for the designers to exercise their art. (By the way, this amount of description is not advised; it's better to be brief.) The designers might ask what inspired you to write the play. They're trying to find a central metaphor or image (i.e., production concept) that they can build their design around. When asked this question, try to put into words the feelings, events, and particularly images that galvanized your need to write the play. Here is what playwright Michel de Ghelderode wrote about his play *Escurial*:

> Think of painting. This play is painting become theater... I was inspired to write *Escurial* after I saw two canvases of the Spanish School at the Louvre. An El Greco and a Velasquez on the same wall and not far from each other... El Greco inspired an anxious, haggard, visibly degenerate, pulmonary "King John"—in brief, a beautiful, clinical specimen. El Greco's brush brought forth a terrible, disquieting, unforgettable character—and I dreamt of him. Velasquez inspired a magnificent dwarf, swollen with blood and instinct. To bring these two monsters together was all that was needed. The play was the outcome.

Notice again, the playwright has given the designer a great deal to work with, but has not told the designer exactly what to design. Give your impressions, but leave it up to the designers to make the set, costumes, and lights work. If you say, "Oh no, that door has got to be on the right side, because that's the way I've always pictured it," you're stepping on the designer's right to design. (Unless there's a strictly functional reason for putting the door there.) Remember: If the designer doesn't follow your concept, your problem is with the director, not the designer.

EVERYONE'S A CRITIC (AND SOME GET PAID)

Jean Racine (1639-1699), the French neoclassicist playwright, wrote: "They [critics] always look forward to some successful work in order to attack it—not out of jealousy, for on what grounds could they be jealous?—but in the hope that they will force someone to take the trouble to reply to their criticism, and that they will thus be rescued from that obscurity to which their own works would have everlastingly condemned them."

No matter how secluded playwrights may be, they still have a deep desire to please, and because of this, brutal critics have been the undoing of many. A playwright may win the critics' hearts with a first success, only to have the next play panned. Tennessee Williams could do no wrong, according to the critics in the fifties, and yet could do no right in the sixties. It's sad to think that years of hard work can come down to one performance: Will the critics like it? More than likely they won't. According to the critics, the vast majority of plays fail; but critics are a jaded and often pretentious lot, so when the reviews come out, try not to put too much weight in them. If you're overjoyed by a good review, you'll be all the more horrified by a pan. Above all, don't let the critics destroy your desire to write. Don't respond to them defensively or write nasty letters. Just let it go, learn what you can, and keep writing. Many plays that are now considered classics were vilified when first reviewed. It may be true that your play sucks; but it may also be true that you've challenged the status quo and broken new ground—which is, after all, the point of it all.

IT'S A PRODUCTION

When a production fails, there can be a great deal of finger-pointing, particularly if it's the play's first production. In his book *Mis-Directing the Play*, Terry McCabe says that the director's fundamental obligation to the playwright is to make sure that "if the play is going down in flames...it's the playwright's fault." In a perfect world, we agree. If the actors, designers, and director do their job perfectly, any failure then must fall on the playwright. Unfortunately, actors, designers, and directors are seldom perfect, and too often their imperfections are wrongly blamed on the playwright. The only way a playwright can correct this situation is to write a script that is actor-proof, director-proof, and designer-proof. This last sentence may be condemned by actors, directors, and designers who think it means that we're demeaning their ability or creative contribution. We don't mean it this way. By making a script actor- , director- , and designer-proof, we mean that the script is so good, so complete, so inspiring that even an average actor, director, and designer can do it justice. You don't want to write a play that can only be staged by artists of extraordinary imagination and talents.

Gregory Boyd, artistic director of The Alley Theatre, once asked, "In terms of a theatrical production, what is the primary focus of the production? Is it service to a text that exists, is it interpretation of that text, or is the text merely one of the elements that come together to make a theatrical event, and no more or less important than costume or scenery or acting or music or sound?" The answer to this critical question depends on the playwright. A weak playwright will allow his script to become no more or less important than the costume or scenery, while an uncompromising and demanding playwright will make all the other elements of production subservient to her script. Only a playwright who knows when and how to rewrite, to compromise, to stand strong, and, most of all, to inspire will make all the elements of production seamless extensions of her script. The playwright may be a member of the ensemble, but he or she is also the ensemble's primary inspiration and reason for being.

Conclusion

****

When people are confronted with a real work of art—
then they discover that they don't believe what they thought
they believed all along. In a way, the great art, the great subversive art,
is art that makes you realize that you don't think what you thought you did.

David Hare

****

Why write plays? There's more money to be made in screenwriting (if you're lucky). There's more fame to be had in acting (again, luck applies). And your life will be much easier if you become a lawyer. (Luck? Who needs it!) So why do it? The answer is simple: We write plays because we have something to say and we don't want our message corrupted by the powers that be. We write because we want to be artists, not just entertainers. And there's a profound difference between art and entertainment that sometimes gets lost in our pop-culture-dominated world. *The Oxford English Dictionary* says that entertainment is "the action of occupying attention agreeably; that which affords interest or amusement." The key word here is "agreeably." Entertainment lets you see an agreeable mirror of yourself, your values, and your ideas about how the world is or should be. The foremost purpose of entertainment is to reaffirm the audience's values and confirm their belief systems. Art may, in the end, also reaffirm and confirm, but artists, unlike entertainers, do not make it their principal purpose to reaffirm the audience's values. Instead, playwrights create in order to challenge themselves and their audiences. Of course, playwrights want their audiences to understand and appreciate their work—that's why they listen to criticism and weigh the audiences' reaction and feedback—but the audience's opinion does not play a part in the *creation* of their work. In other words, playwrights don't poll or consult their audience *before* deciding what to create (as television and movie people often do). They don't set out with the singular purpose of pleasing their audience at the expense of their own thoughts, visions, or voices. As writer Roxana Robinson put it, "My own reasons for writing, for setting down the story, are to a large extent selfish. With each story…I am trying simply to work something out for myself. You, the reader, play no part here: This is a private matter."

The audience plays no part in art; or, more precisely, the audience's *values* play no part. By values we mean the principles, standards, or qualities considered desirable within a given society. When those values are reaffirmed (put into a positive light and upheld as valid and true), we are entertained. As Stephen Sondheim, considered to be one of the finest composers of our time, said, "You get your tickets for *The Lion King* a year in advance, and essentially a family comes as if to a picnic, and they pass on to their children the idea that that's what the theater is—a spectacular musical you see once a year, a stage version of a movie. It has nothing to do with theater at all. It has to do with seeing what is familiar. We live in a recycled culture."

Entertainment sets out to purposefully reaffirm and recycle our culture; that's why so many movies are remakes or sequels to other popular movies. Some books on screenwriting even advise writers to stay away from any subject that may be considered controversial or that would make the audience think. Jurgen Wolff and Kerry Cox in their how-to book *Successful Script Writing* advise screenwriters to shun subjects that are contentious. They state, "Doing a film about child abuse is not controversial—who's in favor of child abuse? Doing a film about abortion that really takes a stand one way or the other would be controversial —and therefore has a slim chance of getting on the air." In other words, subjects that might make the audience think or would challenge their values have little chance of being made and so are inappropriate material for the screenwriter. In his book, *Life the Movie*, Neal Gabler describes Hollywood films as a "rearrangement of our problems into shapes which tame them, which disperse them to the margins of our attention." In other words, entertainment is the art of escape. Art, on the other hand, makes us confront our problems. Entertainment fulfills your expectations; art surprises you and makes you think. Entertainment makes the audience feel good about who they are and what they believe, it gives the audience the impression that their actions are justified and that change is not needed. Art, on the other hand, doesn't care about society's values, so the audience's actions are not always vindicated.

Again, this isn't to say that art can't be entertaining. *Oklahoma!* is spectacular entertainment that is also a work of art. Neil Simon is both entertaining and an artist, as was the most popular playwright of his or any other time, William Shakespeare. Pleasing the audience isn't a sin. But it isn't the point of art, either. An artist is concerned with what he or she perceives to be true. If that's also entertaining, fine. If it's not, too bad. It may be that challenging work will ultimately be seen as affirming and safe, as has happened with the Impressionist painters, who were thoroughly reviled at the time they were creating what are now undeniably the most accepted and popular images in our culture. But they didn't know things would turn out that way. They were after what they felt was a new and true way of seeing the world, and they set out to change how others saw the world, too. (That they succeeded is beside the point.) And that is what art is about.

A playwright's job, as an artist, is to be true to her own vision and to challenge the audience to see things anew, in the light of that vision—to make them think. As the great Enlightenment playwright Voltaire said, "We only half live if we dare only half think."

In the United States, we produce more entertainment than any other country on earth. Even our food has become entertaining. As playwright David Mamet says, "If food is nourishment, the purpose of which is to fuel the body, it's not hard to choose the broccoli. If food is entertainment, who would not choose the French fries? The fast-food chains thrive through corruption of basic human need for nourishment into a need of entertainment." Neal Gabler calls the United States the "Republic of Entertainment." There's nothing wrong with being entertained, but never before in history has there been so much entertainment concentrated in a single population. What happens when a society has so much entertainment? When entertainment invades every aspect of our lives? What happens when our values are constantly reinforced? What happens when a society, with a simple flick of a remote, can find a program that makes them feel good about who they are and what they believe? In Nazi Germany, the Soviet Union, and Maoist China, art as self-congratulatory entertainment was actively promoted, and anything that deviated from their reinforced belief systems was banned as "degenerate." In ancient Rome, when the Empire was falling into disarray, the Caesars distracted the masses with gaudy displays of gladiatorial carnage that promoted the sense of absolute Roman superiority. Totalitarian leaders (like studio executives) knew very well what would happen if entertainment supplanted art: People would stop thinking for themselves and accept what was told (or sold) to them. That's why the writers and artists were sent to the gulags, the provinces, or worse—to Off-Off-Broadway. The result, then as now, was that society became increasingly apathetic and programmed, but more importantly, intolerant of new ideas, new points of view, and other people's opinions of how the world was or should be. The great philosopher Ludwig Wittgenstein (1889-1951) said that philosophical illnesses usually stem from dietary insufficiency. A diet of only one philosophy, religion, or way of looking at the world leads to philosophical illness and a limited view of the world. Theater, art, and playwrights are here to cure that dietary insufficiency.

A playwright's goal is to keep people thinking for themselves, by forcing them to re-examine what they accept as the truth, whether in the political or purely personal arena. It's to help us understand ourselves and our world. One of the highest forms of intelligence is the ability to see life through someone else's eyes. The art of playwriting lets us see through someone else's point of view. It does not set out to reaffirm or entertain, but to eliminate the sameness that breeds ignorance and to enrich our experience of life.

And that's why we write plays.

Appendices

Appendix A

We thank our friend and fellow playwright Erik Ramsey for the following exegesis on script analysis.

OVERCOMING THE NAKED CHIROPRACTOR:
How Not to Navigate the Professional Script Analysis Process
By an Anonymous LORT B Script Analyst

Whether it be five pages of sample stage directions sent book-rate or a complete musical performed by finger-puppets you burned to DVD and over-nighted for delivery by 10 a.m., the main thing to remember when submitting to a regional or professional theater is that you are actually submitting to something akin to a real live human being: a script "reader" or "analyst." The professional theater this purported human works for might be a famous pillar of the national arts community, which explains why you sent your work. But the script analyst, who is usually the very first person to look at your submission, often isn't even famous enough to be recognized by his or her own dog. It's quite possible that he or she could wear thick eyeglasses, have gout, and/or three menstrual periods a month, and not take kindly to a single-spaced 7-point "Oscura" font you thought was thematically integral.

Note that even though the script analyst's famed institution just pulled a private million-dollar endowment earmarked for producing plays about the plight of the pavement armadillo, this hypothetical human may still somehow remain underpaid, and therefore edgy and mildly distracted by your illegibly hand-written last-minute changes to the text. This supposed human cog in the theatrical juggernaut might not be inclined to read six paragraphs of character description, rather preferring to see the characters in action immediately, since he or she gets virtually no action in real life. The analyst might even be constantly fighting scurvy due to a lack of health insurance and the dearth of a balanced diet, and therefore occasionally susceptible to making snap judgments when the grammar and spelling aren't even correct on your title page. It's terribly unfortunate, but these professional hands that your submission graces may be stained with borrowed nicotine and caffeine, and therefore jittery enough that the tiny pink plastic paperclip you bound your play with explodes, sending reams down the fire escape where he or she was hiding from the landlord. Regrettably, the fact that your script "flutters" as it falls to the pavement will not be considered "integral dramatic action" in the final written analysis of your play.

Importantly, this theoretical human being and script analyst is rarely the actual artistic director, or even close to the powerful Cerberus-like personage he or she is often imagined to be. Note that the differences between the front-line script analyst and the actual artistic director are both profound and subtle: The artistic director makes major production decisions and does his or her laundry in the costume shop in order to pay off the $51,686.11 worth of student loans still owed at age 47, whereas the script reader only proffers strong opinions about your play and often must steal actual items from the costume shop in order to avoid a "third-strike" public indecency rap. Artistic directors aspire to produce major new theatrical triumphs that jump directly to Broadway, both for personal artistic satisfaction and the hope that they can afford a used Hyundai someday; script analysts aspire to finding that hit play in the stacks so that they can afford to pretend to aspire whatsoever.

All kidding aside, very often this quasi-human of first contact for your script is really a harmless subspecies, sometimes scornfully referred to as a "subverted playwright"—a relatively promising playwright who would certainly rather be crafting his or her own play adaptation of Sartre's *Nausea* as symbolized by a one-handed banjo player who works in a Des Moines pork-rendering facility. Subverted or not, playwright or not, this theater professional has agreed to read and respond to other people's new work in exchange for magic beans. However, contrary to popular opinion, magic beans do not make for magic farts. Therefore, in order to pay July's rent by October first, this professional reader may have to review your work while also on the clock at the night desk of an oily convention-center hotel at three in the morning. Unfortunately, dealing with belligerently drunk and corpulent chiropractors skipping nude through the hotel lobby is something your submission may literally have to overcome.

When submitting, many playwrights instinctively sense those "naked chiropractors," and the other innate elements of professional theater listed above. This often generates an urge to overcompensate with snazzy fonts and the shine and hue of multicolor clip-art on the cover. But as desperate as the submitting playwright may be to gain initial attention, it is far more imperative to make this "reader" or "dramatic analyst" or "dramaturg" or "artistic assistant" simply *comfortable* in order to retain his attention. And the reader's comfort always begins with details as small as proper spelling, grammar, and no evidence of sticky brown fingerprints that force the reader to sniff and decide whether it's chocolate, blood—or worse.

Many scripts, including "agent-ed submissions," arrive with visual or verbal pyrotechnics and inducements plastered on a script or clipped inside the cover, such as letters of reference to the fact that the writer knows the former artistic director's nephew from high school. Such inducements, if they work at all, only get a script in the door; but they are wholly wasted on the analyst whose *job* it is to read and respond to the submission regardless of its associations. Professional readers do not need to be induced or enticed to pick up a script; however, a seriously overwrought reader may be looking for a reason to put down a script—your radically new page layout ingeniously designed to save paper and incite glaucoma, for example. The urge to creatively cajole an analyst into liking your work is best spent on the contents of the script itself rather than artful support materials and gilt-edged résumés. There is, of course, the apocryphal story of the playwright who taped a ten-spot to the middle of page 184 of his epic-length, 187-page submission, with a handwritten note saying, "This is for you, for having actually read my whole play." The ploy very nearly worked. But the script analyst's conscience got the better of him and he taped three pennies to the page where the ten dollar bill had been, placed the script in the supplied SASE, and sent it back with a note reading: "Thanks. Here's your change."

Finally, upon finishing the play, the analyst will write a page or two of "coverage" explaining how good a story it is, so that the artistic director might come down from the ledge and become interested in reading it; or, conversely, write a paragraph about how his or her time could have been better spent polishing the ubiquitous silver bell on the hotel counter, which naked chiropractors feel compelled to ring even when an employee is clearly present and prepared to supply a spare room key. The basic format a script reader employs for responding in writing to a play varies according to the size, temperament, malicious whims, and needs of the institution. Typically, the written response or "coverage" is broken into sections such as "summation," "synopsis," "characters," "themes," "intended audience," and "recommendation." Sometimes a response worksheet is supplied to the reader to streamline and corral the analyst's natural urge to either effuse or bemoan. Below are sample coverages actually submitted by a mysteriously lucid reader to a LORT B theater. The first is a play that will likely never see professional production, and probably causes angina in lab animals:

Submission Evaluation For: (Anonymous LORT B)
Title: (omitted), Author: (omitted)
Evaluated By: Erik Ramsey

PLAY: This script isn't so much a play as it
is a kind of reader's theater with unintended
ritualistic performance aspects. According to the
stage directions, the characters strike formal poses
(akin to presidential portraiture, although that's
not how it is described in the script) and address
the audience in long monologues about who they are,
where they come from, and the pertinent history of
the time of Nixon and "Watergate." There is little
to no dramatic action in the piece, and the vast
majority of it, while interesting history, is too
static. In essence, the characters do not perform the
historical events surrounding the Watergate break-
in, nor do they interact, but rather recount events
in monologue form, adding stiffly "mimed" stage
activity on occasion. The subject matter of the long
monologues is meticulously researched and accurate,
and (fortunately) each character sees the events
in slightly different ways, producing a slightly
different version. However, the discrepancies in
their recounting fail to create enough dramatic
tension to sustain audience interest. There is little
to no sense of theatricality, unless one wants to
consider G. Gordon Liddy "standing with his arms
akimbo" for eight straight pages to be interesting
spectacle.

SYNOPSIS: Nixon explains his background and how he
came to be president for several pages, then Ford
explains the positive things that came of Nixon's
foreign policy, then Sirica, Haldeman, Mitchell,
Dean, Magruder, and Liddy each take turns telling the
events as they saw them from the time of the break-in
on June 17, 1972, to Nixon's resignation.

THEMES: The script doesn't seem to propose an
intentional theme; however, there is an oblique
suggestion that one small misdeed can slowly snowball
(e.g., "Oh the tangled webs we weave…").

CHARACTERS: There are no real characters; instead
we have talking heads that don't seem to have human
drives but rather prefer to stand around with 20/20
hindsight explaining what happened. No one even gets

thirsty after recounting for endless minutes. Nixon's
cadence, delivery, and language choice are very
little indistinguishable from Ford's; were someone to
see this piece who had never heard the Nixon tapes,
he would assume Nixon used the same boy-scout idiom
Ford employed.

AUDIENCE: This piece might be of some interest to
high school history or civics classes as a learning
tool, though the numerous famous texts on the
subject are far more enlightening (e.g., Woodward and
Bernstein's *All The President's Men* and John Dean's
Blind Ambition).

RECOMMENDATION: Pass.

* * * * *

The following sample coverage was written for a play that eventually won
awards, continues to be widely produced, and may well also cause angina, though
for very different reasons:

Submission Evaluation For: (Anonymous LORT B)
Title: (omitted), Author: (omitted)
Evaluated By: Erik Ramsey

PLAY: _____ is a very dark, satirical look
at the public education system in America. This
play leaves no socio-educational topic unscathed—
pedophilic pedagogy, the ridiculous extremes of
left-wing political correctness and right-wing
religious agendas, meddling school boards, teacher
pay, school funding, and physical violence in the
classroom. Virtually every angle on the failures of
public education is sharply satirized and, therefore,
elucidated in a witty and theatrical manner.

The play specifically focuses on the plight of the
teacher trying to survive with some ideals intact
when faced with a blizzard of bureaucratic bumbling,
P.C. policing, and religious/social dogma. It begs
the question: In a world that wants to change the
nature of the word "teacher" to mean "facilitator,"
are we not asking educators to become the surrogate
parents to our children, the "end-all, be-all" in
the development of our nation's future, while at
the same time bullying them, stigmatizing them, and
paying them less than we pay the average garbage man?

(How did it come to be that we pay the person who cares for our children's teeth ten times the amount that we pay the person who edifies our children's minds? And when your child develops a cavity, do we blame the dentist? No. So why do we tend to blame the teacher when the child fails a quiz?) The play does not suggest that all teachers are good souls becoming martyrs to the labyrinth of ethical red-tape—but it does ask how truly talented and idealistic educators can possibly remain so in a system predisposed to eviscerate the very passion that schoolchildren need the most.

Note: One element of the script as it now stands may need to be watched carefully during development and production. The "pedophilic principal" sub-plot is capable of drawing a lot of focus from the more primary plotline, which is Janet's journey; if produced without a great deal of care, it could potentially overwhelm the play. This is NOT a play about pedophilia.

SYNOPSIS: The play addresses the audience as if we are the elementary schoolchildren ourselves, the teachers and administrators breaking the fourth wall and prodding us to participate in the old call-and-response routine of "Good morning, Ms. Greenberg," etc. We follow the lead character, the naïve, fresh-faced Janet through her first year of teaching as she learns the political ropes, is manipulated, threatened, and eventually jaded to the point where in order to save her soul she has to quit teaching and become a waitress at Red Lobster. Sub-plots include: The principal's pedophilia induces a mentally challenged child to commit murder on school grounds; the machinations of the school board to accommodate both the politically correct and the religious right; and an old fashioned McCarthy-style witch hunt.

THEMES: In trying to serve everyone's interest completely, none are served at all.

CHARACTERS: Janet, a fresh-faced idealist in her first year as a teacher, is the primary character here, and she is drawn somewhat more realistically, as our access point in the play. The truly satirized/ broad characters belong to the "entrenched" class:

Principal "Pettlogg," the pedophile; various veteran teachers who fall on either side of the fence—either sycophants trying to move up into administration or burn-outs too jaded to even care; administrators ruled by a lust for power and a willingness to prostitute their ideals to please every sector of the public in order to keep that power.

AUDIENCE: An audience for this play must be willing to be challenged to look the topic squarely in the eye, laugh about it to avoid weeping, then do something about it. It should be required viewing for all schoolboard members, and every parent who thinks that their hard-earned tax dollars alone ought to be enough to build their children into productive members of society.

RECOMMENDATION: Artistic management should seriously consider this play. It is both truly entertaining and deeply thoughtful.

* * * * *

Coverage is seldom, if ever, shown to the playwright, though many writers will request it in vain, and some go so far as to have a friend with informal ties to the theater in question sneak into the inner sanctum to photocopy the coverage surreptitiously on the theater's own decrepit copy machines—only to be caught in the act and escorted off the grounds by some guy who once auditioned to play Stanley Kowalski but only ended up strong-arming his way to a receptionist position. There is actually a good reason for this privacy, even if it does drive certain local playwrights to larcenous hi-jinx: coverage is *not* a critique intended to help the playwright make the play better, but rather to help artistic management quickly decide what they must read, might read, and won't read. It is often brutally blunt, and is not considered the infallible last word on the piece in question. And almost every theater has a skeleton in their filing cabinets: The now-famous play that got away.

If it seems as though it might be almost insurmountable to overcome the "naked chiropractor" effect and the notion that one of your direct competitors, a clearly demented but promising playwright, gets to have a say in the professional progress of your script … Well, it is. But one shouldn't lose sleep, or lunch, over it. Play readers on the front lines often don't last long unless they bring their bosses something of value to produce, or at least consider producing while they sip Folgers Crystals from disintegrating week-old Starbucks paper cups. As cynical as the process may sound, that poor bastard of a script analyst is actually desperate for your submission to succeed so that he or she can gain some measure of success for having "found" it. And woe betides the analyst who has a bad day and pans a genius script that is subsequently produced first elsewhere to great acclaim. The main method for a script analyst to climb further up the artistic staff —before he or she dies of tetanus or is quietly fired—is to find a few plays that really show promise. Of course, armed with the knowledge above, it would seem that plays lampooning naked chiropractors skipping through the lobbies of oily convention-center hotels might catapult your script all the way onto the artistic director's to-do list. Don't do it.

Erik Ramsey is a playwright, Head of the BFA Playwriting Program at Ohio University, and professional new play development dramaturg. He is also ostensibly the author of the above treatise, but prefers to retain an element of plausible deniability.

Appendix B

SAMPLE CHARACTER SKETCHES
(Written by Todd McCullough)

Some playwrights find it helpful to write character sketches in order to create their characters. Here are several examples of useful sketches.

BARRY

Barry Spatz is 38 years old. He was born outside Denver, in Aurora, Colorado, the son of Larry and Karen Spatz. He has an older brother, Ted. His childhood was what could be called "happy," spent playing football with his brother and the neighborhood kids. When Barry was 10, he went through a one-week period when he spoke and behaved as though he was a superhero leading a double life. The period ended abruptly one night at the dinner table when his father hit him on the back of the head. His upbringing was moderately religious, the family attending church on those Sundays when the Broncos weren't playing.

After graduating high school with mediocre grades, Barry moved to Denver, where he worked several jobs, including baggage man at the airport, short-order cook, and even delivery man helping out in his brother's Rent-To-Own appliance store. Finally, he took a position on the assembly line at Yale Automotive Factory. His brother Ted would joke, "You're the only Spatz to go to Yale." While moderately funny at the first telling, it quickly lost its charm as it was repeated at every family gathering.

Barry's father died in 1989 of heart failure, and his mother passed away four years later, in 1993. In 1999, Barry was permanently injured when a piece of machinery fell on his right foot, sending him to the hospital for a week and giving him a slight limp. Since then, he's collected a meager disability check and lived in a small bachelor apartment.

In terms of meaningful relationships, Barry has none to speak of really. His first kiss came at age 22, when Sandy Barber, an acquaintance of his brother's (who was then already married to his wife, Pam) made out with Barry in a bathroom for 58 seconds at a party thrown at Ted and Pam's house. While Barry attributes the incident to "being a cut-up after six Pabst Blue Ribbons," the truth is that Miss Barber was paid a sum of twenty dollars by Ted to "make out with my little brother for a full minute." Thirteen years later, Barry still doesn't know this. He dated another woman, Dusty LaPage, a co-worker at Yale, for four days in the fall of 1997. The relationship was never consummated and ended awkwardly when Dusty pretended not to know who Barry was. It stands as the most recent romantic liaison Barry Spatz has had.

Barry's favorite album is The Grass Roots' *Temptation Eyes*, and his interests include television, eating, and the Denver Broncos.

CAROL

Carol Sweeney, 35, was born Carol Snodgrass in Butte, Montana. An only child, she was the daughter of Hal and Marjorie Snodgrass. Marjorie was the bread-winner in the family, working as a guidance counselor at the local high school. Hal, a self-proclaimed "Part-Time Fix-It Man and Full-Time Dreamer," spent most of his days listening to The Nitty Gritty Dirt Band and smoking marijuana in the garage.

Carol was a shy girl in grade school and had few friends. In high school, she blossomed a little and was assistant editor of the school's yearbook. Her can-do attitude, coupled with her desperate need to be liked, got her voted "Most Likely To Do You a Favor" by her peers. Also of note is a poem Carol wrote her senior year entitled "The Best Times of Our Lives," which was put in the yearbook. An avid writer, Carol was once referred to by her English teacher, Emma Simms, as "Sylvia Plath, but not as deep." It is a compliment Carol cherishes to this day.

After high school, Carol attended community college in Helena, where she received an Associate's Degree in Communications. Upon looking for a job, she went through a brief episode of depression when she realized that the degree was useless. At age 22, looking for opportunities beyond what Montana had to offer, she decided to move to a larger city. With Canada to the north and the sprawling wasteland of Wyoming to the south, she moved to Denver. Once there, she went through a series of jobs, including waitress, server, and cocktail waitress. It was during this time that she wrote her first collection of poems, *The Pickle Jar*. Though only ever shown to family and close personal friends, the book was met with harsh criticism.

Carol had a moderately productive dating life. She lost her virginity the night of her senior prom to Tommy Knopfler. Though she considered the moment "magical," she learned from Tommy at their ten-year high school reunion that the whole event was Tommy's way of seeing if he was gay. The experiment was a disaster on both accounts. After a string of tepid relationships and misunderstood friendships throughout her twenties, Carol met Darryl Sweeney in 1998 at Tele-Talk, a telemarketing company downtown where the two of them worked. They were married in 2000. Carol wrote both of their vows. However, the marriage was short-lived and Darryl, without warning, took off in 2002. Embarrassed and lonely, Carol told everyone that he had been kidnapped, and, after a period of a few months, that the kidnappers had murdered him.

Carol's favorite album is Simon & Garfunkel's *Parsley, Sage, Rosemary & Thyme*. Her interests include reading, writing, and herbalism.

NEIL

Neil Flanagan, 44, was born and raised in Boulder, Colorado. The son of Jack Flanagan, a failed novelist, and Therese Flanagan, a librarian, Neil was raised with a love of the English language. He had read many of the classics by the time he left middle school and had dismayed many of his teachers with his theory that, all things being equal, The Little Engine That Could probably couldn't. His love affair with literature and problems with authority figures continued throughout middle school, when he was given a week's detention for an unauthorized lunch-time production of *Lysistrata* in the school's cafeteria.

Tragedy struck when, in 1976, Neil's father committed suicide, the result of a crumbling marriage, lack of literary success, and repeated denial of enrollment in Allen Ginsberg's Naropa Institute. The incident stole much of Neil's youthful jubilance and planted the bitter seeds of cynicism and self-destructiveness that would blossom later.

After graduating salutatorian from high school, Neil matriculated at Brown University, majoring in English literature with an emphasis in the works of Milton. He stayed at Brown through his Master's Degree and was offered a teaching position in the English Department. However, the offer was withdrawn when Neil was quoted in the student newspaper as saying the Department Head was "buggering the student body." Though he explained that the comment was intended in a metaphorical way, he was nevertheless refused employment. Soon after, Denver City College approached Neil with a teaching position. He accepted and moved there with his wife, Clara.

Neil met Clara Huxley during his graduate studies at a mixer, when, having read a short paper of Neil's on Nabokov's *Lolita*, she threw a drink in his face. Clara, a psychology major and staunch feminist, thought Neil's assertion that the novel's titular character was a "cocktease" to be particularly distasteful. The two argued all night and, shortly before dawn, made love at Huxley's apartment. They were married shortly after.

Following the move to Denver, a step down in academic prestige in Neil's eyes, Neil began drinking heavily. In 1999, after years in a soulless marriage, Clara left Neil upon learning of a drunken tryst between him and a graduate assistant. At the end of the bitter divorce proceedings, Clara retained custody of their daughter, Cassandra. That night, in a drunken stupor, Neil passed out with a lit cigarette in his mouth, creating a huge fire, which left him badly scarred.

Neil's favorite album is The Beatles' *Revolver*. His interests include literature, cinema, and alcohol.

John

John Spatz, 14½, is the son of Ted and Pam Spatz. Much of his childhood was spent in front of the television, as his parents groomed him to be a Broncos Superfan. His name, though somewhat innocuous, is a testament to his parents' fervent belief that John Elway, if not a better man than Jesus, is capable of putting many more points on the board. An only child, he's been the object of his parents' complete attention. In terms of his mother and her cooking, this has resulted in a slight obesity problem, which John combats as best he can by referring to himself as "husky" and avoiding tight clothing.

Another large influence on John is his uncle, Barry, who dotes on him as much as if he were his own son. Among the many shared activities they enjoy are watching the Broncos Training Camp, trading Broncos football cards, and "putting one over on Mom" by stopping for Big Macs on the drive home after school, which Barry has provided since his accident left him jobless.

John has only a handful of friends, most of which have been similarly pushed to the fringes of popularity at school. In terms of the opposite sex, John has had no initiation other than the scrambled information imparted by a quasi-functioning Playboy Channel. His knowledge was further confused by his father, who, when John was 13, made an incomprehensible attempt at a sex talk. As a result, John knows only that the act of lovemaking and the desire of a football coach to "score" are somehow inextricably linked and that "false starts" are bad, but sometimes happen to the best of players.

John's favorite album is anything by Britney Spears. His interests include the Broncos, football in general, and, for reasons he's not sure of, a documentary he saw in school about Josephine Baker.

Appendix C

FORMATTING TEMPLATE

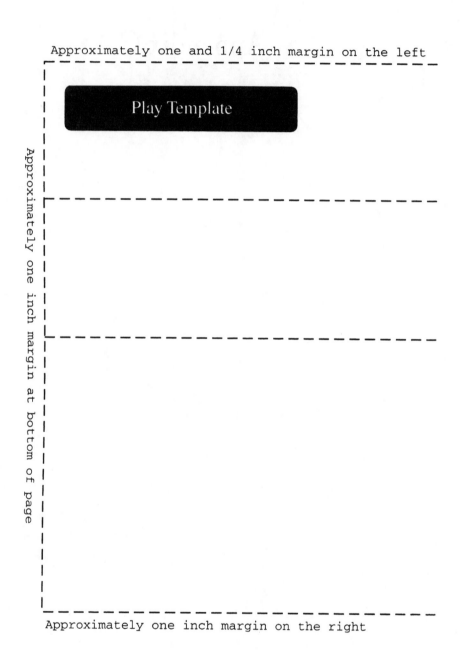

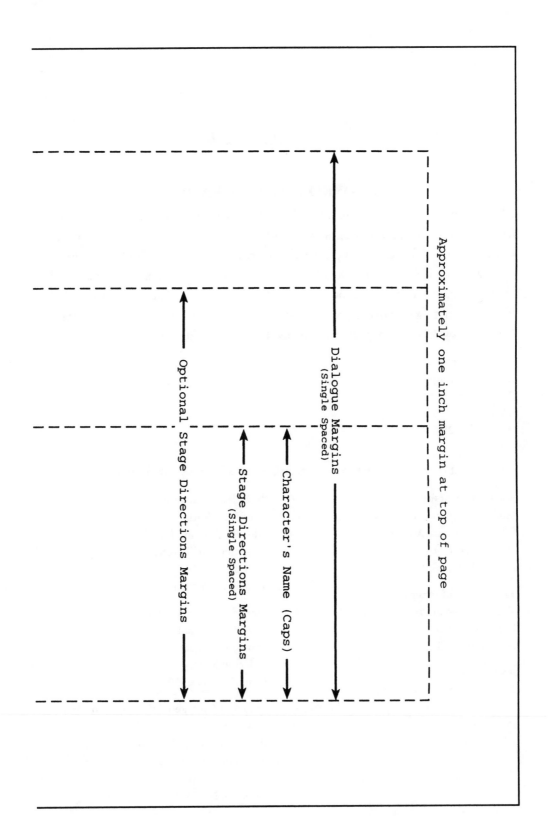

Approximately one inch margin at top of page

Dialogue Margins
(Single Spaced)

Character's Name (Caps)

Stage Directions Margins
(Single Spaced)

Optional Stage Directions Margins

Appendix D

PLAYWRITING PROGRAMS

The university systems in the United States and Canada are rare in that they have professional training programs for playwrights. It all started in 1947, when George Pierce Baker offered a playwriting workshop at Harvard. Today, hundreds of playwriting classes are taught all over the United States. A list of graduate and undergraduate programs can be found in *The Playwright's Companion*. A detailed list of playwriting schools, degrees, programs, and classes is found in *The Student's Guide to Playwriting Opportunites* published by Theatre Directories:

Theatre Directories
American Theatre Works, Inc.
P.O. Box 519
Dorset, VT 05251
(802) 867-2223

Here's a list of some of the top playwriting schools in the United States:

Boston University
MFA Program in Playwriting
School of Theatre Arts
One Sherborn St.
Boston, MA 02215

Yale School of Drama
MFA Program in Playwriting
P.O. Box 208325
New Haven, CT 06520

Brown University
MFA Program in Playwriting
Department of Theatre, Speech, and Dance
Providence, RI 02912

Brooklyn College of the City University of New York
MFA Program in Playwriting
Department of Theater
2900 Bedford Ave.
Brooklyn, NY 11210

Sarah Lawrence College
MFA Program in Playwriting
Program in Theater Arts
1 Mead Way
Bronxville, NY 10708-5999

Brooklyn College of the City University of New York
MFA Program in Playwriting
Department of Theater
2900 Bedford Ave.
Brooklyn, NY 11210

Carnegie Mellon University
School of Drama
MFA Program in Playwriting
Purnell Center for the Arts
5000 Forbes Ave.
Pittsburgh, PA 15213

The Catholic University of America
MFA Program in Playwriting
Department of Drama
620 Michigan Ave. N.E.
Washington, DC 20064

Columbia University
MFA Program in Playwriting
Theatre Division
2960 Broadway
New York, NY 10025

The Actors Studio
MFA Program in Playwriting
New School University
68 Fifth Ave.
New York, NY 10011

New York University
Tisch School
Department of Dramatic Writing
721 Broadway, 7th Floor
New York, NY 10003

Rutgers, The State University of New Jersey-New Brunswick
MFA Program in Playwriting
Theatre Arts Department
Mason Gross School of the Arts
New Brunswick, NJ 08903

Smith College
MFA Program in Playwriting
Department of Theatre
1 College St.
Northampton, MA 01063

Kent State University
MFA Program in Playwriting
School of Theatre and Dance
Kent, OH, 44242

Southern Illinois University Carbondale
MFA Program in Playwriting
Theater Department
Carbondale, IL 62901

DePaul University
MFA Program in Playwriting
The Theatre School
2135 N. Kenmore
Chicago, IL 60614

Indiana University
MFA Program in Playwriting
Department of Theatre and Drama
275 N. Jordan Ave.
Bloomington, IN 47405

Ohio University
Professional Playwriting Program
School of Theatre, Kantner Hall
Athens, OH 45701

Wayne State University
MFA Program in Playwriting
Theatre Department
4841 Cass Ave.
Detroit, MI 48201

University of Virginia
MFA Program in Playwriting
Department of Drama
Culbreth Road
Charlottesville, VA 22903

University of Georgia
MFA Program in Playwriting
Drama and Theatre Program
Athens, GA 30602

The University of Iowa
MFA Program in Playwriting
Department of Theatre Arts
The University of Iowa
100 Theatre Building
Iowa City, IA 52242

University of Missouri-Columbia
MFA Program in Playwriting
Department of Theatre
129 Fine Arts Building
Columbia, MO 65211

Texas Tech University
MFA Program in Playwriting
Department of Theatre and Dance
Box 42061
Lubbock, TX 79409

University of Arkansas
MFA Program in Playwriting
Department of Drama
Fayetteville, AR 72701

University of Houston
MFA Program in Playwriting
School of Theatre
4800 Calhoun Rd.
Houston, TX 77204

University of Nevada, Las Vegas
MFA Program in Playwriting
Department of Theatre Arts
4505 Maryland Pkwy.
Las Vegas, NV 89154

University of New Mexico
MFA Program in Playwriting
College of Fine Arts
MSC04 2570
1 University of New Mexico
Albuquerque, NM 87131-0001

University of New Orleans
MFA Creative Writing Workshop Program
UNO Liberal Arts Building, Room 201
New Orleans, LA 70148

The University of Texas at Austin
MFA Program in Playwriting
Department of Theatre and Dance
Austin, TX 78712

University of California, Los Angeles
MFA Program in Playwriting
103G E. Melnitz
Box 951622
Los Angeles, CA 90095-1622

University of California, Riverside
MFA Program in Creative Writing
900 University Ave.
Riverside, CA 92521

University of Southern California
MFA Program in Playwriting
Los Angeles, CA 90089

Arizona State University
MFA Program in Playwriting
Department of Theater
Box 872002
Tempe, AZ 85287

California Institute of the Arts
MFA Program in Playwriting
School of Theatre
24700 McBean Parkway
Valencia, CA 91355

University of California, Davis
MFA Program in Playwriting
One Shields Ave.
Davis, CA 95616-8572

University of California, San Diego
MFA Program in Playwriting
Department of Theatre and Dance
La Jolla, CA 92093

Bibliography

William Archer, *Play-Making, A Manual of Craftsmanship*; Dodd, Mead & Co., New York, 1912.

American Theatre Magazine; Theatre Communications Group, New York.

Aristotle, *Physics* (Translated by Philip Henry Wicksteed & Francis Macdonald Cornford); Harvard University Press, Cambridge, 1963.

Aristotle, *Poetics* (Translated by James Hutton); Norton, New York, 1982.

Alan Ayckbourn, *The Crafty Art of Playmaking*; Faber and Faber, London, 2002.

George Pierce Baker, *Dramatic Technique*; Da Capo Press, New York, 1976.

David Ball, *Backwards & Forwards*; Southern Illinois University Press, Carbondale, 1998.

Augusto Boal, *Theatre of the Oppressed*; Theatre Communications Group, New York, 1985.

Anne Bogart, *A Director Prepares*; Routledge, New York, 2001.

Albert Camus, *The Myth of Sisyphus*; Vintage (reissue edition), New York, 1991.

Bert Cardullo and Peter Lang, *What Is Dramaturgy?*; P. Lang, New York, 1995.

Toby Cole, editor, *Playwrights on Playwriting: The Meaning and Making of Modern Drama from Ibsen to Ionesco*; Hill and Wang, New York, 1960.

William Wallace Cook, *Plotto*; Ellis Publishing Company, Battle Creek, MI, 1928.

Lisa Collier Cool, *How To Write Irresistible Query Letters*; Writer's Digest Books, Cincinnati, 1987.

Mihaly Csikszentmihalyi, *Creativity*; HarperCollins Publishers, New York, 1996.

William Missouri Downs and Lou Anne Wright, *Playwriting: From Formula to Form*, Harcourt Brace College Publishers, Fort Worth, 1998.

The Dramatist (the bi-monthly magazine of The Dramatist Guild); The Dramatist Guild of America, New York.

The Dramatists Guild's *Resource Directory* (Gregory Bossler, editor); The Dramatist Guild of America, New York, annual periodical.

Dramatists Sourcebook; Theatre Communications Group, New York, 1981-2004.

Will Durant, *Rousseau and Revolution*; MJF Books, New York, 1967.

Lajos Egri, *The Art of Dramatic Writing*; Touchstone Books, Carmichael, CA, 1972.

Valerie Eliot, editor, *Letters Of T.S. Eliot*; Harcourt Brace Jovanovich, San Diego, 1988.

Ralph Waldo Emerson, "Compensation," *Essays and Lectures*; Library of America, New York, 1983.

Cordon Farrell, *The Power of the Playwright's Vision*; Heinemann, Portsmouth, 2001.

Jeffrey Hatcher, *The Art & Craft of Playwriting*; Story Press, Toronto, 2000.

Václav Havel, *The Art of the Impossible*; Alfred A. Knopf Inc., New York, 1997

Insight for Playwrights; monthly periodical edited by Rachel Ladutke, Merrick, NY.

Wendell Johnson, *People in Quandaries*; Harper & Row, New York, 1946.

Robert Edmund Jones, *The Dramatic Imagination*; Theatre Arts Books, New York, 1941.

Walter Kerr, *How Not to Write a Play*; Dramatic Publishing, Woodstock, IL, 1998.

John Howard Lawson, *Theory and Technique of Playwriting*; G. P. Putnam's Sons, New York, 1949.

Jeane Luere and Sidney Berger, editors, *Playwright Versus Director: Authorial Intentions and Performance Interpretations*; Greenwood Press, Westport, CT, 1994.

David Mamet, *Three Uses of the Knife*; Columbia University Press, New York, 1998.

Terry McCabe, *Mis-Directing the Play*; Ivan R. Dee, Chicago, 2001.

Robert McKee, *Story*; Regan Books, New York, 1997.

Georges Polti, *The Thirty-Six Dramatic Situations*; The Writer Inc., Boston, 1993.

Blaise Pascal, *Pascal Selections* (The Great Philosophers), ed. Richard H. Popkin; Macmillan, New York, 1989.

Peter Jason Riley, *The New Tax Guide for Artists of Every Persuasion: Actors, Directors, Musicians, Singers and Other Show-Biz Folk, Visual Artists and Writers*; Limelight Editions, New York, 2002.

Jean-Jacques Rousseau, *Confessions*; The Heritage Press, New York, 1955.

Jean-Jacques Rousseau, *Letter to M. d'Alembert on the Theatre* (translated by Allan Bloom); Cornell University Press, Ithaca, NY, 1960.

Bertrand Russell, *A History of Western Philosophy*; Modern Library, New York, 1945.

Bertrand Russell, *Mysticism and Logic*; Barnes & Noble Books, Totowa, NJ, 1981.

Robin Russin and William Missouri Downs, *Screenplay: Writing the Picture*; Silman-James Press, Los Angeles, 2003.

Jean-Paul Sartre, "Portrait of the Antisemite," *Existentialism from Dostoevsky to Sartre*, edited by Walter Kaufmann, Penguin Group, Canada, 1981.

Dana Singer, *Stage Writers Handbook*; Theatre Communications Group, New York, 1997.

Tom Stoppard and Mel Gussow, *Conversations With Stoppard*; Grove Press, New York, 1996.

Jeffrey Sweet, *Solving Your Script: Tools and Techniques for the Playwright*; Heinemann, Portsmouth, NH, 2001.

Konstantin Stanislavski, *An Actor Prepares*, Theatre Arts Books, New York, 1936.

Konstantin Stanislavski, *Building a Character*, Theatre Arts Books, New York, 1949.

Konstantin Stanislavski, *Creating a Role*, Theatre Arts Books, New York, 1961.

Louis Torres and Michelle Marder Kamhi, *What Art Is: The Esthetic Theory of Ayn Rand*; Open Court, Chicago, 2000.

Chris Vogler, *The Writer's Journey*; Michael Wiese Productions, Studio City, 1992.

Eudora Welty, *One Writer's Beginnings*; Harvard University Press, Cambridge, 1984.

Michael Wright, *Playwriting in Process: Thinking and Working Theatrically*; Heinemann, Portsmouth, NH, 1997.

Index

Abbott, George, x
abbreviations, in dialogue, 183
Absurdism, 9, 40–46, 56
    roots of, 43–44
    writing, 44–46
accepting failure, 93–94
The Accidental Death of an Anarchist (Fo), 40
action
    defined, 7–8
    motivation for, 118
activities vs. dramatic action, 119
actors
    as source for rewrites, 296–97
    working with, 296–97
The Actor's Nightmare (Durang), 99
acts, 95, 97–99
    last page of, 191
adaptations, 203–4
The Adding Machine (Rice), 39
advance payment, 283
Aeschylus, 63, 64
    Agamemnon, ix
African ritual drama, 49
Agamemnon (Aeschylus), ix
agents, 172, 255, 272
    getting, 276–78
    playwriting, 277
Albee, Edward, 22, 212–13
    Who's Afraid of Virginia Woolf?, 156, 289
alienation drama, 48–52
    backgrounds of, 50–51
    writing, 51–52
"alienation effect," 49–50
The Alley Theatre, 302
alliteration, 161, 162
Amadeus (Shaffer), 17, 124, 128, 136, 156
American College Theatre Festival Ten-Minute Play
    Contest, 218
American Theatre, 213
Anderson, Maxwell, xiiv, 84
Anderson, Robert, 280, 289
Angels in America (Kushner), 47, 48, 201
Anne of the Thousand Days, xiiv
antagonist, 135–36
    ghosts, 127
    initiation of conflict, 133
    as magnified aspect of protagonist's shadow, 136
    need to empathize with, 123
    as shadow of protagonist, 136
Apology (Plato), 57
Archer, William, 55, 85, 87
    Play Making: A Manual of Craftmanship, 74, 97

Aristophanes: *Lysistrata*, 104
Aristotelian drama, 48–49
Aristotelianism, 41–42
Aristotle
    "a certain magnitude," 1
    character subservient to plot, 62–63
    definition of character flaw, 125
    definition of opening event, 65–66
    essential structural methods, 48–49
    four causes, 41
    Physics, 41
    plot over character, 111
    Poetics, x, 15, 26, 48–49, 57
    six essential components of drama, 57
    spectacle, 59–60
    tragedy, 72
    unity, 60
art
    and audience, 304
    as discipline, 88
    function of, 62
    as self-congratulatory entertainment, 305
    vs. entertainment, 303
The Art & Craft of Playwriting (Hatcher), 118–19, 120
Art (Hampton), 98
artistic director, 285, 310
artistic meetings, 292
The Art of Dramatic Writing (Egri), 1, 61
asides, 28, 155
assistant stage manager (A.S.M.), 285
atheism, 45
audience
    and art, 304
    communicating to, 20
    reactions during readings, 208
    speaking directly to, 52
audition, 207
authenticity, 29
author's rights, 281–82
avant-garde theater, x
Ayckbourn, Alan, 1, 23, 55
    The Craft of Playmaking, 26
    The Norman Conquests, 135, 137

backstory, 150
*Backwards & Forwards: A Technical Manual for Reading
    Plays* (Ball), 8, 118, 154
Baker, George Pierce, 111, 324
    Dramatic Technique, x, 83, 95
The Bald Soprano (Ionesco), 44
Ball, David: *Backwards & Forwards: A Technical Manual
    for Reading Plays*, 8, 118, 154

Barefoot in the Park (Simon), 24
Bay Area Playwrights Festival, 212
beat (parenthetical), 184
beats, 97, 147–50
    charting, 150
Beckett, Samuel
    Endgame, 44
    Happy Days, 44
    Krapp's Last Tape, 44
    Waiting for Godot, 44, 59, 133, 289
beginnings, of formula plays, 64–65
Bethe, Hans, 93, 215
Betrayal (Pinter), 21
binding, for submission script, 171
black comedies, 24
blackouts, 100
Blake, William, 35
Blind Date (Campbell), 220–31
    comments on, 231–36
blocking, 185, 187
blocking rehearsals, 298
The Bloodknot, 17
Bloom, Alan, 59
Boal, Augusto: *Theater of the Oppressed*, 51
Bogart, Anne: *A Director Prepares*, 110
bold lettering, in script, 180
Boyd, Gregory, 302
The Brady Bunch, 24
brainstorming, 6, 93
Brecht, Bertold
    alienation, 48–52
    Epic Theater, 11
    Mother Courage and Her Children, 47
Breed, Donna, 208
Broadway, dominance by recycled spectacles, 255
Brodsky, Joseph, 4
Brooks, Mel, 23, 116
Brown, Rosellen, 141
Bruce, Lenny, 28
buddy movies, 133
budget, 16
Bus Stop (Inge), 84

The Cabinet of Dr. Caligari, 39
Cain, James M., 290–91
camera angles, 14
Campbell, Clifton: *Emerald Tree Boa*, 215–16
Campbell, Joseph, 2
    The Hero with a Thousand Faces, 64, 73, 132
Campbell, Thomas Michael: *Blind Date*, 218, 220–31
Camus, Albert: *The Myth of Sisyphus*, 43
capitalism, 31
capital letters, in script, 180
Cardullo, Bert, 215
Carlin, George, 28
Carnegie Mellon University, as America's first theater
        school, x
casting, 292
casting method, of writing dialogue, 160
Cast of Characters page, 174–77, 178
"casts to type," 207
catalyst, 122–23
catharsis, 25, 49, 72–73, 119
Cat on a Hot Tin Roof (Williams), 161, 172, 289

Catron, Louis: *Playwriting*, 18
Cats, 7, 50, 58
cause-and-effect logic, 30, 32, 60, 65, 71
central conflict, 11
Cezanne, Paul, 39
change, in characters, 32
Chaplin, Charlie, 40
character arc, 128–29
character descriptions, 95, 174. See also character
        sketches, sample
character-driven plays, 74, 75–82
character flaw, 126, 134
characters, 57
    abstractions from reality, 120
    in action, 117–29
    always attempt to turn negative into positive, 123
    as aspects of the writer, 112, 130–32
    avoiding doubles, 137–38
    background information, 122
    based on "real people," 8, 119
    believability, 130
    change in over course of play, 25, 32
    conflict of need and desire, 128
    (de)constructing, 113–15
    defined, 111
    dominant emotion, 116
    functions, 132–37
    internal conflict, 127–28
    journey of self-revelation, 126
    knowing, 138–39
    limited self-knowledge, 125–26
    methods used to create, 112
    must need or want something, 122
    names, 95, 96, 131–32, 180
    profound choices faced, 120–21
    realist, 30
    traits, 115–16
    types, 2–3
    understandable motivations, 122–23
    who do not change, 129
character biographies (character studies), 112
character's ghost, 126
character sketches, sample, 317–20
character's voice, 160–69
character vs. plot, 62–64, 82–83
Chaucer, Geoffrey: *The Miller's Tale*, 23
Chekhov, Anton, 118
    The Cherry Orchard, 9, 31, 121, 289
    "gun on the wall," 61, 86, 176
    The Seagull, 31
    The Three Sisters, 31
    Uncle Vanya, 31
Childress v. Taylor, 202
A Chorus Line, 60
Churchill, Caryl: *Cloud 9*, 50
cinematic thinking, 13–15
Circle Rep, 209, 210
The Civil Wars (Wilson), 12, 45
Claris Filemaker, 268
clichés, 116, 169
cliché traps, 84
climax, 10, 72, 80
closed-shop unions, 256
close-ups, 14

Cloud 9 (Churchill), 50
Clurman, Harold, 199, 217, 290
co-authors, 200, 202
coincidence, 32–33
cold readings, 199, 207, 208
Coleridge, Samuel Taylor, "willing suspension of
    disbelief," 49
collaboration, 279
    and copyright, 201–3
Collins, Wilkie, 85
comedy, 22–25
    catharsis, 73
    prevalent types of, 23–24
    situation comedy (sitcoms), 24–25
    stand-up, 28, 133
    and tragedy, mixing, 26
comic effect, 204–5
comic flaw, 126
comic timing, 60
commas, in dialogue, 182
communism, 30
Community for Creative Non-Violence v. Read, 203
complication, 68, 69
compromise, 58
conclusionary statements, avoiding, 163–65
The Condemned of Altona (Sartre), 44
confessional performance, 28–29
Confessions (Rousseau), 35
confidants, 155–56
conflict, 10, 58, 68
    avoidance of in real life, 119
    central, 11
    directed, 5–6
    and exposition, 152–53
    imminent, 69
    initiation of by antagonist, 133
    internal, 127–28
construction crew, 284
contact information, on submission script, 172
contracts, 281
    problems, 283–84
    standard, 281
contrivance, 12
Cook, William Wallace: *Plotto,* 2
copyright, 199–205, 281
    how to obtain, 201
    importance of, 201–3
    and parody, 204–5
    plays based on real people, 204
    protects expression of idea, not idea, 200
    resources, 205
    retained by playwrights, xiv
    term on co-authored works, 200
copyright notice, 173
Copyright Office, Library of Congress, 201
Corpus Christi (McNally), 89
costume changes, 100
The Count of Monte Cristo (Dumas), ix, 94
cover, of submission script, 172
coverage, 311–15
cover letters, 257, 260–63
    sample, 262
Cox, Kerry, 304
The Craft of Playmaking (Ayckbourn), 26

creative director, 287–88
creativity, 89–90, 215
    and critical thinking, 91–92
    and technique, 90–91
Creativity (Csikszentmihalyi), 93, 215
crew chief(s), 284
Crimes of the Heart (Henley), 98
crisis, 1, 10, 68, 69
critics, 301
The Crucible (Miller), 33, 289
Csikszentmihalyi, Mihaly: *Creativity,* 93, 215
cue-to-cue rehearsals, 299
cycle plays, 47
Cyrano de Bergerac (Rostand), 34

dark comedies, 24, 289
dark moment, 70–71
Darwin, Charles, 29
    The Origins of Species by Means of Natural Selection, 30
deadlines, 83
Death of a Salesman (Miller), 26, 31, 40, 124, 126, 135
Deathtrap, 124
(de)construction method, 112, 113
dedication page, 173–74
democratic socialism, 30
description, 117
designers, working with, 299–300
Desire Under the Elms (O'Neill), set description for,
    299–300
deus ex machina, 34–35, 71
development process, 199, 212–17
    benefits of, 214–15
    and copyrighting, 203
    developed to death, 212–14
    drawbacks, 215–17
    rewriting, 205–6
dialects, 167–68
dialogue, 8, 80
    as action, 142
    to avoid, 168–69
    begins with characters' need to speak, 141–42
    building blocks of, 141–47
    casting call method of writing, 160
    difficulty of writing, 140
    how characters listen and react, 142–45
    interpretation and misinterpretation, 145
    must advance the story, 86
    structure of, 147–50
    subtext, 145–47
    tempo, 162–63
dialogue, formatting in script, 180–85
    abbreviations, 183
    capitals, bold lettering, underlining, and italics,
        180–81
    commas, 182
    double dash, 181
    ellipsis, 181
    exclamation point, 181–82
    hyphens, 182
    interrupted by a stage direction, 187–88
    parentheticals, 183–85
dialogue sample, 263, 267
diary entry, 26
Dickens, Charles, 117

diction, 57
didactic plays, 104
Dietz, Steven, 213, 295
digital formatting, 191–96
The Dinning Room (Gurney), 23
directed conflict, 5–6
direct experience, 3
directing, by playwright, 295–96
directing technique, 296
director/playwright relationship
    conflicts, 290
    during rehearsals, 292–94
A Director Prepares (Bogart), 110
directors, 65, 285, 286–92
    choosing and approving, 287–89
    creative, 287–88
    interpretive, 287, 288
    playwrights as, 295–96
    responsibilities, 286
    and rewrites, 289–91
    television, 286
Dirty Harry, xiiv
disillusionment, 128
Disney Corporation, 200
disturbance, 66
A Doll's House (Ibsen), x, 27–28, 29, 121, 126, 128, 129, 156
Don Quixote, 135
door-slamming farces, 24
double-casting, 174
double dash, in script, 181
double gesture, 137
drama
    derivation of word, 117–18
    six essential components of, 57
dramatic action, 8, 118–19, 121
dramatic climax, 10, 72, 80
The Dramatic Imagination (Jones), 37
dramatic peaks, 10
dramatic principles, 56–57, 82
dramatic questions, answering with new dramatic
    questions, 85
dramatic rules vs. dramatic principles, 56–57
Dramatic Technique (Baker), x, 83, 95
dramatic traps, 84
"Dramatis Personae," 174
The Dramatist, 89, 212, 256, 279, 297
Dramatists Guild, 33, 202, 256–57
    casting rules, 292
    copyright information, 205
    help with contracts, 276
    as open-shop union, 256
    pre-approved standard contracts, 281
    Resource Directory, 33, 207, 217, 258, 259, 263, 267, 277
Dramatists Play Service, 187
Dramatists Sourcebook (Dramatists Guild), 33, 207, 217, 258, 259, 263, 267, 277
dramatization, 2
dramaturgs, 201, 214–15, 285
A Dream Play (Strindberg), 56
dress rehearsals, 299
Dumas, Alexandre, 87
    The Count of Monte Cristo, ix, 94
    The Three Musketeers, 94

Dumb and Dumber, 23
Durang, Christopher
    The Actor's Nightmare, 99
    Sister Mary Ignatius Explains It All For You, 99
Durant, Will: *Rousseau and Revolution*, 36

Eastern theater, 51
Eastwood, Clint, xiiv
Edgar, David, 12, 47
Edison, Thomas, 29
Edson, Margaret: *Wit*, 212
Egri, Lajos
    The Art of Dramatic Writing, 1, 61
    on avoidance of preaching, 18
    on character, 63
    character biographies, 114
    on character change, 128–29
    on hard work of playwriting, 4
    on the inciting incident, 66
    on organizing premise, 104
    on premise, 3
Eisenstein, Linda: *Seventeen Surefire Ways to Get Your Script Rejected*, 272–74
electric lights, 29
The Elephant Man (Pomerance), 60
Eliot, T. S., 62
ellipsis, in script, 181
El Theatro Campesino, 51
e-mail attachments, 267
e-mail queries, 267
Emerald Tree Boa (Campbell), 215–16
emotional content, 5–6
emotional truth, 59
empathy, required to create a character, 112, 130–31, 139
Endgame (Beckett), 44
endings, of formula plays, 71–73
Endymion (Keats), 35
An Enemy of the People, 119
Enlightenment, and cause-and-effect logic, 27
enlightenment, in formula plays, 71
ensemble, theater, 284–85
ensemble plays, 133
Ensler, Eve: *The Vagina Monologues* (Ensler), 17, 28, 133, 157
entertainment, 59
    as the art of escape, 304–5
    recycling of culture, 304, 305
    vs. art, 303
environment, 103
epic narratives, 11
Epic Theater, 11, 15, 46–48
    beginnings, 47
    staging, 48
    writing, 47–48
epiphany, 128
Equity-waiver, 283
Equus (Shaffer), 17, 60
Erickson, Karen, 202–3, 219
    comments on *Blind Date* (Campbell), 231–32
    comments on *Forever Blue* (McCullough), 247–48
    Much Ado, 202
    Prairie Voices, 202–3
    Time Machine, 202

Escurial (Ghelderode), 300
The Eumenides (Aeschylus), 134
Euripides: *Medea*, 56, 67, 124
evaluation forms, 268–71
event, 65–66
exclamation point, in script, 181–82
exclusive option, 282–83
Existentialism, 42, 43, 45
experience, of playwright, 3–5
experimental theater, 11
exposition
    avoiding obvious, 150–59
    and conflict, 152–53
    limiting to relevant only, 159
    link between present situation and relevant issues
        from the past, 154
    need-to-know basis, 154, 159
    propelling of present situation, 154–55
    repeating, 159
Expressionism, 31, 37–40
    backgrounds of, 39–40
    writing, 40

failure, accepting, 93–94
fair use, 204
false monologues, 157
Fantastiks (Jones), 50
farce, 17, 24, 101
A Farewell to Arms (Hemingway), 96
Farrelly Brothers, 23, 24
fatalism, 42–43, 44–45
Fates, 63
Faulkner, William: *The Sound and the Fury*, 96
Faust (Goethe), 34, 47
feedback, 275
Feiffer, Jules: *Little Murders*, 24
Festival of Dionysus, 286
A Few Good Men (Sorkin), 126, 127
filler, 168
FinalDraft, 191
final dress rehearsals, 299
Finding Nemo, 86
first draft, 110
Fitzgerald, F. Scott, 76, 116
flavor-of-the-month plays, 17
"fly on the wall," 138
Fo, Dario
    The Accidental Death of an Anarchist, 40
    Orgasmo Adulto Escapes from the Zoo, 40
following up, submission scripts, 274
font, 171, 172
foreshadowing, 86
Forever Blue or, The Pregnancy Test (McCullough), 237–46
    comments on, 247–51
formatting, of script, 170–71, 179–80, 257
    dialogue, 180–85
    digital, 191–96
    last page, 191
    stage directions, 185–90
formatting template, 322–23
formula plays, 34–35, 64–73
    beginning, 64–65
    catharsis, 72–73
    climax, 72

endings, 71–73
enlightenment, 71–72
event, 65–66
    inciting incident, 66
    middle, 68–71
    rising action, 69–70
    three Cs, 68–69
    trap of, 73–74
Forrest Gump, 110
For Whom the Bell Tolls (Hemingway), 96
Frayne, Michael: *Noises Off*, 24
Freakazoid (Leguizamo), 133
"A Free Man's Worship" (Russell), 42
free verse (non-formula writing), 75–82
French farce, 60
French scenes, 95, 97, 101–2
Freud, Sigmund, 29, 30, 33
Friends of Active Copyright Education (F.A.C.E.), 205
Froebel, Freidrich, 35
front matter, of submission script, 172–78
full-length one-act play, 98

Gabler, Neal: *Life the Movie*, 304, 305
Gabridge, Patrick, 257
Gate-Keeper, 137
generalities, in dialogue, 163–65
germinal idea, 1
Ghelderode, Michel de: *Escurial*, 300
Gibson, Mel, 296
Gielgud, Sir John, 296
Gladiator, 96
The Glass Menagerie (Williams), 95–96, 158
Glengarry Glen Ross (Mamet), 84, 126, 128
God Said "Ha!" (Sweeney), 133
Goethe, Johann Wolfgang von, 35
    Faust, 34, 47
    formula for play analysis, 211
Gorky, Maxim: *The Lower Depths*, 31
Great Depression, 43
Greek Chorus, 137
Greek mythology, 63
Greek theater, 57
    play festivals, 22
    playwrights as philosopher-poets, 4
Greek Tragedies, 25
gross, percentage of, 281
Grotowski, Jerzy, 14–15
group dynamics, 284–85
Group Theatre, 217
Gurney, A. R., 23

The Hairy Ape (O'Neill), 39–40
half-ideas, 6–8, 12–13, 16
half-rejection letter, 275
Hamlet (Shakespeare), 60, 115, 204
    action, 8
    difficult decisions, 120
    ghost, 126
    internal conflict, 127
    Polonius, 163
    premise, 3
Hampton, Christopher
    Art, 98
    The Philanthropist, 21

Hansberry, Lorraine: *A Raisin in the Sun* (Hansberry), 65, 66, 67, 68, 70, 72, 73
Happy Days (Beckett), 44
Hare, David, 55, 303
Hart, Moss, 23
Harvard, as first school to offer playwriting course, x
Hatch, Orrin, 256
Hatcher, Jeffrey: *The Art & Craft of Playwriting*, 118–19, 120
Havel, Václav, 55–56
Hawthorne, Nathaniel, 35
Hedda Gabler (Ibsen), 29
Hegelian dialectics, 11
Hegland, Kenney F.: *Trial and Practice Skills*, 159
The Heidi Chronicles (Wasserstein), 47
Heine, Heinrich, 35
Hellman, Lillian, 213, 290
Hemingway, Ernest
    A Farewell to Arms, 96
    For Whom the Bell Tolls, 96
Henley, Beth, 98
Herakleitos, 128
heredity, 30
Hernan (Hugo), 35
hero. *See* protagonist
hero's journey, 138
hilarious theater, 42, 43, 45–46
Hollywood film industry, 34, 304
hook, 68
Hopkins, Arthur, 131
house manager(s), 284
Hugo, Victor
    Hernani, 35
    Les Misérables, 34, 35
Humanist movement, 27
Hunter, Lew, 172
Hwang, David, 288–89
    M. Butterfly, 289
hyphens, in dialogue, 182

Ibsen, Henrik
    A Doll's House, x, 27–28, 29, 121, 126, 128, 129, 156
    Hedda Gabler, 29
ideas
    evaluating, 1
    necessary characteristics of, 6
    originality of, 2
    scope, 15
    vs. plot and character, 2
imagery, 165–66
imitation, xvi, 169
imminent conflict, 69
The Importance of Being Earnest (Wilde), 3, 126, 135
Impressionism, 31, 39, 304–5
improvisation, 297
inciting incident, 66
Indian religious epics, 49
indirect experience, 4
indirect verbal strategies, 142
individualism, 35
Inge, William
    Bus Stop, 84
    Picnic, 290
Inherit the Wind (Lawrence and Lee), 128, 129

inkjet printer, 171
The Insider, 110
Inside the Actor's Studio, 23
Insight for Playwrights (Dramatists Guild), 33, 207, 217, 257–58, 258, 259, 263, 267
intellectual truth, 59
intention, playwright's, 211
intermissions, 97, 98
internal conflict, 127–28
interpretive director, 287, 288
interruption, 85
Ionesco, Eugene: *Rhinoceros*, 44
Irish theater, ix
irony, in naming characters, 132
italics, in script, 180
Izzard, Eddie, 28

J. B. (MacLeish), 290
Jacobs, Emmett, 97
James, Henry, ix
James, William, 30
Japanese Kabuki plays, 49, 56
Johnson, Wendell: *People in Quandaries*, 92–93
joint authors, 200, 202
joint protagonists, 133
Jones, Robert Edmund: *The Dramatic Imagination*, 37
Jones, Tom: *Fantastiks*, 50
Jonson, Ben: *Timber; Or, Discoveries Made upon Men and Matters*, 199
Jung, Carl, 132

Kabuki plays, 49, 56
Kafka, Franz, 39
    Metamorphosis, 44
Kahn, David, 208
Kamhi, Michelle Marder, 61
Kasdan, Lawrence, x
Kaufman, George, 23
Kaufman, Moises, 212
Kazan, Elia, 289, 293
Keats, John: *Endymion*, 35
Kennedy, Ted, 256
Key Largo (Anderson), 84
Kindergarten, 35–36
King Lear (Shakespeare), 59, 67, 128
Kissinger, Henry, 204
Kitchen-Sink Realism, 33
Krapp's Last Tape (Beckett), 44
Kushner, Tony, x, 202, 255
    Angels in America, 47, 48, 201

Laing, Ronald D., 43
Lang, Fritz, 39, 40
Lang, Peter, 215
The Laramie Project (Kaufman), 17, 212
Larson, Jonathan, 202
laser printer, 171
Laundry & Bourbon (McLure), 99
Lawson, John Howard, 63, 118
    Loud Speaker, 118
    Roger Bloomer, 118
Lawson, John Howard: *Theory and Technique of Playwriting*, 58
Lees, Russell: *Nixon's Nixon*, 204

legal protections, 280–84
Leguizamo, John, 28
    Freakazoid, 133
Les Misérables (Hugo), 34, 35
Letter to M. d'Alembert on the Theatre (Rousseau), 59
Library of Congress website, 205
life studies, 169
Life the Movie (Gabler), 304
linear progression, defined, 11
"line readings," 296
The Lion King, 58, 304
literary managers, 214–15
The Little Mermaid, xiii
Little Murders (Feiffer), 24
The Living Theatre, 51
London, Todd, 279
Lone Star (McLure), 99
Long Day's Journey into Night (O'Neill), 84, 165–66
Loomer, Lisa: *The Waiting Room*, 133
Loud Speaker (Lawson), 118
Love! Valour! Compassion! (McNally), 89
The Lower Depths (Gorky), 31
Lyrical Ballads (Wordsworth), 35
Lysistrata (Aristophanes), 104

M. Butterfly (Hwang), 289
Macbeth (Shakespeare), 15, 48, 137, 161–62
Machiavelli, Niccolo: *Mandragola*, 155
MacLeish, Archibald, 290
Maeterlinck, Maurice, 118
"The Magic If," 130
Mahabharata, 11
The Maids (Genet), 133
Mailer, Norman, ix
mailing etiquette, 257
major decision, 66–68
Major Dramatic Question (MDQ), x, xi, 68, 85
Mamet, David, 305
    distinctive tempo, 162
    Glengarry Glen Ross, 126
    Three Uses of the Knife, 2, 10, 18, 32
Mandragola (Machiavelli), 155
Man Ray, 39
The Man who Came to Dinner (Hart and Kaufman), 23
margins, 179
Mark Taper Forum's New Work Festival, 212, 215–16
Marvin's Room (McPherson), 65, 66, 67
    catharsis, 73
    climax, 72
    dark moment, 70
    enlightenment, 72
    rising action, 70
Marx, Karl, 29, 30–31
Marxism, 11
masks, 137
Mason, Jackie, 28
McCabe, Terry, 291
    Mis-Directing the Play, 279, 301
McCullough, Todd, 218, 317–20
    Forever Blue or, The Pregnancy Test, 237–46
McIntyre, Dennis, x
McKee, Robert, 152
    Story, 117
McLeish, Archibald: *J. B.*, 290

McLure, James
    Laundry & Bourbon, 99
    Lone Star, 99
McNally, Terrence, 287, 297
    Corpus Christi, 89
    Love! Valour! Compassion!, 89
McPherson, Scott: *Marvin's Room*, 65, 66, 67, 70, 72
Medea (Euripides), 56, 67, 124
melodrama, 34, 37
Memento, 86
Menander, 24
mental action, 8
mentors, 296
Metamorphosis (Kafka), 44
metaphors, 165
Method Acting, 147
Metropolis, 39, 40
Meyerhold, Vsevolod Emilievich, 295
MFA directing programs, 294
MFA in playwriting, 324–26
Mickey Mouse, 200
Microsoft Excel, 268
Microsoft Word, 171, 191
middle, of formula play, 68–71
A Midsummer Night's Dream (Shakespeare), 69, 125–26, 133
Midwest Play-Labs, 212
Milius, John, xiv
Miller, Arthur, x, 20, 140, 279, 289
    The Crucible, 33, 289
    Death of a Salesman, 26, 31, 40, 124, 126, 135
    Playwrights on Playwriting, 125
    selective realism, 31
    Timebends, 290
The Miller's Tale (Chaucer), 23
Mill Mountain Theatre New Play Competition Reader
    Critique Report, 270–71
mini-climax, 102
Miracle cycles, 11
Mis-Directing the Play (McCabe), 279, 301
Miss Julie (Strindberg), 98
Miss Saigon, 14, 60
Modern Times, 40
Molière, ix, xiii, 200
Monet, Claude, 39
monologistic theater, 28–29
monologues, 155, 156–58
moral ambiguity, 67
Moscow Art Theatre, 147, 289
Mother Courage and Her Children (Brecht), 47
motivation, of characters, 122–23
motivation, to write, 20–21, 94
movies
    cooption of expressionism, 39
    effect on theater, ix, 37
Moyers, Bill, 73
Much Ado About Nothing (Shakespeare), 161
Much Ado (Erickson), 202
Munch, Edvard: *The Scream*, 39
Murray, Joel, 219
    comments on *Blind Date* (Campbell), 232–33
    comments on *Forever Blue* (McCullough), 248–49
The Music Man (Willson), xv, 137
Myers, Mike, 23

Mystery cycles, 11
Mysticism and Logic (Russell), 42
mythic archetypes, 132
The Myth of Sisyphus (Camus), 43

name-calling, in dialogue, 168–69
name-recognition, 276
narrators, 158
National Festival of New Canadian Plays, 212
naturalism, 31, 39
need vs. desire, 128
negative feedback, value of, 210–11
networking, 275–76, 277
New Dramatists Theatre, 279
New Lyceum, 29
new-play development programs, 212, 217
Nicholas Nickleby (Dickens), 12
Nicholas Nickleby (Edgar), 47
nickelodeons, 37
Nietzsche, Friedrich, 41, 43
'*Night Mother* (Norman), 74–75
Nixon's Nixon (Lees), 204
No Exit (Sartre), 44
Noises Off (Frayne), 24
non-Aristotelian plays, 49
nonexclusive option, 283
non-formula writing, 75–82
non-linear theater, x
Norman, Marsha: '*Night Mother,* 74–75
The Norman Conquests (Ayckbourn), 135, 137
note-sessions, 210–11
The Notorious Mrs. Ebbsmit (Pinero), 95
Nottage, Lynn, x
Not Without My Daughter (Rintels), 136

O'Brien, Richard, 50–51
O'Casey, Sean, 218
   The Plough and the Stars, 28
The Odd Couple (Simon), 24
Odets, Clifford, 290
Oedipus Rex (Sophocles)
   catharsis, 73
   climax, 72
   dark moment, 70
   enlightenment, 72
   the event, 65
   the inciting incident, 66
   need vs. desire, 128
   offstage action, 85
   protagonist, 134, 135
   rising action, 70
   trap, 84
off book, 298
off (parenthetical), 184
offstage action, 84–85
Off Stage (parenthetical), 184
Oklahoma!, 304
one-act play
   full-length, 98
   short, 98–99
O'Neill, Eugene, ix, x, 165–66, 290
   The Hairy Ape, 39–40
   Long Day's Journey into Night, 84, 165–66
   set description for *Desire Under the Elms,* 299–300

O'Neill Playwrights Conference, 212, 216
One Writer's Beginnings (Welty), 156
opening nights, 299
open-shop unions, 256
opera, 117
options, 282–83
Orgasmo Adulto Escapes from the Zoo (Fo), 40
The Origins of Species by Means of Natural Selection
   (Darwin), 30
O.S. (parenthetical), 184
Ostrow, Stuart, 94
Othello (Shakespeare), 135, 136
Our Town (Wilder), 50, 158
outline, 94, 95
Overcoming the Naked Chiropractor: How Not to Navigate
   the Professional Script Analysis Process
   (Ramsey), 309–16

page numbers, of script, 179–80
page one, of script, 179
paper, for submission script, 171
parentheticals, in dialogue, 183–85
parody, 204–5
Pascal, Blaise: *Pensées,* 34
Pasteur, Louis, 90
pathos, 27
pause (parenthetical), 184
Peking Opera, 51
People in Quandaries (Johnson), 92–93
percentage of gross, 281
performance art, 133
Performance Theory (Schechner), 290
Phantom of the Opera, 50
The Philanthropist (Hampton), 21
philosophy, 4–5
photography, 29, 39
Picnic (Inge), 290
Pinero, Arthur
   The Notorious Mrs. Ebbsmit, 95
   The Second Mrs.Tanqueray, 95
Pinter, Harold: *Betrayal,* 21
Pirandello, Luigi: *Six Characters in Search of an Author,*
   63
pitch, 75–76, 260–61
pity and fear, 72
place, of play, 95, 103, 174, 176
Plato
   Apology, 57
   The Republic, 50
plausibility, 12, 32, 33
play, formatting body of, 179–80
   last page, 191
play analysis, formula for, 211
"playmaking," 55
play-reading series, 207
play template, 322–23
playwright/director relationship, during rehearsals,
   292–94
playwrights
   attending rehearsals, 291, 294–95
   as directors, 295–96
   homepages, 172, 276
   individual experience, 3–5
   as literary scientists, 31

marginalization, 290
ownership of play, xiv, 203, 256
"problem," 294
purpose, 211
rights, 281–82
The Playwright's Companion, 324
Playwrights Licensing Antitrust Initiative, 256
Playwrights on Playwriting (Miller), 125
playwriting, 109–10
    as art of communication, 20
    binge method, 110
    having a place to write, 109
    learning as a professional skill, ix–x
    non-formula, 75–82
    as one of last bastions of individual expression,
        xiii–xiv
    schedule, 109
    schools of thought, 22, 26
    as therapy, 21
playwriting agent, 277
Playwriting (Catron), 18
playwriting contests, 257, 258
playwriting programs, 324–26
plot, 57
    and formula, 64
    and structure, 2
    vs. character, 82–83
plot-based plays, 82
plot points, 74, 77, 78, 79, 80–81
plot structure. *See* structure
Plotto (Cook), 2
plot twist, 97
The Plough and the Stars (O'Casey), 28
Poetic Realism, 31
point of attack, 67–68
Polish Laboratory Theater, 14
Pollock, Jackson, 55
Polti, George: *The Thirty-Six Dramatic Situations*, 2
"poor man's copyright," 201
"poor theater," 14–15
Portrait of the Antisemite (Sartre), 44
positive motivation, 123
post-Impressionism, 39
post-reading discussions, 208–11
Prairie Voices (Erickson), 202–3
pre-blocking, 298
premise, 3, 63, 104–5
    defining, 19–20
previews, 299
printers, 171
private readings, 207
problem plays, 18, 20, 27, 32
problem playwright, 294
problem-solving, 92–93
producers, 65, 284–85
The Producers (Brooks and Meehan), 116
production, 301
production meetings, 292
prologue, 127
propaganda plays, 104
protagonist, 133–35
    active, 67
    always instigates the climax, 72
    defined, 16

    internal deadline, 83–84
    position of disadvantage, 66
    primary function, 133–34
    romantic, 36–37
    writer's too close identification with, 131
Proust, Marcel: *Remembrance of Things Past*, 3
Pryor, Richard, 28
psychology, 29, 30
psychotherapy, 29
public domain, 200, 203
publicity meetings, 292
public readings, 207–8
published plays, stage directions, 186–87
punctuation, in script, 181–82
purpose, playwright's, 211

query, 260, 263, 267
query postcards, 274
quest story, 138

Racine, Jean, 301
radio, effect on theater, ix
A Raisin in the Sun (Hansberry)
    catharsis, 73
    climax, 72
    dark moment, 70
    enlightenment, 72
    the event, 65
    inciting incident, 66
    major decision, 67, 68
    rising action, 70
Ramayana, 11
Ramsey, Erik: *Overcoming the Naked Chiropractor: How
        Not to Navigate the Professional Script Analysis
        Process*, 309–16
Rand, Ayn, 61
readings, 206–8
    audience reactions, 208
    post-reading discussions, 208–11
Realism, 26–33, 39
    backgrounds of, 29–31
    defined, 27
    Kitchen-Sink, 33
    of movies, 37
    selective, 33
    sets, 33
    tragic, 27
    writing, 31–33
realistic illumination, 29
real people, plays based on, 204
The Real Thing (Stoppard), 21, 58–59
rear-projection imagery, 60
regional theater movement, 212
rehearsal reports, 295
rehearsals, 294–95
    attendance by playwright, 291, 294–95
    blocking, 297
    cue-to-cue, 299
    dress, 299
    final dress, 299
    off book, 298
    playwright/director relationship during, 292–94
    previews, 299
    run-through, 298

special, 298
speed-through, 298
table work, 297
tech, 299
types of, 297–99
working, 298
rehearsed readings, 199
Reinhart, Gordon, 219
    comments on *Blind Date* (Campbell), 233–35
    comments on *Forever Blue* (McCullough), 249–50
rejection, 278
rejection letters, 275
religion, 62
religious epics, 49
religious theater, 11
The Remains of the Day (film), 121
Renaissance, 27
    critics, 155
    dramatic rules, 56–57
Renaissance Italy, 97
Renoir, Auguste, 39
Rent (Larson), 202
The Republic (Plato), 50
research, 131
Resource Directory (Dramatists Guild), 33, 207, 258, 259,
    263, 267
The Respectful Prostitute (Sartre), 44
résumé, 263, 277
rewriting, 199, 205–6, 282
Rhinoceros (Ionesco), 44
rhythm
    in dialogue, 161–63
    as problem for playwriting students, x
Rice, Elmer: *The Adding Machine*, 39
Richard III (Shakespeare), 127
Riders to the Sea (Synge), x
Riesner, Dean, xiiv
Ring Cycle (Wagner), 47
Rintels, David: *Not Without My Daughter*, 136
rising action, 68, 69–70
Ristad, Eric, 45
ritual drama, 49
Roaring Twenties, 43
The Robbers (Schiller), 35
Rock, Chris, 28
The Rocky Horror Picture Show, 50–51
Roger Bloomer (Lawson), 118
Romanticism, 33–37
    beginnings, 35–36
    protagonist, 36–37
    scope of, 36
    writing, 36–37
Romeo and Juliet (Shakespeare), 33–34
    balcony scene, 69
    catharsis, 73
    climax, 72
    dark moment, 70
    the event, 65
    inciting incident, 66
    Major Dramatic Question, 68
    rising action, 70
    signposts, 86
    time lock, 84
    unfinished business, 126

Rosencrantz and Guildenstern Are Dead (Stoppard), 4, 59,
    133, 204
Rostand, Edmond, 34
Roth, Eric, 110
Rousseau, Jean-Jacques
    Confessions, 35
    Letter to M. d'Alembert on the Theatre, 59
Rousseau and Revolution (Durant, Will), 36
Rowe, Kenneth Thorpe
    Major Dramatic Question, x, xi
    Write That Play, x
royalties, 281
run-through, 298
Russell, Bertrand
    "A Free Man's Worship," 42
    Mysticism and Logic, 42
Russin, Robin
    comments on *Blind Date* (Campbell), 235–36
    comments on *Forever Blue* (McCullough), 250–51

Same Time, Next Year (Slade), 15
Samuel French, 187
San Francisco Mime Troupe, 51
Sarcey, Francisque, 84
Sarcey's principle of offstage action, 84–85
Sartre, Jean-Paul
    The Condemned of Altona, 44
    No Exit, 44
    Portrait of the Antisemite, 44
Saturday Night Live, 18, 204
scansion, 161
scenario, 94–95, 102
    sample, 105–9
scenes, 95, 97–99
    changes, 100
    last page of, 191
    making, 100–101
scenes list page, 177
Schechner, Richard: *Performance Theory*, 290
Schiller, Friedrich von: *The Robbers*, 35
science, 62
scientific methods, 30
The Scream (Munch), 39
screenplays, 100
screenwriters, xiiv, 256
Scribe, Eugene, 34–35
script. *See* submission script
script analysis, 309–16
script analyst, 309–11, 315–16
script-in-hand performances, 199
Scriptwork: A Director's Approach to New Play Development
    (Breed and Kahn), 208
The Seagull (Chekhov), 31
seamstresses, 284
secondary characters, 131
The Second Mrs. Tanqueray (Pinero), 95
Selective Realism, 31, 33
self-addressed return envelope (SASE), 260
self-addressed stamped postcard (SASP), 260, 265–66
self-doubt, 127
self-knowledge, of characters, 125–26
self-pity, 116
self-promotion, xvi, 255, 275–76
self-understanding, 73

"sense memories," 5
sentimental comedy, 23–24
set changes, 100
set description, 176–77
sets, realism, 33
setting, of play, 95, 103–4, 174, 176, 177
setup, 86
Seventeen Surefire Ways to Get Your Script Rejected
    (Eisenstein), 272–74
Shaffer, Peter
    Amadeus, 17, 124, 128, 136, 156
    Equus, 17, 60
"shaggy-dog story," 71
Shakespeare, William
    as actor, ix
    borrowing of plots, 2
    fart jokes, 23
    Hamlet, 3, 8, 60, 115, 120, 126, 127, 163, 204
    King Lear, 59, 67, 128
    and limits of self-knowledge, 125
    MacBeth, 15, 48, 137, 161–62
    A Midsummer Night's Dream, 69, 125–26, 133
    Much Ado About Nothing, 161
    Othello, 135, 136
    rhythms of language, 161
    Richard III, 127
    Romeo and Juliet (Shakespeare), 33–34, 65, 66, 68,
        69, 70, 72, 73, 84, 86, 126
    scenes, 100
    stage directions, 186
    staging, 48
    The Tempest, 84, 137
    The Winter's Tale, 186
Shape-Shifter, 137
Shaw, George Bernard, 68, 186
Shelley, Percy Bysshe, 35
Shepard, Sam: *The Tooth of Crime*, 40
Sheridan, R. B., 170
short one-acts, 98–99
signing fee, 278
signpost, 86–87
silent monologue, 117
similes, 165
Simon, Neil, 24, 64, 304
simultaneous submissions, 277
Singer, Dana: *Stage Writers Handbook*, 280, 282, 283, 284
Sister Mary Ignatius Explains It All For You (Durang), 99
situation comedy (sitcoms), 24–25
Six Characters in Search of an Author (Pirandello), 63
skit, 18
"small penis" rule, 205
small workshop productions, 199
solicited script, 259
soliloquies, 28, 155, 156–58
Sondheim, Stephen, 304
song, 57
Sonny Bono Copyright Term Extension Act, 200
Sophocles, 63. See also *Oedipus Rex*
Sorkin, Aaron: *A Few Good Men*, 126, 127
The Sound and the Fury (Faulkner), 96
sounds, in dialogue, 160–62
special rehearsals, 298
spectacle, 37, 57, 58, 59–60
speech rhythm, 161–63

speed-through, 298
spiral (strip or Velo) bindings, 171
stage, restrictions of, 14
stage directions
    alienationist drama, 52
    to avoid, 188
    character descriptions, 187
    formatting, 185–90
    interrupting dialogue, 187–88
    must work on the page and the stage, 188
stage manager (S.M.), 284, 285
stage reading, 207–8
stage reality, 61
Stage Writers Handbook (Singer), 280, 282, 283, 284
staging, 177
    of epic plays, 48
stand-up comedy, 28, 133
Stanislavski, Konstantin, 5, 109, 147, 163, 289
    "The Magic If," 130
Starry Night (Van Gogh), 39
Star Spangled Girl (Simon), 24
Star Wars, 34
static characters, 112
step outline, 94, 97
stereotypes, 116–17, 163
Stewart, Potter, 19
stock characters, 24
stock conventions, 116
Stoppard, Tom
    The Real Thing, 58–59
    Rosencrantz and Guildenstern Are Dead, 4, 59, 133,
        204
story building, techniques of, 83–87
Story (McKee), 117
storytelling, 64, 73
A Streetcar Named Desire (Williams), 26, 96, 154, 172, 187
Strindberg, August, 39
    A Dream Play, 56
    Miss Julie, 98
strip binding, 171
structural unity, 58, 60–62
structure, xv, 55–62, 82
    conflict, 58
    spectacle, 59–60
    truth, 58–59
    unity, 60–62
The Student's Guide to Playwriting Opportunities, 324
"Sturm und Drang" (Storm and Stress), 35
style sheets, 191
subconscious, in expressionist plays, 38
subconscious motivations, 30
submission record, 267–68
submission script, 259–60, 311
    Cast of Characters page, 174–77, 178
    character names, 180
    dialogue, formatting of, 180–85
    digital formatting, 191–96
    formatting, 170–71
    front matter, 172–78
    last page, 191
    last page of scene, act, and play, 191
    the look, 171
    the play, 179–80
    sample page, 189–90

scenes list page, 177
stage directions, 185–90
time/place/setting page(s), 175–77
widows, 191
subplot, 137
subsidiary rights, 282
subtext, 142, 145–47
sub-themes, 104
Successful Script Writing (Wolff and Cox), 304
Sundance, 212, 216
supporting roles, 137
Sweeney, Julia, 28
    God Said "Ha!", 133
symbolic acts, 51–52
Synge, John Millington: *Riders to the Sea*, x
synopsis, 263–64

table work, 297–99
Talbot, Fox, 29
talking therapy, 33
Tarantino, Quentin, 2
Tchaikovsky, Pyotr, 60–61
The Tech, 45
technical director(s), 284
technique, xv
    and creativity, 90–91
    directing, 296
    story building, 83–87
tech rehearsals, 299
teleology, 41
television, effect on theater, ix
television directors, 286
television sitcoms, 24–25
The Tempest (Shakespeare), 84, 137
template, formatting, 322–23
templates, 191
tempo, 162–63
Ten Big Copyright Myths Explained, 205
ten-minute plays, 99
    dissected and discussed, 218–51
"10 Percent Rule," 67
theater, only art form in which medium and subject are
    the same, 7
theater ensemble, 284–85
Theater of the Oppressed (Boal), 51
theaters
    Internet addresses, 259
    play evaluation forms, 268–71
Theatre Communications Group, 258, 259, 280
Theatre Directories, 324
Theatre Profiles, 259
theatrical conventions, 50
theme, 3, 19, 20, 26, 63, 95, 104–5
Theory and Technique of Playwriting (Lawson), 58
therapy, playwriting as, 21
Thespis, 286
Thomas Aquinas, Saint, 41
Thompson, Lynn, 202
thought, 57
three-act plays, 97–98
The Three Musketeers (Dumas), 94
The Three Sisters (Chekhov), 31
Three Uses of the Knife (Mamet), 2, 10, 18, 32
through-line, 11

Timber; Or, Discoveries Made upon Men and Matters
    (Jonson), 199
time, of play, 95, 174
Timebends (Miller), 290
time lock, 83–84
Time Machine (Erickson), 202
time/place/setting page(s), 175–77
title, 172
title file, 96
title page, 172–73
    sample, 175
Tolstoy, Leo: *War and Peace*, 11, 47
Tomlin, Lily, 28
The Tooth of Crime (Shepard), 40
Torres, Louis, 61
trademark laws, 200
tragedy, x, 22–23, 25–26, 72
    Aristotle on, 72
    and comedy, mixing, 26
    of the common man, 25–26
    dark moment, 71
tragic flaw, 126
tragic realism, 27
trap, 84
traveling angels, 129
Trial and Practice Skills (Hegland), 159
Trickster, 137
Trinity Theatre, Chicago, 202–3
true character, 117
truth, 58–59
two-act plays, 98

Uncle Vanya (Chekhov), 31
underlining, in script, 180
underlying rights, 203–4
uniqueness, 21
United States Copyright office website, 201
unities, 56–57
    of action, 11, 19, 57
    of place, 56–57
    structural, 58, 60–62
    of time, 56
universal mythic prototypes, 2
universal truths, 36, 37
University of Michigan, x
unpublished plays, formatting of, 170–71
unsolicited scripts, 259
unstageability, 13–15
ushers, 284
Ustinov, Peter, 23
Utah Playfest Reader's Response Form, 268–69

The Vagina Monologues (Ensler), 17, 28, 133, 157
Van Gogh, Vincent: *Starry Night*, 39
Velo binding, 171
verbal pitch, 276
verbal scene painting, 48
verisimilitude, 155, 156
visual impact, 60
Vogler, Chris, 135
    masks, 137
    The Writer's Journey, 2, 132, 138
Voltaire, 305
Vonnegut, Kurt, 1

Wagner, Richard: *Ring Cycle*, 47
Waiting for Godot (Beckett), 44, 59, 133, 289
The Waiting Room (Loomer), 133
Walter, Richard, 10
War and Peace (Tolstoy), 11, 47
Wasserstein, Wendy: *The Heidi Chronicles*, 47
webpages, playwright's, 172, 276
Welty, Eudora: *One Writer's Beginnings*, 156
Westerns, 71
What Art Is: The Esthetic Theory of Ayn Rand (Torres and
      Kamhi), 61
What Is Dramaturgy? (Cardullo and Lang), 215
Who's Afraid of Virginia Woolf? (Albee), 156, 289
widows, 191
Wiene, Robert, 39
Wilde, Oscar, 23
    The Importance of Being Earnest, 3, 126, 135
Wilder, Thornton: *Our Town*, 50, 158
Williams, Karin, 257
Williams, Tennessee, x, 26, 158, 289
    critics and, 301
    master of the right sound, 161–62, 161–63
    master of titles, 172
    Poetic Realism, 31
    A Streetcar Named Desire, 26, 96, 154, 172, 187
    working titles, 95–96
"willing suspension of disbelief," 49
Willson, Meredith: *The Music Man*, xv
Wilson, Lanford, x
Wilson, Robert: *The Civil Wars*, 12, 45
Winnie the Pooh, 200
The Winter's Tale (Shakespeare), 186
Wit (Edson), 212
Wittgenstein, Ludwig, 305
Wolff, Jurgen, 304
Woolrich, Cornell, 33
word-processing programs, 191
Wordsworth, William: *Lyrical Ballads*, 35
working rehearsals, 298
working title, 95–96
workshop productions, 199
World War I, 43
World War II, 43
The Writer, 258
writer's block, 88–89
Writers Guild of America, 256
Writer's Market, 258
Write That Play (Rowe), x
"Write what you know," 19
writing
    Absurdism, 44–46
    alienation drama, 51–52
    dialogue, 140, 160
    Epic Theater, 47–48
    Expressionism, 40
    Realism, 31–33
    Romanticism, 36–37
    . *See* playwriting

Yale School of Drama, x

About the Authors

William Missouri Downs earned an MFA in Screenwriting from UCLA and an MFA in acting from the University of Illinois. For several years, he studied playwriting under Lanford Wilson and Milan Stitt at Circle Repertory Theatre in New York.

He has authored a dozen plays, including *Kabuki Medea*, which won the Bay Area Critics Award for best production in San Francisco and the Jefferson Award for best production in Chicago. He also wrote *Jewish Sports Heroes and Texas Intellectuals*, which took first place at The Mill Mountain Theatre's Festival of New Plays, and *Innocent Thoughts*, winner of the National Playwrights Award from the Unicorn Theatre in Kansas City. His plays have been produced from New York to Singapore, from the Kennedy Center to the Berkeley Rep. When working in Hollywood, he wrote for such NBC sitcoms as *My Two Dads*, *Amen*, and *Fresh Prince of Bel Air* and won the Jack Nicholson Award for screenwriting.

Mr. Downs is the co-author of the books *Screenplay: Writing the Picture*, published by Silman-James Press, and *Setting the Stage* (Wadsworth). He is also the head of playwriting at the University of Wyoming, where he has been honored with a dozen teaching and research awards. Plays written by his student playwrights have been published by Dramatists, Harcourt, and Samuel French and have won numerous awards from the American College Theater Festival, including the National Student Playwriting Award, the national Musical Theater Award, and the national Mark Twain Comedy Playwriting Award.

Robin U. Russin was educated at Harvard, Oxford, Rhode Island School of Design, and UCLA, where he received an MFA in screenwriting. A Rhodes Scholar and member of Phi Beta Kappa, he has written for film, theater, television, and various national publications. He has twice won the Jack Nicholson Award for screenwriting, and was a finalist in the Script P.I.M.P. Competition.

Mr. Russin's screenwriting credits include the number-one box-office feature *On Deadly Ground*, an eco-thriller starring Steven Seagal and Michael Caine (co-written with Ed Horowitz). He has also sold or optioned other original spec scripts to both studio and independent producers and produced the independent feature *Shark in a Bottle*. For television, he has written, produced, and directed numerous segments and specials for *America's Most Wanted* as well as written for a half-hour animated series. He was Senior Producer of ABC's hour-long primetime series *Vital Signs*, co-producer of a Fox-TV one-hour dramatic special, and co-producer of an ABC movie of the week.

His stageplay *Painted Eggs* was produced at the Harman Avenue Theater in Los Angeles. Mr. Russin is co-author of the book *Screenplay: Writing the Picture* (Silman-James Press) and a professor of screenwriting at the University of California, Riverside.